Copyright ©2022 by **Laura Howell**. All rights reserved.

This document is intended to provide accurate and trustworthy information regar‑
issue at hand.

From a Declaration of Principles accepted and approved by a Committee of the American Bar Association and a Committee of Publishers and Associations in equal measure.

Electronic or printed reproduction, duplication, or transmission of any portion of this document is strictly prohibited. All privileges reserved

The information contained in this document is claimed to be accurate and reliable; however, any liability, whether due to negligence or otherwise, arising from the use or misuse of any policies, procedures, or instructions is the sole and complete responsibility of the recipient reader. Under no circumstances will the publisher be held liable for any direct or indirect restitution, damages, or financial loss resulting from the information contained herein.

Copyrights not held by the publisher belong to the respective authors.

This information is provided solely for educational purposes and is therefore universal. The information is presented without a contract or any type of assurance of guarantee.

The trademarks are used without permission, and their publication is done so without the trademark owner's consent or support. All trademarks and brands mentioned in this book are for illustrative purposes only and are the property of their respective owners, who are not affiliated with this document.

All rights reserved by **Laura Howell**

Table of Contents

ANTI-INFLAMMATORY DIET FOR BEGINNERS 2022

800+ Delicious, Quick & Easy Recipes to Live Healthier, Reduce your Body Inflammation, and Balance Hormones.
30-day Meal Plan Included

Laura Howell

CHAPTER 3: STAPLES, SAUCES, DIPS, AND DRESSINGS 38

CHAPTER 4: BEANS AND GRAINS 46

CHAPTER 7: MEAT RECIPES: BEEF, PORK, LAMB, POULTRY 84

CHAPTER 8: STEWS AND SOUPS 97

Introduction

WHAT IS ANTI-INFLAMMATORY DIET?

An anti-inflammatory meal consists of foods that diminish inflammatory reactions. A diet that is anti-inflammatory contains expanded amounts of antioxidants, which are receptive molecules in food that lessen the number of free radicals. Free radicals harm cells and increase the danger of specific diseases.

Numerous mainstream diets, as of now, pursue anti-inflammatory standards. Different foods are utilized in an unexpected way, some advancing inflammation and others decreasing it. The reason for the anti-inflammatory diet is to advance ideal well-being and mending by picking foods that decrease inflammation. If one can effectively control the exorbitant inflammation through characteristic methods (such as through diet), it decreases dependence on anti-inflammatory drugs that have undesirable and unfortunate symptoms and do not address the hidden problem. While anti-inflammatory medications (for example, NSAIDs) are a handy solution to ease inflammations, they debilitate the safe framework by harming the gastrointestinal tract, which assumes a significant job in an invulnerable framework. When all is said and done, an anti-inflammatory diet consists of new, entire foods that do not contain triggers for inflammation and are loaded with molecules that kill inflammation in your body.

SYMPTOMS OF CHRONIC INFLAMMATION

The symptoms associated with acute inflammation are generally short-term (e.g., pain, swelling). In contrast, symptoms associated with chronic inflammation include slow to develop symptoms (e.g., high blood pressure, which can lead to heart disease). Although it is still not fully understood, most studies suggest that chronic inflammation may be the root of many diseases. This is because inflammation can manifest itself in so many ways in the human body. In this section, you will get to discover the not-pretty-obvious and obvious inflammation signs.

Normal

Most often, the symptoms of inflammation are pretty obvious, and they demand your undivided attention. These symptoms include:

- Heat
- Redness
- Soreness and pain
- Swelling

Silent

Inflammation signs are not always obvious. Most people do not realize that the symptoms they are going through are directly linked to chronic inflammation. Some pretty common signs of inflammation are:

Disease	Possible symptoms
Heart disease	Fatigue, high blood pressure, chest fluttering, sweating, and dizziness
Inflammatory bowel disease	Constipation, poor appetite, mucus or blood in stool, fatigue, night sweating, diarrhea, nausea
Obesity	Blood sugar imbalance, sweating, snoring, excess weight
Rheumatoid Arthritis	Joint stiffness, weight loss, weakness, fatigue
Osteoarthritis	Morning stiffness
Allergies	Digestive issues, food intolerance, dizziness, bedwetting, watery eyes, runny nose, mental fogginess
Asthma	Mucus, coughing
Lupus	Fever, fatigue, light sensitivity, anemia, hair loss
Hashimoto diseases	Cold sensitivity, weight gain, thinning hair, fatigue, depression, dry skin
Diabetes	Increased urination, thirst, and hunger
Cancer	Fever, fatigue, weight loss
Celiac disease	Fever, fatigue, weight loss
Multiple sclerosis	Weakness, tingling, dizziness, blurred vision
Skin condition	Family allergen history, digestive issues
Headaches	Dull acne, blurred vision, nausea
Brain disorder	Behavioral changes, decreased cognitive functioning, anxiety, insulin resistance, memory loss.

HEALTH RISKS OF CHRONIC INFLAMMATION

Anti-inflammatory medications are prescribed to reduce symptoms of inflammation in the body. The medications works by blocking or neutralizing factors that cause inflammation in various parts of the body. However, it is essential to know that anti-inflammation drugs are not without risks, most notably an increased risk for heart attack and stroke.

The health risks associated with anti-inflammatories include:

- Heart Attack: Taking anti-inflammatory drugs increases your risk of having a heart attack by 18%. If you've been taking anti-inflammatories for three years, you have a 23% higher risk for heart disease. In addition, doctors say that the heart protection offered by aspirin is less effective in people who regularly take anti-inflammatory drugs.
- Stroke: People who take one type of anti-inflammatory medication called COX 2 inhibitor have a 24% higher risk for stroke. Additionally, people who take corticosteroids are at risk for hemorrhagic stroke.
- Kidney Damage: A study of almost 90,000 patients found that those taking anti-inflammatories were 25% more likely to develop kidney damage.
- Pneumonia: A study of people who had recently been hospitalized for pneumonia shows that those who took anti-inflammatory medications were 34% more likely to die from the illness within six months.
- Impaired Wound Healing: A recent study of people who had undergone colon surgery found that those taking COX 2 inhibitors were twice as likely to have an incisional surgical site infection. Another recent study of people with gout showed that those who took ibuprofen for three weeks after surgery had slower healing times, with more than twice as much pain on movement.
- Congestive Heart Failure: When our heart is unable to pump blood effectively—more than half of the people who have this illness die within five years. A recent study shows that those with chronic heart failure are prescribed anti-inflammatories more than twice as often as those without.
- Rheumatoid Arthritis: People with rheumatoid arthritis are more likely to take anti-inflammatories for pain than those with other types of arthritis. Moreover, they are expected to be hospitalized for gastrointestinal reflux when the stomach acid backs up the throat or esophagus.
- Eye Damage: A recent study of over 100,000 patients found that people who took anti-inflammatories for arthritis or asthma were 60% more likely to develop cataracts. Similarly, people who take high doses of NSAIDs are almost twice as likely to develop macular degeneration, which is damage to the macula in the eye.
- Blood Clots: Anti-inflammatories increase your risk for blood clots by anywhere from 50% to 400%. Those who take anti-inflammatories have a three times greater risk of developing a blood clot in the leg or arm.
- Infections: Anti-inflammatories can damage your natural defenses against infections by somehow inhibiting the immune system. A recent study of cancer patients found that those who take antimicrobial drugs have much higher hospitalization rates due to urinary tract infections and pneumonia.
- Weight Gain: Weight gain can be caused by taking anti-inflammatories for arthritis or asthma. The most commonly prescribed anti-inflammatories are NSAIDs (non-steroidal anti-inflammatory drugs), including over 30 different medications. Over 50% of all adults in the US take an NSAID for at least one week every year.
- Blood Sugar - Taking anti-inflammatories can cause blood sugar to either rise or fall by as much as 40 mg within one week of taking them.
- Pregnancy Complications: Women who take aspirin or other anti-inflammatories during pregnancy increase their risk of miscarriage. Additionally, the use of anti-inflammatories during pregnancy causes preterm birth and low birth weight.
- Cognitive Deficits: Older adults who take NSAIDs are almost twice as likely to develop Alzheimer's Disease. This risk is compounded when people take high doses of the medications every day for long periods.

COMMON CHRONIC INFLAMMATION TREATMENTS

Some inflammation treatments include:

Nonsteroidal Anti-inflammatory Drugs (NSAIDs) – the NSAIDs drug group works by blocking specific enzyme groups hence preventing the creation of chemicals that cause inflammation. Ibuprofen and aspirin are two pretty popular NSAIDs. However, long-term consumption of this drugs can ultimately increase getting stomach ulcers; hence you should be careful.

Corticosteroids – Some genes are activated during an inflammation process, so this drug simply deactivates these genes, hence reducing inflammation.

Acetaminophen –Acetaminophen, also called paracetamol and Tylenol, helps to manage pain caused by chronic conditions. However, it does not address or prevent inflammation.

Some lifestyle practices that your doctor might recommend to keep inflammation under control:

Rest – Getting an excellent night's sleep helps reduce inflammation, boost memory repairs, and heal tissue. Plus, it keeps your appetite under control. It would help if you hence aimed to sleep for a minimum of 8 hours every night. Consider staying off any electronic device, screens an hour before your bedtime.

Anti-inflammatory diets – A tremendous and nutritious diet loaded with fruits, vegetables, healthy fats, fiber, antioxidants, clean water, and proteins play a massive role in managing inflammation.

Consult a medical practitioner to gain more information on targeted and specific strategies that you can apply to fight inflammation.

GETTING INTO THE ANTI-INFLAMMATORY DIET

Starting an anti-inflammatory diet can be difficult. There are many rules to follow, foods to avoid, and advice to follow. That's what makes it so successful, though! It helps you get rid of the wrong foods for you and ensures that you will give your body the good stuff by eliminating the wrong thing.; all in the hope of reducing the amount of inflammation and the adverse health effects in your body.

As a beginner, you may be a little confused about how to start with this diet plan. But don't let this stop you! Below are tips to help you be sure you can get the most out of your anti-inflammatory diet!

- Eat more plants. Explore and enjoy the wide range of fruits and vegetables that provide fiber, antioxidants, and other nutrients to support optimal health. These low-calorie foods combat cellular damage, promote digestion, and help maintain a healthy weight range, which keeps inflammation in check as well.
- Discover whole and ancient grains. Ancient grains are those that predate modern varieties created through selective breeding and hybridization—think oats, chia, barley, sorghum, bulgur, quinoa, and the like. These and whole grains retain fiber, antioxidants, and other nutrients that promote a healthy immune response. If whole grains are new to you, try mixing them 50/50 with your usual choice to begin dining the anti-inflammatory way, such as white rice with brown rice, quinoa with couscous, or whole-wheat bread crumbs with white.
- Choose healthy fats. Plant-based options like olive oil contain unsaturated fats that support immunity. These are preferable to proinflammatory trans fats and saturated fats from animal products, like butter and bacon. Look for omega-3 fats, such as fish and walnuts, to directly reduce inflammation.
- Enjoy nuts and seeds. These little bites provide healthy fats and protein, as well as valuable micronutrients and fiber. Plus, their flavor and crunchiness enhance any meal or snack.
- Add flavor with herbs and spices. Turmeric, ginger, and garlic are anti-inflammatory powerhouses. Have fun exploring these and countless other options for their deep flavors and unique benefits.
- Support your microbiome. High-fiber foods like whole grains and beans provide nourishment for your useful gut bacteria to thrive. Fermented foods such as yogurt, kimchi, and pickles keep the "communities" of bacteria in your digestive system balanced to help fight inflammation and disease.
- Consume power beverages. Coffee and unsweetened green or black tea offer antioxidant compounds that promote resilience against cell damage. Enjoy red wine on occasion, if you like, to maximize anti-inflammatory benefits. Plain water is always a great choice for keeping your body hydrated and energized—vary the flavor and benefits by tossing in some cut fruit or herbs.
- Eat fewer processed foods. Highly processed foods are often high in added sugars, refined grains, sodium, and detrimental fats. These types of foods are proinflammatory and also increase one's risk for weight gain and other diseases. If you haven't yet, become a label reader to increase your awareness of what's in these foods—it may surprise and inspire you to run toward the whole foods sections of the store.
- Consume less meat. When you want meat, choose and prepare it carefully. Many meats have undesirable amounts of unhealthy fats, and some are pumped full of sodium during processing. Use cooking methods that do not blacken the meat, such as grilling, as the blackened parts that occur have compounds that can contribute to inflammation.
- Relax! Stress is a significant contributor to inflammation and disease—in fact, chronic elevation of the stress hormone cortisol leads to ongoing negative impacts on health. Get more sleep, boost your physical activity, and try new activities such as mindfulness meditation—these all help manage stress and keep inflammation down.

ANTI-INFLAMMATORY DIET FOOD LIST

As you can already tell, food list is at the heart of this particular diet, so you need to understand which foods are allowed and which are not.

You should be happy to know, though, that despite there being some manner of restrictions when it comes to certain food groups, you will still have the option to enjoy a great number of absolutely delicious meals to help you rejuvenate your body.

To keep things simple and easy for you to understand, let me break down the food list into separate food groups and let you know what foods you should go for and avoid.

Beans and Legumes

What to eat

- Black-eyed peas
- Red beans
- Pinto beans
- Lentils
- Chickpeas
- Black beans

What not to eat

- Nothing, in particular, to be aware of.

Fruits

What to eat

- Blueberries
- Blackberries
- Raspberries
- Strawberries
- Dark red grapes
- Cherries
- Coconut
- Avocado

- Citrus fruits

What not to eat

- Nothing, in particular, to be aware of.

Allium Vegetables

What to eat

- Onion
- Garlic
- Chives
- Shallots
- Leeks
- Green onions

What not to eat

- Nothing, in particular, to be aware of.

Vegetables

What to eat

- Cauliflower
- Broccoli
- Cabbage
- Dark leafy greens
- Mustard greens
- Collard greens
- Lettuce
- Spinach
- Mushrooms
- Squash

What not to eat

- Nothing, in particular, to be aware of.

Nightshade Vegetables

What to eat

- Tomatoes
- Bell pepper
- Eggplant
- potatoes

What not to eat

- Nothing, in particular, to be aware of. However, some individuals are a bit sensitive to certain Nightshade vegetables, so make sure to keep that in check.

Herbs and Spices

What to eat

- Thyme
- Rosemary
- Cinnamon
- Basil
- Garlic
- Ginger
- Turmeric
- Chili peppers
- Paprika

What not to eat

- Nothing, in particular, to be aware of.

Animal and Fish Products

What to eat

- Oily fish, such as herring
- Salmon
- Tuna
- Mackerel
- Sardines
- Lean meats, such as chicken breast/fat-free lean beef

What not to eat

- Make sure to avoid processed meats, such as sausages, since they contain a good amount of nitrates.

Fats

What to eat

- Coconut oil
- Avocado oil
- Olive oil
- Almond butter/oil
- Pine nuts
- Pistachios
- Walnuts
- Cocoa
- Chocolates

What not to eat

- Fried foods
- Vegetable oil
- Soybean oil
- Margarine
- Shortening
- Lard
- Whole milk
- Dairy butter
- Low Fat: butter

Drinks

What to eat

- Green tea
- Healthy Smoothies
- Red wine is in a very moderate amount

What not to eat

- Sugary beverages
- Excessive alcohol

Carbohydrates

What to eat

- Unrefined whole grains
- Whole wheat bread
- Brown rice
- Oatmeal

What not to eat

- Refined carbs
- Pastries
- White bread
- French fries
- Artificial sugar

CHAPTER 1: Breakfast

1. ANTI-INFLAMMATORY PORRIDGE

Preparation time: 10 minutes
Cooking time: 25 minutes
Servings: 2
Ingredients:

- ¾ cup Almond Milk, unsweetened
- 2 tbsp. Hemp Seeds
- 2 tbsp. Chia Seeds, whole
- ¼ cup Walnuts, halved
- ¼ cup Almond Butter
- ¼ cup Coconut Flakes, unsweetened & toasted
- ¼ cup Coconut Milk
- ½ tsp. Turmeric Powder
- Dash of Black Pepper, grounded, as needed
- ½ tsp. Cinnamon
- 1 tbsp. Extra Virgin Olive Oil

Directions:

1. To start with, heat a large saucepan over medium heat.
2. To this, put in the hemp seeds, flaked coconut, and chopped walnuts.
3. Roast for 2 minutes or until toasted.
4. Once the coconut-seed mixture is roasted, transfer to a bowl and set it aside.
5. Then, heat almond milk and coconut milk in a wide saucepan over medium heat.
6. Once it becomes hot but not boiling, remove from the heat. Stir in almond butter and coconut oil to it. Mix.
7. Now, add chia seeds, pepper powder, turmeric powder, and salt to the milk. Combine.
8. Keep it aside for 5 minutes and then add half of the roasted coconut mixture. Mix.
9. Finally, transfer to a serving bowl and top with the remaining coconut mixture.
10. Serve immediately.
11. Tip: If possible, try adding bee pollen for enhanced taste.

Per serving: Calories: 575Kcal; Protein: 14.8g; Carbohydrates: 6g; Fat: 50.2g

2. GINGERBREAD OATMEAL

Preparation time: 10 minutes
Cooking time: 30 minutes
Servings: 4
Ingredients:

- ¼ tsp. Cardamom, grounded
- 4 cups Water
- ¼ tsp. Allspice
- 1 cup Steel Cut Oats
- 1/8 tsp. Nutmeg
- 1 ½ tbsp. Cinnamon, grounded
- ¼ tsp. Ginger, grounded
- ¼ tsp. Coriander, grounded
- Maple Syrup, if desired
- ¼ tsp. Cloves

Directions:

1. Place all ingredients in a huge saucepan over medium-high heat and stir well.
2. Next, cook them for 6 to 7 minutes or until cooked.
3. Once finished, add the maple syrup.
4. Top it with dried fruits of your choice if desired.
5. Serve it hot or cold.
6. Tip: Avoid those spices which you don't prefer.

Per serving: Calories: 175Kcal; Protein: 6g; Carbohydrates: 32g; Fat: 32g

3. ROASTED ALMONDS

Preparation time: 5 minutes
Cooking time: 10 minutes
Servings: 32
Ingredients:

- 2 cups whole almonds
- 1 tbs. chili powder
- ½ tsp. ground cinnamon
- ½ tsp. ground cumin
- ½ tsp. ground coriander
- Salt and freshly ground black pepper, to taste
- 1 tbs. extra-virgin organic olive oil

Directions:

1. Preheat the oven to 350 deg. F. Line a baking dish with a parchment paper.
2. In a bowl, add all ingredients and toss to coat well.
3. Transfer the almond mixture into prepared baking dish in a single layer.
4. Roast for around 10 minutes, flipping twice inside the middle way.
5. Remove from oven and make aside to cool down completely before serving.
6. You can preserve these roasted almonds in airtight jar.

Per serving: Calories: 62Kcal; Protein: 2g; Carbohydrates: 12g; Fat: 5g

4. ROASTED PUMPKIN SEEDS

Preparation time: 10 minutes
Cooking time: 20 minutes
Servings: 4
Ingredients:

- 1 cup pumpkin seeds, washed and dried
- 2 tsp. garam masala
- 1/3 tsp. red chili powder
- ¼ tsp. ground turmeric
- Salt, to taste
- 3 tbsp. coconut oil, meted
- ½ tbs. fresh lemon juice

Directions:

1. Preheat the oven to 350 deg. F.
2. In a bowl, add all ingredients except lemon juice and toss to coat well.
3. Transfer the almond mixture right into a baking sheet.
4. Roast for approximately twenty or so minutes, flipping occasionally.
5. Remove from oven and put aside to cool completely before serving.
6. Drizzle with freshly squeezed lemon juice and serve.

Per serving: Calories: 136Kcal; Protein: 25g; Carbohydrates: 15g; Fat: 4g

5. QUICK BURRITO

Preparation time: 10 minutes
Cooking time: 11 minutes
Servings: 1
Ingredients:

- 1/4-pound beef meat; ground
- 1 tsp. sweet paprika
- 1 tsp. cumin; ground
- 1 tsp. onion powder
- 1 small red onion; julienned 3 eggs
- 1 tsp. coconut oil
- 1 tsp. garlic powder
- 1 tsp. cilantro; chopped.
- Salt and black pepper to the taste.

Directions:

1. Heat up a pan over medium heat; add beef and brown for a few minutes
2. Add salt, pepper, cumin, garlic and onion powder and paprika; stir, cook for 4 minutes more and take off heat.
3. Using a bowl, mix the eggs with salt and pepper and whisk well. Heat a pan with the oil over medium heat; add egg, spread evenly and cook for 6 minutes Transfer your egg burrito to a plate, divide beef mix, add onion and cilantro, roll and serve

Per serving: Calories: 280Kcal; Protein: 14g; Carbohydrates: 7g; Fat: 5g

6. SPICED POPCORN

Preparation time: 5 minutes
Cooking time: 2 minutes
Servings: 2-3
Ingredients:

- 3 tbsp. coconut oil
- ½ cup popping corn
- 1 tbsp. olive oil
- 1 tsp. ground turmeric
- ¼ tsp. garlic powder
- Salt, to taste

Directions:

1. In a pan, melt coconut oil on medium-high heat.
2. Add popping corn and cover the pan tightly.
3. Cook, shaking the pan occasionally for around 1-2 minutes or till corn kernels begin to pop.
4. Remove from heat and transfer right into a large heatproof bowl.
5. Add essential olive oil and spices and mix well.
6. Serve immediately.

Per serving: Calories: 200Kcal; Protein: 6g; Carbohydrates: 12g; Fat: 4g

7. CUCUMBER BITES

Preparation time: 15 minutes
Cooking time: 0 minutes
Servings: 4
Ingredients:

- ½ cup prepared hummus
- 2 tsp. nutritional yeast
- ¼-½ tsp. ground turmeric
- Pinch of red pepper cayenne
- Pinch of salt
- 1 cucumber, cut diagonally into ¼-½-inch thick slices
- 1 tsp. black sesame seeds
- Fresh mint leaves, for garnishing

Directions:

1. In a bowl, mix together hummus, turmeric, cayenne and salt.
2. Transfer the hummus mixture in the pastry bag and spread on each cucumber slice.
3. Serve while using garnishing of sesame seeds and mint leaves.

Per serving: Calories: 203Kcal; Protein: 8g; Carbohydrates: 20g; Fat: 4g

8. SPINACH FRITTERS

Preparation time: 15 minutes
Cooking time: 5 minutes
Servings: 2-3
Ingredients:

- 2 cups chickpea flour
- ¾ tsp. white sesame seeds
- ½ tsp. garam masala powder
- ½ tsp. red chili powder
- ¼ tsp. ground cumin
- 2 pinches of baking soda
- Salt, to taste
- 1 cup water
- 12-14 fresh spinach leaves
- Olive oil, for frying

Directions:

1. In a mixing bowl, add all ingredients except spinach and oil and mix till an easy mixture forms.
2. In a sizable skillet, heat oil on medium heat.
3. Dip each spinach leaf in chickpea flour mixture evenly and place in the hot oil in batches.
4. Cook, flipping occasionally for about 3-5 minutes or till golden brown from each side.
5. Transfer the fritters onto paper towel lined plate.

Per serving: Calories: 211Kcal; Protein: 9g; Carbohydrates: 13g; Fat: 2g

9. CRISPY CHICKEN FINGERS

Preparation time: 15 minutes
Cooking time: 18 minutes
Servings: 4-6
Ingredients:

- 2/3 cup almond meal
- ½ tsp. ground turmeric
- ½ tsp. red pepper cayenne
- ½ tsp. paprika
- ½ tsp. garlic powder
- Salt and freshly ground black pepper, to taste
- 1 egg
- 1-pound skinless, boneless chicken breasts, cut into strips

Directions:

1. Preheat the oven to 375 deg. F. Line a substantial baking sheet with parchment paper.
2. In a shallow bowl, beat the egg.
3. In another shallow dish, mix together almond meal and spices.
4. Coat each chicken strip with egg after which roll into spice mixture evenly.
5. Arrange the chicken strips onto prepared baking sheet in the single layer.
6. Bake for approximately 16-18 minutes.

Per serving: Calories: 236Kcal; Protein: 37g; Carbohydrates: 26g; Fat: 10g

10. DELICATE RICE WITH COCONUT AND BERRIES

Preparation time: 10 minutes
Cooking time: 30 minutes
Servings: 4
Ingredients:

- 1 cup water
- 1 cup coconut milk
- 1 tsp. salt
- 2 dates, pitted and chopped
- 1 cup blueberries, or raspberries, fresh and divided
- ¼ cup slivered almonds, toasted and divided
- ½ cup coconut, shaved and divided

Directions:

1. Combine the basmati rice, water, coconut milk, salt, and date pieces in a medium saucepan over high heat.
2. Mix well until the mixture comes to a boil. For 20 to 30 minutes, lower the heat to simmer and cook, without stirring, or until the rice is tender.
3. Drop the rice in four bowls and top each serving with ¼ cup of blueberries, 1 tbs. of almonds, and 2 tbsp. of coconut.

Per serving: Calories: 281Kcal; Protein: 6g; Carbohydrates: 49g; Fat: 8g

11. COLD OATMEAL WITH APPLE AND CINNAMON

Preparation time: 10 minutes
Cooking time: 10 minutes
Servings: 4-6
Ingredients:

- 1 cups coconut milk
- ¼ cup no-added-sugar apple juice
- 1 tbs. apple cider vinegar
- 1 apple, cored and chopped

- Dash ground cinnamon

Directions:

1. Stir together the oats, coconut milk, apple juice, and vinegar in a medium bowl.
2. Cover and refrigerate overnight.
3. Stir in the chopped apple and season the cold oatmeal with cinnamon the next morning.

Per serving: Calories: 213Kcal; Protein: 6g; Carbohydrates: 39g; Fat: 4g

12. APPETIZING CREPES WITH BERRIES

Preparation time: 15 minutes

Cooking time: 5 minutes

Servings: 4-6

Ingredients:

- 1 cup buckwheat flour
- ½ tsp. sea salt
- 2 tbsp. coconut oil (1 tbs. melted)
- 1½ cups almond milk, or water
- 1 egg
- 1 tsp. vanilla extract
- 3 cups fresh berries, divided
- 6 tbsp. Chia Jam, divided

Directions:

1. Whisk together the buckwheat flour, salt, 1 tbs. of melted coconut oil, almond milk, egg, and vanilla in a small bowl until smooth.
2. Melt the remaining 1 tbs. of coconut oil in a large (12-inch) nonstick skillet over medium-high heat. Tilt the pan, coating it evenly with the melted oil.
3. Into the skillet, ladle ¼ cup of batter, and tilt it to coat evenly with the batter.
4. Cook for 2 minutes, or until the edges begin to curl up. Flip the crêpe and cook for 1 minute on the second side using a spatula. Transfer the crêpe to a plate.
5. Continue to make crêpes with the remaining batter. You should have 4 to 6 crêpes.
6. Place 1 crêpe on a plate, top with ½ cup of berries and 1 tbs. of Chia Jam. Fold the crêpe over the filling. Repeat with the remaining crêpes and serve.

Per serving: Calories: 242Kcal; Protein: 7g; Carbohydrates: 33g; Fat: 11g

13. BEAUTIFUL BUCKWHEAT WAFFLES

Preparation time: 15 minutes

Cooking time: 6 minutes

Servings: 4

Ingredients:

- 1½ cups buckwheat flour
- ½ cup brown rice flour
- 2 tsp. baking powder
- 1 tsp. baking soda
- ½ tsp. sea salt
- 1 egg
- 1 tbs. maple syrup
- 2 tsp. vanilla extract
- 1 cup water
- 1½ cups almond milk
- Coconut oil

Directions:

1. Whisk together the buckwheat flour, rice flour, baking powder, baking soda, and salt in a medium bowl.
2. Add the maple syrup, egg, and vanilla to the dry ingredients. Slowly whisk in the water and almond milk until the batter is completely smooth. Let the batter sit for 10 minutes to thicken slightly.
3. Stir well before using because the buckwheat may settle in the bottom of the bowl while resting.
4. Heat the waffle iron and brush it with coconut oil.
5. Add the batter to the waffle iron and cook.

Per serving: Calories: 282Kcal; Protein: 9g; Carbohydrates: 55g; Fat: 4g

14. OATS WITH BERRIES

Preparation time: 10 minutes

Cooking time: 30 minutes

Servings: 4

Ingredients:

- 1 cup Steel Cut Oats
- Dash of Salt
- 3 cups Water
- For toppings:
- ½ cup Berries of your choice
- ¼ cup Nuts or Seeds of your choice like Almonds or Hemp Seeds

Directions:

1. To begin with, place the oats in a small saucepan and heat it over medium-high heat.
2. Now, toast it for 3 minutes while stirring the pan frequently.
3. Next, pour water to the saucepan and mix well.
4. Allow the mixture to boil. Lower the heat.
5. Allow it to cook for 23 to 25 minutes or until the oats are cooked and tender.
6. Once done cooking, transfer the mixture to the serving bowl and top it with the berries and seeds.

7. Serve it warm or cold.
8. Tip: If you desire, you can add sweeteners like maple syrup or coconut sugar or stevia to it.

Per serving: Calories: 118Kcal; Protein: 4.1g; Carbohydrates: 16.5g; Fat: 4.4g;

15. SPINACH AVOCADO SMOOTHIE

Preparation time: 5 minutes

Cooking time: 5 minutes

Servings: 1

Ingredients:

- ¼ of 1 avocado
- 1 cup plain yoghurt, non-fat:
- 2 tbsp. water
- 1 cup spinach, fresh
- 1 tsp. honey
- 1 banana, frozen

Directions:

1. Start by blending all the ingredients needed to make the smoothie in a high-speed blender for 2 to 3 minutes or until you get a smooth and creamy mixture.
2. Next, transfer the mixture to a serving glass.
3. Serve and enjoy.

Tip: If you don't prefer to use yogurt, you can use unsweetened almond milk.

Per serving: Calories: 357Kcal; Protein: 17.7g; Carbohydrates: 57.8g; Fat: 8.2g

16. GOLDEN MILK

Preparation time: 5 minutes

Cooking time: 5 minutes

Servings: 2

Ingredients:

- 1 tbsp. coconut oil
- 1 ½ cups coconut milk, light
- pinch of pepper
- 1 ½ cups almond milk, unsweetened
- ¼ tsp. ginger, grated
- 1 ½ tsp. turmeric, grounded
- ¼ tsp. cinnamon, grounded
- sweetener of your choice, as needed

Directions:

1. To make this healthy beverage, you need to place all the ingredients in a medium-sized saucepan and mix it well.
2. After that, heat it over medium heat for 3 to 4 minutes or until it is hot but not boiling. Stir continuously.
3. Taste for seasoning. Add more sweetener or spice as required by you.

4. Finally, transfer the milk to the serving glass and enjoy it.

Tip: Instead of cinnamon powder, you can also use the cinnamon stick, which can be discarded at the end if you prefer a much more intense flavor.

Per serving: Calories: 205Kcal; Protein: 3.2g; Carbohydrates: 8.9g; Fat: 19.5g

17. GRANOLA

Preparation time: 10 minutes
Cooking time: 60 minutes
Servings: 2
Ingredients:

- ½ cup flax seeds, grounded
- 1 cup almonds, whole & raw
- ½ cup ginger, grated
- 1 cup pumpkin seeds, raw
- ½ tsp. salt
- 1 cup shredded coconut, unsweetened
- ¾ cup water
- 1 cup oat bran
- ½ cup coconut oil, melted
- 1 cup dried cherries, pitted
- 4 tsp. turmeric powder

Directions:

1. First, preheat the oven to 300 deg. F.
2. Next, combine dried cherries, almonds, grounded flax, pumpkin seeds, coconut, salt, and turmeric in a large mixing bowl until mixed well.
3. After that, mix ginger, coconut oil, and water in the blender and blend for 30 to 40 seconds or until well incorporated.
4. Now, spoon in the coconut oil mixture to the nut mixture. Mix well.
5. Then, transfer the mixture to a parchment paper-lined baking sheet and spread it across evenly.
6. Bake for 50 to 60 minutes while checking on it once or twice.
7. Allow it to cool completely and enjoy it.

Tip: Substitute dried cherries with raisins if preferred.

Per serving: Calories: 225Kcal; Protein: 6g; Carbohydrates: 18g; Fat: 16g

18. OVERNIGHT COCONUT CHIA OATS

Preparation time: 10 minutes
Cooking time: 60 minutes
Servings: 1 to 2

Ingredients:

- ½ cup coconut milk, unsweetened
- 2 tsp. chia seeds
- 1 ½ cups old fashioned oats, whole grain
- ½ tsp. cinnamon, grounded
- 1 cup almond milk, unsweetened
- ½ tsp. cinnamon, grounded
- 2 tsp. date syrup
- ½ tsp. black pepper, grounded
- 1 tsp. turmeric, grounded

Directions:

1. To start with, keep the oats in the mason jar.
2. After that, mix the rest of the ingredients in a medium bowl until combined well.
3. Then, pour the mixture to the jars and stir well.
4. Now, close the jar and place it in the refrigerator overnight.
5. In the morning, stir the mixture and then enjoy it.

Tip: You can top it with toasted nuts or berries.

Per serving: Calories: 335Kcal; Protein: 8g; Carbohydrates: 34.1g; Fat: 19.9g

19. BLUEBERRY HEMP SEED SMOOTHIE

Preparation time: 10 minutes
Cooking time: 5 minutes
Servings: 1
Ingredients:

- 1 ¼ cup Blueberries, frozen
- 1 ¼ cup plant-based milk of your choice
- 2 tbsp. hemp seeds
- 1 tsp. spirulina
- 1 scoop of protein: powder

Directions:

1. Put all the ingredients needed to make the smoothie in a high-speed blender and blend them for 2 minutes or until smooth.
2. Transfer the mixture to a serving glass and enjoy it.

Tip: Instead of blueberries, you can use any berries of your choice.

Per serving: Calories: 493Kcal; Protein: 37.8g; Carbohydrates: 46.3g; Fat: 19.6g

20. SPICED MORNING CHIA PUDDING

Preparation time: 10 minutes
Cooking time: 5 minutes
Servings: 1

Ingredients:

- ½ tsp. cinnamon
- 1 ½ cups cashew milk
- 1/8 tsp. cardamom, grounded
- 1/3 cup chia seeds
- 1/8 tsp. cloves, grounded
- 2 tbsp. maple syrup
- 1 tsp. turmeric

Directions:

1. To begin with, combine all the ingredients in a medium bowl until well mixed.
2. Next, spoon the mixture into a container and allow it to sit overnight.
3. In the morning, transfer to a cup and serve with toppings of your choice.

Tip: You can top it with toppings of your choice like coconut flakes or seeds etc.

Per serving: Calories: 237Kcal; Protein: 8.1g; Carbohydrates: 28.9g; Fat: 8.1g

21. GREEN SMOOTHIE

Preparation time: 10 minutes
Cooking time: 10 minutes
Servings: 1
Ingredients:

- 2 cups kale
- 1 tbsp. chia seeds
- ½ of 1 banana, medium
- 1 cup pineapple chunks, frozen
- ¼ tsp. turmeric
- 1 cup green tea, brewed & cooled
- 1 scoop of protein: powder
- 2/3 cup cucumber, cut into chunks
- 3 mint leaves
- ½ cup mango, cut into chunks
- ½-inch ginger, sliced
- ice cubes, if needed

Directions:

1. Place all the ingredients in a high-speed blender, excluding the chia seeds, and blend them for 2 to 3 minutes or until smooth.
2. Next, put in the chia seeds and blend them for a further 1 minute.
3. Finally, transfer to a serving glass and enjoy it.

Tip: You can substitute kale with spinach if desired.

Per serving: Calories: 445Kcal; Protein: 31.9g; Carbohydrates: 73.7g; Fat: 7.2g

22. OATMEAL PANCAKES

Preparation time: 10 minutes
Cooking time: 25 minutes
Servings: 2

Ingredients:

- 1 ½ cups rolled oats, whole-grain
- 2 eggs, large & pastured
- 2 tsp. baking powder
- 1 banana, ripe
- 2 tbsp. water
- ¼ cup maple syrup
- 1 tsp. vanilla extract
- 2 tbsp. extra virgin olive oil

Directions:

1. To make this delicious breakfast dish, you need to first blend all the ingredients in a high-speed blender for a minute or two or until you get a smooth batter. Tip: To blend easily, pour egg, banana, and all other liquid ingredients first and finally add oats at the end.
2. Now, take a huge skillet and heat it over medium-low heat.
3. Once the skillet is hot, ¼ cup of the batter into it and cook it for around 3 to 4 minutes per side or until bubbles start appearing in the middle portion.
4. Turn the pancake and cook the other side also.
5. Serve warm.

Tip: You can pair it with maple syrup and fruits.

Per serving: Calories: 201Kcal; Protein: 5g; Carbohydrates: 28g; Fat: 8g

23. SWEET POTATO CRANBERRY BREAKFAST BARS

Preparation time: 10 minutes

Cooking time: 40 minutes

Servings: 8

Ingredients:

- 1 ½ cups sweet potato puree
- 2 tbsp. coconut oil, melted
- 2 tbsp. maple syrup
- 2 eggs, pasture-raised
- 1 cup almond meal
- 1/3 cup coconut flour
- 1 ½ tsp. baking soda
- 1 cup fresh cranberry, pitted and chopped
- ¼ cup water

Directions:

1. Preheat the oven to 350F.
2. Grease a 9-inch baking tray with coconut oil. Set aside.
3. In a mixing bowl, combine the sweet potato puree, water, coconut oil, maple syrup, and eggs.
4. In another bowl, sift the almond flour, coconut flour, and baking soda.

5. Slowly add the dry ingredients to the wet ingredients. Use a spatula to fold and mix all ingredients.
6. Pour into the prepared baking pan and press the cranberries on top.
7. Place in the oven and bake for 40 minutes or until a toothpick inserted in the middle comes out clean.
8. Allow to rest or cool before removing from the pan.

Per serving: Calories: 98Kcal; Protein: 3g; Carbohydrates: 9g; Fat: 6g

24. SAVORY BREAKFAST PANCAKES

Preparation time: 5 minutes

Cooking time: 6 minutes

Servings: 4

Ingredients:

- ½ cup almond flour
- ½ cup tapioca flour
- 1 cup coconut milk
- ½ tsp. chili powder
- ¼ tsp. turmeric powder
- ½ red onion, chopped
- 1 handful cilantro leaves, chopped
- ½ inch ginger, grated
- 1 tsp. salt
- ¼ tsp. ground black pepper

Directions:

1. In a mixing bowl, mix all ingredients until well-combined.
2. Heat a pan on low medium heat and grease with oil.
3. Pour ¼ cup of batter onto the pan and spread the mixture to create a pancake.
4. Fry for 3 minutes per side.
5. Repeat until the batter is done.

Per serving: Calories: 108Kcal; Protein: 2g; Carbohydrates: 20g; Fat: 2g

25. SCRAMBLED EGGS WITH SMOKED SALMON

Preparation time: 10 minutes

Cooking time: 10 minutes

Servings: 2

Ingredients:

- 4 eggs
- 2 tbsp. coconut ilk
- Fresh chives, chopped
- 4 slices of wild-caught smoked salmon, chopped
- salt to taste

Directions:

1. In a bowl, whisk the egg, coconut milk, and chives.

2. Grease the skillet with oil and heat over medium low heat.
3. Pour the egg mixture and scramble the eggs while cooking.
4. When the eggs start to settle, add in the smoked salmon and cook for 2 more minutes.

Per serving: Calories: 349Kcal; Protein: 29g; Carbohydrates: 3g; Fat: 23g

26. RASPBERRY GRAPEFRUIT SMOOTHIE

Preparation time: 5 minutes

Cooking time: 0 minutes

Servings: 1

Ingredients:

- Juice from grapefruit, freshly squeezed
- 1 banana, peeled and sliced
- 1 cup raspberries

Directions:

1. Put all ingredients in a blender and pulse until smooth.
2. Chill before serving.

Per serving: Calories: 381Kcal; Protein: 4g; Carbohydrates: 96g; Fat: 0.8g

27. BREAKFAST BURGERS WITH AVOCADO BUNS

Preparation time: 10 minutes

Cooking time: 5 minutes

Servings: 1

Ingredients:

- 1 ripe avocado
- 1 egg, pasture-raised
- 1 red onion slice
- 1 tomato slice
- 1 lettuce leaf
- Sesame seed for garnish
- salt to taste

Directions:

1. Peel the avocado and remove the seed. Slice the avocado into half. This will serve as the bun. Set aside.
2. Grease a skillet over medium flame and fry the egg sunny side up for 5 minutes or until set.
3. Assemble the breakfast burger by placing on top of one avocado half with the egg, red onion, tomato, and lettuce leaf. Top with the remaining avocado bun.
4. Garnish with sesame seeds on top and season with salt to taste.

Per serving: Calories: 458Kcal; Protein: 13g; Carbohydrates: 20g; Fat: 39g

28. GREEN ON GREEN SMOOTHIE

Preparation time: 5 minutes
Cooking time: 0 minutes
Servings: 1
Ingredients:

- 1 cup packed baby spinach
- ½ green apple
- 1 tbs. maple syrup
- ¼ tsp. ground cinnamon
- 1 cup unsweetened almond milk
- ½ cup ice

Directions:

1. In a blender, combine all the ingredients. Blend them until smooth.
2. Serve.

RECIPE TIP: If you can eat nuts, a handful of raw pistachios blended with the rest of the ingredients adds a rich, buttery flavor and boosts protein.

Per serving: Calories: 130Kcal; Protein: 2g; Carbohydrates: 23g; Fat: 4g

29. POACHED EGGS

Preparation time: 10 minutes
Cooking time: 40 minutes
Servings: 4
Ingredients:

- 3 tomatoes; chopped.
- 2 garlic cloves; minced
- 1 tbs. ghee 1/4 tsp. chili powder
- 1 tbs. cilantro; chopped. 6 eggs
- 1 white onion; chopped.
- 1 red bell pepper; chopped.
- 1 tsp. paprika
- 1 tsp. cumin
- 1 Serrano pepper; chopped.
- Salt and black pepper to the taste.

Directions:

1. Warm a pan with the ghee over medium heat
2. Add onion in the pan and stir and cook for 10 minutes, then add Serrano pepper, red bell pepper, and garlic, and stir and cook for 10 minute more.
3. Add salt, tomatoes, pepper, chili powder, cumin and paprika, and let it cook for 10 minutes more.
4. Crack eggs into the pan, season them with salt and pepper, cover pan and cook for 6 minutes more.
5. Sprinkle cilantro at the end and serve. Enjoy!

Per serving: Calories: 300Kcal; Protein: 14g; Carbohydrates: 22g; Fat: 12g

30. CHIA PUDDING WITH OATS, STRAWBERRIES, AND KIWI

Preparation time: 25 minutes
Cooking time: 0 minutes
Servings: 2
Ingredients:

- 2 cups unsweetened almond milk
- 1 cup chia seeds
- ¼ cup maple syrup
- ½ tsp. vanilla extract
- ½ cup toasted oats
- 4 large strawberries, sliced
- 1 kiwi, peeled and sliced

Directions:

1. In a quart-size jar with a tight-fitting lid, combine the milk, chia seeds, maple syrup, and vanilla.
2. Cover and shake well, then set aside for at least 15 minutes for the pudding to thicken. (You can do this the night before and refridgerate overnight.)
3. Divide the pudding between two serving dishes, top with the toasted oats, strawberries, and kiwi, and serve.

Per serving: Calories: 360Kcal; Protein: 8g; Carbohydrates: 60g; Fat: 11g

31. BUCKWHEAT GRANOLA

Preparation time: 15 minutes
Cooking time: 10 minutes
Servings: 6
Ingredients:

- 3 cups buckwheat groats
- ½ cup coarsely chopped pecans
- 1 cup extra-virgin olive oil
- ¼ cup maple syrup
- 1 tsp. vanilla extract
- ¼ tsp. salt

Directions:

1. Preheat the oven to 350°F.
2. In a medium bowl, combine the buckwheat, pecans, oil, maple syrup, vanilla, and salt. Mix well to evenly coat the buckwheat with the oil and maple syrup.
3. Spread the mixture on a rimmed baking sheet and place in the oven.
4. After 5 minutes, remove the baking sheet from the oven. Using a spatula, stir the mixture around so it will bake evenly. Return to the oven and bake until the granola is lightly toasted, about 5 minutes more.
5. Allow to cool completely before serving.

RECIPE TIP: If you'd like to add dried fruit to this granola, add it after baking and cooling the granola. Once cool, the granola can be stored at room temperature in an airtight container for up to 6 weeks.

Per serving: Calories: 490Kcal; Protein: 11g; Carbohydrates: 71g; Fat: 21g

32. HIGH-PROTEIN BREAKFAST BOWL

Preparation time: 5 minutes
Cooking time: 0 minutes
Servings: 1
Ingredients:

- 1 1/2 tbsp. plant-based protein powder
- 1/4 cup of blueberries
- 1/4 cup of raspberries
- 1 small banana (sliced)
- 1 small sweet potato (baked)

Directions:

1. Set out the flesh of the baked sweet potato and place it in a bowl.
2. Use a fork to mash the flesh until you get the consistency you desire.
3. Add the protein powder. Mix until well combined.
4. Arrange the blueberries, raspberries, and banana slices in layers on top of the mashed sweet potato.
5. Top with your desired toppings.
6. Warm for about 15 minutes before serving.

Per serving: Calories: 290Kcal; Protein: 10.36g; Carbohydrates: 65.13g; Fat: 0.85g

33. SALMON CAKES BENEDICT WITH LEMON-TURMERIC AIOLI

Preparation time: 10 minutes
Cooking time: 20 minutes
Servings: 4
Ingredients:

- 1 (8-ounce) wild-caught salmon fillet, finely chopped, or canned salmon
- 2 tbsp. minced red onion
- 2 tbsp. Anti-Inflammatory Mayo
- 1 cup almond flour
- 1 tsp. garlic powder
- 1 tsp. ground cumin
- 1 tsp. salt
- ½ tsp. ground turmeric
- ½ tsp. freshly ground black pepper
- Grated zest and juice of 1 lime
- ½ cup extra-virgin olive oil, divided
- 4 large eggs
- ¼ cup lemon-turmeric aioli, for serving
- smoked paprika, for serving
- lemon wedges, for serving

Directions:

1. In a huge bowl, combine the salmon and onion. Add the mayo and mix well.
2. In a mini bowl, whisk together the almond flour, garlic powder, cumin, salt, turmeric, and pepper.
3. Add the flour mixture and lime zest and juice to the salmon and mix well.
4. Form the mixture into four patties, about 2 inches in diameter. Let sit for 15 minutes.
5. In a cast-iron skillet, heat 4 tbsp. of olive oil over medium heat. Add the patties and fry for 2 to 3 minutes per side, until they are browned on each side.
6. Cover the skillet, reduce the heat to low, and cook for another 6 to 8 minutes, or until the patties are set in the center. Remove from the skillet and keep warm.
7. In the same skillet, working in two batches, heat 2 tbsp. of olive oil over medium-high heat. Slowly crack two eggs separately into the oil, try to keep them from touching, and fry for around 1 to 3 minutes on each side, depending on desired doneness. For a runnier egg, fry until just set, about 1 minute on each side.
8. Repeat with the remaining 2 tbsp. of olive oil and two eggs.
9. To serve, top each salmon cake with a fried egg and 1 tbs. of aioli. Sprinkle with paprika and serve with a lemon wedge.

Per serving: Calories: 645Kcal; Protein: 22g; Carbohydrates: 5g; Fat: 61g

34. VEGAN "FRITTATA"

Preparation time: 15 minutes
Cooking time: 20 minutes
Servings: 6
Ingredients:

- 1½ cups garbanzo bean flour
- 1 tsp. salt
- 1 tsp. ground turmeric
- ½ tsp. ground cumin
- 1 tsp. chopped fresh sage
- 1½ cups water
- 2 tbsp. extra-virgin olive oil
- 1 zucchini, sliced
- 2 scallions, sliced

Directions:

1. Preheat the oven to 350°F.
2. In a medium-sized bowl, whisk together the garbanzo bean flour, salt, turmeric, cumin, and sage.

3. Slowly add the water, stirring constantly to prevent the batter from getting lumpy. Set aside.
4. In an oven-safe skillet, heat the oil over high heat. Sauté the zucchini until softened, 2 to 3 minutes. Stir in the scallions, then spoon the batter over the vegetables.
5. Place the skillet in the oven and bake until firm when jiggled slightly, 20 to 25 minutes.
6. Serve warm or at room temperature.

RECIPE TIP: Store in the refrigerator for a week, or consider freezing this dish in individual-size portions for handy grab-and-go work lunches.

Per serving: Calories: 140Kcal; Protein: 6g; Carbohydrates: 15g; Fat: 6g

35. SPINACH FRITTATA

Preparation time: 10 minutes
Cooking time: 12 minutes
Servings: 2
Ingredients:

- 2 cups of baby spinach
- 1 tsp. of garlic powder
- 2 tbsp. of extra-virgin olive oil
- 8 beaten eggs
- 1/2 tsp. of sea salt
- 2 tbsp. of grated parmesan cheese
- 1/8 tsp. black pepper

Directions:

1. Preheat the broiler to the highest setting.
2. Heat the olive oil in a big ovenproof skillet or pan (well-seasoned cast iron fits well) over medium-high heat until it starts shimmering.
3. Cook, stirring regularly, for around 3 minutes after introducing the spinach.
4. Whisk together the eggs, salt, garlic powder, and pepper in a medium mixing cup. Carefully pour the egg mixture over the spinach and cook for 3 minutes, or until the edges of the eggs begin to set.
5. Gently raise the eggs away from the pan's sides with a rubber spatula. Enable the uncooked egg to flow into the pan's edges by tilting it. Cook for another 2 or 3 minutes, just until the sides are solid.
6. Place the pan under the broiler and cover with the Parmesan cheese. Preheat the oven to broil for around 3 minutes, or before the top puffs up.
7. To eat, break into wedges.

Per serving: Calories: 203Kcal; Protein: 13g; Carbohydrates: 203g; Fat: 13g

36. MUSHROOM AND BELL PEPPER OMELET

Preparation time: 10 minutes
Cooking time: 10 minutes
Servings: 2
Ingredients:

- 1 sliced red bell pepper
- 6 beaten eggs
- 1/8 tsp. ground black pepper
- 2 tbsp. of extra virgin olive oil
- 1 cup of sliced mushrooms
- 1/2 a tsp. of sea salt

Directions:

1. Heat the olive oil in a broad non-stick pan over medium heat until it shimmers.
2. Combine the mushrooms and red bell pepper in a mixing dish. Cook, stirring regularly, for around 4 minutes, or until tender.
3. Whisk together the salt, eggs, and pepper in a medium mixing cup. Set the eggs over the vegetables and cook for around 3 minutes, or until the edges of the eggs begin to set.
4. Gently raise the eggs away from the pan's sides with a rubber spatula. Allow the uncooked egg to flow to the pan's edges by tilting it. Cook for 2 to 5 minutes until the edges and core of the eggs are set.
5. Set the omelet in half with a spatula. To eat, break into wedges.

Per serving: Calories: 336Kcal; Protein: 18g; Carbohydrates: 7g; Fat: 27g

37. YOGURT, BERRY, AND WALNUT PARFAIT

Preparation time: 10 minutes
Cooking time: 0 minutes
Servings: 2
Ingredients:

- 2 tbsp. of honey
- 2 cups of Plain unsweetened coconut yogurt or plain unsweetened yogurt or almond yogurt
- 1 cup of fresh blueberries
- 1/2 cup of walnut pieces
- 1 cup of fresh raspberries

Directions:

1. Stir the yogurt and honey together. Divide into two bowls.
2. Sprinkle in blueberries and raspberries along with a quarter cup of chopped walnuts.

Per serving: Calories: 505Kcal; Protein: 23g; Carbohydrates: 56g; Fat: 22g

38. GREEN TEA AND GINGER SHAKE

Preparation time: 5 minutes
Cooking time: 0 minutes
Servings: 2
Ingredients:

- 2 tbsp. of honey
- 2 tbsp. of grated ginger
- 2 tbsp. of matcha (green tea) powder
- 2 cups of skim milk
- 2 scoops of Low-fat Vanilla ice cream

Directions:

1. In a blender, merge all the ingredients and blend until smooth.
2. Serve.

Per serving: Calories: 340Kcal; Protein: 11g; Carbohydrates: 56g; Fat: 7g

39. PLUM, PEAR AND BERRY-BAKED BROWN RICE

Preparation time: 12 minutes
Cooking time: 30 minutes
Servings: 2
Ingredients:

- 1-cup water
- 1/2-cup brown rice
- A pinch of cinnamon
- 1/2-tsp pure vanilla extract
- 2-Tbsps pure maple syrup (divided)
- Sliced fruits: berries, pears, or plums
- A pinch of salt (optional)

Directions:

1. Preheat your oven at 400F.
2. Bring the water and brown rice mixture to a boil in a pot placed over medium-high heat. Stir in the cinnamon and vanilla extract. Reduce the heat to medium-low. Simmer for 18 minutes, or until the brown rice is tender.
3. Fill two oven-safe bowls with equal portions of the rice. Pour a tbs. of maple syrup into each bowl. Top the bowls with the sliced fruits and sprinkle over a pinch of salt.
4. Put the bowls in the oven. Bake for 12 minutes, or until the fruits start caramelizing and the syrup begins bubbling.

Per serving: Calories: 227Kcal; Protein: 14g; Carbohydrates: 32g; Fat: 6.3g

40. WAFFLES WHIPPED WITH PERFECT PLANTAINS PAIR

Preparation time: 12 minutes
Cooking time: 10 minutes
Servings: 2
Ingredients:

- 2-cups large plantains, medium-ripe, peeled and sliced
- 21/2-tbsps coconut oil, melted
- 1-tsp apple cider vinegar
- 1-tsp pure vanilla extract
- 1-tsp cinnamon
- 1/2-tsp baking soda
- 1/2-tsp sea salt
- Choice of fresh fruit, maple syrup, and whipped coconut cream for serving

Directions:

1. Preheat your waffle iron to level 5 on its dial.
2. Combine the plantain and oil in your blender. Puree to a smooth consistency. Add the apple cider vinegar, vanilla, and cinnamon. Blend again on high speed until thoroughly combined. Add the baking soda and salt. Using a spatula, stir the mixture until forming a batter. Set aside.
3. Grease your waffle iron and pour 1/3 cup of the batter. Cook until the waffle turns brown to your liking.
4. Repeat until forming the batter. Ensure to grease the iron before pouring the batter. Stack the cooked waffles on a wire rack.
5. To serve, top each waffle with fresh fruit of your choice. Drizzle with the syrup, and then, garnish with the whipped coconut cream.

Per serving: Calories: 805Kcal; Protein: 40g; Carbohydrates: 108g; Fat: 26g

41. SCRAMBLED EGGS WITH MACKEREL

Preparation time: 5 minutes
Cooking time: 10 minutes
Servings: 4
Ingredients:

- 6 large eggs
- 2 ounces goat cheese, at room temperature
- 7 tbsp. extra-virgin olive oil, divided
- 1 tsp. garlic powder
- ½ tsp. freshly ground black pepper
- 2 Roma tomatoes, finely chopped
- 2 tbsp. minced onion
- 1 (4-ounce) can olive oil–packed mackerel, chopped and oil reserved
- ¼ cup chopped pitted Kalamata or Spanish green olives
- 2 tbsp. chopped fresh parsley, oregano, rosemary, or cilantro

Directions:

1. In a small bowl, whisk together the eggs, goat cheese, 2 tbsp. of olive oil, garlic powder, and pepper.
2. In a medium-sized nonstick skillet, heat 1 tbs. of olive oil over medium-low heat. Add the tomatoes and onion and sauté for 2 to 3 minutes, until they are soft and the water from the tomato has evaporated. Add the egg mixture to the skillet and scramble, stirring constantly with a spatula, for 3 to 4 minutes, until the eggs are set and creamy.
3. Remove the skillet from the heat and stir in the mackerel and reserved oil, olives, and parsley. Serve warm with each serving drizzled with an additional 1 tbs. of olive oil.

Per serving: Calories: 479Kcal; Protein: 17g; Carbohydrates: 3g; Fat: 45g

42. COCONUT MILK SMOOTHIE BOWL

Preparation time: 5 minutes
Cooking time: 0 minutes
Servings: 2
Ingredients:

- 1 cup full-fat: canned coconut milk
- ½ cup frozen mixed berries
- 2 scoops unflavored collagen protein powder
- 2 tbsp. shredded unsweetened coconut
- 2 tbsp. chia or hemp seeds
- 2 tbsp. chopped macadamia nuts
- Grated lime zest (optional)

Directions:

1. Place the coconut milk, berries, and protein powder in a blender and process until very smooth.
2. Divide the mixture between bowls. Top each with 1 tbs. of shredded coconut, 1 tbs. of seeds, and 1 tbs. of nuts. Garnish with lime zest (if using) and serve immediately.

Per serving: Calories: 408Kcal; Protein: 16g; Carbohydrates: 9g; Fat: 33g

43. CHERRY-COCONUT PANCAKES

Preparation time: 5 minutes
Cooking time: 25 minutes
Servings: 3

Ingredients:

- 1 cup fresh or frozen dark cherries, thawed and coarsely chopped
- 1 tbs. water or lemon juice
- 1 tsp. vanilla extract, divided
- 2 to 4 tsp. monk fruit extract or powdered sugar-free sweetener (optional)
- ½ cup almond meal
- ½ cup coconut flour
- ¼ cup ground flaxseed
- 1 tsp. baking powder
- ½ tsp. ground cinnamon
- ½ cup heavy whipping cream
- 1 large egg
- 2 tbsp. coconut oil, divided

Directions:

1. In a small saucepan, heat the cherries, water, and ½ tsp. of vanilla over medium-high heat for 5 to 6 minutes, until bubbly, adding more water if the mixture is too thick. Stir in the sweetener (if using). Using a fork, mash the cherries and whisk until the mixture is smooth. Remove from the heat and set aside.
2. In a huge bowl, combine the almond meal, coconut flour, flaxseed, baking powder, and cinnamon and whisk to combine.
3. Add the cream, egg, 1 tbs. of coconut oil, the remaining ½ tsp. of vanilla, and a quarter of the cherry syrup mixture, whisking to combine well.
4. In large nonstick skillet, heat the remaining 1 tbs. of coconut oil over medium-low heat. Using about 2 tbsp. of batter for each, form three pancakes.
5. Cook for 4 to 5 minutes, until bubbles begin to form, then flip. Cook for about 2 to 3 minutes on the second side, until the pancakes are golden brown. Repeat this process with the remaining batter. You should get six large pancakes.
6. Serve warm drizzled with the remaining cherry syrup.

Per serving: Calories: 511Kcal; Protein: 12g; Carbohydrates: 27g; Fat: 41g

44. PUMPKIN PIE YOGURT BOWL

Preparation time: 10 minutes
Cooking time: 0 minutes
Servings: 1
Ingredients:

- 1 tbs. heavy whipping cream
- ½ cup plain whole milk Greek yogurt
- 1 tbs. unsweetened pumpkin puree

- 1 tsp. pumpkin pie spice
- 1 to 2 tsp. monk fruit extract or sugar-free sweetener (optional)
- ½ tsp. vanilla extract
- 2 tbsp. coarsely chopped pecans

Directions:

1. In a small bowl, using an immersion blender or whisk, whisk the cream for 2 to 3 minutes, until thick and doubled in volume. Set aside.
2. In a medium bowl, mix together the yogurt, pumpkin, pumpkin pie spice, sweetener (if using), and vanilla.
3. Top the yogurt mixture with the pecans and whipped cream and serve.

Per serving: Calories: 266Kcal; Protein: 20g; Carbohydrates: 9g; Fat: 20g

45. GREEK YOGURT OAT PANCAKES

Preparation time: 15 minutes
Cooking time: 10 minutes
Servings: 2
Ingredients:

- 6 egg whites (or ¾ cup liquid egg whites)
- 1 cup rolled oats
- 1 cup plain nonfat Greek yogurt
- 1 medium banana, peeled and sliced
- 1 tsp. ground cinnamon
- 1 tsp. baking powder

Directions:

1. Blend all of the listed fixing using a blender. Warm a griddle over medium heat. Spray the skillet with nonstick cooking spray.
2. Put 1/3 cup of the mixture or batter onto the griddle. Allow to cook and flip when bubbles on the top burst, about 5 minutes. Cook again within a minute until golden brown. Repeat with the remaining batter. Divide between two serving plates and enjoy.

Per serving: Calories: 318Kcal; Protein: 28g; Carbohydrates: 4g; Fat: 4g

46. SCRAMBLED EGG AND VEGGIE BREAKFAST QUESADILLAS

Preparation time: 15 minutes
Cooking time: 15 minutes
Servings: 2
Ingredients:

- 2 eggs
- 2 egg whites
- 2 to 4 tbsp. nonfat or low-fat milk
- ¼ tsp. freshly ground black pepper

- 1 large tomato, chopped
- 2 tbsp. chopped cilantro
- ½ cup canned black beans, rinsed and drained
- 1½ tbsp. olive oil, divided
- 4 corn tortillas
- ½ avocado, peeled, pitted, and thinly sliced

Directions:

1. Mix the eggs, egg whites, milk, and black pepper in a bowl. Using an electric mixer, beat until smooth. To the same bowl, add the tomato, cilantro, and black beans, and fold into the eggs with a spoon.
2. Warm-up half of the olive oil in a medium pan over medium heat. Add the scrambled egg mixture and cook for a few minutes, stirring, until cooked through. Remove from the pan.
3. Divide the scrambled-egg mixture between the tortillas, layering only on one half of the tortilla. Top with avocado slices and fold the tortillas in half.
4. Heat the remaining oil over medium heat, and add one of the folded tortillas to the pan. Cook within 1 to 2 minutes on each side or until browned. Repeat with remaining tortillas. Serve immediately.

Per serving: Calories: 445Kcal; Protein: 19g; Carbohydrates: 42g; Fat: 24g

47. STUFFED BREAKFAST PEPPERS

Preparation time: 15 minutes
Cooking time: 45 minutes
Servings: 4
Ingredients:

- 4 bell peppers (any color)
- 1 (16-ounce) bag frozen spinach
- 4 eggs
- ¼ cup shredded low-fat cheese (optional)
- Freshly ground black pepper

Directions:

1. Preheat the oven to 400°F. Line a baking dish with aluminum foil. Cut the tops off the pepper, then discard the seeds. Discard the tops and seeds. Put the peppers in the baking dish, and bake for about 15 minutes.
2. While the peppers bake, defrost the spinach and drain off the excess moisture. Remove the peppers, then stuff the bottoms evenly with the defrosted spinach.
3. Crack an egg over the spinach inside each pepper. Top each egg with a tbs. of the cheese (if using) and

season with black pepper to taste. Bake within 15 to 20 minutes, or until the egg whites are set and opaque.

Per serving: Calories: 136Kcal; Protein: 11g; Carbohydrates: 15g; Fat: 5g

48. MUFFINS WITH STRAWBERRIES

Preparation time: 10 minutes
Cooking time: 0 minutes
Servings: 4
Ingredients:

- 1 tsp. lemon zest, grated
- 12 ounces low-fat, soft, cream cheese
- 2 cups strawberries, sliced
- 1 tbs. stevia
- 8 whole-wheat English muffins, toasted

Directions:

1. Combine the cream cheese, stevia, and lemon zest in a food processor and pulse until smooth.
2. Spread 1 tbs. of this mixture on 1 muffin half
3. Top with some of the sliced strawberries.
4. Repeat the process with the rest of the muffin.
5. Halves and serve for breakfast. Enjoy!

Per serving: Calories: 150Kcal; Protein: 2g; Carbohydrates: 23g; Fat: 7g

49. STEEL CUT OAT BLUEBERRY PANCAKES

Preparation time: 15 minutes
Cooking time: 15 minutes
Servings: 4
Ingredients:

- 1½ c. Water
- ½ c. steel-cut oats
- 1/8 tsp. Salt
- 1 c. Whole wheat Flour
- ½ tsp. Baking powder
- ½ tsp. Baking soda
- 1 Egg
- 1 c. Milk
- ½ c. Greek yogurt
- 1 c. Frozen Blueberries
- ¾ c. Agave Nectar

Directions:

1. Combine your oats, salt, and water in a medium saucepan, stir, and allow to come to a boil over high heat. Adjust the heat to low, and allow to simmer for about 10 min, or until oats get tender. Set aside.

2. Combine all your remaining ingredients, except agave nectar, in a medium bowl, then fold in oats. Preheat your skillet, and lightly grease it. Cook ¼ cup of milk batter at a time for about 3 minutes per side. Garnish with agave nectar.

Per serving: Calories: 257Kcal; Protein: 14g; Carbohydrates: 46g; Fat: 7g

50. MUSHROOMS AND CHEESE OMELET

Preparation time: 10 minutes
Cooking time: 15 minutes
Servings: 4
Ingredients:

- 2 tbsp. olive oil
- A pinch of black pepper
- 3 ounces mushrooms, sliced
- 1 cup baby spinach, chopped
- 3 eggs, whisked
- 2 tbsp. low-fat cheese, grated
- 1 small avocado, peeled, pitted, and cubed
- 1 tbsp. parsley, chopped

Directions:

1. Add mushrooms to a cooking pan, stir, cook them for 5 minutes and transfer to a bowl on a heated pan with the oil over medium-high heat.
2. Heat-up the same pan over medium-high heat, add eggs and black pepper, spread into the pan, cook within 7 minutes, and transfer to a plate.
3. Spread mushrooms, spinach, avocado, and cheese on half of the omelet, fold the other half over this mix, sprinkle parsley on top, and serve.

Per serving: Calories: 136Kcal; Protein: 16g; Carbohydrates: 5g; Fat: 5g

51. EGG WHITE BREAKFAST MIX

Preparation time: 10 minutes
Cooking time: 10 minutes
Servings: 4
Ingredients:

- 1 yellow onion, chopped
- 3 plum tomatoes, chopped
- 10 ounces spinach, chopped
- A pinch of black pepper
- 2 tbsp. water
- 12 egg whites
- Cooking spray

Directions:

1. Mix the egg whites with water and pepper in a bowl. Grease a pan with cooking spray, heat up over medium heat, add ¼ of the egg whites,

..spread into the pan, and cook for 2 minutes.
2. Spoon ¼ of the spinach, tomatoes, and onion, fold, and add to a plate.
3. Serve for breakfast. Enjoy!

Per serving: Calories: 31Kcal; Protein: 3g; Carbohydrates: 0g; Fat: 2g

52. SWEET POTATO BANANA TOAST

Preparation time: 15 minutes
Cooking time: 2 5 minutes
Servings: 4
Ingredients:

- 3 sweet potato, unpeeled
- 2 ripe banana, sliced
- Ground cinnamon to taste
- 5 tbsp. peanut butter

Directions:

1. Cut the sweet potato into 14-inch thick slices lengthwise.
2. Toast the sweet potato slices for about 5 minutes on high, or until cooked through.
3. Depending on your toaster settings, you may need to repeat this step many times. Enjoy by topping with your preferred toppings.

Per serving: Calories: 137Kcal; Protein: 2g; Carbohydrates: 32g; Fat: 0g

53. APPLE-APRICOT BROWN RICE BREAKFAST PORRIDGE

Preparation time: 15 minutes
Cooking time: 8 minutes
Servings: 4
Ingredients:

- 3 cups cooked brown rice
- 1¾ cups nonfat or low-fat milk
- 2 tbsp. lightly packed brown sugar
- 4 dried apricots, chopped
- 1 medium apple, cored and diced
- ¾ tsp. ground cinnamon
- ¾ tsp. vanilla extract

Directions:

1. Combine the rice, milk, sugar, apricots, apple, and cinnamon in a medium saucepan. Boil it on medium heat, lower the heat down slightly and cook within 2 to 3 minutes.
2. Turn it off, then stir in the vanilla extract. Serve warm.

Per serving: Calories: 260Kcal; Protein: 7g; Carbohydrates: 57g; Fat: 2g

54. STEEL-CUT OATMEAL WITH PLUMS AND PEAR

Preparation time: 15 minutes
Cooking time: 25 minutes
Servings: 4
Ingredients:

- 2 cups of water
- 1 cup nonfat or low-fat milk
- 1 cup steel-cut oats
- 1 cup dried plums, chopped
- 1 medium pear, cored, and skin removed, diced
- 4 tbsp. almonds, roughly chopped

Directions:

1. Mix the water, milk, plus oats in a medium pot and bring to a boil over high heat. Reduce the heat and cover. Simmer for about 10 minutes, stirring occasionally.
2. Add the plums and pear, and cover. Simmer for another 10 minutes. Turn off the heat and let stand within 5 minutes until all of the liquid is absorbed. To serve, top each portion with a sprinkling of almonds.

Per serving: Calories: 307Kcal; Protein: 9g; Carbohydrates: 58g; Fat: 6g

55. FRENCH TOAST WITH APPLESAUCE

Preparation time: 5 minutes
Cooking time: 5 minutes
Servings: 6
Ingredients:

- ¼ c. unsweetened applesauce
- ½ c. skim milk
- 2 packets Stevia
- 2 eggs
- 6 slices whole-wheat bread
- 2 tsp. cinnamon, ground

Directions:

1. Mix well sugar, applesauce, cinnamon, eggs, and milk in a mixing bowl.
2. Soak the bread into the applesauce mixture until wet, and then warm a large nonstick skillet over a medium fire.
3. Place moistened bread on one side and unsoaked bread on the other.
4. Cook in a single layer within 2-3 minutes per side on medium-low fire or until lightly browned. Serve and enjoy.

Per serving: Calories: 122.6Kcal; Protein: 6.5g; Protein: 6.5g; Fat: 2.6g

56. BANANA-PEANUT BUTTER AND GREENS SMOOTHIE

Preparation time: 5 minutes
Cooking time: 0 minutes
Servings: 1
Ingredients:

- 1 c. chopped and packed Romaine lettuce
- 1 frozen medium banana
- 1 tbsp. all-natural peanut butter
- 1 c. cold almond milk

Directions:

1. In a heavy-duty blender, add all ingredients. Puree until smooth and creamy. Serve and enjoy.

Per serving: Calories: 349.3Kcal; Protein: 8.1g; Carbohydrates: 57.4g; Fat: 9.7g

57. LIGHTWEIGHT BISCUITS

Preparation time: 5 minutes
Cooking time: 5 minutes
Servings: 1
Ingredients:

- 1 egg white
- 1 c. white whole-wheat flour
- 4 tbsps. non-hydrogenated vegetable shortening
- 1 tbsp. sugar
- 2/3 c. low-fat milk
- 1 c. unbleached all-purpose flour
- 4 tsp.
- Sodium-free baking powder

Directions:

1. Warm oven to 450°F. Put the flour, sugar, plus baking powder into a mixing bowl and mix. Split the shortening into the batter using your fingers until it resembles coarse crumbs. Put the egg white plus milk and stir to combine.
2. Place the dough out onto a lightly floured surface and knead 1 minute.
3. Roll dough to ¾ inch thickness and cut into 12 rounds. Place rounds on the baking sheet. Bake 10 minutes, then remove the baking sheet and place biscuits on a wire rack to cool.

Per serving: Calories: 118Kcal; Protein: 3g; Carbohydrates: 16g; Fat:4g

58. BREAKFAST FRUITS BOWLS

Preparation time: 10 minutes
Cooking time: 0 minutes
Servings: 2
Ingredients:

- 1 cup mango, chopped
- 1 banana, sliced
- 1 cup pineapple, chopped

- 1 cup almond milk

Directions:

1. Mix the mango with the banana, pineapple, and almond milk in a bowl, stir, divide into smaller bowls, and serve.

Per serving: Calories: 10Kcal; Protein: 0g; Carbohydrates: 0g; Fat: 1g

59. PUMPKIN COOKIES

Preparation time: 10 minutes
Cooking time: 25 minutes
Servings: 6
Ingredients:

- 2 cups whole wheat flour
- 1 cup old-fashioned oats
- 1 tsp. baking soda
- 1 tsp. pumpkin pie spice
- 15 ounces pumpkin puree
- 1 cup coconut oil, melted
- 1 cup of coconut sugar
- 1 egg
- ½ cup pepitas, roasted
- ½ cup cherries, dried

Directions:

1. Mix the flour the oats, baking soda, pumpkin spice, pumpkin puree, oil, sugar, egg, pepitas, and cherries in a bowl, stir well, shape medium cookies out of this mix, arrange them all on a baking sheet, then bake within 25 minutes at 350 degrees F.
2. Serve the cookies for breakfast.

Per serving: Calories: 150Kcal; Protein: 1g; Carbohydrates: 24g; Fat: 8g

60. VEGGIE SCRAMBLE

Preparation time: 10 minutes
Cooking time: 2 minutes
Servings: 1
Ingredients:

- 1 egg
- 1 tbs. water
- ¼ cup broccoli, chopped
- ¼ cup mushrooms, chopped
- A pinch of black pepper
- 1 tbs. low-fat mozzarella, shredded
- 1 tbs. walnuts, chopped
- Cooking spray

Directions:

1. Grease a ramekin with cooking spray, add the egg, water, pepper, mushrooms, and broccoli, and whisk well.
2. Let it cook in the microwave and for 2 minutes.
3. Add mozzarella and walnuts on top and serve for breakfast.

Per serving: Calories: 128Kcal; Protein: 9g;
Carbohydrates: 24g; Fat: 0g

CHAPTER 2: Vegetables and Sides

61. CITRUS COUSCOUS WITH HERB

Preparation time: 5 minutes
Cooking time: 15 minutes
Servings: 2
Ingredients:

- 1/3 cup couscous
- ¼ cup of water
- 4 tbsp. orange juice
- ¼ orange, chopped
- 1 tsp. Italian seasonings
- 1/3 tsp. salt
- ½ tsp. butter

Directions:

1. Fill the pan with water and orange juice.
2. Combine the orange, Italian seasoning, and salt in a mixing bowl.
3. Bring the liquid to a boil, then turn off the heat.
4. Stir in the butter and couscous. Close the cover after giving it a good stir.
5. Set aside for 10 minutes to allow the couscous to absorb the liquid.

Per serving: Calories: 149Kcal; Protein: 4.1g; Carbohydrates: 28.5g; Fat: 1.9g

62. SALAD WITH VINAIGRETTE

Preparation time: 25 minutes
Cooking time: 0 minutes
Servings: 4
Ingredients:

For the vinaigrette:

- Olive oil – ½ cup
- Balsamic vinegar - 4 Tbsps.
- Chopped fresh oregano – 2 Tbsps.
- Pinch red pepper flakes
- Ground black pepper

For the salad:

- Shredded green leaf lettuce – 4 cups
- Carrot – 1, shredded
- Fresh green beans – ¾ cup, cut into 1-inch pieces
- Large radishes – 3, sliced thin

Directions:

1. To make the vinaigrette: put the vinaigrette ingredients in a bowl and whisk.
2. In another bowl, make the salad, pitch together with the carrot, lettuce, green beans, and radishes.
3. Add the vinaigrette to the vegetables. Toss to coat.

4. Arrange the salad on plates and serve.

Per serving: Calories: 273Kcal; Protein: 1g; Carbohydrates: 7g; Fat: 27g

63. SALAD WITH LEMON DRESSING

Preparation time: 10 minutes
Cooking time: 0 minutes
Servings: 4
Ingredients:

- Heavy cream – ¼ cup
- Freshly squeezed lemon juice – ¼ cup
- Granulated sugar – 2 tbsps.
- chopped fresh dill – 2 tbsps.
- finely chopped scallion – 2 tbsps. green part only
- Ground black pepper – ¼ tsp.
- English cucumber – 1, sliced thin
- Shredded green cabbage – 2 cups

Directions:

1. In a small bowl, mixing the lemon juice, cream, sugar, dill, scallion, and pepper until well blended.
2. In a large bowl, toss together the cucumber and cabbage.
3. Place the salad in the refrigerator and chill for 1 hour.
4. Stir before serving.

Per serving: Calories: 99Kcal; Protein: 2g; Carbohydrates: 13g; Fat: 6g

64. SHRIMP WITH SALSA

Preparation time: 15 minutes
Cooking time: 10 minutes
Servings: 4
Ingredients:

- Olive oil – 2 tbsp.
- large shrimp – 6 ounces, peeled and deveined, tails left on
- Minced garlic – 1 tsp.
- Chopped English cucumber – ½ cup
- Chopped mango – ½ cup
- Zest of 1 lime
- Juice of 1 lime
- Ground black pepper
- Lime wedges for garnish

Directions:

1. Soak four wooden skewers in water for 30 minutes.
2. Preheat the barbecue to medium heat.

3. In a bowl, toss together the olive oil, shrimp, and garlic.
4. Thread the shrimp onto the skewers, about four shrimp per skewer.
5. In a bowl, stir together the mango, cucumber, lime zest, and lime juice, and season the salsa lightly with pepper. Set aside.
6. Grill the shrimp for 10 minutes, turning once or until the shrimp is opaque and cooked through.
7. Season the shrimp lightly with pepper.
8. Serve the shrimp on the cucumber salsa with lime wedges on the side.

Per serving: Calories: 120Kcal; Protein: 9g; Carbohydrates: 4g; Fat: 8g

65. THYME WITH HONEY-ROASTED CARROTS

Preparation time: 5 minutes
Cooking time: 30 minutes
Servings: 4
Ingredients:

- 1/5 lb. carrots, with the tops
- 1 tbs. of honey
- 2 tbsp. of olive oil
- ½ tsp. thyme, dried
- ½ tsp. of sea salt

Directions:

1. Preheat the oven to 425 degrees °F.
2. Ensure that the baking sheet is lined with parchment paper.
3. Combine the carrots, honey, oil, thyme, and salt in a mixing bowl. Apply a thick coat of paint.
4. Keep everything in a single layer. Preheat the oven to 350°F and bake for 30 minutes.
5. Before serving, set aside to cool.

Per serving: Calories: 85Kcal; Protein: 1g; Carbohydrates: 6g; Fat: 8g

66. ROASTED PARSNIPS

Preparation time: 5 minutes
Cooking time: 30 minutes
Servings: 4
Ingredients:

- 1 tbs. of extra-virgin olive oil
- 2 lbs. parsnips
- 1 tsp. of kosher salt
- 1-1/2 tsp. of Italian seasoning
- Chopped parsley for garnishing

Directions:

1. Preheat the oven to 400 degrees °F.

2. Peel the parsnips and set aside. Make one-inch slices out of them.

3. In a mixing dish, combine the seasoning, salt, and oil.

4. Put this on a baking pan and spread it out. It should be done in a single layer.

5. Cook for 30 minutes at 350°F. Every ten minutes, give it a good stir.

6. Place on a platter. Serve with parsley as a garnish.

Per serving: Calories: 124Kcal; Protein: 2g; Carbohydrates: 20g; Fat: 4g

67. GREEN BEANS

Preparation time: 5 minutes
Cooking time: 15 minutes
Servings: 6
Ingredients:

- ½ tsp. of red pepper flakes
- 3 garlic cloves, minced
- 3 tbsp. of water
- 1 tsp. kosher salt
- 1 lbs. green beans, trimmed
- 3 tbsp. of extra-virgin olive oil

Directions:

1. In a medium-sized skillet, heat the oil.

2. Add the pepper flake to the mix. Toss in the olive oil and stir to coat.

3. Add the green beans to the mix and cook for7 minutes in the oven

4. Be sure to stir frequently. In some locations, the beans should be brown.

5. Add the garlic and salt. Cook for 1 minute, stirring constantly.

6. Immediately pour water and cover, and cook for 1 minute more, covered.

Per serving: Calories: 82Kcal; Protein: 1g; Carbohydrates: 6g; Fat: 6g

68. TEX-MEX COLE SLAW

Preparation time: 15 minutes
Cooking time: 0 minutes
Servings: 12
Ingredients:

- Black beans, cooked – 2 cups
- Grape tomatoes, sliced in half – 1.5 cups
- Grilled corn kernels – 1.5 cups
- Jalapeno, seeded and minced – 1
- Cilantro, chopped – .5 cup
- Bell pepper, diced – 1
- Coleslaw cabbage mix – 16 ounces
- Lime juice – 3 tbsp.
- Light sour cream - .66 cup

- Olive oil mayonnaise, reduced-Fat: – 1 cup
- Chili powder – 1 tbs.
- Cumin, ground – 1 tsp.
- Onion powder – 1 tsp.
- Garlic powder – 1 tsp.

Directions:

1. Mix the sour cream, mayonnaise, lime juice, garlic powder, onion powder, cumin, and chili powder in a bowl to create the dressing.

2. In a large bowl, toss the vegetables and then add in the prepared dressing and toss again until evenly coated. Chill the mixture in the fridge for thirty minutes to twelve hours before serving.

Per serving: Calories: 50Kcal; Protein: 3g; Carbohydrates: 10g; Fat: 1g

69. ROASTED OKRA

Preparation time: 15 minutes
Cooking time: 20 minutes
Servings: 4
Ingredients:

- Okra, fresh – 1 pound
- Extra virgin olive oil – 2 tbsp.
- Cayenne pepper, ground - .125 tsp.
- Paprika – 1 tsp.
- Garlic powder - .25 tsp.

Directions:

1. Warm the oven to Fahrenheit 450 degrees and prepare a large baking sheet. Cut the okra into pieces appropriate 1/2-inch in size.

2. Place the okra on the baking pan and top it with the olive oil and seasonings, giving it a good toss until evenly coated. Roast the okra in the heated oven until it is tender and lightly browned and seared. Serve immediately while hot.

Per serving: Calories: 65Kcal; Protein: 2g; Carbohydrates: 6g; Fat: 5g

70. BROWN SUGAR GLAZED CARROTS

Preparation time: 15 minutes
Cooking time: 25 minutes
Servings: 6
Ingredients:

- Carrots, sliced into 1-inch pieces – 2 pounds
- Light olive oil - .33 cup
- Truvia Brown Sugar Blend - .25 cup
- Black pepper, ground - .25 tsp.

Directions:

1. Warm the oven to Fahrenheit 400 degrees and prepare a large baking

sheet. Toss the carrots with the oil, Truvia, and black pepper until evenly coated and then spread them out on the prepared baking sheet.

2. Place the carrots in the oven and allow them to roast until tender, about twenty to twenty-five minutes. Halfway through the cooking time, give the carrots a good serve. Remove the carrots from the oven and serve them alone or topped with fresh parsley.

Per serving: Calories: 110Kcal; Protein: 1g; Carbohydrates: 16g; Fat: 4g

71. OVEN-ROASTED BEETS WITH HONEY RICOTTA

Preparation time: 15 minutes
Cooking time: 40 minutes
Servings: 6
Ingredients:

- Purple beets – 1 pound
- Golden beets – 1 pound
- Ricotta cheese, low-fat- .5 cup
- Extra virgin olive oil – 3 tbsp.
- Honey – 1 tbs.
- Rosemary, fresh, chopped – 1 tsp.
- Black pepper, ground - .25 tsp.

Directions:

1. Warm the oven to Fahrenheit 375 degrees and prepare a large baking sheet by lining it with kitchen parchment. Slice the beets into 1/2-inch cubes before tossing them with the extra virgin olive oil and black pepper.

2. Put the beets on the prepared baking sheet and allow them to roast until tender, about thirty-five to forty minutes. Halfway through the cooking process, flip the beets over.

3. Meanwhile, in a small bowl, whisk the ricotta with the rosemary and honey. Put in the fridge until ready to serve. Once the beets are done cooking, serve them topped with the ricotta mixture, and enjoy.

Per serving: Calories: 195Kcal; Protein: 8g; Carbohydrates: 24g; Fat: 8g

72. EASY CARROTS MIX

Preparation time: 10 minutes
Cooking time: 40 minutes
Servings: 6
Ingredients:

- 15 carrots, halved lengthwise
- 2 tbsp. coconut sugar
- ¼ cup olive oil
- ½ tsp. rosemary, dried
- ½ tsp. garlic powder

- A pinch of black pepper

Directions:

1. In a bowl, combine the carrots with the sugar, oil, rosemary, garlic powder, and black pepper, toss well, spread on a lined baking sheet, introduce in the oven and bake at 400 degrees F for 40 minutes.
2. Serve.

Per serving: Calories: 60Kcal; Protein: 2g; Carbohydrates: 9g; Fat: 0g

73. TASTY GRILLED ASPARAGUS

Preparation time: 10 minutes
Cooking time: 6 minutes
Servings: 4
Ingredients:

- 2 pounds asparagus, trimmed
- 2 tbsp. olive oil
- A pinch of salt and black pepper

Directions:

1. In a bowl, combine the asparagus with salt, pepper, and oil and toss well.
2. Place the asparagus on a preheated grill over medium-high heat, cook for 3 minutes on each side, then serve.

Per serving: Calories: 50Kcal; Protein: 5g; Carbohydrates: 8g; Fat: 1g

74. LIMA BEANS DISH

Preparation time: 10 minutes
Cooking time: 5 hours
Servings: 10
Ingredients:

- 1 green bell pepper, chopped
- 1 sweet red pepper, chopped
- 1 and ½ cups tomato sauce, salt-free
- 1 yellow onion, chopped
- ½ cup of water
- 16 ounces canned kidney beans, no-salt-added, drained and rinsed
- 16 ounces canned black-eyed peas, no-salt-added, drained and rinsed
- 15 ounces corn
- 15 ounces canned lima beans, no-salt-added, drained and rinsed
- 15 oz canned black beans, no-salt-added, drained
- 2 celery ribs, chopped
- 2 bay leaves
- 1 tsp. ground mustard
- 1 tbs. cider vinegar

Directions:

1. In a slow cooker, mix the tomato sauce with the celery, onion, green bell pepper, water, red pepper bay leaves, vinegar, mustard, kidney

beans, corn, black-eyed peas, Lima beans, and black beans, cook on Low within 5 hours.

2. Discard bay leaves, divide the whole mix between plates, and serve.

Per serving: Calories: 602Kcal; Protein: 33g; Carbohydrates: 117.7g; Fat: 4.8g

75. ROASTED CARROTS

Preparation time: 10 minutes
Cooking time: 40 minutes
Servings: 4
Ingredients:

- 1 onion, peeled & cut
- 8 carrots, peeled & cut
- 1 tsp. thyme, chopped
- 2 tbsp. of extra-virgin olive oil
- ½ tsp. rosemary, chopped
- ¼ tsp. ground pepper
- ½ tsp. salt

Directions:

1. Preheat your oven to 425 °F.
2. In a bowl mix the carrots, onions, rosemary, thyme, pepper, and salt.
3. Spread on your baking sheet, and roast for 40 minutes.
4. The onions and carrots should be browning and tender.

Per serving: Calories: 126Kcal; Protein: 2g; Carbohydrates: 16g; Fat: 6g

76. TOMATO BULGUR

Preparation time: 7 minutes
Cooking time: 20 minutes
Servings: 2
Ingredients:

- ½ cup bulgur
- 1 tsp. tomato paste
- ½ white onion, diced
- 2 tbsp. coconut oil
- 1 ½ cup chicken stock

Directions:

1. Toss coconut oil in the pan and melt it.
2. Add diced onion and roast it until light brown.
3. Then add bulgur and stir well.
4. Cook bulgur in coconut oil for 3 minutes.
5. Then add tomato paste and mix up bulgur until homogenous.
6. Add chicken stock.
7. Close the lid and cook bulgur for 15 minutes over the medium heat.
8. The cooked bulgur should soak all liquid.

Per serving: Calories: 257Kcal; Protein: 5.2g; Carbohydrates: 30.2g; Fat: 14.5g

77. MOROCCAN STYLE COUSCOUS

Preparation time: 10 minutes
Cooking time: 10 minutes
Servings: 4
Ingredients:

- 1 cup yellow couscous
- ½ tsp. ground cardamom
- 1 cup chicken stock
- 1 tbs. butter
- 1 tsp. salt
- ½ tsp. red pepper

Directions:

1. Toss butter in the pan and melt it.
2. Add couscous and roast it for 1 minute over the high heat.
3. Then add ground cardamom, salt, and red pepper. Stir it well.
4. Pour the chicken stock and bring the mixture to boil.
5. Simmer couscous for 5 minutes with the closed lid.

Per serving: Calories: 196Kcal; Protein: 5.9g; Carbohydrates: 35g; Fat: 3.4g

78. CAULIFLOWER BROCCOLI MASH

Preparation time: 5 minutes
Cooking time: 10 minutes
Servings: 6
Ingredients:

- 1 large head cauliflower, cut into chunks
- 1 small head broccoli, cut into florets
- 3 tbsp. extra virgin olive oil
- 1 tsp. salt
- Pepper, to taste

Directions:

1. Take a pot and add oil then heat it.
2. Add the cauliflower and broccoli.
3. Season with salt and pepper to taste.
4. Keep stirring to make vegetable soft.
5. Add water if needed.
6. When it is already cooked, use a food processor or a potato masher to puree the vegetables.
7. Serve and enjoy!

Per serving: Calories: 39Kcal; Protein: 0.89g; Carbohydrates: 2g; Fat: 3g

79. ROASTED CURRIED CAULIFLOWER

Preparation time: 5 minutes
Cooking time: 30 minutes
Servings: 4

Ingredients:

- 1 large head cauliflower, cut into florets
- 1 tsp. curry powder
- 1 and ½ tbs. olive oil
- 1 tsp. cumin seeds
- 1 tsp. mustard seeds
- ¾ tsp. salt

Directions:

1. Preheat your oven to 375 deg. F.
2. Grease a baking sheet with cooking spray.
3. Take a bowl and place all ingredients.
4. Toss to coat well.
5. Arrange the vegetable on a baking sheet.
6. Roast for 30 minutes.
7. Serve and enjoy!

Per serving: Calories: 67Kcal; Protein: 2g; Carbohydrates: 4g; Fat: 6g

80. CARAMELIZED PEARS AND ONIONS

Preparation time: 5 minutes
Cooking time: 35 minutes
Servings: 4
Ingredients:

- 2 red onions, cut into wedges
- 2 firm red pears, cored and quartered
- 1 tbs. olive oil
- Salt and pepper, to taste

Directions:

1. Preheat your oven to 425 deg. F.
2. Place the onions, and pears on a baking tray, and drizzle with olive oil.
3. Season with salt and pepper.
4. Bake in the oven for 35 minutes.
5. Serve and enjoy!

Per serving: Calories: 101Kcal; Protein: 1g; Carbohydrates: 17g; Fat: 4g

81. SPICY ROASTED BRUSSELS SPROUTS

Preparation time: 5 minutes
Cooking time: 30 minutes
Servings: 4
Ingredients:

- 1 and ¼ pound Brussels sprouts, cut into florets
- ½ cup kimchi with juice
- 2 tbsp. olive oil
- Salt and pepper, to taste

Directions:

1. Set the oven to 425 F.

2. Toss the Brussels sprouts with pepper, salt, and oil.
3. Bake in the oven for 25 minutes.
4. Remove from oven and mix with kimchi.
5. Return to the oven.
6. Cook for 5 minutes.
7. Serve and enjoy!

Per serving: Calories: 135Kcal; Protein: 5g; Carbohydrates: 16g; Fat: 7g

82. COOL GARBANZO AND SPINACH BEANS

Preparation time: 5-10 minutes
Cooking time: 0 minute
Servings: 4
Ingredients:

- 12 ounces garbanzo beans
- 1 tbs. olive oil
- ½ onion, diced
- ½ tsp. cumin
- 10 ounces spinach, chopped

Directions:

1. Take a skillet and add olive oil.
2. Place it over medium-low heat.
3. Add onions, garbanzo and cook for 5 minutes.
4. Stir in cumin, garbanzo beans, spinach and season with sunflower seeds.
5. Use a spoon to smash gently.
6. Cook thoroughly.
7. Serve and enjoy!

Per serving: Calories: 90Kcal; Protein: 4g; Carbohydrates: 11g; Fat: 4g

83. STIR-FRIED ALMOND AND SPINACH

Preparation time: 10 minutes
Cooking time: 15 minutes
Servings: 2
Ingredients:

- 34 pounds spinach
- 3 tbsp. almonds
- Salt to taste
- 1 tbs. coconut oil

Directions:

1. Put oil to a large pot and place it on high heat.
2. Add spinach and let it cook, stirring frequently.
3. Once the spinach is cooked and tender, season with salt and stir.
4. Add almonds and enjoy!

Per serving: Calories: 150Kcal; Protein: 8g; Carbohydrates: 10g; Fat: 12g

84. SPICY WASABI MAYONNAISE

Preparation time: 15 minutes
Cooking time: 0 minute
Servings: 4
Ingredients:

- ½ tbs. wasabi paste
- 1 cup mayonnaise

Directions:

1. Take a bowl and mix wasabi paste and mayonnaise.
2. Mix well.
3. Let it chill, use as needed.
4. Serve and enjoy.

Per serving: Calories: 388Kcal; Protein: 1g; Carbohydrates: 1g; Fat: 42g

85. ROASTED PORTOBELLOS WITH ROSEMARY

Preparation time: 5 minutes
Cooking time: 15 minutes
Servings: 4
Ingredients:

- 8 portobello mushroom, trimmed
- 1 sprig rosemary, torn
- 2 tbsp. fresh lemon juice
- ¼ cup extra virgin olive oil
- 1 clove garlic, minced
- Salt and pepper, to taste

Directions:

1. Preheat your oven to 450 deg. F.
2. Take a bowl and add all ingredients.
3. Toss to coat.
4. Place the mushroom in a baking sheet stem side up.
5. Roast in the oven for around 15 minutes.
6. Serve and enjoy!

Per serving: Calories: 63Kcal; Protein: 1g; Carbohydrates: 2g; Fat: 6g

86. TURMERIC ENDIVES

Preparation time: 10 minutes
Cooking time: 20 minutes
Servings: 4
Ingredients:

- 2 endives, halved lengthwise
- 2 tbsp. olive oil
- 1 tsp. rosemary, dried
- ½ tsp. turmeric powder
- A pinch of black pepper

Directions:

1. Mix the endives with the oil and the other ingredients in a baking pan, toss gently, bake at 400 degrees F within 20 minutes.
2. Serve as a side dish.

Per serving: Calories: 64Kcal; Protein: 0.2g; Carbohydrates: 0.8g; Fat: 7.1g

87. PARMESAN ENDIVES

Preparation time: 10 minutes

Cooking time: 20 minutes

Servings: 4

Ingredients:

- 4 endives, halved lengthwise
- 1 tbs. lemon juice
- 1 tbs. lemon zest, grated
- 2 tbsp. fat-free parmesan, grated
- 2 tbsp. olive oil
- A pinch of black pepper

Directions:

1. In a baking dish, combine the endives with the lemon juice and the other ingredients except for the parmesan and toss.
2. Sprinkle the parmesan on top, bake the endives at 400 degrees F for 20 minutes, and serve.

Per serving: Calories: 71Kcal; Protein: 0.9g; Carbohydrates: 2.2g; Fat: 7.1g

88. LEMON ASPARAGUS

Preparation time: 10 minutes

Cooking time: 20 minutes

Servings: 4

Ingredients:

- 1-pound asparagus, trimmed
- 2 tbsp. basil pesto
- 1 tbs. lemon juice
- A pinch of black pepper
- 3 tbsp. olive oil
- 2 tbsp. cilantro, chopped

Directions:

1. Arrange the asparagus n a lined baking sheet, add the pesto and the other ingredients, toss, bake at 400 degrees F within 20 minutes.
2. Serve as a side dish.

Per serving: Calories: 114Kcal; Protein: 2.6g; Carbohydrates: 4.5g; Fat: 10.7g

89. LIME CARROTS

Preparation time: 10 minutes

Cooking time: 30 minutes

Servings: 4

Ingredients:

- 1-pound baby carrots, trimmed
- 1 tbs. sweet paprika
- 1 tsp. lime juice
- 3 tbsp. olive oil
- A pinch of black pepper
- 1 tsp. sesame seeds

Directions:

1. Arrange the carrots on a lined baking sheet, add the paprika and the other ingredients except for the sesame seeds, toss, bake at 400 degrees F within 30 minutes.
2. Divide the carrots between plates, sprinkle sesame seeds on top and serve as a side dish.

Per serving: Calories: 139Kcal; Protein: 1.1g; Carbohydrates: 10.5g; Fat: 11.2g

90. GARLIC POTATO PAN

Preparation time: 10 minutes

Cooking time: 1 hour

Servings: 8

Ingredients:

- 1-pound gold potatoes, peeled and cut into wedges
- 2 tbsp. olive oil
- 1 red onion, chopped
- 2 garlic cloves, minced
- 2 cups coconut cream
- 1 tbs. thyme, chopped
- ¼ tsp. nutmeg, ground
- ½ cup low-fatparmesan, grated

Directions:

1. Heat-up a pan with the oil over medium heat, put the onion plus the garlic, and sauté for 5 minutes. Add the potatoes and brown them for 5 minutes more.
2. Add the cream and the rest of the ingredients, toss gently, bring to a simmer and cook over medium heat within 40 minutes more. Divide the mix between plates and serve as a side dish.

Per serving: Calories: 230Kcal; Protein: 3.6g; Carbohydrates: 14.3g; Fat: 19.1g

91. BALSAMIC CABBAGE

Preparation time: 10 minutes

Cooking time: 20 minutes

Servings: 4

Ingredients:

- 1-pound green cabbage, roughly shredded
- 2 tbsp. olive oil
- A pinch of black pepper
- 1 shallot, chopped
- 2 garlic cloves, minced
- 2 tbsp. balsamic vinegar
- 2 tsp. hot paprika
- 1 tsp. sesame seeds

Directions:

1. Heat-up a pan with the oil over medium heat, add the shallot and the garlic, and sauté for 5 minutes.

2. Add the cabbage and the other ingredients, toss, cook over medium heat for 15 minutes, divide between plates and serve.

Per serving: Calories: 100Kcal; Protein: 1.8g; Carbohydrates: 8.2g; Fat: 7.5g

92. CHILI BROCCOLI

Preparation time: 10 minutes

Cooking time: 30 minutes

Servings: 4

Ingredients:

- 2 tbsp. olive oil
- 1-pound broccoli florets
- 2 garlic cloves, minced
- 2 tbsp. chili sauce
- 1 tbs. lemon juice
- A pinch of black pepper
- 2 tbsp. cilantro, chopped

Directions:

1. In a baking pan, combine the broccoli with the oil, garlic, and the other, toss a bit, and bake at 400 degrees F for 30 minutes.
2. Divide the mix between plates and serve as a side dish.

Per serving: Calories: 103Kcal; Protein: 3.4g; Carbohydrates: 8.3g; Fat: 7.4g

93. HOT BRUSSELS SPROUTS

Preparation time: 10 minutes

Cooking time: 25 minutes

Servings: 4

Ingredients:

- 1 tbs. olive oil
- 1-pound Brussels sprouts, trimmed and halved
- 2 garlic cloves, minced
- ½ cup low-fatmozzarella, shredded
- A pinch of pepper flakes, crushed

Directions:

1. In a baking dish, mix the Brussels sprouts with the oil and the other ingredients except for the cheese and toss.
2. Sprinkle the cheese on top, introduce in the oven and bake at 400 degrees F for 25 minutes.
3. Divide between plates and have it as a side dish.

Per serving: Calories: 111Kcal; Protein: 10g; Carbohydrates: 11.6g; Fat: 3.9g

94. PAPRIKA BRUSSELS SPROUTS

Preparation time: 10 minutes

Cooking time: 25 minutes

Servings: 4

Ingredients:

- 2 tbsp. olive oil
- 1-pound Brussels sprouts, trimmed and halved
- 3 green onions, chopped
- 2 garlic cloves, minced
- 1 tbs. balsamic vinegar
- 1 tbs. sweet paprika
- A pinch of black pepper

Directions:

1. In a baking pan, combine the Brussels sprouts with the oil and the other ingredients, toss and bake at 400 degrees F within 25 minutes.
2. Divide the mix between plates and serve.

Per serving: Calories: 121Kcal; Protein: 4.4g; Carbohydrates: 12.6g; Fat: 7.6g

95. CREAMY CAULIFLOWER MASH

Preparation time: 10 minutes
Cooking time: 25 minutes
Servings: 4
Ingredients:

- 2 pounds cauliflower florets
- ½ cup of coconut milk
- A pinch of black pepper
- ½ cup low-fatsour cream
- 1 tbs. cilantro, chopped
- 1 tbs. chives, chopped

Directions:

1. Put the cauliflower in a pot, add water to cover, bring to a boil over medium heat, and cook for 25 minutes and drain.
2. Mash the cauliflower, add the milk, black pepper, and the cream, whisk well, divide between plates, sprinkle the rest of the ingredients on top, and serve.

Per serving: Calories: 188Kcal; Protein: 6.1g; Carbohydrates: 15g; Fat: 13.4g

96. RADISH AND OLIVES SALAD

Preparation time: 5 minutes
Cooking time: 0 minutes
Servings: 4
Ingredients:

- 2 green onions, sliced
- 1-pound radishes, cubed
- 2 tbsp. balsamic vinegar
- 2 tbs. olive oil
- 1 tsp. chili powder
- 1 cup black olives, pitted and halved
- A pinch of black pepper

Directions:

1. Mix radishes with the onions and the other ingredients in a large salad bowl, toss, and serve as a side dish.

Per serving: Calories: 123Kcal; Protein: 1.3g; Carbohydrates: 6.9g; Fat: 10.8g

97. BASIL OLIVES MIX

Preparation time: 5 minutes
Cooking time: 0 minutes
Servings: 4
Ingredients:

- 2 tbsp. olive oil
- 1 tbs. balsamic vinegar
- A pinch of black pepper
- 4 cups corn
- 2 cups black olives, pitted and halved
- 1 red onion, chopped
- ½ cup cherry tomatoes halved
- 1 tbs. basil, chopped
- 1 tbs. jalapeno, chopped
- 2 cups romaine lettuce, shredded

Directions:

1. Mix the corn with the olives, lettuce, and the other ingredients in a large bowl, toss well, divide between plates and have it as a side dish.

Per serving: Calories: 290Kcal; Protein: 6.2g; Carbohydrates: 37.6g; Fat: 16.1g

98. ARTICHOKE AND KALE STUFFED MUSHROOMS

Preparation time: 15 minutes
Cooking time: 28 minutes
Servings: 4
Ingredients:

- 16 large white button mushrooms, stemmed
- 2 tsps. olive oil
- 1 tsp. bottled minced garlic
- ½ cup finely chopped sweet onion
- 1 cup chopped water-packed canned artichoke hearts
- 2 cups finely shredded kale
- 1 tsp. chopped fresh basil
- 1 tsp. chopped fresh oregano
- ⅛ tsp. sea salt

Directions:

1. Preheat the oven to 375 deg. F (190°C).
2. On a baking sheet, hollow-side up to arrange the mushroom caps.
3. Warm the olive oil in a large saucepan, over medium-high heat.
4. Stir in the garlic and onion. Sauté until tender, about 3 minutes.
5. Add the artichoke hearts, kale, basil, oregano, and sea salt. Sauté until the kale is wilted, about 5 minutes.
6. Squeeze the liquid out of the filling into the skillet with the back of a spoon and divide the mixture evenly among the mushroom caps.
7. Bake until the mushrooms are tender, about 20 minutes. Serve warm.

Per serving: Calories: 75Kcal; Protein: 5g; Fat: 3g; Carbohydrates: 11g

99. AVOCADO CUCUMBER SUSHI

Preparation time: 20 minutes
Cooking time: 15 minutes
Servings: 4
Ingredients:

- 1½ cups dry quinoa
- 6 nori sheets
- 3 avocados, halved, pitted, and sliced thin, divided
- 1 small cucumber, halved, seeded, and cut into matchsticks, divided
- 3 cups water, plus additional for rolling
- ½ tsp. salt
- Coconut aminos, for dipping (optional)

Directions:

1. In a fine-mesh sieve, rinse the quinoa.
2. Add the rinsed quinoa, water, and salt into a medium pot, bring to a boil over high heat. Reduce the heat to low. Cover and simmer for 15 minutes. Use a fork to fluff the quinoa.
3. Lay out 1 nori sheet on a cutting board, spread ½ cup of quinoa over the sheet, leaving 2 to 3 inches uncovered at the top.
4. Put 5 or 6 avocado slices across the bottom of the nori sheet in a row. Add 5 or 6 cucumber matchsticks on top.
5. From the bottom, roll up the nori sheet tightly. Dab the uncovered top with water to seal the roll.
6. Cut the sushi roll into 6 pieces.
7. Repeat with the remaining 5 nori sheets, quinoa, and vegetables.
8. After all is done, serve the sushi with the coconut aminos (if using).

Per serving: Calories: 557Kcal; Protein: 13 g; Carbohydrates: 57g; Fat: 33g

100. PERSIMMON SALAD

Preparation time: 10 minutes
Cooking time: 0 minutes
Servings: 4
Ingredients:

- Seeds from 1 pomegranate
- 2 persimmons, cored and sliced
- 5 cups baby arugula
- 6 tbsp. green onions, chopped
- 4 navel oranges, cut into segments
- ¼ cup white vinegar
- 1/3 cup olive oil
- 3 tbsp. pine nuts
- 1 and ½ tsp. orange zest, grated
- 2 tbsp. orange juice
- 1 tbs. coconut sugar
- ½ shallot, chopped
- A pinch of cinnamon powder

Directions:

1. In a salad bowl, combine the pomegranate seeds with persimmons, arugula, green onions, and oranges and toss.
2. n another bowl, combine the vinegar with the oil, pine nuts, orange zest, orange juice, sugar, shallot, and cinnamon, whisk well, add to the salad, toss and serve as a side dish.

Per serving: Calories: 310Kcal; Protein: 7g; Carbohydrates: 33g; Fat: 16g

101. AVOCADO SIDE SALAD

Preparation time: 10 minutes
Cooking time: 0 minutes
Servings: 4
Ingredients:

- 4 blood oranges, slice into segments
- 2 tbsp. olive oil
- A pinch of red pepper, crushed
- 2 avocados, peeled, cut into wedges
- 1 and ½ cups baby arugula
- 1 tbs. lemon juice

Directions:

1. Mix the oranges with the oil, red pepper, avocados, arugula, almonds, and lemon juice in a bowl, and then serve.

Per serving: Calories: 146Kcal; Protein: 15g; Carbohydrates: 8g; Fat: 7g

102. CREAM DREDGED CORN PLATTER

Preparation time: 10 minutes
Cooking time: 4 hours
Servings: 3
Ingredients:

- 3 cups corn
- 2 ounces cream cheese, cubed
- 2 tbsp. milk
- 2 tbsp. whipping cream
- 2 tbsp. butter, melted
- Salt and pepper as needed
- 1 tbs. green onion, chopped

Directions:

1. Add corn, cream cheese, milk, whipping cream, butter, salt and pepper to your Slow Cooker.
2. Give it a nice toss to mix everything well.
3. Place lid and cook on LOW for 4 hours.
4. Divide the mix amongst serving platters.
5. Serve and enjoy!

Per serving: Calories: 261Kcal; Protein: 6g; Carbohydrates: 17g; Fat: 11g;

103. EXUBERANT SWEET POTATOES

Preparation time: 5 minutes
Cooking time: 7-8 hours
Servings: 4
Ingredients:

- 6 sweet potatoes, washed and dried

Directions:

1. Loosely ball up 7-8 pieces of aluminum foil in the bottom of your Slow Cooker, covering about half of the surface area.
2. Prick each potato 6-8 times using a fork.
3. Wrap each potato with foil and seal them.
4. Place wrapped potatoes in the cooker on top of the foil bed.
5. Place lid and cook on LOW for 7-8 hours.
6. Use tongs to remove the potatoes and unwrap them.
7. Serve and enjoy!

Per serving: Calories: 129Kcal; Carbohydrates: 30g; Protein: 2g; Fat: 0g

104. ETHIOPIAN CABBAGE DELIGHT

Preparation time: 15 minutes
Cooking time: 6-8 hours
Servings: 6
Ingredients:

- ½ cup water
- 1 head green cabbage, cored and chopped
- 1 pound sweet potatoes, peeled and chopped
- 3 carrots, peeled and chopped
- 1 onion, sliced
- 1 tsp. extra virgin olive oil
- ½ tsp. ground turmeric
- ½ tsp. ground cumin
- ¼ tsp. ground ginger

Directions:

1. Add water to your Slow Cooker.
2. Take a medium bowl and add cabbage, carrots, sweet potatoes, onion and mix.
3. Add olive oil, turmeric, ginger, cumin and toss until the veggies are fully coated.
4. Transfer veggie mix to your Slow Cooker.
5. Cover and cook over low heat for 5-7 hours.
6. Serve and enjoy!

Per serving: Calories: 155Kcal; Protein: 4g; Carbohydrates: 35g; Fat: 2g

105. KALE, MUSHROOM, WALNUT, AND AVOCADO

Preparation time: 10 minutes
Cooking time: 15 minutes
Servings: 2–3
Ingredients:

- 6 kale leaves, chopped
- 10 crushed walnuts
- ¼ onion, diced
- ¼ red bell pepper, diced
- ½ plum tomato, sliced
- 20 mushrooms, sliced
- ½–1 tbsp. avocado oil
- Dressing:
- 1 tbsp. key lime juice
- 1 tbsp. sesame oil
- 1 plum tomato
- ⅛ tsp. sea salt
- ¼ avocado

Directions:

1. Dressing: Blend the lime juice, sesame oil, plum tomato, salt, and avocado together until smooth. Sauté the mushrooms in the avocado oil.
2. Let cool afterward. Mix the kale, walnuts, onion, pepper, tomato, and mushrooms together.
3. Pour the dressing into the salad, then toss it well until it evenly coats the entire salad.

Per serving: Calories: 87Kcal; Protein: 10g; Carbohydrates: 22g; Fat: 1g

106. MIX-MIX ALKALINE VEGGIE

Preparation time: 5 minutes
Cooking time: 10 minutes
Servings: 2
Ingredients:

- 15 kale leaves, chopped
- 1 C. watercress leaves
- 1 cucumber, diced
- 2 tbsp. fresh dill, finely chopped
- ¼ red onion, chopped
- 5–10 olives, sliced
- ¼ red bell pepper, chopped
- ¼ green bell pepper, chopped
- 1 tbsp. 100% date sugar syrup
- 3 tbsp. water
- ⅛ tsp. sea salt

Directions:

1. Mix the date sugar syrup, water, and salt together. Stir the remaining ingredients together in a bowl. Massage in date syrup mix with the vegetables.
2. Toss and serve.

Per serving: Calories: 102Kcal; Protein: 11g; Carbohydrates: 6g; Fat: 1g

107. BROCCOLI SALAD

Preparation time: 15 minutes
Cooking time: 20 minutes
Servings: 4
Ingredients:
For the Salad:

- Kosher salt
- 3 broccoli heads
- ½ C. Cheddar, shredded
- ¼ red onion
- ¼ C. almond, toasted
- 3 slices bacon
- 2 tbsp. fresh chives

For the dressing:

- ⅔ C. mayonnaise
- 3 tbsp. apple cider
- 1 tbsp. Dijon mustard
- Kosher salt
- Black paper, ground

Directions:

1. Heat 6 C. of salted water in a medium pot. Then prepare a large bowl with ice water. Mix in the broccoli florets and cook until tender. Take it out from the pan, and transfer the mix to the bowl with ice water. When it cools down, drain the broccoli.
2. Whisk all the dressing ingredients and season it well to your desired taste. Then mix all the salad ingredients in a separate bowl and pour the dressing. Toss it well until fully coated. Let it chill before serving.

Per serving: Calories: 150Kcal; Protein: 19g; Carbohydrates: 5g; Fat: 2g

108. TOMATO, CUCUMBER AND RED ONION SALAD

Preparation time: 20 minutes
Cooking time: 0 minute
Servings: 4
Ingredients:

- 2 large cucumbers
- 3 large tomatoes
- ⅔ C. red onion, chopped
- ⅓ C. balsamic vinegar
- ½ tbsp. white sugar
- 3 tbsp. extra virgin coconut oil
- Salt and pepper to taste
- Fresh basil for garnish

Directions:

1. Combine all the ingredients and toss them well until fully coated.
2. Seasonthe to your taste.

Per serving: Calories: 105Kcal; Protein: 18g; Carbohydrates: 30g; Fat: 8g

109. HOT CABBAGE QUARTET SALAD

Preparation time: 5 minutes
Cooking time: 15 minutes
Servings: 4
Ingredients:

- 3 tbsp. extra-virgin olive oil
- ½ yellow onion, rinsed, and finely chopped
- 8 oz. cabbage, rinsed, and shredded
- 8 oz. broccoli, rinsed, and cut into medium-sized pieces
- 8 oz. Bok choy, rinsed and chopped
- 8 oz. Brussels sprouts, rinsed and halved
- 1 tbsp. celery, rinsed, and finely chopped
- 1½ tsp. fresh thyme leaves, rinsed and finely chopped
- 1 tsp. garlic powder
- ½ tsp. Himalayan pink salt, plus more as needed
- ½ tsp. black pepper, freshly ground
- ¾ C. water, filtered
- 1 tbsp. lemon juice, freshly squeezed

Directions:

1. Coat the interior of an electric pressure cooker with olive oil. In the pot, combine the onion, cabbage, broccoli, bok choy, Brussels sprouts, celery, thyme, garlic powder, salt, and pepper. Stir well. Add the water, and stir again.
2. Seal the lid into place, set Manual and High Pressure, and cook for 6 minutes.
3. When the beep sounds, quickly release the pressure by pressing "Cancel" and twisting the steam valve to the Venting position. Carefully remove the lid and transfer the vegetables to a serving bowl.
4. Taste and season with salt, as needed. Drizzle with the lemon juice and serve.

Per serving:
Calories: 144.7Kcal; Protein: 12g; Carbohydrates: 9.86g; Fat: 10.49g

110. TABBOULEH SALAD

Preparation time: 20 minutes
Cooking time: 15 minutes
Servings: 4
Ingredients:

- 2 C. water, filtered
- 1 C. millet, rinsed
- ⅓ C. extra-virgin olive oil
- Juice of 1 lemon
- 1 large garlic clove, crushed
- 1½ tsp. Himalayan pink salt, divided
- 2 large tomatoes, rinsed and finely diced
- 3 scallions, white parts only, rinsed and thinly sliced
- ½ English cucumber, rinsed and finely diced
- ¾ C. fresh mint, rinsed and finely chopped
- 1½ C. fresh parsley, rinsed and finely chopped

Directions:

1. Boil water over high heat. Add the millet and turn the heat to low. Cover the pan and cook for 15 minutes.
2. Remove the pan from the heat and mash the millet with a fork. Let cool with the lid off for 15 minutes. It should be firm but not crunchy or mushy.
3. Meanwhile, in a small bowl, whisk the olive oil, lemon juice, garlic, and ½ tsp. of salt. Let sit.
4. In a large bowl, combine the tomatoes, scallions, cucumber, mint, and parsley. Add the cooled millet. Pour the dressing over and mix well. Taste and season with the remaining 1 tsp. of salt, as needed.

Per serving: Calories: 360Kcal; Protein: 8g; Carbohydrates: 44g; Fat: 20g

111. GUACAMOLE SALAD

Preparation time: 10 minutes
Cooking time: 0 minute
Servings: 2
Ingredients:

- 2 avocados, halved and pitted
- ½ C. red onion, diced
- ½ C. fresh cilantro, rinsed and chopped
- Juice of ½ lime
- ½ tsp. onion powder
- ½ tsp. cayenne, ground
- ½ tsp. Himalayan pink salt
- 1 tomato, rinsed and diced

Directions:

1. Take the avocado flesh into a medium bowl. Stir in the red onion, cilantro, lime juice, onion powder, cayenne, and salt. Mash everything until smooth.
2. Add the tomato, mix well, and serve.

Per serving: Calories: 450Kcal; Protein: 16g; Carbohydrates: 27g; Fat: 40g

112. BUCKWHEAT SALAD

Preparation time: 10 minutes
Cooking time: 15 minutes
Servings: 2
Ingredients:

- 1 C. raw buckwheat, rinsed
- 2 C. water
- 2 handfuls fresh baby spinach leaves, rinsed
- Handful fresh basil leaves, rinsed
- 2 scallions, white parts only, rinsed and chopped
- Zest of 1 lemon
- Juice of ½ lemon
- ½ red onion, finely chopped
- Himalayan pink salt
- Black pepper, freshly ground
- ¼ C. extra-virgin olive oil
- 1 red chili, rinsed and thinly sliced
- 2 tbsp. mixed sprouts, rinsed
- 1 ripe avocado, peeled, pitted, and sliced
- 1½ oz. feta cheese (optional)

Directions:

1. Mix the buckwheat and water, then bring it to a boil over high heat. Reduce the heat to simmer and cook for 15 minutes, or until soft. Remove from the heat and let cool.
2. Meanwhile, in a food processor, combine the baby spinach, basil, scallions, lemon zest, and lemon juice, and process for 30 seconds. Stir the herb mixture into the cooled buckwheat.
3. Add the red onion and season with salt and pepper. Arrange the buckwheat on a platter. Drizzle with the olive oil and scatter on the chopped chili and sprouts. Top with the sliced avocado, crumble the feta over top (if using), and serve.

Per serving: Calories: 685Kcal; Fiber: 16g; Carbohydrates: 43g; Fat: 54g

113. MIXED SPROUTS SALAD

Preparation time: 10 minutes
Cooking time: 0 minute
Servings: 2
Ingredients:

- 1–2 tbsp. coconut oil
- Juice of 1 lemon
- Handful fresh chives, rinsed and chopped
- Handful fresh dill, rinsed and chopped
- Handful fresh parsley, rinsed and chopped
- ½ tsp. Himalayan pink salt
- ½ tsp. black pepper, freshly ground
- 1 scallion, rinsed and chopped
- 1 cucumber, rinsed and chopped
- ½ C. mixed sprouts of choice (alfalfa, radish, broccoli, mung bean, cress, etc.), rinsed

Directions:

1. In a blender, combine the coconut oil, lemon juice, chives, dill, parsley, salt, and pepper, and blend until mainly smooth.
2. Transfer to a medium bowl. Stir in the scallion, cucumber, and sprouts to coat, and serve.

Per serving: Calories: 168Kcal; Protein: 20g; Carbohydrates: 12g; Fat: 14g

114. SWEET POTATO SALAD

Preparation time: 15 minutes
Cooking time: 5 minutes
Servings: 2
Ingredients:

- For the dressing:
- ½ C. sesame oil
- 2 tbsp. coconut oil
- 2 tbsp. light soy sauce
- 1 tbsp. coconut sugar or raw honey
- 1 garlic clove, crushed

For the salad:

- 5 ½ oz. fresh baby spinach leaves, rinsed
- 1 red onion, rinsed and finely chopped
- 1 tomato, rinsed, seeded, and chopped
- 1 tbsp. coconut oil
- 1 large sweet potato, scrubbed, peeled, and diced

Directions:
To make the dressing:

1. In a small mixing bowl, whisk the sesame oil, coconut oil, soy sauce, coconut sugar, and garlic until blended. Set aside.

To make the salad:

2. In a large bowl, gently toss together the baby spinach, red onion, and tomato. Set aside.
3. In a medium skillet over medium heat, heat the coconut oil. Add the sweet potato and cook for 3–5 minutes, stirring, until golden brown. Using a slotted spoon, add the sweet potato to the salad and gently stir to combine.
4. Pour the dressing over the salad, gently toss again to coat, and serve.

Per serving: Calories: 550Kcal; Protein 42g; Carbohydrates: 20g; Fat: 52g

115. WALDORF SALAD

Preparation time: 15 minutes plus overnight to soak
Cooking time: 0 minute
Servings: 2
Ingredients:
For the dressing:

- 1 ripe avocado, peeled and pitted
- 1 tsp. Dijon mustard
- ½ tsp. Himalayan pink salt
- Freshly ground black pepper
- Juice of ½ lemon

For the salad:

- 2 C. chickpeas, canned, rinsed and drained, or cooked, drained, and cooled
- 1 C. sunflower seeds, soaked in filtered water overnight, drained
- 2 apples, rinsed, cored, and chopped
- ½ red onion, rinsed and diced
- 1 celery stalk, rinsed and diced
- 1–2 tsp. fresh dill, chopped and rinsed

Directions:
To make the dressing:

1. In a small bowl, using a fork, mash together the avocado, mustard, salt, pepper, and lemon juice. Set aside

To make the salad:

2. In a large bowl, stir together the chickpeas, sunflower seeds, and dressing until well combined. Stir in the apples, red onion, and celery. Top with the fresh dill and serve.

Per serving: Calories: 700Kcal; Protein: 28g; Carbohydrates: 80g; Fat: 40g

116. STUFFED BELL PEPPERS

Preparation time: 10 minutes
Cooking time: 15 minutes
Servings: 1–2
Ingredients:

- 1 C. quinoa
- 1 ½ C. water
- 2 green bell peppers
- 1 lb. oyster or another mushroom
- 1 tbsp. grapeseed or avocado oil
- ½ red bell peppers chopped fine
- ½ tsp. basil
- ½ tsp. dill
- ½ tsp. sea salt
- ⅛ tsp. cayenne pepper

Directions:

1. Soak quinoa for 5–10 minutes and rinse. Combine quinoa and water in a saucepan. Let it boil, then adjust the heat to low and cook for 15–20 minutes. Set aside.
2. Remove stem, cut off tops, and hollow out the green bell peppers. Steam in a steamer until softened. Sauté mushrooms in oil over medium heat. It is important not to cook on high heat to maintain the integrity of the oil and food. Remove mushrooms from pan at let cool.
3. Combine cooked quinoa, mushrooms, and spices and mix. Stuff green bell peppers with e quinoa mix and serve.

Per serving: Calories: 98Kcal; Protein: 7.9g; Carbohydrates: 18g; Fat: 6g

117. SEASONED WILD RICE

Preparation time: 5 minutes
Cooking time: 25 minutes
Servings: 1–2

- **Ingredients:**
- 1 C. wild rice (soak wild rice overnight)
- 2–3 C. water (3 C. water if you didn't soak the rice overnight)
- 1 tbsp. coconut oil
- 2 tsp. oregano
- ½ tsp. sea salt
- ⅛ tsp. cayenne pepper
- 2–3 scallions, chopped

- 1 plum tomato, chopped

Directions:

1. Soaking the rice in water overnight reduces the cooking time for the rice.
2. Transfer all the ingredients to a saucepan over high heat and let them come to a boil.
3. Cover saucepan and reduce to a simmer and allow the water to absorb into the rice. If you soaked the rice overnight, cook the rice for 25 minutes.
4. If you did not soak the rice overnight, cook for 50–60 minutes.

Per serving: Calories: 150Kcal; Protein: 25g; Carbohydrates: 16g; Fat: 4g

118. ROASTED LARGE CAP PORTOBELLO MUSHROOMS AND YELLOW SQUASH

Preparation time: 10 minutes
Cooking time: 30 minutes
Servings: 1–2
Ingredients:

- 3 large Portobello mushrooms
- 9 ½ inch slices yellow squash
- Avocado oil (brush on front and back of mushrooms)
- ½ lime
- Spices (coriander, cayenne pepper, oregano, sea salt)

Directions:

1. Pull off the Portobello mushroom stems and scoop out the fins with a spoon. Brush on avocado oil on the front and back of the mushrooms. Squeeze a little lime over the tops of the mushrooms.
2. Sprinkle the spices on the mushrooms and yellow squash but keep the mushrooms and squash separate. Heat oven to 400°F. Place mushrooms on the roasting pan, scooped outside facing up. Cook for 10 minutes.
3. Carefully remove the pan and mushrooms, and add 3 seasoned yellow squash slices to each mushroom top.
4. Put the roasting pan back into the oven. Cook the mushrooms and squash for another 10 minutes. Remove from oven and serve hot.

Per serving: Calories: 108Kcal; Protein: 5.9g; Carbohydrates: 8g; Fat: 4g

119. SIMPLY CHAYOTE SQUASH

Preparation time: 10 minutes
Cooking time: 20 minutes
Servings: 1
Ingredients:

- 1 chayote squash
- ¼ tsp. coconut oil
- Dash cayenne pepper
- Dash sea salt

Directions:

1. Wash and cut chayote squash in half. The seed can be eaten, and it has a nice texture. Add chayote, oil, and enough water to cover the chayote in a saucepan.
2. Boil for 20 minutes until the fork can penetrate the squash, but the squash should still maintain some firmness. Remove from water. Season it well with cayenne pepper and salt.
3. Serve as a light snack or part of a dish.

Per serving: Calories: 117Kcal; Protein: 14g; Carbohydrates: 12g; Fat: 6g

120. VEGETABLE MEDLEY SAUTÉ

Preparation time: 10 minutes
Cooking time: 15 minutes
Servings: 4
Ingredients:

- 1 cup mushrooms, sliced
- 1 zucchini, sliced
- 1 yellow squash, sliced
- 1 red pepper, chopped
- 1 green pepper, chopped
- 2 plum tomatoes, chopped
- ½ red onion, finely chopped
- ½ cup chayote, finely chopped
- 3 tbsp. grape-seed oil or avocado oil
- ⅛ tsp. cayenne pepper
- ⅛ tsp. sea salt

Directions:

1. Cook the oil in a saucepan over medium heat. Let the oil get hot.
2. Add in mushrooms and onions and sauté for 4 minutes.
3. Add in the rest of the vegetables and spices and sauté for 8–10 minutes.

Per serving: Calories: 115Kcal; Protein: 21g; Carbohydrates: 20g; Fat: 10g

CHAPTER 3: Staples, Sauces, Dips, and Dressings

121. OLIVES AND FETA DRESSING

Preparation time: 10 minutes
Cooking time: 0 minutes
Servings: 16
Ingredients:

- 3 tbsp. feta cheese, crumbled
- 3 tbsp. Kalamata olives, pitted and chopped
- 2 tbsp. yellow onion, chopped
- 1 garlic clove, chopped
- 6–8 drops liquid stevia
- 1 tbsp. Dijon mustard
- 3 tbsp. fresh lemon juice
- 3 tbsp. olive oil
- 1 tsp. oregano, dried and crushed
- Salt and black pepper, ground, as required

Directions:

1. Put all together with the ingredients in a blender and pulse until smooth.
2. Serve immediately.

Per serving: Calories: 31Kcal; Protein: 0.6g; Carbohydrate: 0.8g; Fat: 3.1g

122. CREAMY MUSTARD DRESSING

Preparation time: 10 minutes
Cooking time: 0 minutes
Servings: 8
Ingredients:

- ½ C. sour cream
- ¼ C. water
- ¼ C. Dijon mustard
- 1 tbsp. organic apple cider vinegar
- 1 tbsp. Erythritol, granulated

Directions:

1. Put all together the ingredients in a large bowl and beat until well combined.
2. Serve immediately.

Per serving: Calories: 36Kcal; Protein: 0.8g; Carbohydrate: 1.1g; Fat: 3.3g

123. TOMATO ONION SAUCE

Preparation time: 10 minutes
Cooking time: 10 minutes
Servings: 8
Ingredients:

- 2 large tomatoes, roughly chopped
- 1 C. tomato sauce, sugar-free
- 2 onions, chopped
- 2 garlic cloves, crushed
- 2 tbsp. tomato paste
- 3 tbsp. olive oil

Spices:

- 2 tsp. stevia powder
- ½ tsp. thyme, dried
- 1 tsp. salt

Directions:

1. Warm the oil on the "Sauté" mode. Put the onions and garlic and sauté for 3–4 minutes.
2. Then add tomatoes and season with stevia, salt, and dried thyme. Put about ¼ C. of water and simmer until tomatoes have softened and most of the liquid has evaporated.
3. Stir in tomato paste, then put tomato sauce. Mix and continue to cook for 1–2 minutes more. Optionally, season using some more salt, thyme, or some herbs.

Per serving: Calories: 76Kcal; Protein: 1.3g; Carbohydrates: 5.2g; Fat: 5.5g

124. CRAB AND CARROT DIP

Preparation time: 20 minutes
Cooking time: 0 minutes
Servings: 1 ½ cups
Ingredients:

- 1 cup mascarpone cheese
- Two tbsp. freshly squeezed lemon juice
- ½ cup lump crab meat, drained
- 1 cup grated carrots
- Four scallions, both green and white parts, chopped

Directions:

1. In a medium bowl, beat the mascarpone and lemon juice until smooth.
2. Look over the crab, removing any bits of cartilage and discarding.
3. Stir the crab, carrots, and scallions into the mascarpone mixture.
4. Serve immediately or cover and chill for 4 to 6 hours before serving.

Per serving: Calories: 194Kcal; Protein: 5g; Carbohydrates: 4g; Fat: 18g

125. RED CABBAGE SAUERKRAUT

Preparation time: 10 minutes
Cooking time: 30 minutes
Servings: 6
Ingredients:

- 85g; red cabbage
- 1 ½ tsp. caraway seeds
- 2 tsp. salt

Directions:

1. Remove the outer leaves and dense core of the cabbage. Dice remaining leaves roughly. Toast with salt.
2. Leave the cabbage to sweat for 30 minutes. Add caraway seeds.
3. Place the cabbage and its juices in a jar. Compress tightly and set aside for 30 minutes.
4. Pour filtered water until 1 inch of the jar is covered. Seal with a fermentation lid.
5. Leave the cabbage to ferment until it gets a tangy taste. Refrigerate for 2 months.

Per serving: Calories: 298Kcal; Protein: 5g; Carbohydrates: 20g; Fat: 12g

126. CRANBERRY SAUCE

Preparation time: 10 minutes
Cooking time: 40 minutes
Servings: 3
Ingredients:

- 15g; cranberries, dried
- 2 tsp. red wine
- 125 ml cranberry juice
- 2 tsp. white sugar
- 1 ½ tsp. corn starch
- ½ tsp. orange zest
- ⅛ tsp. salt
- Water

Directions:

1. Soak cranberries in boiling water while covered for 30 minutes.
2. Drain excess water and place cranberries in a food processor with cranberry juice. Blend until relatively smooth.
3. Mix corn starch and water. Transfer mixture to a saucepan together with sugar, wine, zest, and salt.
4. Heat over medium-low flame for 5 minutes. Stir occasionally.
5. Pour sauce in a bowl and refrigerate to chill.

Per serving: Calories: 350Kcal; Protein: 26g; Carbohydrates: 8g; Fat: 8g

127. CHOCOLATE DIPPING SAUCE

Preparation time: 10 minutes
Cooking time: 10 minutes
Servings: 6
Ingredients:

- 8g; dark chocolate, chopped

- 1 tbsp. butter
- 63 ml almond milk
- 4 tsp. white sugar

Directions:

1. Heat chocolate, butter, sugar over low heat. Stir continuously until melted.
2. Add milk and stir well.

Per serving: Calories: 250Kcal; Protein: 17g; Carbohydrates: 8g; Fat: 8g

128. CELERY-ONION VINAIGRETTE

Preparation time: 15 minutes
Cooking time: 0 minutes
Servings: 4

Ingredients:

- 1 tbsp. celery, finely chopped
- 1 tbsp. red onion, finely chopped
- 4 garlic cloves, minced
- ½ C. red wine vinegar
- 1 tbsp. extra virgin olive oil

Directions:

1. Prepare the dressing by mixing the pepper, celery, onion, olive oil, garlic, and vinegar in a small bowl. Whisk well to combine.
2. Let it sit for at least 30 minutes to let flavors blend.
3. Serve and enjoy with your favorite salad greens.

Per serving: Calories: 41Kcal; Protein: 0.2g; Carbohydrates: 1.4g; Fat: 3.4g

129. COWBOY SAUCE

Preparation time: 10 minutes
Cooking time: 10 minutes
Servings: 6

Ingredients:

- 1 stick butter
- 2 cloves garlic, minced
- 1 tbsp. fresh horseradish, grated
- 1 tsp. thyme, dried
- 1 tsp. paprika powder
- Salt and pepper to taste
- ¼ C. water

Directions:

1. Place all ingredients in a pot and bring to a simmer.
2. Simmer for 10 minutes.
3. Adjust seasoning to taste.

Per serving: Calories: 194Kcal; Protein: 1.3g; Carbohydrates: 0.9g; Fat: 20.6g

130. BLUE CHEESE DRESSING

Preparation time: 10 minutes
Cooking time: 0 minutes
Servings: 24

Ingredients:

- 1 C. blue cheese, crumbled
- 1 C. sour cream
- 1 C. mayonnaise
- 2–4 drops liquid stevia
- 2 tsp. fresh lemon juice
- 2 tsp. Worcestershire sauce
- 1 tsp. hot pepper sauce
- 2 tbsp. fresh parsley, chopped
- Salt and black pepper, ground, as required

Directions:

1. Put all together the ingredients in a large bowl and beat until well combined.
2. Refrigerate to chill before serving.

Per serving: Calories: 101Kcal; Protein: 1.5g; Carbohydrate: 0.7g; Fat: 10.3g

131. CURRY HONEY VINAIGRETTE

Preparation time: 10 minutes
Cooking time: 0minutes
Servings: ¾ cup / 180 ml

Ingredients:

- 2 tsps. honey
- ¼ cup (60 ml) lime juice
- 2 tsps. curry powder, plus more as needed
- ¼ tsp. cayenne pepper
- ½ tsp. freshly ground black pepper
- ½ cup (120 ml) organic canola oil
- Kosher salt

Directions:

1. In a small bowl, add the honey, lime juice, curry powder, cayenne and black pepper. Whisk them together until smooth. Then whisk in the canola oil slowly until combined. Use salt to season. Taste, adding more salt or spice if desired.
2. Place in an airtight glass container, and store in the refrigerator for up to 1 week. Just before serving, whisk again to re-emulsify.

Per serving: Calories: 237Kcal; Protein: 2.92g; Carbohydrates: 40 g; Fat: 9.38g

132. GARLIC PARSLEY VINAIGRETTE WITH RED WINE VINEGAR

Preparation time: 5 minutes
Cooking time: 0minutes
Servings: about ½ cup

Ingredients:

- 1 garlic clove, minced
- ½ cup lightly packed fresh parsley, finely chopped
- 3 tbsps. red wine vinegar
- ⅓ cup extra-virgin olive oil
- ¼ tsp. salt, plus additional as needed

Directions:

1. Add the garlic, parsley, red wine vinegar, olive oil, and salt to a small jar, combine them together. Seal the jar and shake until mixed.
2. Taste the vinaigrette and adjust the seasoning as necessary.
3. Keep in the refrigerator.

Per serving: Calories: 93Kcal; Protein: 0g; Carbohydrates: 0g; Fat: 11g

133. GARLIC TAHINI SAUCE WITH LEMON

Preparation time: 10 minutes
Cooking time: 0minutes
Servings: 1 cup

Ingredients:

- ½ cup tahini
- 1 garlic clove, minced
- juice of 1 lemon
- zest of 1 lemon
- ½ tsp. salt, plus additional as needed
- ½ cup warm water, plus additional as needed

Directions:

1. Stir together the tahini and garlic into a small bowl.
2. Stir in the lemon juice, lemon zest, and salt. Mix well.
3. Add ½ cup of warm water, whisk until well mixed and creamy (If the sauce is too thick add more water.)
4. Taste the sauce and adjust the seasoning as necessary.
5. Store in a sealed container and place in the refrigerator.

Per serving: Calories: 180Kcal; Protein: 5g; Carbohydrates: 7g; Fat: 16g

134. GARLICKY CHIPOTLE AND HONEY VINAIGRETTE

Preparation time: 10 minutes
Cooking time: 0minutes
Servings: 1 ¼ cups / 300 ml

Ingredients:

- 1 tbsp. honey
- 2 tsps. to 2 tbsps. chipotle paste
- ½ cup (120 ml) lime juice
- 2 garlic cloves, smashed and peeled
- ½ cup (120 ml) organic canola oil
- Kosher salt

- Freshly ground black pepper (optional)

Directions:

1. In a blender, add the honey, 2 tsps. of the chipotle paste, lime juice, garlic and ½ tsp salt. Blend until combined. Turn on low speed, pour in the canola oil slowly, blending until combined. Taste, adding more salt or pepper or chipotle paste if desired.
2. Place in an airtight glass container, and store in the refrigerator for up to 1 week. Just before serving, shake it to re-emulsify.

Per serving: Calories: 276Kcal; Protein: 3.42g; Carbohydrates: 52g; Fat: 8g

135. GARLICKY GREEN OLIVE TAPENADE

Preparation time: 10 minutes
Cooking time: 0minutes
Servings: 1 cup
Ingredients:

- ¼ cup extra-virgin olive oil
- 2 garlic cloves
- ¼ cup freshly squeezed lemon juice
- 1 cup pitted green olives
- Pinch dried rosemary
- Salt
- Freshly ground black pepper

Directions:

1. Add the olive oil, garlic, lemon juice, olives and rosemary into a food processor, then use the pepper and salt to season.
2. Process them until the mixture is a little chunky, almost smooth.
3. Place in an airtight container and store in the refrigerator. The tapenade will keep for several weeks.

Per serving: Calories: 73Kcal; Protein: 0g; Carbohydrates: 2g; Fat: 8g

136. HONEY LEMON JUICE

Preparation time: 10 minutes
Cooking time: 0minutes
Servings: 1 cup
Ingredients:

- 1 cup water
- ¼ cup fresh lemon juice
- 2 tbsps. honey
- 2 tsps. fresh ginger root, grated

Directions:

1. In an airtight jar, mix all the ingredients and shake, stir until the honey dissolves..

2. Refrigerate for about 24 hours before using so the ginger can permeate the mixture.
3. Cover and store in the refrigerator at least a week.

Per serving: Calories: 20Kcal; Protein: 0g; Carbohydrates: 5g; Fat: 0g

137. ITALIAN GREMOLATA SAUCE

Preparation time: 10 minutes
Cooking time: 0minutes
Servings: 1 cup
Ingredients:

- 2 tbsps. olive oil
- ¾ cup finely chopped fresh parsley
- 2 tsps. bottled minced garlic
- Juice of 2 lemons (or 6 tbsps.)
- Zest of 2 lemons (optional)
- ¼ tsp. sea salt

Directions:

1. Add the olive oil, parsley, garlic, lemon juice, lemon zest (if using) and sea salt into a small bowl, stir them together until well combined.
2. Transfer into a sealed container, and store in the refrigerator for up to 4 days.

Per serving: Calories: 33Kcal; Protein: 0g; Carbohydrates: 1g; Fat: 4g

138. ROASTED GARLIC LEMON DIP

Preparation time: 5 minutes
Cooking time: 30 minutes
Servings: 3
Ingredients:

- 3 medium lemons
- 3 cloves garlic, peeled and smashed
- 5 tbsp. olive oil, divided
- ½ tsp. kosher salt
- Pepper to taste
- Salt
- Pepper

Directions:

1. Bring the rack to the center of the oven then heat to 400°F.
2. Cut the lemons in half crosswise and take off the seeds. Put the lemons cut-side up in a small baking dish. Add the garlic and drizzle with 2 tbsp. of the oil.
3. Roast until the lemons are tender and lightly browned, about 30 minutes. Take off the baking dish to a wire rack.
4. Once the lemons are cool enough to handle, squeeze the juice into the baking dish. Discard the lemon pieces and any remaining seeds. Put

the contents of the baking dish, including the garlic, into a blender or mini food processor. Put the remaining 3 tbsp. oil and salt. Process until the garlic is completely puréed, and the sauce is emulsified and slightly thickened. Serve warm or at room temperature.

Per serving: Calories: 165Kcal; Protein: 4.6g; Carbohydrates: 4.8g; Fat: 17g

139. HOISIN SAUCE

Preparation time: 10 minutes
Cooking time: 0 minutes
Servings: 8
Ingredients:

- 4 tbsp. low-sodium soy sauce
- 2 tbsp. natural peanut butter
- 1 tbsp. Erythritol
- 2 tsp. balsamic vinegar
- 2 tsp. sesame oil
- 1 tsp. Sriracha
- 1 garlic clove, peeled
- Black pepper, ground, as required

Directions:

1. Put all the ingredients together in a food processor and pulse until smooth.
2. Preserve in the refrigerator by placing it into an airtight container.

Per serving: Calories: 39Kcal; Protein: 1.8g; Carbohydrate: 1.5g; Fat: 3.1g

140. SWEET CHILI SAUCE

Preparation time: 10 minutes
Cooking time: 40 minutes
Servings: 3
Ingredients:

- 25g; mild red chili
- 375 ml white vinegar
- 31g; white sugar

Directions:

1. Chop 5g; red chilies roughly. Place chili bits in a food processor.
2. Slice remaining chilies in half and remove the seeds. Chop chilies roughly and add them to the food processor together with ½ C. vinegar.
3. Blend until chilies are reduced to fine bits.
4. Put the mixture in a saucepan. Add the remaining amount of vinegar and sugar. Heat on low flame while stirring continuously for 5 minutes.
5. Turn up the flame to high. Once the sauce is boiling, turn down the heat to medium.
6. Simmer for 25 minutes. Stir occasionally.

Per serving: Calories: 250Kcal; Protein: 17g; Carbohydrates: 8g; Fat: 8g

141. CHOCOLATE COCONUT FUDGE SAUCE

Preparation time: 10 minutes
Cooking time: 10 minutes
Servings: 3
Ingredients:

- 165 ml coconut cream
- 1 tsp. vanilla extract
- 4 tbsp. Dutch cocoa powder
- 250 ml almond milk
- 3 tbsp. coconut oil
- 15g; brown sugar

Directions:

1. Put cocoa powder, milk, coconut cream, and brown sugar in a blender. Process for 30 seconds.
2. Transfer mixture into a saucepan. Simmer while stirring occasionally over medium-low heat for 15 minutes.
3. Add vanilla extract and coconut oil and stir. Simmer for 4 more minutes.
4. Refrigerate for 20 minutes.

Per serving: Calories: 185Kcal; Protein: 11g; Carbohydrates: 4g; Fat: 12g

142. TARTAR SAUCE

Preparation time: 10 minutes
Cooking time: 10 minutes
Servings: 3
Ingredients:

- 2 tbsp. pickles, chopped
- ½ C. mayonnaise
- 1 tsp. shallot, chopped
- 1 tbsp. white wine vinegar
- 1 tbsp. capers, chopped
- ½ tsp. dry mustard powder
- 1 tbsp. parsley, chopped
- Black pepper

Directions:

1. Drop all of the ingredients in a bowl and mix well.
2. Adjust seasoning as desired.

Per serving: Calories: 385Kcal; Protein: 7g; Carbohydrates: 4g; Fat: 12g

143. HOMEMADE GRAVY

Preparation time: 10 minutes
Cooking time: 1 hour 30 minutes
Servings: 3
Ingredients:

- 24g; carrot
- 1.5 l. water, boiling

- 12g; green leek leaves, chopped
- 4 tbsp. corn starch
- 4 sprigs rosemary
- 5 bay leaves
- 8 chicken wings
- 5 sage leaves
- Salt and pepper
- Olive oil

Directions:

1. Slice the chicken wings and break up the bones. Place chicken meat and bones in a roasting tray together with carrots, herbs, and leek leaves.
2. Drizzle oil over the contents of the tray. Season with black pepper and salt. Toss to coat.
3. Bake for an hour in a preheated oven at 200°C.
4. Place the roasting tray over low heat and grind the contents together. Pour water into the tray. Increase the flame to high and allow to boil for 10 minutes.
5. Place corn starch in warm water. Stir well.
6. Reduce heat. Add corn starch mixture to the gravy.
7. Simmer for 25 minutes. Season to taste.
8. Filter the gravy using a sieve.

Per serving: Calories: 298Kcal; Protein: 5g; Carbohydrates: 20g; Fat: 12g

144. ANTI-INFLAMMATORY SALAD DRESSING

Preparation time: 10 minutes
Cooking time: 3 minutes
Servings: 4
Ingredients:

- 1 tbs. of chia seeds
- ¼ cup of raw cherries
- 1 tbs. of apple cider vinegar
- 2/3 cup dairy-free cashew milk
- ½ tsp. turmeric, ground
- ½ tsp. ginger, minced
- 1 tbs. of raw honey
- 1/8 tsp. of mustard powder
- ½ tsp. curry powder
- 1/8 tsp. of black pepper and salt

Directions:

1. Put the chia seeds and milk in a food processor. Grind and mix.
2. Place this mix in your blender. Add some more cashew milk.
3. Blend for a minute.
4. Now add the vinegar, honey, ginger, turmeric, curry, pepper, salt, and mustard.
5. Puree for a minute. Adjust the seasoning if needed.

6. Refrigerate for half an hour.
7. Whisk or blend before pouring on your salad.

Per serving: Calories58Kcal; Protein; 1g; Carbohydrates: 2g; Fat: 5g

145. GINGER AND TURMERIC DRESSING

Preparation time: 5 minutes
Cooking time: 5 minutes
Servings: 10
Ingredients:

- 2 tsp. ginger, skin removed
- 1/5 lb. of lemon juice
- 2 tsp. turmeric, ground
- 1 clove of garlic
- 3 tbsp. of extra-virgin olive oil
- 1 tsp. of honey
- 1 tbs. of apple cider vinegar
- Black pepper and Himalayan salt to taste

Directions:

1. Keep all the ingredients in your blender.
2. Mix to combine well.
3. Adjust the seasoning if needed.
4. Pour over roasted vegetables or salad.

Per serving: Calories: 61Kcal; Protein: 1g; Carbohydrates: 3g; Fat: 7g

146. YOGURT DIP

Preparation time: 10 minutes
Cooking time: 0 minute
Servings: 6
Ingredients:

- 2 tbsp. pistachios, toasted and chopped
- 2 cups Greek yogurt
- A pinch of salt and white pepper
- 1 tbs. kalamata olives, pitted and chopped
- 2 tbsp. mint, chopped
- ¼ cup zaatar spice
- 1/3 cup olive oil
- ¼ cup pomegranate seeds

Directions:

1. Blend the yogurt with the pistachios and the remaining ingredients, and whisk well
2. Serve with pita chips on the side and split it into tiny cups.

Per serving: Calories: 294Kcal; Protein: 10g; Carbohydrates: 2g; Fat: 18g

147. GARLIC RANCH DIP

Preparation time: 10 minutes
Cooking time: 0 minutes
Servings: 4
Ingredients:

- ¼ Cup anti-inflammatory mayonnaise
- ¼ cup buttermilk
- 3 garlic cloves, minced
- 1 tbs. chopped fresh chives
- 1 tbs. chopped fresh dill
- ½ tsp. of sea salt
- ¼ tsp. freshly ground black pepper

Directions:

1. In a little bowl, stir together the mayonnaise, buttermilk, garlic, chives, dill, salt, and pepper.

Per serving: Calories: 69Kcal; Protein: 1g; Carbohydrates: 6g; Fat: 5g

148. HOMEMADE GINGER PINEAPPLE TERIYAKI SAUCE

Preparation time: 20 minutes
Cooking time: 0 minutes
Servings: 4
Ingredients:

- 2 tbsps. maple syrup
- ¼ cup low-sodium soy sauce
- 1 tsp. garlic powder
- ¼ cup pineapple juice
- 1 tbsp. grated fresh ginger
- 1 tbsp. arrowroot powder

Directions:

1. Add all the ingredients into a small bowl, whisk them together until well combined.
2. Place the mixture into a tightly sealed container, and store in the refrigerator for up to 5 days.

Per serving: Calories: 41Kcal; Protein: 1g; Carbohydrates: 10g; Fat: 0g

149. ROASTED GARLIC DIP

Preparation time: 10 minutes
Cooking time: 10 minutes
Servings: 2-3
Ingredients:

- 1 head garlic
- ½ tbs. olive oil

Directions:

1. Slice the top off the garlic.
2. Drizzle with the olive oil.
3. Add to the air fryer.
4. Set it to roast, and let it cook at 390 °F for 20 minutes.
5. Peel the garlic.

6. Transfer to a food processor.
7. Pulse until smooth.

Per serving: Calories: 207Kcal; Protein: 9g; Carbohydrates: 17g; Fat: 12g

150. CASHEW YOGURT

Preparation time: 12 hours and 5 minutes
Cooking time: 0 minutes
Servings: 8
Ingredients:

- 3 probiotic supplements
- 2 2/3 cups cashews, unsalted, soaked in warm water for 15 minutes
- 1/4 tsp. sea salt
- 4 tbs. lemon juice
- 1 1/2 cup water

Directions:

1. Drain the cashews, add them into the food processor, then add remaining ingredients, except for probiotic supplements, and pulse for 2 minutes until smooth.
2. Tip the mixture in a bowl, add probiotic supplements, stir until mixed, then cover the bowl with a cheesecloth and let it stand for 12 hours in a dark and cool room.
3. Serve straight away.

Per serving: Calories: 252Kcal; Protein: 8.3g; Carbohydrates: 14.1g; Fat: 19.8g

151. ARTICHOKE SPINACH DIP

Preparation time: 5 minutes
Cooking time: 3 minutes
Servings: 3 ½ cups
Ingredients:

- 1 (10-ounce package spinach, chopped
- ⅓ cup nutritional yeast
- 2 (8-ounce jars marinated artichoke hearts
- ½ teaspoon Tabasco sauce
- 3 scallions, minced
- 1 tablespoon fresh lemon juice
- 1 cup vegan cream cheese
- ½ teaspoon salt

Directions:

1. Drain the artichoke hearts. Chop them finely.
2. Add the scallions, lemon juice, salt, artichoke hearts, sauce, spinach and yeast in an instant pot.
3. Cover and cook for about 3 minutes.
4. Add the cheese and stir well.
5. Serve warm.

Per serving: Calories: 194Kcal; Protein: 7g; Carbohydrates: 2g; Fat: 10g

152. CHICKPEA AND ARTICHOKE MUSHROOM PÂTÉ

Preparation time: 15 minutes
Cooking time: 1 minutes
Servings: 6-8
Ingredients:

- 2 cups canned artichoke hearts, drained
- 1½ cups cooked chickpeas
- 3 garlic cloves, chopped
- 1 tablespoon fresh lemon juice
- 1 tsp. dried basil
- ½ cup raw cashews, soaked overnight and drained
- 1 cup chopped mushrooms
- Shredded fresh basil leaves, for garnish
- 1 cup crumbled extra-firm tofu
- Salt and black pepper
- Paprika, for garnish

Directions:

1. In an instant pot add some oil and toss the garlic, mushroom and artichokes for 1 minute.
2. Drain them to get rid of excess liquid.
3. Add the cashews and tofu in a blender and blend until smooth.
4. Add the artichoke mixture, lemon juice, salt, chickpeas, basil and pepper.
5. Blend again and pour into a loaf pan.
6. Cover with aluminum foil and poke some holes on top.
7. Add to your instant pot and cook for about 3 minutes.
8. Let it cool and refrigerate until served.
9. Garnish using basil, paprika.

Per serving: Calories: 260Kcal; Protein: 12g; Carbohydrates: 29g; Fat: 12 g

153. BUFFALO DIP

Preparation time: 20 minutes
Cooking time: 20 minutes
Servings: 4
Ingredients:

- 2 cups cashews
- 2 tsp. garlic powder
- 1 1/2 tsp. salt
- 2 tsp. onion powder
- 3 tbsp. lemon juice
- 1 cup buffalo sauce
- 1 cup of water
- 14-ounce artichoke hearts, packed in water, drained

Directions:

1. Switch on the oven, then set it to 375 degrees F and let it preheat.
2. Meanwhile, pour 3 cups of boiling water in a bowl, add cashews and let soak for 5 minutes.
3. Drain the cashew, transfer them into the blender, pour in water, add lemon juice and all the seasoning and blend until smooth.
4. Add artichokes and buffalo sauce, process until chunky mixture comes together, and then transfer the dip to an ovenproof dish.
5. Bake for 20 minutes and then serve.

Per serving: Calories: 100Kcal; Protein: 10g; Carbohydrates: 18g; Fat: 8g

154. EGG WHITES -GARLIC SAUCE

Preparation time: 10 minutes
Cooking time: 0 minutes
Servings: 2 cups
Ingredients:

- 1 (12-ounce) cooked organic egg whites
- 2 garlic cloves, crushed
- ½ cup fresh basil, chopped
- 1 tbsp. fresh lemon juice
- ½ cup coconut oil
- 1 tsp. salt
- ¼ tsp. ground black pepper

Directions:

1. Combine the egg whites, garlic, basil, lemon juice, coconut oil, salt and pepper in a blender.
2. Stir until smooth. If too thick, thin with a bit of water.
3. Refrigerate in an airtight container at least 5 days.

Per serving: Calories: 120Kcal; Protein: 6g; Carbohydrates: 5g; Fat: 10g

155. TZATZIKI - CUCUMBER YOGURT SAUCE

Preparation time: 8 minutes
Cooking time: 0minutes
Servings: 2
Ingredients:

- ⅓ cup olive oil
- ⅔ cup Coconut Yogurt
- 2 cups roughly chopped seedless cucumber (1 large cucumber)
- 2 cloves garlic, peeled
- Juice of 2 lemons
- 1 tbsp. dried dill weed
- 1 tsp. fine Himalayan salt
- 1½ tsps. ground black pepper

Directions:

1. In a blender, add all the ingredients. Blend until smooth.
2. Place in a glass jar with a tight-fitting lid, and store in the refrigerator for up to 1 week. Shake well and use.

Per serving: Calories 132Kcal; Protein 0.5g; Carbohydrate 2.9g; Fat 13.5g

156. GARLICKY HONEY-MUSTARD SAUCE WITH SESAME OIL

Preparation time: 10 minutes
Cooking time: 0 minutes
Servings: 1
Ingredients:

- ½ cup raw honey or maple syrup
- ½ cup Dijon mustard
- 1 tsp. toasted sesame oil
- 1 garlic clove, minced

Directions:

1. Add the honey, Dijon, sesame oil, and garlic to a small bowl, whisk until combined.
2. Store in an airtight container and chill in the refrigerator.

Per serving: Calories: 67Kcal; Protein: 1g; Carbohydrates: 14g; Fat: 1g

157. HEALTHY AVOCADO DRESSING

Preparation time: 10 minutes
Cooking time: 5 minutes
Servings: 2 cups
Ingredients:

- ¼ cup yogurt
- ¼ tsp. coriander
- 1 tbsp. lemon juice
- 1 ripe avocado
- 1 green onion, chopped

Directions:

1. Put the avocado, yogurt, lemon juice, green onions, and coriander in a food processor and stir at high speed until smooth.
2. Put the mixture in an airtight container, close the lid and put it in the refrigerator.

Per serving: Calories: 33Kcal; Protein: 0g; Carbohydrates: 2g; Fat: 3g

158. SIMPLE BERRY VINAIGRETTE

Preparation time: 15 minutes
Cooking time: 5 minutes
Servings: 1 ½ cups
Ingredients:

- ½ cup balsamic vinegar
- 1 tbsp. lemon or lime zest
- 2 tbsps. freshly squeezed lemon or lime juice
- ⅓ cup extra-virgin olive oil
- 1 cup berries, fresh or frozen, no added sugar (thawed if frozen)
- 1 tbsp. raw honey or maple syrup
- 1 tsp. salt
- ½ tsp. freshly ground black pepper
- 1 tbsp. Dijon mustard

Directions:

1. Put the berries, balsamic vinegar, olive oil, lemon juice, honey, lemon zest, Dijon mustard, salt, and pepper in a blender, and beat into a puree.
2. Put the puree in an airtight container and put it in the refrigerator for up to five days.

Per serving: Calories: 73Kcal; Protein: 0g; Carbohydrates: 3g; Fat: 7g

159. BARBECUE TAHINI SAUCE

Preparation time: 5 minutes
Cooking time: 0 minutes
Servings: 8
Ingredients:

- 6 tbsp. tahini
- 3/4 tsp. garlic powder
- 1/8 tsp. red chili powder
- 2 tsp. maple syrup
- 1/4 tsp. salt
- 3 tsp. molasses
- 3 tsp. apple cider vinegar
- 1/4 tsp. liquid smoke
- 10 tsp. tomato paste
- 1/2 cup water

Directions:

1. Drop all the ingredients in a food processor or blender. Pulse for 3 to 5 minutes at high speed until smooth.
2. Pour the sauce in a bowl and then serve.

Per serving: Calories: 86Kcal; Protein: 2g; Carbohydrates: 7g; Fat: 5g

160. BOLOGNESE SAUCE

Preparation time: 55 minutes
Cooking time: 0 minutes
Servings: 8
Ingredients:

- ½ of small green bell pepper, chopped
- 1 stalk of celery, chopped
- 1 small carrot, chopped
- 1 medium white onion, peeled, chopped
- 2 tsp. minced garlic
- 1/2 tsp. crushed red pepper flakes
- 3 tbsp. olive oil

- 8-ounce tempeh, crumbled
- 8 ounces white mushrooms, chopped
- 1/2 cup dried red lentils
- 28-ounce crushed tomatoes
- 28-ounce whole tomatoes, chopped
- 1 tsp. dried oregano
- 1/2 tsp. fennel seed
- 1/2 tsp. ground black pepper
- 1/2 tsp. salt
- 1 tsp. dried basil
- 1/4 cup chopped parsley
- 1 bay leaf
- 6-ounce tomato paste
- 1 cup dry red wine

Directions:

1. Take a Dutch oven, place it over medium heat, add oil, and when hot, add the first six ingredients, stir and cook: for 5 minutes until sauté.
2. Then switch heat to medium-high level, add two ingredients after olive oil, stir and cook for 3 minutes.
3. Switch heat to medium-low level, stir in tomato paste, and continue cooking for 2 minutes.
4. Add remaining ingredients except for lentils, stir and bring the mixture to boil.
5. Switch heat to the low level, simmer sauce for 10 minutes, covering the pan partially, then add lentils and continue cooking for 20 minutes until tender.
6. Serve sauce with cooked pasta.

Per serving: Calories: 208.8Kcal; Protein: 10.6g; Carbohydrates: 17.8g; Fat: 12g

161. CHIPOTLE BEAN CHEESY DIP

Preparation time:10 minutes
Cooking time: 0 minutes
Servings: 3 cups
Ingredients:

- 2cups pinto beans, cooked, mashed
- 1tablespoon chipotle chiles in adobo, minced
- ¼cup water
- ½cup shredded vegan cheddar cheese
- ¾cup tomato salsa
- 1teaspoon chili powder
- Salt

Directions:

1. In a bowl combine the mashed beans, chipotle chile, salsa, chili powder and water in an instant pot.
2. Mix well and cover with lid.
3. Cook for about 5 minutes.

4. Add the cheddar cheese and salt and serve warm.
5. Drain the tomatoes and add to a blender.

Per serving: Calories: 217Kcal; Protein: 9g; Carbohydrates: 3g; Fat: 19g

162. CILANTRO AND PARSLEY HOT SAUCE

Preparation time: 5 minutes
Cooking time: 0 minutes
Servings: 4
Ingredients:

- 2 cups of parsley and cilantro leaves with stems
- 4 Thai bird chilies, destemmed, deseeded, torn
- 2 tsp. minced garlic
- 1 tsp. salt
- 1/4 tsp. coriander seed, ground
- 1/4 tsp. ground black pepper
- 1/2 tsp. cumin seeds, ground
- 3 green cardamom pods, toasted, ground
- 1/2 cup olive oil

Directions:

1. Take a spice blender or a food processor, place all the ingredients in it, and process for 5 minutes until the smooth paste comes together.
2. Serve straight away.

Per serving: Calories: 130Kcal; Protein: 1g; Carbohydrates: 2g; Fat: 14 g

163. ALMOND CARROT SPREAD

Preparation time: 10 minutes
Cooking time: 0 minutes
Servings: 2 cups
Ingredients:

- 3 carrots, peeled and cut into chunks
- 1 tbsp. pure maple syrup
- ½ cup almonds
- 2 tbsps. freshly squeezed lemon juice
- ½ tsp. ground cardamom
- Sea salt

Directions:

1. Place the carrots in a food processor, process until very finely chopped.
2. Combine the maple syrup, almonds, lemon juice, and cardamom in the processor and process until smooth.
3. With sea salt to season the spread, transfer to a lidded container. Place in the refrigerator and chill for up to 6 days.

Per serving: Calories: 26Kcal; Protein: 1 g; Carbohydrates: 3g; Fat: 2g

164. BEST CAESAR SALAD DRESSING

Preparation time: 10 minutes
Cooking time: 0 minutes
Servings: 1 cup
Ingredients:

- 3 tbsps. apple cider vinegar
- ¾ cup extra-virgin olive oil
- 2 garlic cloves, minced
- 2 anchovy fillets
- ½ tsp. salt
- Freshly ground black pepper

Directions:

1. Add the cider vinegar, olive oil, garlic, anchovies, salt and pepper into a blender or food processor, purée them.
2. Place in an airtight container, and store in the refrigerator for up to one week.

Per serving: Calories: 166Kcal; Protein: 0 g; Carbohydrates: 0 g; Fat: 19g

165. CASHEW CREAM WITH LEMON AND DILL

Preparation time: 10 minutes
Cooking time: 0minutes
Servings: 1 cup
Ingredients:

- ¾ cup cashews (soaked in water for at least 4 hours)
- zest of 1 lemon
- juice of 1 lemon
- 2 tbsps. chopped fresh dill
- ¼ tsp. salt, plus additional as needed
- ¼ cup water

Directions:

1. Place the cashews into a mesh sieve, drain and rinse well.
2. Add the cashews, water, lemon juice, and lemon zest into a blender, blend until smooth and creamy. Then mix in the dill and salt. Blend again.
3. Taste the cream and adjust the seasoning as necessary.
4. Place the cream in the refrigerator and chill for at least 1 hour. Allow the cream to be thicken in the refrigerator.

Per serving: Calories: 38Kcal; Protein: 1g; Carbohydrates: 2g; Fat: 3g

166. CREAMY HERB DRESSING

Preparation time: 5 minutes
Cooking time: 0minutes
Servings: 1 cup

Ingredients:

- 8 ounces (227 g) plain coconut yogurt
- 2 tbsps. freshly squeezed lemon juice
- 2 tbsps. chopped fresh parsley
- 1 tbsp. snipped fresh chives
- ½ tsp. salt
- Pinch freshly ground black pepper

Directions:

1. Add all ingredients into a mini bowl, whisk them together.
2. Refrigerate for 5 to 7 days into an airtight container.

Per serving: Calories: 14Kcal; Protein: 0g; Carbohydrates: 2g; Fat: 1g

167. MUSTARD TURMERIC DRESSING

Preparation time: 15 minutes or fewer
Cooking time: 0minutes
Servings: 4 to 6
Ingredients:

- ¼ cup extra-virgin olive oil
- 1½ tbsps. raw honey
- 1 tbsp. apple cider vinegar
- 1 tsp. ground turmeric
- 1 tsp. Dijon mustard
- ½ tsp. ground ginger
- 2 tbsps. water
- 2 tbsps. freshly squeezed lemon juice
- ¼ tsp. sea salt
- Pinch freshly ground black pepper

Directions:

1. Add all ingredients into a mini bowl, whisk well to combine.

2. Place in an airtight container and keep in the refrigerator.

Per serving: Calories: 151Kcal; Protein: 0g; Carbohydrates: 8g; Fat: 14g

168. SIMPLE GARLIC AIOLI

Preparation time: 5 minutes
Cooking time: 0 minutes
Servings: 4
Ingredients:

- 3 garlic cloves, finely minced
- ½ cup anti-inflammatory mayonnaise

Directions:

1. Add the garlic mayonnaise into a small bowl, whisk them tocombine.
2. Transfer the mixture into a tightly sealed container, and store in the refrigerator for up to 4 days.

Per serving: Calories: 169Kcal; Protein: 1g; Carbohydrates: 1g; Fat: 20g

169. SPICY APPLESAUCE

Preparation time: 10 minutes
Cooking time: 10 minutes
Servings: 2 cups
Ingredients:

- 1 tbsp. almond oil
- 4 apples, peeled, cored, diced
- 1 tbsp. honey
- ½ cup white raisins
- 1 tbsp. apple cider vinegar
- 1 small onion, diced
- 1 tsp. ground cinnamon
- ½ tsp. ground cardamom
- ½ tsp. ground ginger
- ½ tsp. salt

Directions:

1. In a saucepan, warm the oil over low heat.
2. Combine the apples, honey, raisins, vinegar, onion, cinnamon, cardamom, ginger and salt, cook briefly, until the apples begin to release their juices.
3. Bring to a simmer, cover then cook for about 5 to 10 minutes, until the apples are tender.
4. Set aside until completely cool.

Per serving: Calories: 120Kcal; Protein: 1g; Carbohydrates: 24g; Fat: 2g

170. SPICY LEMON DRESSING

Preparation time: 10 minutes
Cooking time: 0 minutes
Servings: 1 ½ cups
Ingredients:

- 1 cup extra-virgin olive oil
- ¼ cup fresh lemon juice
- 1 tsp. lemon zest, grated
- 1 tbsp. honey
- 1 tsp. Dijon mustard
- 1 shallot, sliced
- 1 tsp. salt
- ¼ tsp. pepper

Directions:

1. Combine the olive oil, lemon juice, lemon zest, honey, Dijon, shallot, salt and pepper in a blender.
2. Stir until smooth.
3. Refrigerate in an airtight container at least 5 days.

Per serving: Calories: 180Kcal; Protein: 0g; Carbohydrates: 2g; Fat: 20g

CHAPTER 4: Beans and Grains

171. QUINOA FLORENTINE

Preparation time: 5 minutes
Cooking time: 25 minutes
Servings: 4
Ingredients:

- 2 tbsp. extra-virgin olive oil
- 1 onion, chopped
- 3 cups fresh baby spinach
- 2 garlic cloves, minced
- 2 cups quinoa, rinsed well
- 4 cups no-salt-added vegetable broth
- ½ tsp. sea salt
- ⅛ tsp. freshly ground black pepper

Directions:

1. In a huge pot over medium-high heat, heat the olive oil until it shimmers.
2. Add onion and spinach. Cook for 3 minutes.
3. Add garlic and cook for 30 seconds.
4. Stir in the remaining ingredients. Bring to a boil and simmer on low for 15 to 20 minutes, until the liquid is absorbed. Fluff with a fork.

Per serving: Calories: 403 Kcal; Protein: 13g; Carbohydrates: 62g; Fat: 1g

172. BROWN RICE WITH BELL PEPPERS

Preparation time: 10 minutes
Cooking time: 10 minutes
Servings: 4
Ingredients:

- 2 tbsp. extra-virgin olive oil
- 1 red bell pepper, chopped
- 1 green bell pepper, chopped
- 1 onion, chopped
- 2 cups cooked brown rice
- 2 tbsp. low-sodium soy sauce

Directions:

1. In a huge nonstick skillet over medium-high heat, heat the olive oil until it shimmers.
2. Add bell peppers and onion. Cook for about 7 minutes, until brown.
3. Add the rice and the soy sauce.
4. Cook for about 3 minutes, until the rice warms through.

Per serving: Calories: 266Kcal; Protein: 5g; Carbohydrates: 44g; Fat: 8g

173. LENTILS WITH TOMATOES AND TURMERIC

Preparation time: 10 minutes
Cooking time: 10 minutes
Servings: 4
Ingredients:

- 3 tbsp. extra-virgin olive oil
- 1 onion, finely chopped
- 1 tbs. ground turmeric
- 1 tsp. garlic powder
- 1 (14-ounce / 397-g) can lentils, drained
- 1 (14-ounce / 397-g) can chopped tomatoes, drained
- ½ tsp. sea salt
- ¼ tsp. freshly ground black pepper

Directions:

1. In a huge pot over medium-high heat, heat the olive oil until it shimmers.
2. Add the onion and turmeric, and cook for about 5 minutes.
3. Add the garlic powder, lentils, tomatoes, salt, and pepper. Cook for 5 minutes. Serve garnished with additional olive oil, if desired.

Per serving: Calories: 248Kcal; Protein: 12g; Carbohydrates: 34g; Fat: 8g

174. BLACK BEAN CHILI WITH GARLIC AND TOMATOES

Preparation time: 10 minutes
Cooking time: 20 minutes
Servings: 4
Ingredients:

- 2 tbsp. extra-virgin olive oil
- 1 onion, chopped
- 2 (28-ounce / 794-g) cans chopped tomatoes, undrained
- 2 (14-ounce / 397-g) cans black beans, drained
- 1 tbs. chili powder
- 1 tsp. garlic powder
- ½ tsp. sea salt

Directions:

1. In a huge pot over medium-high, heat the olive oil until it shimmers.
2. Add the onion. Cook for about 5 minutes, stirring occasionally, until soft.
3. Stir in the remaining ingredients. Bring to a simmer on medium for 15 minutes.

Per serving: Calories: 481Kcal; Protein: 25g; Carbohydrates: 60g; Fat: 10g

175. CELERY AND TURMERIC LENTILS

Preparation time: 10 minutes
Cooking time: 10 minutes
Servings: 4
Ingredients:

- 2 tbsp. olive oil
- 1 celery stalk, chopped
- 1 onion, chopped
- 1 tbs. ground turmeric
- 1 tsp. garlic powder
- 1 (14-ounce / 397-g) can lentils, drained
- 1 (14-ounce / 397-g) can diced tomatoes
- Sea salt and pepper to taste

Directions:

1. Warm the olive oil in your pot over medium heat and place the onion, celery, and turmeric.
2. Cook for 5 minutes until tender. Stir in garlic powder, lentils, tomatoes, salt, and pepper and cook for 5 more minutes.
3. Serve immediately.

Per serving: Calories: 285Kcal; Protein: 16g; Carbohydrates: 35g; Fat: 9g

176. HOT QUINOA FLORENTINE

Preparation time: 15 minutes
Cooking time: 25 minutes
Servings: 4
Ingredients:

- ½ tsp. crushed red pepper
- 2 tbsp. olive oil
- 1 onion, chopped
- 3 cups fresh baby spinach
- 2 garlic cloves, minced
- 2 cups quinoa
- 4 cups vegetable broth
- Sea salt and pepper to taste

Directions:

1. Warm the olive oil in your pot over medium heat, place the onion and spinach, and cook for 3 minutes.
2. Stir in garlic and crushed red pepper and cook for another 30 seconds.
3. Mix in quinoa, vegetable broth, salt, and pepper, bring to a boil, low the heat, and simmer for 15 to 20 minutes until the liquid is absorbed.
4. Fluff the quinoa and serve.

Per serving: Calories: 404Kcal; Protein: 13g; Carbohydrates: 62g; Fat: 12g

177. GRANDMA'S BLACK BEAN CHILI

Preparation time: 15 minutes
Cooking time: 20 minutes
Servings: 4
Ingredients:

- 2 tbsp. olive oil
- 1 tsp. smoked paprika
- 1 onion, chopped
- 2 (28-ounce / 794-g) cans diced tomatoes
- 2 (14-ounce / 397-g) cans black beans
- 1 chili pepper, chopped
- 1 tsp. garlic powder
- ½ tsp. sea salt

Directions:

1. Warm the olive oil in your pot over medium heat, place the onion, and cook for 5 minutes until tender.
2. Mix in tomatoes, black beans, chili pepper, garlic powder, smoked paprika, and salt and bring to a simmer. Then lower the heat and cook for 15 more minutes. Serve warm.

Per serving: Calories: 338Kcal; Protein: 17g; Carbohydrates: 54g; Fat: 9g

178. GARBANZO AND KIDNEY BEAN SALAD

Preparation time: 10 minutes
Cooking time: 0 minutes
Servings: 4
Ingredients:

- 1 (15 oz) can kidney beans, drained
- 1 (15.5 oz) can garbanzo beans, drained
- 1 lemon, zested and juiced
- 1 medium tomato, chopped
- 1 tsp. capers, rinsed and drained
- 1/2 cup chopped fresh parsley
- 1/2 tsp. salt, or to taste
- 1/4 cup chopped red onion
- 3 tbsp. extra virgin olive oil

Directions:

1. In a salad bowl, whisk lemon juice, olive oil and salt well until dissolved.
2. Stir in garbanzo, kidney beans, tomato, red onion, parsley, and capers. Toss well to coat.
3. Allow flavors to mix for 30 minutes by setting in the fridge.
4. Mix again before serving.

Per serving: Calories: 329Kcal; Protein: 12.1g; Carbohydrates: 46.6g; Fat: 12.0g

179. RICE AND CURRANT SALAD MEDITERRANEAN STYLE

Preparation time: 20 minutes
Cooking time: 50 minutes
Servings: 4
Ingredients:

- 1 cup basmati rice
- salt
- 2 1/2 Tablespoons lemon juice
- 1 tsp. grated orange zest
- 2 Tablespoons fresh orange juice
- 1/4 cup olive oil
- 1/2 tsp. cinnamon
- Salt and pepper to taste
- 4 chopped green onions
- 1/2 cup dried currants
- 3/4 cup shelled pistachios or almonds
- 1/4 cup chopped fresh parsley

Directions:

1. Place a nonstick pot on medium high fire and add rice. Toast rice until opaque and starts to smell, around 10 minutes.
2. Add 4 quarts of boiling water to pot and 2 tsp salt. Boil until tender, around 8 minutes uncovered.
3. Drain the rice and spread out on a lined cookie sheet to cool completely.
4. In a large salad bowl, whisk well the oil, juices and spices. Add salt and pepper to taste.
5. Add half of the green onions, half of parsley, currants, and nuts.
6. Toss with the cooled rice and let stand for at least 20 minutes.
7. If needed, adjust seasoning with pepper and salt.
8. Garnish with remaining parsley and green onions.

Per serving: Calories: 450Kcal; Protein: 9.0g; Carbohydrates: 50.0g; Fat: 24.0g

180. STUFFED TOMATOES WITH GREEN CHILI

Preparation time: 10 minutes
Cooking time: 55 minutes
Servings: 6
Ingredients:

- 4 oz Colby-Jack shredded cheese
- ¼ cup water
- 1 cup uncooked quinoa
- 6 large ripe tomatoes
- ¼ tsp freshly ground black pepper
- ¾ tsp ground cumin
- 1 tsp salt, divided
- 1 tbsp fresh lime juice

- 1 tbsp olive oil
- 1 tbsp chopped fresh oregano
- 1 cup chopped onion
- 2 cups fresh corn kernels
- 2 poblano chilies

Directions:

1. Preheat broiler to high.
2. Slice the chilies lengthwise and press on a baking sheet lined with foil. Broil for 8 minutes. Remove from oven then let cool for 10 minutes. Peel the chilies and chop coarsely and place in medium sized bowl.
3. Place onion and corn in baking sheet and broil for ten minutes. Stir two times while broiling. Remove from oven and mix in with chopped chilies.
4. Add black pepper, cumin, ¼ tsp salt, lime juice, oil and oregano. Mix well.
5. Cut off the tops of tomatoes and set aside. Leave the tomato shell intact as you scoop out the tomato pulp.
6. Drain tomato pulp as you press down with a spoon. Reserve 1 ¼ cups of tomato pulp liquid and discard the rest. Invert the tomato shells on a wire rack for 30 mins and then wipe the insides dry with a paper towel.
7. Season with ½ tsp salt the tomato pulp.
8. On a sieve over a bowl, place quinoa. Add water until it covers quinoa. Rub quinoa grains for 30 seconds together with your hands; rinse and drain. Repeat this procedure two times and drain well at the end.
9. In medium saucepan, bring to a boil remaining salt, ¼ cup water, quinoa and tomato liquid.
10. Once boiling, reduce heat then simmer for 15 minutes or until liquid is fully absorbed. Remove from heat then fluff quinoa with fork. Transfer and mix well the quinoa with the corn mixture.
11. Spoon ¾ cup of the quinoa-corn mixture into the tomato shells, top with cheese and cover with the tomato top. Bake in a preheated 350 deg. F oven for 15 minutes and then broil high for another 1.5 minutes.

Per serving: Calories: 276Kcal; Protein: 13.4g; Carbohydrates: 46.3g; Fat: 4.1g

181. RED WINE RISOTTO

Preparation time: 30 minutes
Cooking time: 25 minutes
Servings: 8
Ingredients:

- Pepper to taste
- 1 cup finely shredded Parmigian-Reggiano cheese, divided
- 2 tsp tomato paste
- 1 ¾ cups dry red wine
- ¼ tsp salt
- 1 ½ cups Italian 'risotto' rice
- 2 cloves garlic, minced
- 1 medium onion, freshly chopped
- 2 tbsp extra-virgin olive oil
- 4 ½ cups reduced sodium beef broth

Directions:

1. On medium high fire, bring to a simmer broth in a medium fry pan. Lower fire so broth is steaming but not simmering.
2. On medium low heat, place a Dutch oven and heat oil.
3. Sauté onions for 5 minutes. Add garlic and cook for 2 minutes.
4. Add rice, mix well, and season with salt.
5. Into rice, add a generous splash of wine and ½ cup of broth.
6. Lower fire to a gentle simmer, cook until liquid is fully absorbed while stirring rice every once in a while.
7. Add another splash of wine and ½ cup of broth. Stirring once in a while.
8. Add tomato paste and stir to mix well.
9. Continue cooking and adding wine and broth until broth is used up.
10. Once done cooking, turn off fire and stir in pepper and ¾ cup cheese.
11. To serve, sprinkle with remaining cheese and enjoy.

Per serving: Calories: 231Kcal; Protein: 7.9g; Carbohydrates: 33.9g; Fat: 5.7g

182. CHICKEN PASTA PARMESAN

Preparation time: 10 minutes
Cooking time: 20 minutes
Servings: 1
Ingredients:

- ¼ cup prepared marinara sauce
- ½ cup cooked whole wheat spaghetti
- 1 oz reduced Fat: mozzarella cheese, grated
- 1 tbsp olive oil
- 2 tbsp seasoned dry breadcrumbs
- 4 oz skinless chicken breast

Directions:

1. On medium high fire, place an ovenproof skillet and heat oil.
2. Pan fry chicken for 3 to 5 minutes per side or until cooked through.

3. Pour marinara sauce, stir and continue cooking for 3 minutes.
4. Turn off fire, add mozzarella and breadcrumbs on top.
5. Pop into a preheated broiler on high and broil for 10 minutes or until breadcrumbs are browned and mozzarella is melted.
6. Remove from broiler, serve and enjoy.

Per serving: Calories: 529Kcal; Protein: 38g; Carbohydrates: 34.4g; Fat: 26.6g

183. ORANGE, DATES AND ASPARAGUS ON QUINOA SALAD

Preparation time: 10 minutes
Cooking time: 25 minutes
Servings: 8
Ingredients:

- ¼ cup chopped pecans, toasted
- ½ cup white onion, finely chopped
- ½ jalapeno pepper, diced
- ½ lb. asparagus, sliced into 2-inch lengths, steamed and chilled
- ½ tsp salt
- 1 cup fresh orange sections
- 1 cup uncooked quinoa
- 1 tsp olive oil
- 2 cups water
- 2 tbsp minced red onion
- 5 dates, pitted and chopped
- ¼ tsp freshly ground black pepper
- ¼ tsp salt
- 1 garlic clove, minced
- 1 tbsp extra virgin olive oil
- 2 tbsp chopped fresh mint
- 2 tbsp fresh lemon juice
- Mint sprigs – optional

Directions:

1. On medium high fire, place a large nonstick pan and heat 1 tsp oil.
2. Add white onion and sauté for two minutes.
3. Add quinoa and sauté for 5 minutes.
4. Add salt and water. Bring to a boil, once boiling, slow fire to a simmer and cook for 15 minutes while covered.
5. Turn off fire and leave for 15 minutes, to let quinoa absorb the remaining water.
6. Transfer quinoa to a large salad bowl. Add jalapeno pepper, asparagus, dates, red onion, pecans and oranges. Toss to combine.
7. Make the dressing by mixing garlic, pepper, salt, olive oil and lemon juice in a small bowl.

8. Pour dressing into quinoa salad along with chopped mint, mix well.
9. If desired, garnish with mint sprigs before serving.

Per serving: Calories: 265.2Kcal; Protein: 14.6g; Carbohydrates: 28.3g; Fat: 10.4g

184. CINNAMON QUINOA BARS

Preparation time: 20 minutes
Cooking time: 30 minutes
Servings: 4
Ingredients:

- 2 ½ cups cooked quinoa
- 4 large eggs
- 1/3 cup unsweetened almond milk
- 1/3 cup pure maple syrup
- Seeds from ½ whole vanilla bean pod or 1 tbsp vanilla extract
- 1 ½ tbsp cinnamon
- 1/4 tsp salt

Directions:

1. Preheat oven to 375oF.
2. Into a large mixing bowl, mix all ingredients and mix well.
3. In an 8 x 8 baking pan, cover with parchment paper.
4. Pour batter evenly into baking dish.
5. Bake for 25-30 minutes, or until the mixture has set. Because the eggs are properly cooked, they should not wobble when softly shaken.
6. Remove as quickly as possible from pan and parchment paper onto cooling rack.
7. Cut into 4 pieces.
8. Enjoy on its own, with a small spread of nut butter or almond or let it cool to enjoy the next morning.

Per serving: Calories: 285; Protein: 8.5g; Carbohydrates: 46.2g; Fat: 7.4g

185. BASIC BEANS

Preparation time: 30 minutes
Cooking time: 7 to 8 hours
Servings: 6 cups
Ingredients:

- 1 pound (45g;) dried beans, soaked for at least 8 hours
- Water

Directions:

1. Drain and rinse the beans well. Put them in slow cooker and cover with 2 inches of fresh water.
2. Cover and cook on low for 7 to 8 hours, or until soft and cooked through. Drain and serve.

Per serving: Calories: 259Kcal; Protein: 15g; Carbohydrates: 48g; Fat: 0g

186. INDIAN BUTTER CHICKPEAS

Preparation time: 15 minutes
Cooking time: 6 to 8 hours
Servings: 4 to 6
Ingredients:

- 1 tbs. coconut oil
- 1 medium onion, diced
- 1 pound (45g;) dried chickpeas, soaked in water overnight, drained, and rinsed
- 2 cups full-Fat: coconut milk
- 1 (14½-ounce / 411-g) can crushed tomatoes
- 2 tbsp. almond butter
- 2 tbsp. curry powder
- 1½ tsp. garlic powder
- 1 tsp. ground ginger
- ½ tsp. sea salt
- ½ tsp. ground cumin
- ½ tsp. chili powder

Directions:

1. Coat the slow cooker with coconut oil.
2. Layer the onion along the bottom of the slow cooker.
3. Add the remaining ingredients and stir to combine.
4. Cover and cook on low for 6 to 8 hours, until the chickpeas are soft, and serve.

Per serving: Calories: 720Kcal; Protein: 27g; Carbohydrates: 86g; Fiber: 19g

187. BASIC QUINOA

Preparation time: 15 minutes
Cooking time: 4 to 6 hours
Servings: 4 to 6
Ingredients:

- 2 cups quinoa, rinsed well
- 4 cups vegetable broth

Directions:

1. In slow cooker, combine the quinoa and broth.
2. Cover and cook on low for 4 to 6 hours. Fluff with a fork, cool, and serve.

Per serving: Calories: 335Kcal; Protein: 12g; Carbohydrates: 61g; Fat: 5g

188. MEDITERRANEAN QUINOA WITH PEPERONCINI

Preparation time: 15 minutes
Cooking time: 6 to 8 hours
Servings: 4 to 6
Ingredients:

- 1½ cups quinoa, rinsed well
- 3 cups vegetable broth

- ½ tsp. sea salt
- ½ tsp. garlic powder
- ¼ tsp. dried oregano
- ¼ tsp. dried basil leaves
- Freshly ground black pepper, to taste
- 3 cups arugula
- ½ cup diced tomatoes
- ⅓ cup sliced peperoncini
- ¼ cup freshly squeezed lemon juice
- 3 tbsp. extra-virgin olive oil

Directions:

1. In slow cooker, combine the first seven ingredients.
2. Cover and cook on low for about 6 to 8 hours.
3. In a huge bowl, toss together the remaining ingredients.
4. When the quinoa is done, add it to the arugula salad, mix well, and serve.

Per serving: Calories: 359Kcal; Protein: 10g; Carbohydrates: 50g; Fat: 14g

189. COCONUT BROWN RICE

Preparation time: 15 minutes
Cooking time: 3 hours
Servings: 4 to 6
Ingredients:

- 2 cups brown rice, soaked in water overnight, drained, and rinsed
- 3 cups water
- 1½ cups full-Fat: coconut milk
- 1 tsp. sea salt
- ½ tsp. ground ginger
- Freshly ground black pepper, to taste

Directions:

1. In slow cooker, combine all the ingredients and stir to combine.
2. Cover then cook on high for 3 hours and serve.

Per serving: Calories: 479Kcal; Protein: 9g; Carbohydrates: 73g; Fat: 19g

190. HERBED HARVEST RICE

Preparation time: 15 minutes
Cooking time: 3 hours
Servings: 4 to 6
Ingredients:

- 2 cups brown rice, soaked in water overnight, drained, and rinsed
- ½ small onion, chopped
- 4 cups vegetable broth
- 2 tbsp. extra-virgin olive oil
- ½ tsp. dried thyme leaves
- ½ tsp. garlic powder
- ½ cup cooked sliced mushrooms

- ½ cup dried cranberries
- ½ cup toasted pecans

Directions:

1. In slow cooker, combine the rice, onion, broth, olive oil, thyme, and garlic powder. Stir well.
2. Cover then cook on high for 3 hours.
3. Stir in the mushrooms, cranberries, and pecans, and serve.

Per serving: Calories: 546Kcal; Protein: 10g; Carbohydrates: 88g; Fat: 20g

191. SPANISH RICE

Preparation time: 15 minutes
Cooking time: 5 to 6 hours
Servings: 4 to 6
Ingredients:

- 2 cups white rice
- 2 cups vegetable broth
- 2 tbsp. extra-virgin olive oil
- 1 (14½-ounce / 411-g) can crushed tomatoes
- 1 (4-ounce / 113-g) can Hatch green chiles
- ½ medium onion, diced
- 1 tsp. sea salt
- ½ tsp. ground cumin
- ½ tsp. garlic powder
- ½ tsp. chili powder
- ½ tsp. dried oregano
- Freshly ground black pepper, to taste

Directions:

1. In slow cooker, combine all the ingredients and stir.
2. Cover then cook on low for 5 to 6 hours, fluff, and serve.

Per serving: Calories: 406Kcal; Protein: 8g; Carbohydrates: 79g; Fat: 7g

192. MUSHROOM RISOTTO WITH SPRING PEAS

Preparation time: 15 minutes
Cooking time: 2 to 3 hours
Servings: 4 to 6
Ingredients:

- 1½ cups Arborio rice
- 1 cup English peas
- 1 small shallot, minced
- ¼ cup dried porcini mushrooms
- 4½ cups broth of choice (choose vegetable to keep it vegan)
- 1 tbs. freshly squeezed lemon juice
- ½ tsp. garlic powder
- ½ tsp. sea salt

Directions:

1. In slow cooker, combine all the ingredients and stir to mix well.
2. Cover then cook on high for 2 to 3 hours and serve.

Per serving: Calories: 382Kcal; Protein: 12g; Carbohydrates: 79g; Fat: 1g

193. RED LENTIL CURRY WITH CAULIFLOWER AND YAMS

Preparation time: 30 minutes
Cooking time: 45 minutes
Servings: 6
Ingredients:

- 2 tbsp. organic canola oil
- 1 yellow onion, diced
- 2 tsp. grated fresh ginger
- 2 garlic cloves, minced
- 1 tbs. red curry paste (optional if nightshade-sensitive)
- 1 tsp. garam masala
- Kosher salt, to taste
- Freshly ground black pepper
- 4 cups water
- 1 (14-ounce / 397-g) can unsweetened coconut milk
- 2 tbsp. lime juice
- 1 tbs. agave nectar
- 1½ cups red lentils
- 2 small garnet yams, diced
- 1 small head cauliflower, cutted in florets
- Steamed brown rice for serving (optional)
- Cilantro for garnish

Directions:

1. In a stockpot over medium heat, cook onion in canola oil until soft. Turn the heat to low and cook ginger and garlic until fragrant. Add the curry paste (if using), garam masala, 1 tsp. salt, and ½ tsp. pepper and cook for 1 minute.
2. Add water, turn the heat to medium-high, and bring to a boil, scraping up the browned bits on the bottom. Add coconut milk, lime juice, agave nectar, and lentils and bring to a boil. Cover then simmer on medium-low for 10 minutes.
3. Add yams and cauliflower, cover, and simmer for 15 minutes. Season with salt and pepper. Serve over rice, and garnish with cilantroif desired.

Per serving: Calories: 394Kcal; Protein: 14g; Carbohydrates: 41g; Fat: 22g

194. SWEET POTATO CHILI

Preparation time: 25 minutes
Cooking time: 15 minutes
Servings: 4
Ingredients:

- 15 ounces (42g;) canned black beans
- 2 cups veggie broth
- 28 ounces (79g;) canned diced tomatoes
- 15 ounces (42g;) canned kidney beans
- 2 sweet potatoes, chopped
- 1 red onion, chopped
- 1 red bell pepper, chopped
- 1 green bell pepper, chopped
- 1 tbs. olive oil
- 1 tbs. chili powder
- ¼ tsp. cinnamon
- 1 tsp. cumin
- 2 tsp. cocoa powder
- 1 tsp. cayenne pepper
- Sea salt to taste

Directions:

1. Heat the olive oil in your Instant Pot on "Sauté".
2. Add the onions, peppers, and sweet potatoes. Cook until the onions become translucent. Stir in the rest of the ingredients.
3. Cover and cook for 12 minutes on "Manual" setting.
4. Once the cooking is complete, let the pressure release naturally for 5 minutes. Serve hot.

Per serving: Calories: 365Kcal; Protein: 16g; Carbohydrates: 62g; Fat: 4g

195. BEAN AND RICE CASSEROLE

Preparation time: 10 minutes
Cooking time: 35 minutes
Servings: 4
Ingredients:

- 1 cup soaked black beans
- 2 cups water
- 2 tsp. onion powder
- 2 tsp. chili powder, optional
- 2 cups brown rice
- 6 ounces (17g;) tomato paste
- 1 tsp. minced garlic
- 1 tsp. sea salt

Directions:

1. Combine all the ingredients in your Instant Pot. Choose the "Manual" setting and seal the lid. Cook for 35 minutes on high pressure.
2. Once the cooking is complete, let the pressure release for 5 minutes. Then perform a quick pressure release. Serve hot.

Per serving: Calories: 444Kcal; Protein: 20g; Carbohydrates: 82g; Fat: 4g

196. BEAN AND SPINACH CASSEROLE

Preparation time: 20 minutes
Cooking time: 30 minutes
Servings: 6
Ingredients:

- ½ cup whole-wheat bread crumbs
- 1 (15½-ounce / 439-g) can Great Northern beans
- 1 (15½-ounce / 439-g) can Navy beans
- 3 tbsp. olive oil
- 1 onion, chopped
- 2 carrots, chopped
- 1 celery stalk, chopped
- 2 garlic cloves, minced
- 1 cup baby spinach
- 3 tomatoes, chopped
- 1 cup vegetable broth
- 1 tbs. parsley, chopped
- 1 tsp. dried thyme
- Sea salt and pepper to taste

Directions:

1. Preheat your oven to 380 °F (193 °F). Heat the oil in a skillet over medium heat.
2. Place in onion, carrots, celery, and garlic. Sauté for 5 minutes.
3. Remove into a greased casserole.
4. Add in beans, spinach, tomatoes, broth, parsley, thyme, salt, and pepper and stir to combine.
5. Cover with foil then bake in the oven for 15 minutes. Take out the casserole from the oven, remove the foil, and spread the bread crumbs all over.
6. Bake for another 10 minutes until the top is crispy and golden. Serve warm.

Per serving: Calories: 332Kcal; Protein: 16g; Carbohydrates: 49g; Fat: 8g

197. QUINOA A LA PUTTANESCA

Preparation time: 20 minutes
Cooking time: 15 minutes
Servings: 4
Ingredients:

- 1 cup brown quinoa
- 2 cups water
- Sea salt to taste
- 4 cups tomatoes, diced
- 4 pitted green olives, sliced
- 4 Kalamata olives, sliced
- 1½ tbsp. capers

- 2 garlic cloves, minced
- 1 tbs. olive oil
- 1 tbs. chopped parsley
- ¼ cup chopped basil
- ⅛ tsp. red chili flakes

Directions:

1. Add quinoa, water, and salt to a medium pot and cook for 15 minutes. In a bowl, mix tomatoes, green olives, olives, capers, garlic, olive oil, parsley, basil, and red chili flakes.
2. Allow sitting for 5 minutes. Serve.

Per serving: Calories: 231Kcal; Protein: 7g; Carbohydrates: 35g; Fat: 7g

198. HERBY QUINOA WITH WALNUTS

Preparation time: 20 minutes
Cooking time: 10 to 15 minutes
Servings: 4
Ingredients:

- 2 minced sun-dried tomatoes
- 1 cup quinoa
- 2 cups vegetable broth
- 2 garlic cloves, minced
- ¼ cup chopped chives
- 2 tbsp. chopped parsley
- 2 tbsp. chopped basil
- 2 tbsp. chopped mint
- 1 tbs. olive oil
- ½ tsp. lemon zest
- 1 tbs. lemon juice
- 2 tbsp. minced walnuts

Directions:

1. In a pot, combine quinoa, vegetable broth, and garlic.
2. Boil until the quinoa is tender and the liquid absorbs, 10 to 15 minutes.
3. Stir in chives, parsley, basil, mint, tomatoes, olive oil, zest, lemon juice, and walnuts. Warm for 5 minutes. Serve.

Per serving: Calories: 308Kcal; Protein: 28g; Carbohydrates: 31g; Fat: 8g

199. HOT PAPRIKA LENTILS

Preparation time: 10 minutes
Cooking time: 20 minutes
Servings: 6
Ingredients:

- 1 onion, chopped
- 3 tbsp. olive oil
- 1 tbs. hot paprika
- 2¼ cups lentils, drained
- 2 garlic cloves, minced
- ½ tsp. dried thyme
- Salt and black pepper to taste

Directions:

1. Warm the oil in your pot over medium heat.
2. Place the onion and garlic and sauté for 3 minutes. Add in paprika, salt, pepper, 5 cups water, lentils, and thyme.
3. Bring to a boil, lower the heat and simmer for 15 minutes, stirring often.

Per serving: Calories: 111Kcal; Protein: 3g; Carbohydrates: 9g; Fat: 7g

200. CHIPOTLE KIDNEY BEAN CHILI

Preparation time: 20 minutes
Cooking time: 25 minutes
Servings: 4

- 2 tbsp. olive oil
- 1 onion, chopped
- 2 garlic cloves, minced
- 1 (16-ounce / 454-g) can tomato sauce
- 1 tbs. chili powder
- 1 chipotle chili, minced
- 1 tsp. ground cumin
- ½ tsp. dried marjoram
- 1 (15½-ounce / 439-g) can kidney beans
- Sea salt and pepper to taste
- ½ tsp. cayenne pepper

Directions:

1. Warm the oil in your pot over medium heat. Place in onion and garlic and sauté for 3 minutes.
2. Put in tomato sauce, chipotle chili, chili powder, cumin, cayenne pepper, marjoram, salt, and pepper and cook for 5 minutes. Stir in kidney beans and 2 cups of water.
3. Bring to a boil, thenturn the heat to low and simmer for 15 minutes, stirring often.

Per serving: Calories: 271Kcal; Protein: 6g; Carbohydrates: 37g; Fat: 11g

201. TENDER FARRO

Preparation time: 8 minutes
Cooking time: 40 minutes
Servings: 4
Ingredients:

- 1 cup farro
- 3 cups beef broth
- 1 tsp. salt
- 1 tbs. almond butter
- 1 tbs. dried dill

Directions:

1. Place farro in the pan.
2. Add beef broth, dried dill, and salt.

3. Close the lid and bringthe mixture to boil.
4. Then boil it for 35 minutes over the medium-low heat.
5. Open the lid and add almond butter.
6. Mix up the cooked farro well.

Per serving: Calories: 95Kcal; Protein: 6.4g; Carbohydrates: 10.1g; Fat: 3.3g

202. RED BEANS AND RICE

Preparation time: 15 minutes
Cooking time: 45 minutes
Servings: 2
Ingredients:

- ½ cup dry brown rice
- 1 cup water, plus ¼ cup
- 1 can red beans, drained
- 1 tbs. ground cumin
- Juice of 1 lime
- 4 handfuls of fresh spinach
- Optional toppings: avocado, chopped tomatoes, Greek yogurt, onions

Directions:

1. Mix rice plus water in a pot and bring to a boil. Cover then place heat to a low simmer. Cook within 30 to 40 minutes or according to package directions.
2. Meanwhile, add the beans, ¼ cup of water, cumin, and lime juice to a medium skillet. Simmer within 5 to 7 minutes.
3. Once the liquid is mostly gone, remove from the heat and add the spinach. Cover and let spinach wilt slightly, 2 to 3 minutes. Mix in with the beans. Serve beans with rice. Add toppings, if using.

Per serving: Calories: 232Kcal; Protein: 13g; Carbohydrate: 41g; Fat: 2g

203. BROWN RICE PILAF

Preparation time: 5 minutes
Cooking time: 10 minutes
Servings: 4
Ingredients:

- 1 cup low-sodium vegetable broth
- ½ tbs. olive oil
- 1 clove garlic, minced
- 1 scallion, thinly sliced
- 1 tbs. minced onion flakes
- 1 cup instant brown rice
- 1/8 tsp. freshly ground black pepper

Directions:

1. Mix the vegetable broth, olive oil, garlic, scallion, and minced onion flakes in a saucepan and boil. Put

rice, then boil it again, adjust the heat and simmer within 10 minutes.

2. Remove and let stand within 5 minutes. Fluff with a fork then season with black pepper.

Per serving: Calories: 100Kcal; Protein: 2g; Carbohydrate: 19g; Fat: 2g

204. HOT COCONUT BEANS WITH VEGETABLES

Preparation time: 15 minutes
Cooking time: 10 minutes
Servings: 4
Ingredients:

- 2 tbsp. olive oil
- 1 onion, chopped
- 1 red bell pepper, chopped
- 2 garlic cloves, minced
- 1 tbs. hot powder
- 1 (13½-ounce / 383-g) can coconut milk
- 2 (15½-ounce / 439-g) cans white beans
- 1 (14½-ounce / 411-g) can diced tomatoes
- 3 cups fresh baby spinach
- Sea salt and pepper to taste
- Chopped toasted walnuts

Directions:

1. Warm the oil in your pot over medium heat. Place in onion, garlic, hot powder, and bell pepper and sauté for 5 minutes, stirring occasionally.
2. Put in the coconut milk and whisk until well mixed.
3. Add in white beans, tomatoes, spinach, salt, and pepper and cook for 5 minutes until the spinach wilts.
4. Garnish with walnuts and serve.

Per serving: Calories: 578Kcal; Protein: 11g; Carbohydrates: 48g; Fat: 38g

205. SOUTHERN BEAN BOWL

Preparation time: 15 minutes
Cooking time: 0 minutes
Servings: 4
Ingredients:

- 1 tomato, chopped
- 1 red bell pepper, chopped
- 1 green bell pepper, chopped
- 1 small red onion, sliced
- 1 (14½-ounce / 411-g) can black-eyed peas
- 1 (14½-ounce / 411-g) can black beans
- ¼ cup capers
- 2 avocados, pitted
- 1 tbs. lemon juice

- ¼ cup sake
- 1 tsp. dried oregano
- Sea salt to taste
- 2 tbsp. olive oil
- 1 cup leafy greens, chopped

Directions:

1. In a bowl, mix the tomato, peppers, onion, black-eyed peas, beans, and capers.
2. Put the avocados, lemon juice, sake, olive oil, oregano, and salt in a food processor and blitz until smooth. Add the dressing to the bean bowl and toss to combine.
3. Top with leafy greens to serve.

Per serving: Calories: 412Kcal; Protein: 7g; Carbohydrates: 48g; Fat: 21g

206. HABANERO PINTO BEAN AND BELL PEPPER POT

Preparation time: 10 minutes
Cooking time: 15 minutes
Servings: 6
Ingredients:

- 1 tsp. olive oil
- 2 red bell peppers, diced
- 1 habanero pepper, minced
- 2 (14½-ounce / 411-g) cans pinto beans
- ½ cup vegetable broth
- 1 tsp. ground cumin
- 1 tsp. chili powder
- Sea salt and pepper to taste

Directions:

1. Warm the oil in your pot over medium heat.
2. Place in bell and habanero peppers. Sauté for 5 minutes until tender. Add beans, broth, cumin, chili powder, salt, and pepper.
3. Bring to a boil, then lower the heat and cook more for about 10 minutes.

Per serving: Calories: 141Kcal; Protein: 7g; Carbohydrates: 23g; Fat: 2g

207. KIDNEY BEANS TACO SOUP

Preparation time: 5 minutes
Cooking time: 6 hours
Servings: 6
Ingredients:

- 1 lb. ground beef
- 1 cup onion, chopped
- Two cans of kidney beans
- One can corn
- 1 (15 oz.) can tomato
- 1 (15 oz.) can tomato sauce
- Black pepper, to taste
- 2 1/2 cups water

Directions:

1. Add the beef, onion, beans, and the rest of the ingredients to a slow cooker.
2. Cover the beans-corn mixture and cook for 6 hours at low temperature.
3. Serve warm.

Per serving: Calories: 228Kcal; Protein: 27.5g; Carbohydrates: 17.6g; Fat: 5.3g

208. CHICKEN GREEN BEANS SOUP

Preparation time: 5 minutes
Cooking time: 25 minutes
Servings: 4
Ingredients:

- 1 lb. chicken breasts, boneless, skinless, cubed
- 1 1/2 cups onion, sliced
- 1 1/2 cups celery, chopped
- One tbs. olive oil
- 1 cup carrots, chopped
- 1 cup green beans, chopped
- Three tbsp. flour
- One tsp. dried oregano
- Two tsp. dried basil
- 1/4 tsp. nutmeg
- One tsp. thyme
- 32 oz. chicken broth
- 1/2 cup milk
- 2 cups frozen green peas
- 1/4 tsp. black pepper

Directions:

1. Add the chicken to a skillet and sauté for 6 minutes, then remove it from the heat.
2. Warm up the olive oil in a pan and stir-fry the onion for 5 minutes.
3. Stir in the carrots, flour, green beans, basil, the sautéed chicken, thyme, oregano, and nutmeg.
4. Sauté for approximately 3 minutes, then transfer the ingredients to a large pan.
5. Add the milk and broth and cook until it boils.
6. Stir in the green peas and cook for 5 minutes.
7. Adjust seasoning with pepper and serve warm.

Per serving: Calories: 277Kcal; Protein: 29.5g; Carbohydrates: 17.3g; Fat: 9.6g

209. QUINOA SALMON BOWL

Preparation time: 15 minutes
Cooking time: 0 minutes
Servings: 4

Ingredients:

- 4 cups cooked quinoa
- 1 pound (45g;) cooked salmon, flaked
- 3 cups arugula
- 6 radishes, thinly sliced
- 1 zucchini, sliced into half moons
- 3 scallions, minced
- ½ cup almond oil
- 1 tbs. apple cider vinegar
- 1 tsp. Sriracha or other hot sauce (or more if you like it spicy)
- 1 tsp. salt
- ½ cup toasted slivered almonds (optional)

Directions:

1. Combine the quinoa, salmon, arugula, radishes, zucchini, and scallions in a large bowl.
2. Add the almond oil, vinegar, Sriracha, and salt and mix well.
3. Put the mixture into four separate serving bowls, garnish with the toasted almonds (if using), and serve.

Per serving: Calories: 790Kcal; Protein: 37g; Carbohydrates: 45g; Fat: 52g

210. FIERY QUINOA

Preparation time: 10 minutes
Cooking time: 20 minutes
Servings: 4
Ingredients:

- 1 cup rinsed quinoa
- 2 cups water
- ½ cup coconut, shredded
- ¼ cup hemp seeds
- 2 tbsp. flaxseed
- 1 tsp. cinnamon, ground
- 1 tsp. vanilla extract
- Pinch sea salt
- 1 cup fresh berries of your choice, divided
- ¼ cup hazelnuts, chopped

Directions:

1. Combine the quinoa and water in a medium saucepan over high heat.
2. Bring to a boil then place the heat to a simmer, and cook for 15 to 20 minutes, or until the quinoa is cooked through. It should double or triple in bulk to couscous, and be slightly translucent.
3. Stir in the coconut, hemp seeds, flaxseed, cinnamon, vanilla, and salt.
4. Put the quinoa into four separate bowls and top each serving with ¼ cup of berries and 1 tbs. of hazelnuts.

Per serving: Calories: 286Kcal; Protein: 10g; Carbohydrates: 32g; Fat: 13g

211. BLACK-BEAN SOUP

Preparation time: 15 minutes
Cooking time: 20 minutes
Servings: 4
Ingredients:

- 1 yellow onion
- 1 tbs. olive oil
- 2 cans black beans, drained
- 1 cup diced fresh tomatoes
- 5 cups low-sodium vegetable broth
- ¼ tsp. freshly ground black pepper
- ¼ cup chopped fresh cilantro

Directions:

1. Cook or sauté the onion in the olive oil within 4 to 5 minutes in a large saucepan over medium heat. Put the black beans, tomatoes, vegetable broth, and black pepper. Boil, then adjust heat to simmer within 15 minutes.
2. Remove, then working in batches, ladle the soup into a blender and process until somewhat smooth. Put it back to the pot, add the cilantro, and heat until warmed through. Serve immediately.

Per serving: Calories: 234Kcal; Protein: 11g; Carbohydrate: 37g; Fat: 5g

212. CHUNKY BLACK-BEAN DIP

Preparation time: 5 minutes
Cooking time: 1 minute
Servings: 2
Ingredients:

- 1 (15-ounce) can black beans, drained, with liquid reserved
- ½-can of chipotle peppers in adobo sauce
- ¼ cup plain Greek yogurt
- Freshly ground black pepper

Directions:

1. Combine beans, peppers, and yogurt in a food processor or blender and process until smooth.
2. Add some of the bean liquid, 1 tbs. at a time, for a thinner consistency.
3. Season to taste with black pepper.
4. Serve.

Per serving: Calories: 70Kcal; Protein: 5g; Carbohydrate: 11g; Fat: 1g

213. ASPARAGUS FRIED RICE

Preparation time: 20 minutes
Cooking time: 10 minutes
Servings: 4

Ingredients:

- Three large eggs, beaten
- ½ tsp. ground ginger
- Two tsp. low-sodium soy sauce
- Two tbsp. olive oil
- One onion, diced
- Four garlic cloves, minced
- 1 cup sliced cremini mushrooms
- 1 (10-ounce) package frozen brown rice, thawed
- 8 ounces fresh asparagus, about 15 spears, cut into 1-inch pieces
- One tsp. sesame oil

Directions:

1. Whisk the eggs, ginger, and soy sauce in a small bowl and set aside.
2. In a medium skillet, heat the olive oil or wok over medium heat.
3. Add the onion and garlic and sauté for 2 minutes until tender-crisp.
4. Add the mushrooms and rice; stir-fry for 3 minutes longer.
5. Cook for 2 minutes after adding the asparagus.
6. Move the rice mixture to one side of the skillet and pour in the egg mixture. Stir the eggs until cooked through, 2 to 3 minutes, and stir into the rice mixture.
7. Sprinkle the fried rice with the sesame oil and serve.

Per serving: Calories: 247Kcal; Protein: 9g; Carbohydrates: 25g; Fat: 13g

214. HEALTHY VEGETABLE FRIED RICE

Preparation time: 15 minutes
Cooking time: 10 minutes
Servings: 4
Ingredients:
For the sauce:

- 1/3 cup garlic vinegar
- 1½ tbsp. dark molasses
- 1 tsp. onion powder

For the fried rice:

- 1 tsp. olive oil
- 2 lightly beaten whole eggs + 4 egg whites
- 1 cup of frozen mixed vegetables
- 1 cup frozen edamame
- 2 cups cooked brown rice

Directions:

1. Prepare the sauce by combining the garlic vinegar, molasses, and onion powder in a glass jar. Shake well.
2. Heat-up oil in a large wok or skillet over medium-high heat. Add eggs and egg whites, let cook until the eggs set, for about 1 minute.

3. Break up eggs with a spatula or spoon into small pieces. Add frozen mixed vegetables and frozen edamame. Cook for 4 minutes, stirring frequently.
4. Add the brown rice and sauce to the vegetable-and-egg mixture. Cook for 5 minutes or until heated through. Serve immediately.

Per serving: Calories: 210Kcal; Protein: 13g; Carbohydrate: 28g; Fat: 6g

215. JALAPENO BLACK-EYED PEAS MIX

Preparation time: 10 minutes
Cooking time: 5 hours
Servings: 12
Ingredients:

- 17 ounces black-eyed peas
- 1 sweet red pepper, chopped
- ½ cup sausage, chopped
- 1 yellow onion, chopped
- 1 jalapeno, chopped
- 2 garlic cloves minced
- 6 cups of water
- ½ tsp. cumin, ground
- A pinch of black pepper
- 2 tbsp. cilantro, chopped

Directions:

1. In a slow cooker, mix the peas with the onion, sausage, garlic, red pepper, jalapeno, black pepper, cumin, water, cilantro, cover, and cook low for 5 hours.
2. Serve.

Per serving: Calories: 75Kcal; Protein: 4.3g; Carbohydrates: 7.2g; Fat: 3.5g

216. SOUR CREAM GREEN BEANS

Preparation time: 10 minutes
Cooking time: 4 hours
Servings: 8
Ingredients:

- 15 ounces green beans
- 14 ounces corn
- 4 ounces mushrooms, sliced
- 11 ounces cream of mushroom soup, low-fatand sodium-free
- ½ cup low-fatsour cream
- ½ cup almonds, chopped
- ½ cup low-fatcheddar cheese, shredded

Directions:

1. In a slow cooker, mix the green beans with the corn, mushroom soup, mushrooms, almonds, cheese, sour cream, toss, cover, and cook on Low for 4 hours.

2. Stir one more time, divide between plates and serve as a side dish.

Per serving: Calories: 360Kcal; Protein: 14g; Carbohydrates: 58.3g; Fat: 12.7g

217. QUINOA CURRY

Preparation time: 15 minutes
Cooking time: 4 hours
Servings: 8
Ingredients:

- 1 chopped Sweet Potato
- 2 cups Green Beans
- ½ diced onion (white)
- 1 diced Carrot
- 15 oz Chick Peas (organic and drained)
- 28 oz. Tomatoes (diced)
- 29 oz Coconut Milk
- 2 minced cloves of garlic
- ¼ cup Quinoa
- 1 tbs. Turmeric (ground)
- 1 tbsp. Ginger (grated)
- 1 ½ cups Water
- 1 tsp. of Chili Flakes
- 2 tsp. of Tamari Sauce

Directions:

1. Put all the listed ingredients in the slow cooker.
2. Add 1 cup of water. Stir well.
3. Cook on "high" for 4 hrs.
4. Serve with rice.

Per serving: Calories: 297Kcal; Protein: 2g; Carbohydrates: 9mg; Fat: 1g

218. LEMON AND CILANTRO RICE

Preparation time: 15 minutes
Cooking time: 6 hours
Servings: 4
Ingredients:

- 3 cups vegetable broth (low sodium)
- 1 ½ cups brown rice (uncooked)
- Juice of2 lemons
- 2 tbsp. chopped cilantro

Directions:

1. In a slow cooker, place broth and rice.
2. Cook on "low" for 5 hrs. Check the rice for doneness with a fork.
3. Add the lemon juice and cilantro before serving.

Per serving: Calories: 56Kcal; Protein: 1g; Carbohydrates: 12g; Fats 0.3g

219. CAULIFLOWER CARROT WILD RICE PILAF

Preparation time: 10 minutes
Cooking time: 45 minutes
Servings:4
Ingredients:

- 2 tbsp. olive oil
- 2 cups herbed chicken bone broth
- 1 cup raw wild rice
- 1 tsp. bottled minced garlic
- 1 sweet onion, chopped, or about 1 cup precut packaged onion
- 2 stalks celery, chopped, or about ¾ to 1 cup precut packaged celery
- 2 carrots, peeled, halved lengthwise, and sliced, or about 1 cup precut packaged carrots
- ½ cauliflower head, chopped into small florets, or 2½ to 3 cups precut packaged florets
- 1 tsp. chopped fresh thyme
- Sea salt

Directions:

1. Preheat oven to 350 deg. F (180°C).
2. Use olive oil to lightly grease an 8-by-8-inch baking dish, set it aside.
3. Add the chicken broth and wild rice to a large saucepan, stir them together over high heat, then bring the mixture to a boil. Place the heat to low and simmer until the rice is tender, about 30 minutes.
4. In the meantime, heat the remaining 1 tbs. of olive oil in a large skillet over medium-high heat.
5. Stir in the garlic, onion and celery. Sauté until tender, about 3 minutes.
6. Stir in the carrots and cauliflower, sauté for 5 minutes. Remove the skillet from the heat and set it aside until the rice is done.
7. After the rice is cooked over, transfer to the skillet. Add the thyme and stir. Season with sea salt and spoon the mixture into the prepared dish.
8. Bake until the vegetables are tender (about 15 minutes.)

Per serving: Calories: 213Kcal; Protein: 7g; Carbohydrates: 38 g; Fat: 4 g

220. CREAMY BLACK BEAN DIP WITH VEGGIE STICKS

Preparation time: 15 minutes
Cooking time: 0 minutes
Servings: 4 to 6
Ingredients:

- 2 tbsps. extra-virgin olive oil
- 1 (15-ounce) can black beans, drained and rinsed

- 1 tbsp. chopped fresh cilantro
- 2 scallions, chopped
- 1 tsp. chipotle powder
- 2 tbsps. fresh lime juice
- 1 tsp. salt
- ½ tsp. ground cumin
- 1 cup carrot sticks, for serving
- 1 cup celery sticks, for serving

Directions:

1. In a medium bowl, add the olive oil, black beans, cilantro, scallions, chipotle powder, lime juice, salt and cumin, toss them together until well mixed.
2. Mash the ingredients with a potato masher, until slightly smooth but still lumpy.
3. Serve dipped the vegetable sticks in.

Per serving: Calories: 170Kcal; Protein: 6g; Carbohydrates: 20g; Fat: 7g

221. APPLE QUINOA MUFFINS

Preparation time: 10 minutes

Cooking time: 35 minutes

Servings: 4

Ingredients:

- ½ cup natural, unsweetened applesauce
- 1 cup banana, peeled and mashed
- 1 cup quinoa
- 2 and ½ cups old-fashioned oats
- ½ cup almond milk
- 2 tbsp. stevia
- 1 tsp. vanilla extract
- 1 cup of water
- Cooking spray
- 1 tsp. cinnamon powder
- 1 apple, cored, peeled, and chopped

Directions:

1. Put the water in a small pan, bring to a simmer over medium heat, add quinoa, cook within 15 minutes, fluff with a fork, and transfer to a bowl.
2. Add all ingredients, stir, divide into a muffin pan greases with cooking spray, introduce in the oven, and bake within 20 minutes at 375 degrees F. Serve for breakfast.

Per serving: Calories: 241Kcal; Protein: 5g; Carbohydrates: 31g; Fat: 11g

222. VERY BERRY MUESLI

Preparation time: 15 minutes

Cooking time: 0 minutes

Servings: 2

Ingredients:

- 1 c. Oats
- 1 c. Fruit flavored Yogurt

- ½ c. Milk
- 1/8 tsp. Salt
- ½ c dried Raisins
- ½ c. Chopped Apple
- ½ c. Frozen Blueberries
- ¼ c. chopped Walnuts

Directions:

1. Combine your yogurt, salt, and oats in a medium bowl, mix well, and then cover it tightly. Put in the fridge for at least 6 hours.
2. Add your raisins and apples then gently fold. Top with walnuts and serve. Enjoy!

Per serving: Calories: 195Kcal; Protein: 6g; Carbohydrates: 31g; Fat: 4g

223. CARROT CAKE OVERNIGHT OATS

Preparation time: overnight

Cooking time: 2 minutes

Servings: 1

Ingredients:

- ½ cup rolled oats
- ½ cup plain nonfat or low-fat Greek yogurt
- ½ cup nonfat or low-fat milk
- ¼ cup shredded carrot
- 2 tbsp. raisins
- ½ tsp. ground cinnamon
- 1 to 2 tbsp. chopped walnuts (optional)

Directions:

1. Mix all of the ingredients in a lidded jar, shake well, and refrigerate overnight.
2. Serve.

Per serving: Calories: 331Kcal; Protein: 22g; Carbohydrates: 59g; Fat: 3g

224. QUINOA AND CHICKPEA

Preparation time: 5 minutes

Cooking time: 10 minutes

Servings: 2–3

Ingredients:

- 1 C. quinoa
- 1 ½ C. water
- ¼ tsp. coconut oil
- 4 oz. chickpeas, cooked
- ¼ C. red onion, diced
- ¼ green bell pepper, chopped
- ⅛ tsp. cayenne pepper
- ½ tbsp. coconut oil
- Sea salt (optional)

Directions:

1. Add quinoa, water, and ¼ tsp. coconut oil to the saucepan. Let it boil, then adjust the heat to simmer

until water is absorbed. Remove quinoa from fire and let cool.
2. Add cooked chickpeas, onion, bell pepper, cayenne pepper, and ½ tsp. of coconut oil to a bowl and mix. Stir in cold quinoa.

Per serving: Calories: 87Kcal; Protein: 9.1g; Carbohydrates: 8g; Fat: 4g

225. THAI QUINOA SALAD

Preparation time: 15 minutes

Cooking time: 0 minute

Servings: 2

Ingredients:

For the dressing:

- ⅓ C. water, filtered
- ¼ C. tahini
- 1 date, pitted
- 1 tbsp. sesame seeds
- 1 tbsp. apple cider vinegar
- 2 tsp. tamari
- 1 tsp. lemon juice, freshly squeezed
- 1 tsp. sesame oil, toasted
- 1 tsp. garlic, chopped
- ½ tsp. Himalayan pink salt

For the salad:

- 1 C. quinoa, rinsed and steamed
- 1 C. arugula, rinsed and chopped
- 1 tomato, rinsed and sliced
- ¼ red onion, rinsed and diced

Directions:

To make the dressing:

1. Blend the water, tahini, date, sesame seeds, vinegar, tamari, lemon juice, sesame oil, garlic, and salt at high speed until smooth.

To make the salad:

2. Combine together the quinoa, arugula, tomato, and red onion. Drizzle the dressing, toss it well to coat, and serve.

Per serving: Calories: 558Kcal; Protein: 19g; Carbohydrates: 69g; Fat: 25g

226. VEGETABLE STUFFED QUINOA WITH STEAMED ZUCCHINI

Preparation time: 10 minutes

Cooking time: 15 minutes

Servings: 2–4

Ingredients:

- 1 C. quinoa
- 1 ½ C. water
- 2 tbsp. coconut milk
- ¾ C. mushrooms, chopped
- 1-inch section red bell pepper, chopped
- ¼ onion, chopped

- 1 plum tomato, chopped
- ½ tsp. sea salt
- Spices: a dash of basil, oregano, thyme, red pepper flakes
- ⅓ zucchini, sliced

Directions:
1. Dip the quinoa for at least 5 minutes, strain, and rinse to remove wax. Add all the ingredients (except for the zucchini) to a saucepan and bring to a boil.
2. Lower the heat, then simmer until the water is absorbed. Steam the zucchini slices in a steamer for 5–10 minutes.
3. Plate and serve.

Per serving: Calories: 104Kcal; Protein: 5.8g; Carbohydrates: 9g; Fat: 5g

227. MILLET PILAF

Preparation time: 10 minutes
Cooking time: 15 minutes
Servings: 4
Ingredients:

- 1 cup millet
- 2 tomatoes, rinsed, seeded, and chopped
- 1¾ cups filtered water
- 2 tbsp. extra-virgin olive oil
- ¼ cup chopped dried apricot
- Zest of 1 lemon
- Juice of 1 lemon
- ½ cup fresh parsley, rinsed and chopped
- Himalayan pink salt
- Freshly ground black pepper

Directions:
1. In an electric pressure cooker, combine the millet, tomatoes, and water. Lock the lid into place, select Manual and High Pressure, and cook for 7 minutes.
2. When the beep sounds, quickly release the pressure by pressing 'Cancel' and twisting the steam valve to the Venting position. Carefully remove the lid.
3. Stir in the olive oil, apricot, lemon zest, lemon juice, and parsley. Taste, season with salt and pepper, and serve.

Per serving: Calories: 270Kcal; Protein: 6g; Carbohydrates: 42g; Fat: 8g

228. GREEN BEANS IN OVEN

Preparation time: 5 minutes
Cooking time: 17 minutes
Servings: 3
Ingredients:

- 12 oz. green bean pods
- 1 tbsp. olive oil
- 1/2 tsp. onion powder
- 1/8 tsp. pepper
- 1/8 tsp. salt

Directions:
1. Preheat oven to 350°F. Mix green beans with onion powder, pepper, and oil.
2. Spread the seeds on the baking sheet.
3. Bake for 17 minutes or until you have a delicious aroma in the kitchen.
4. Serve straight away.

Per serving: Calories: 273Kcal; Protein: 8g; Carbohydrates: 7g; Fat: 23g

229. QUINOA TABBOULEH

Preparation time: 8 minutes
Cooking time: 16 minutes
Servings: 6
Ingredients:

- 1 cup quinoa, rinsed
- 1 large English cucumber
- 2 scallions, sliced
- 2 cups cherry tomatoes, halved
- 2/3 cup chopped parsley
- 1/2 cup chopped mint
- ½ tsp. minced garlic
- 1/2 tsp. salt
- ½ tsp. ground black pepper
- 2 tbs. lemon juice
- 1/2 cup olive oil

Directions:
1. Plugin instant pot, insert the inner pot, add quinoa, then pour in water and stir until mixed.
2. Close instant pot with its lid and turn the pressure knob to seal the pot.
3. Select 'manual' button, then set the 'timer' to 1 minute and cook in high pressure, it may take7 minutes.
4. Once the timer stops, select 'cancel' button and do natural pressure release for 10 minutes and then do quick pressure release until pressure nob drops down.

5. Open the instant pot, fluff quinoa with a fork, then spoon it onto a rimmed baking sheet, spread quinoa evenly and let cool.
6. Meanwhile, place lime juice in a small bowl, add garlic and stir until just mixed.
7. Then add salt, black pepper, and olive oil and whisk until combined.
8. Transfer cooled quinoa to a large bowl, add remaining ingredients, then drizzle generously with the prepared lime juice mixture and toss until evenly coated.
9. Taste quinoa to adjust seasoning and then serve.

Per serving: Calories: 283Kcal; Protein: 5g; Carbohydrates: 30.6g; Fat: 21g

230. PINTO BEANS

Preparation time: 6 minutes
Cooking time: 55 minutes
Servings: 10
Ingredients:

- 2 cups pinto beans, dried
- 1 medium white onion
- 1 ½ tsp. minced garlic
- ¾ tsp. salt
- 1/4 tsp. ground black pepper
- 1 tsp. red chili powder
- 1/4 tsp. cumin
- 1 tbs. olive oil
- 1 tsp. chopped cilantro
- 5 ½ cup vegetable stock

Directions:
1. Plugin instant pot, insert the inner pot, press sauté/simmer button, add oil and when hot, add onion and garlic and cook for 3 minutes or until onions begin to soften.
2. Add remaining ingredients, stir well, then press the cancel button, shut the instant pot with its lid and seal the pot.
3. Click 'manual' button, then press the 'timer' to set the cooking time to 45 minutes and cook at high pressure.
4. Once done, click 'cancel' button and do natural pressure release for 10 minutes until pressure nob drops down.
5. Open the instant pot, spoon beans into plates and serve.

Per serving: Calories: 107Kcal; Protein: 8g; Carbohydrates: 11/7g; Fat: 19g

CHAPTER 5: Vegetarian Recipes

231. RUTABAGA LATKES

Preparation time: 15 minutes
Cooking time: 7 minutes
Servings: 4
Ingredients:

- One tsp. hemp seed
- One tsp. ground black pepper
- 7 oz rutabaga, grated
- ½ tsp. ground paprika
- Two tbsp. coconut flour
- One egg, beaten
- One tsp. olive oil

Directions:

1. Mix up together hemp seeds, ground black pepper, ground paprika, and coconut flour.
2. Then add grated rutabaga and beaten egg.
3. Using a fork, combine all the ingredients into the smooth mixture.
4. Preheat the skillet for 2-3 minutes over the high heat.
5. Then reduce the heat till medium and add olive oil.
6. Using a fork, place the small amount of rutabaga mixture in the skillet. Flatten it gently in the shape of latkes.
7. Cook the latkes for 3 minutes from each side.
8. After this, transfer them to the plate and repeat the same steps with the remaining rutabaga mixture.

Per serving: Calories: 64Kcal; Protein: 2.8g; Carbohydrates: 7.1g; Fat: 3.1g

232. GLAZED SNAP PEAS

Preparation time: 10 minutes
Cooking time: 5 minutes
Servings: 2
Ingredients:

- 1 cup snap peas
- Two tsp. Erythritol
- One tsp. butter, melted
- ¾ tsp. ground nutmeg
- ¼ tsp. salt
- 1 cup water for cooking

Directions:

1. Pour water into the pan. Add snap peas and bring them to boil.
2. Boil the snap peas for 5 minutes over medium heat.
3. Then drain water and chill the snap peas.
4. Meanwhile, whisk together ground nutmeg, melted butter, salt, and Erythritol.
5. Preheat the mixture in the microwave oven for 5 seconds.
6. Pour the sweet butter liquid over the snap peas and shake them well.
7. The side dish should be served only warm.

Per serving: Calories: 80Kcal; Protein: 4g; Carbohydrates: 10.9g; Fat: 2.5g

233. STEAMED COLLARD GREENS

Preparation time: 10 minutes
Cooking time: 5 minutes
Servings: 2
Ingredients:

- 2 cups collard greens
- One tbs. lime juice
- One tsp. olive oil
- One tsp. sesame seed
- ½ tsp. chili flakes
- 1 cup water for the steamer

Directions:

1. Chop collard greens roughly.
2. Pour water in the steamer and insert rack.
3. Add collard greens in the steamer bowl and close the lid.
4. Steam the greens for 5 minutes.
5. After this, transfer the steamed collard greens to the salad bowl.
6. Sprinkle it with the lime juice, olive oil, sesame seeds, and chili flakes.
7. Mix up greens with the help of 2 forks and leave to rest for 10 minutes before serving.

Per serving: Calories: 43Kcal; Protein: 1.3g; Carbohydrates: 3.4g; Fat: 3.4g

234. BAKED EGGPLANT SLICES

Preparation time: 15 minutes
Cooking time: 15 minutes
Servings: 3
Ingredients:

- One large eggplant, trimmed
- One tbs. butter softened
- One tsp. minced garlic
- One tsp. salt

Directions:

1. Cut the eggplant and sprinkle it with salt. Mix up well and leave for 10 minutes to make the vegetable "give" bitter juice.
2. After this, dry the eggplant with a paper towel.
3. In the shallow bowl, mix up together minced garlic and softened butter.
4. Brush every eggplant slice with the garlic mixture.
5. Line the baking tray with baking paper—Preheat the oven to 355F.
6. Place the sliced eggplants in the tray to make one layer and transfer it to the oven.
7. Bake the eggplants for 15 minutes. The cooked eggplants will be tender but not soft!

Per serving: Calories: 81Kcal; Protein: 1.9g; Carbohydrates: 11.1g; Fat: 4.2g

235. PESTO AVOCADO

Preparation time: 10 minutes
Cooking time: 10 minutes
Servings: 2
Ingredients:

- One avocado pitted, halved
- 1/3 cup Mozzarella balls, cherry size
- 1 cup fresh basil
- One tbs. walnut
- ¼ tsp. garlic, minced
- ¾ tsp. salt
- ¾ tsp. ground black pepper
- Four tbsp. olive oil
- 1 oz Parmesan, grated
- 1/3 cup cherry tomatoes

Directions:

1. Make pesto sauce: blend salt, minced garlic, walnuts, fresh basil, ground black pepper, and olive oil.
2. When the mixture is smooth, augment grated cheese and pulse it for 3 seconds more.
3. Then scoop ½ flesh from the avocado halves.
4. In the mixing bowl, mix mozzarella balls and cherry tomatoes together.
5. Add pesto sauce and shake well.
6. Preheat the oven to 360F.
7. Fill the avocado halves with the cherry tomato mixture and bake for 10 minutes.

Per serving: Calories: 526Kcal; Protein: 8.2g; Carbohydrates: 11.7g; Fat: 53.2g

236. FAST CABBAGE CAKES

Preparation time: 15 minutes
Cooking time: 10 minutes
Servings: 2
Ingredients:

- 1 cup cauliflower, shredded
- One egg, beaten
- One tsp. salt
- One tsp. ground black pepper
- Two tbsp. almond flour
- One tsp. olive oil

Directions:

1. Blend the shredded cabbage in the blender until you get cabbage rice.
2. Then, mix up cabbage rice with the egg, salt, ground black pepper, and almond flour.
3. Pour olive oil into a skillet and preheat it.
4. Makes small cakes with the help of 2 spoons and place them in the hot oil.
5. Roast the cabbage cakes for 4 minutes on each side over medium-low heat.
6. It is suggested to use a non-stick skillet.

Per serving: Calories: 227Kcal; Protein: 9.9g; Carbohydrates: 9.5g; Fat: 18.6g

237. VEGAN CHILI

Preparation time: 10 minutes
Cooking time: 20 minutes
Servings: 4
Ingredients:

- 1 cup cremini mushrooms, chopped
- One zucchini, chopped
- One bell pepper, diced
- 1/3 cup crushed tomatoes
- 1 oz celery stalk, chopped
- One tsp. chili powder
- One tsp. salt
- ½ tsp. chili flakes
- ½ cup of water
- One tbs. olive oil
- ½ tsp. diced garlic
- ½ tsp. ground black pepper
- One tsp. of cocoa powder
- 2 oz Cheddar cheese, grated

Directions:

1. Pour olive oil into the pan and preheat it.
2. Add chopped mushrooms and roast them for 5 minutes. Stir them from time to time.
3. After this, add chopped zucchini and bell pepper.
4. Sprinkle the vegetables with the chili powder, salt, chili flakes, diced garlic, and ground black pepper.
5. Stir the vegetables and cook them for 5 minutes more.
6. Add crushed tomatoes. Mix well.
7. Bring the mixture to boil and add water and cocoa powder.
8. Add celery stalk.
9. Mix the chili and close the lid.
10. Cook the chili for about 10 minutes over medium-low heat.
11. Transfer the cooked vegan chili to the bowls and top with the grated cheese.

Per serving: Calories: 123Kcal; Protein: 5.6g; Carbohydrates: 7.6g; Fat: 8.6g

238. MUSHROOM TACOS

Preparation time: 10 minutes
Cooking time: 15 minutes
Servings: 6
Ingredients:

- Six collard greens leave
- 2 cups mushrooms, chopped
- One white onion, diced
- One tbs. Taco seasoning
- One tbs. coconut oil
- ½ tsp. salt
- ¼ cup fresh parsley
- One tbs. mayonnaise

Directions:

1. Put the coconut oil in the skillet and melt it.
2. Add chopped mushrooms and diced onion. Mix the ingredients.
3. Close the lid and cook them for 10 minutes.
4. After this, sprinkle the vegetables with Taco seasoning, salt, and add fresh parsley.
5. Mix the mixture and cook for 5 minutes more.
6. Add mayonnaise and stir well.
7. Chill the mushroom mixture a little.
8. Fill the collard green leaves with the mushroom mixture and fold up them.

Per serving: Calories: 52 Kcal; Protein: 1.4g; Carbohydrates: 5.1g; Fat: 3.3g

239. LIME SPINACH AND CHICKPEAS SALAD

Preparation time: 10 minutes
Cooking time: 0 minutes
Servings: 4
Ingredients:

- 16 ounces canned chickpeas, drained and rinsed
- 2 cups baby spinach leaves
- ½ tbs. lime juice
- Two tbsp. olive oil
- One tsp. cumin, ground
- A tweak of sea salt and black pepper
- ½ tsp. chili flakes

Directions:

1. In a bowl, mix the chickpeas with the spinach and the rest of the ingredients, toss and serve cold.

Per serving: Calories: 240Kcal; Protein: 12g; Carbohydrates: 11.6g; Fat: 8.2g

240. CURRIED VEGGIES AND RICE

Preparation time: 12 minutes
Cooking time: 18 minutes
Servings: 4
Ingredients:

- ¼ cup olive oil
- 1 cup long-grain white basmati rice
- Four garlic cloves, minced
- 2½ tsp. curry powder
- ½ cup sliced shiitake mushrooms
- One red bell pepper, chopped
- 1 cup frozen, shelled edamame
- 2 cups low-sodium vegetable broth
- 1/8 tsp. freshly ground black pepper

Directions:

1. Heat the olive oil in a large saucepan over medium temperature.
2. Add the rice, garlic, curry powder, mushrooms, bell pepper, and edamame; cook, stirring, for 2 minutes.
3. Add the broth and black pepper and bring to a boil.
4. Reduce the heat to low, partially cover the pot, and simmer for 15 to 18 minutes or until the rice is tender. Stir and serve.

Per serving: Calories: 347Kcal; Protein: 8g; Carbohydrates: 44g; Fat: 16g

241. SPICY MUSHROOM STIR-FRY

Preparation time: 15 minutes
Cooking time: 10 minutes
Servings: 4
Ingredients:

- 1 cup low-sodium vegetable broth
- Two tbsp. cornstarch
- One tsp. low-sodium soy sauce
- ½ tsp. ground ginger
- 1/8 tsp. cayenne pepper
- Two tbsp. olive oil

- 2 (8-ounce) packages sliced button mushrooms
- One red bell pepper, chopped
- One jalapeño pepper, minced
- 3 cups brown rice that has been cooked in unsalted water
- Two tbsp. sesame oil

Directions:

1. In a mini bowl, whisk together the broth, cornstarch, soy sauce, ginger, and cayenne pepper and set aside.
2. Warm the olive oil in a wok or heavy skillet over high heat.
3. Add the mushrooms and peppers and stir-fry for 3 to 5 minutes or until the vegetables are tender-crisp.
4. Stirring the broth mixture and pouring it into the wok; stir-fry for 3 to 5 minutes longer or until the vegetables are tender and the sauce has thickened. Serve the stir-fry over the hot cooked brown rice and drizzle with the sesame oil.

Per serving: Calories: 361Kcal; Protein: 8g; Carbohydrates: 49g; Fat: 16g

242. SPICY VEGGIE PANCAKES

Preparation time: 20 minutes

Cooking time: 10 minutes

Servings: 4

Ingredients:

- Three tbsp. olive oil, divided
- Two small onions, finely chopped
- One jalapeño pepper, minced
- ¾ cup carrot, grated
- ¾ cup cabbage, finely chopped
- 1½ cups quick-cooking oats
- ¾ cup cooked brown rice
- ¾ cup of water
- ½ cup whole-wheat flour
- One large egg
- One large egg white
- One tsp. baking soda
- ¼ tsp. cayenne pepper

Directions:

1. Warm 2 tsp. oil in a medium skillet over medium temperature.
2. Sauté the onion, jalapeño, carrot, and cabbage for 4 minutes.
3. While the vegetables are cooking, combine the oats, rice, water, flour, egg, egg white, cayenne pepper and baking soda in a medium bowl until well mixed.
4. Add the cooked vegetables to the mixture and stir to combine.
5. Heat the remaining oil in a huges skillet over medium heat.
6. Drop the mixture into the skillet, about 1/3 cup per pancake. Cook

for 4 minutes, or until bubbles form on the pancakes' surface and the edges look cooked, then carefully flip them over.

7. Cook the other side for 3 to 5 minutes or until the pancakes are hot and firm.
8. Repeat with the remaining mixture and serve.

Per serving: Calories: 323 Kcal; Protein: 10g; Carbohydrates: 48g; Fat: 11g

243. EGG AND VEGGIE FAJITAS

Preparation time: 20 minutes

Cooking time: 10 minutes

Servings: 4

Ingredients:

- Three large eggs
- Three egg whites
- Two tsp. chili powder
- One tbs. unsalted butter
- One onion, chopped
- Two garlic cloves, minced
- One jalapeño pepper, minced
- One red bell pepper, chopped
- 1 cup frozen corn, thawed and drained
- 8 (6-inch) corn tortillas

Directions:

1. Whisk the eggs, egg whites, and chili powder in a small bowl until well combined. Set aside.
2. In a large skillet, dissolve the butter over medium temperature.
3. Sauté the onion, garlic, jalapeño, bell pepper, and corn until the vegetables are tender, 3 to 4 minutes.
4. Put the beaten egg mixture into the skillet. Cook, occasionally stirring, until the eggs form large curds and are set, 3 to 5 minutes.
5. Meanwhile, soften the corn tortillas as directed on the package.
6. Divide the egg mixture evenly among the softened corn tortillas. Roll the tortillas up and serve.

Per serving: Calories: 316Kcal; Protein: 14g; Carbohydrates: 35g; Fat: 14g

244. VEGETABLE BIRYANI

Preparation time: 20 minutes

Cooking time: 10 minutes

Servings: 4

Ingredients:

- Two tbsp. olive oil
- One onion, diced
- Four garlic cloves, minced

- One tbs. peeled and grated fresh ginger root
- 1 cup carrot, grated
- 2 cups chopped cauliflower
- 1 cup freezing baby peas, thawed and drained
- Two tsp. curry powder
- 1 cup low-sodium vegetable broth
- 3 cups of frozen cooked brown rice

Directions:

1. In a large skillet, heat the olive oil over medium heat.
2. Add the onion, garlic, and ginger root, then sauté, frequently stirring, until tender-crisp, 2 minutes.
3. Add the carrot, cauliflower, peas, and curry powder and cook for 2 minutes longer.
4. Stir in the vegetable broth and lead to a simmer. Place the heat to low, partially cover the skillet, and simmer for 6 to 7 minutes or until the vegetables are tender.
5. Meanwhile, heat the rice as directed on the package.
6. Stir the rice into the vegetable mixture and serve.

Per serving: Calories: 378 Kcal; Protein: 8g; Carbohydrates: 53g; Fat: 16g

245. PESTO PASTA SALAD

Preparation time: 15 minutes

Cooking time: 15 minutes

Servings: 4

Ingredients:

- 1 cup fresh basil leaves
- ½ cup packed fresh flat-leaf parsley leaves
- ½ cup arugula, chopped
- Two tbsp. Parmesan cheese, grated
- ¼ cup extra-virgin olive oil
- Three tbsp. mayonnaise
- Two tbsp. water
- 12 ounces whole-wheat rotini pasta
- One red bell pepper, chopped
- One medium yellow summer squash, sliced
- 1 cup frozen baby peas melted and drained

Directions:

1. Bring a large pot of water to a boil.
2. Meanwhile, combine the basil, parsley, arugula, cheese, and olive oil in a blender or food processor. Blend until the herbs are finely chopped. Add the mayonnaise and water, then process again. Set aside.
3. Add the pasta to the container of boiling water; cook according to package directions, about 8 to 9

minutes. Drain well, reserving ¼ cup of the cooking liquid.

4. Combine the pesto, pasta, bell pepper, squash, and peas in a large bowl and toss gently, adding enough reserved pasta cooking liquid to make a sauce on the salad. Serve immediately or cover and chill, then serve.

5. Cover and then store in the refrigerator for up to 3 days.

Per serving: Calories: 378Kcal; Protein: 9g; Carbohydrates: 35g; Fat: 24g

246. BARLEY BLUEBERRY AVOCADO SALAD

Preparation time: 15 minutes

Cooking time: 15 minutes

Servings: 4

Ingredients:

- 1 cup quick-cooking barley
- 3 cups low-sodium vegetable broth
- Three tbsp. extra-virgin olive oil
- Two tbsp. freshly squeezed lemon juice
- One tsp. yellow mustard
- One tsp. honey
- ½ avocado, peeled and chopped
- 2 cups blueberries
- ¼ cup crumbled feta cheese

Directions:

1. In a medium saucepan, add the barley and vegetable broth and bring to a simmer.

2. Lower the heat to low, partially cover the pan, and simmer for 10 to 12 minutes or until the barley is tender.

3. In the meantime, whisk together the olive oil, lemon juice, mustard, and honey in a serving bowl until blended.

4. Drain the barley if necessary and add to the bowl; toss to combine.

5. Add the avocado, blueberries, and feta and toss gently. Serve.

Per serving: Calories: 345Kcal; Protein: 7g; Carbohydrates: 44g; Fat: 16g

247. VEGETARIAN GOBI CURRY

Preparation time: 5 minutes

Cooking time: 15 minutes

Servings: 8

Ingredients:

- 2 cups of cauliflower florets
- 2 tbsp. of unsalted butter
- One medium dry white onion, thinly chopped
- ½ cup of green peas (frozen if wish)

- 1 tsp. of fresh ginger, chopped
- 1/2 tsp. of turmeric
- 1 tsp of garam masala
- ¼ tsp. cayenne pepper
- 1 tbsp. of water

Directions:

1. Heat-up a skillet over medium heat with the butter and sauté the onions until caramelized (golden brown).

2. Add the spices, e.g., ginger, garam masala turmeric, and cayenne.

3. Add the cauliflower and the (frozen) peas and stir.

4. Add the water and cover with a lid. Put the heat to a low temperature and let cook covered for about 10 minutes.

5. Serve with white rice.

Per serving: Calories: 91.04Kcal; Protein: 2.19g; Carbohydrate: 7.3g; Fat: 6.4g

248. TOFU HOISIN SAUTÉ

Preparation time: 15 minutes

Cooking time: 20 minutes

Servings: 4

Ingredients:

- Two tbsp. of hoisin sauce
- Two tbsp. of rice vinegar
- One tsp. of cornstarch
- Two tbsp. of olive oil
- 1 (15-ounce) package extra-firm tofu, cut into 1-inch cubes
- 2 cups of unpeeled cubed eggplant
- Two scallions, white and green parts, sliced
- Two tsp. of minced garlic
- One jalapeño pepper, minced
- Two tbsp. of chopped fresh cilantro

Directions:

1. In a mini bowl, whisk together the hoisin sauce, rice vinegar, and cornstarch and set aside.

2. In a big frying pan over high heat, heat the olive oil. Add the tofu, and sauté gently until golden brown, about 10 minutes, and transfer to a plate.

3. Reduce the heat to medium. Add the eggplant, scallions, garlic, jalapeño pepper, and sauté until tender and fragrant, about 6 minutes.

4. Stir in the reserved sauce, and toss until the sauce thickens, about 2 minutes. Stir in the tofu and cilantro, and serve hot.

Per serving: Calories: 105Kcal; Protein: 8g; Carbohydrates: 9g; Fat: 4g

249. SWEET POTATO CURRY

Preparation time: 20 minutes

Cooking time: 20 minutes

Servings: 6

Ingredients:

- Two tsp. of olive oil
- One medium sweet onion, chopped
- One tbs. of grated peeled fresh ginger
- One tsp. of minced fresh garlic
- 2 cups of diced peeled sweet potatoes
- 1 cup of diced carrots
- 1 cup of water
- ½ cup of heavy (whipping) cream
- One tbs. of curry powder
- One tsp. of ground cumin
- Two tbsp. of low-fatplain yogurt
- Two tbsp. of chopped fresh cilantro

Directions:

1. In a large saucepan overheat, heat the olive oil.

2. Add the onion, ginger, and garlic and sauté until softened, about 3 minutes.

3. Add the sweet potatoes, carrots, water, cream, curry powder, and cumin and stir to mix well. Bring the mixture to a boil. Lessen the heat to low, and simmer until the vegetables are tender, about 15 minutes.

4. Serve immediately, topped with the yogurt and cilantro.

Per serving: Calories: 132Kcal; Protein: 1g; Carbohydrates: 13g; Fat: 9g

250. ZUCCHINI NOODLES WITH SPRING VEGETABLES

Preparation time: 20 minutes

Cooking time: 10 minutes

Servings: 6

Ingredients:

- Six zucchinis, cut into long noodles
- 1 cup of halved snow peas
- 1 cup (3-inch pieces) of asparagus
- One tbs. of olive oil
- One tsp. of minced fresh garlic
- One tbs. of freshly squeezed lemon juice
- 1 cup of shredded fresh spinach
- ¾ cup of halved cherry tomatoes
- Two tbsp. of chopped fresh basil leaves

Directions:

1. Fill a medium pan with water, place over medium-high heat, and bring to a boil.

2. Reduce the heat to medium, and blanch the zucchini ribbons, snow

peas, and asparagus by submerging them in the water for 1 minute. Drain and rinse immediately under cold water.

3. Pat the vegetables dry with paper towels and transfer to a large bowl.
4. Place an average skillet over medium heat, and increase the olive oil. Add the garlic, and sauté until tender, about 3 minutes.
5. Add the lemon juice and spinach, and sauté until the spinach is wilted, about 3 minutes.
6. Add the zucchini mixture, the cherry tomatoes, and basil and toss until well combined.
7. Serve immediately.

Per serving: Calories: 52Kcal; Protein: 2g; Carbohydrates: 4g; Fat: 2g

251. LIME ASPARAGUS SPAGHETTI

Preparation time: 5 minutes
Cooking time: 20 minutes
Servings: 6
Ingredients:

- 1 pound of asparagus spears, clipped and cut into 2-inch pieces
- Two tsp. of olive oil
- Two tsp. of minced garlic
- Two tsp. of all-purpose flour
- 1 cup of homemade rice milk (or use unsweetened store-bought) or almond milk
- Juice and zest of ½ lemon
- One tbs. of chopped fresh thyme
- Freshly ground black pepper
- 2 cups of cooked spaghetti
- ¼ cup of grated Parmesan cheese

Directions:

1. Fill a large pan with water, then boil over high heat. Add the asparagus and blanch up until crisp-tender, about 2 minutes. Drain and set away.
2. In a huge skillet over medium-high heat, warm the olive oil. Add the garlic, and sauté until softened, about 2 minutes.
3. Whisk in the flour to create a paste, about 1 minute. Whisk in the rice milk, lemon juice, lemon zest, and thyme.
4. Decrease the heat to medium and cook the sauce, continually whisking, until thickened and creamy, about 3 minutes.
5. Season the sauce with pepper.
6. Stir in the spaghetti and the asparagus.

7. Serve the pasta topped with the Parmesan cheese.

Per serving: Calories: 127 Kcal; Protein: 6g; Carbohydrates: 19g; Fat: 3g

252. BRAISED KALE

Preparation time: 10 minutes
Cooking time: 15 minutes
Servings: 3
Ingredients:

- 2 to 3 tbsp. water
- 1 tbsp. coconut oil
- ½ sliced red pepper
- 2 stalk celery (sliced to ¼-inch thick)
- 5 cups of chopped kale

Directions:

1. Heat a pan over medium heat.
2. Add coconut oil and sauté the celery for at least five minutes.
3. Add the kale and red pepper.
4. Add a tbs. of water.
5. Let the vegetables wilt for a few minutes. Add a tbs. of water if the kale starts to stick to the pan.
6. Serve warm.

Per serving: Calories: 61Kcal; Protein: 1g; Carbohydrates: 3g; Fat: 5g

253. BLACK-EYED PEAS AND GREENS POWER SALAD

Preparation time: 15 minutes
Cooking time: 6 minutes
Servings: 2
Ingredients:

- 1 tbs. olive oil
- 3 cups purple cabbage, chopped
- 5 cups baby spinach
- 1 cup shredded carrots
- 1 can black-eyed peas, drained
- Juice of ½ lemon
- Salt
- Freshly ground black pepper

Directions:

1. In a medium pan, add the oil and cabbage and sauté for 1 to 2 minutes on medium heat. Add in your spinach, cover for 3 to 4 minutes on medium heat, until greens are wilted. Remove from the heat and add to a large bowl.
2. Add in the carrots, black-eyed peas, and a splash of lemon juice. Season with salt and pepper, if desired. Toss and serve.

Per serving: Calories: 320Kcal; Protein: 16g; Carbohydrate: 49g; Fat: 9g

254. BUTTERNUT-SQUASH MACARONI AND CHEESE

Preparation time: 15 minutes
Cooking time: 20 minutes
Servings: 2
Ingredients:

- 1 cup whole-wheat ziti macaroni
- 2 cups peeled and cubed butternut squash
- 1 cup non-fat: or low-fat milk, divided
- Freshly ground black pepper
- 1 tsp. Dijon mustard
- 1 tbs. olive oil
- ¼ cup shredded low-fatcheddar cheese

Directions:

1. Cook the pasta al dente. Put the butternut squash plus ½ cup milk in a medium saucepan and place over medium-high heat. Season with black pepper. Bring it to a simmer. Lower the heat, then cook until fork-tender, 8 to 10 minutes.
2. In a blender, add squash and Dijon mustard. Purée until smooth. In the meantime, place a huge sauté pan over medium heat and add olive oil. Add the squash purée and the remaining ½ cup of milk. Simmer for 5 minutes. Add the cheese and stir to combine.
3. Add the pasta to the sauté pan and stir to combine. Serve immediately.

Per serving: Calories: 373Kcal; Protein: 14g; Carbohydrate: 59g; Fat: 10g

255. PASTA WITH TOMATOES AND PEAS

Preparation time: 15 minutes
Cooking time: 15 minutes
Servings: 2
Ingredients:

- ½ cup whole-grain pasta of choice
- 8 cups water, plus ¼ for finishing
- 1 cup frozen peas
- 1 tbs. olive oil
- 1 cup cherry tomatoes, halved
- ¼ tsp. freshly ground black pepper
- 1 tsp. dried basil
- ¼ cup grated Parmesan cheese (low-sodium)

Directions:

1. Cook the pasta al dente. Add water to the same pot you used to cook the pasta, and when it's boiling, add the peas. Cook for 5 minutes. Drain and set aside.
2. Heat-up the oil in a large skillet over medium heat. Add the cherry

tomatoes, put a lid on the skillet and let the tomatoes soften for about 5 minutes, stirring a few times.

3. Season with black pepper and basil. Toss in the pasta, peas, and ¼ cup of water, stir and remove from the heat. Serve topped with Parmesan.

Per serving: Calories: 266Kcal; Protein: 13g; Carbohydrate: 30g; Fat: 12g

256. BAKED CHICKPEA-AND-ROSEMARY OMELET

Preparation time: 15 minutes
Cooking time: 15 minutes
Servings: 2
Ingredients:

- ½ tbs. olive oil
- 4 eggs
- ¼ cup grated Parmesan cheese
- 1 (15-ounce) can chickpeas, drained and rinsed
- 2 cups packed baby spinach
- 1 cup button mushrooms, chopped
- 2 sprigs rosemary, leaves picked (or 2 tsp. dried rosemary)
- Salt
- Freshly ground black pepper

Directions:

1. Warm oven to 400 F and put a baking tray on the middle shelf. Line an 8-inch springform pan with baking paper and grease generously with olive oil. If you don't have a springform pan, grease an oven-safe skillet (or cast-iron skillet) with olive oil.
2. Lightly whisk the eggs and Parmesan. Place chickpeas in the prepared pan. Layer the spinach and mushrooms on top of the beans. Pour the egg mixture on top and scatter the rosemary. Season to taste with salt and pepper.
3. Place the pan on the preheated tray and bake until golden and puffy and the center feels firm and springy about 15 minutes. Remove from the oven, slice, and serve immediately.

Per serving: Calories: 418 Kcal; Protein: 30g; Carbohydrate: 33g; Fat: 19g

257. CHILLED CUCUMBER-AND-AVOCADO SOUP WITH DILL

Preparation time: 15 minutes
Cooking time: 30 minutes
Servings: 4
Ingredients:

- 2 English cucumbers, peeled and diced, plus ¼ cup reserved for garnish

- 1 avocado, peeled, pitted, and chopped, plus ¼ cup reserved for garnish
- 1½ cups non-fat: or low-fatplain Greek yogurt
- ½ cup of cold water
- 1/3 cup loosely packed dill, plus sprigs for garnish
- 1 tbs. freshly squeezed lemon juice
- ¼ tsp. freshly ground black pepper
- ¼ tsp. salt
- 1 clove garlic

Directions:

1. Purée ingredients in a blender until smooth. If you prefer a thinner soup, add more water until you reach the desired consistency. Divide soup among 4 bowls.
2. Cover with plastic wrap and refrigerate within 30 minutes. Garnish with cucumber, avocado, and dill sprigs, if desired.

Per serving: Calories: 142Kcal; Protein: 11g; Carbohydrate: 12g; Fat: 7g

258. SOUTHWESTERN BEAN-AND-PEPPER SALAD

Preparation time: 6 minutes
Cooking time: 0 minutes
Servings: 4
Ingredients:

- 1 can pinto beans, drained
- 2 bell peppers, cored and chopped
- 1 cup corn kernels
- Salt
- Freshly ground black pepper
- Juice of 2 limes
- 1 tbs. olive oil
- 1 avocado, chopped

Directions:

1. Mix beans, peppers, corn, salt, plus pepper in a large bowl.
2. Press fresh lime juice, then mix in olive oil. Let the salad stand in the fridge within 30 minutes. Add avocado just before serving.

Per serving: Calories: 245 Kcal; Protein: 8g; Carbohydrate: 32g; Fat: 11g

259. CAULIFLOWER MASHED POTATOES

Preparation time: 10 minutes
Cooking time: 10 minutes
Servings: 4
Ingredients:

- 16 cups water (enough to cover cauliflower)
- 1 head cauliflower (about 3 pounds), trimmed and cut into florets

- 2 garlic cloves
- 1 tbs. olive oil
- ¼ tsp. salt
- 1/8 tsp. freshly ground black pepper
- 2 tsp. dried parsley

Directions:

1. Boil a huge pot of water, then the cauliflower and garlic. Cook within 10 minutes, then strain. Move it back to the hot pan, and let it stand within 2 to 3 minutes with the lid on.
2. Put the cauliflower plus garlic in a food processor or blender. Add the olive oil, salt, pepper, and purée until smooth. Taste and adjust the salt and pepper.
3. Remove, then put the parsley, and mix until combined. Garnish with additional olive oil, if desired. Serve immediately.

Per serving: Calories: 87Kcal; Protein: 4g; Carbohydrate: 12g; Fat: 4g

260. SOUTHWEST TOFU SCRAMBLE

Preparation time: 15 minutes
Cooking time: 15 minutes
Servings: 1
Ingredients:

- ½ tbs. olive oil
- ½ red onion, chopped
- 2 cups chopped spinach
- 8 ounces firm tofu, drained well
- 1 tsp. ground cumin
- ½ tsp. garlic powder
- Optional for serving: sliced avocado or sliced tomatoes

Directions:

1. Heat-up the olive oil in a medium skillet over medium heat. Put the onion and cook within 5 minutes. Add the spinach and cover to steam for 2 minutes.
2. Using a spatula, move the veggies to one side of the pan. Crumble the tofu into the open area in the pan, breaking it up with a fork. Add the cumin and garlic to the crumbled tofu and mix well. Sauté for 5 to 7 minutes until the tofu is slightly browned.
3. Serve immediately with whole-grain bread, fruit, or beans. Top with optional sliced avocado and tomato, if using.

Per serving: Calories: 267Kcal; Protein: 23g; Carbohydrate: 13g; Fat: 17g

261. BLACK-BEAN AND VEGETABLE BURRITO

Preparation time: 15 minutes
Cooking time: 15 minutes
Servings: 4
Ingredients:

- ½ tbs. olive oil
- 2 red or green bell peppers, chopped
- 1 zucchini or summer squash, diced
- ½ tsp. chili powder
- 1 tsp. cumin
- Freshly ground black pepper
- 2 cans black beans drained and rinsed
- 1 cup cherry tomatoes, halved
- 4 (8-inch) whole-wheat tortillas
- Optional for serving: spinach, sliced avocado, chopped scallions, or hot sauce

Directions:

1. Heat-up the oil in a large sauté pan over medium heat. Add the bell peppers and sauté until crisp-tender, about 4 minutes.
2. Add the zucchini, chili powder, cumin, and black pepper to taste, and continue to sauté until the vegetables are tender, about 5 minutes.
3. Add the black beans and cherry tomatoes and cook for 5 minutes. Divide between 4 burritos and serve topped with optional ingredients as desired. Enjoy immediately.

Per serving: Calories: 311Kcal; Protein: 19g; Carbohydrate: 52g; Fat: 6g

262. BAKED EGGS IN AVOCADO

Preparation time: 15 minutes
Cooking time: 15 minutes
Servings: 2
Ingredients:

- 2 avocados
- Juice of 2 limes
- Freshly ground black pepper
- 4 eggs
- 2 (8-inch) whole-wheat or corn tortillas, warmed
- Optional for serving: halved cherry tomatoes and chopped cilantro

Directions:

1. Adjust the oven rack to the middle position and preheat the oven to 450°F. Scrape out the center of halved avocado using a spoon about 1½ tablespoons.
2. Press lime juice over the avocados and season with black pepper to taste, and then place it on a baking sheet. Crack an egg into the avocado.
3. Bake within 10 to 15 minutes. Remove from oven and garnish with optional cilantro and cherry tomatoes and serve with warm tortillas.

Per serving: Calories: 534Kcal; Protein: 23g; Carbohydrate: 30g; Fat: 39g

263. HEARTY LENTIL SOUP

Preparation time: 15 minutes
Cooking time: 30 minutes
Servings: 4
Ingredients:

- 1 tbs. olive oil
- 2 carrots, peeled and chopped
- 2 celery stalks, diced
- 1 onion, chopped
- 1 tsp. dried thyme
- ½ tsp. garlic powder
- Freshly ground black pepper
- 1 (28-ounce) can no-salt diced tomatoes, drained
- 1 cup dry lentils
- 5 cups of water
- Salt

Directions:

1. Heat-up the oil in a large Dutch oven or pot over medium heat. Once the oil is simmering, add the carrot, celery, and onion. Cook, often stirring within 5 minutes.
2. Add the thyme, garlic powder, and black pepper. Cook within 30 seconds. Pour in the drained diced tomatoes and cook for a few more minutes, often stirring to enhance their flavor.
3. Put the lentils, water, plus a pinch of salt. Raise the heat then bring to a boil, then partially cover the pot and reduce heat to maintain a gentle simmer.
4. Cook within 30 minutes, or until lentils are tender but still hold their shape. Ladle into serving bowls and serve with a fresh green salad and whole-grain bread.

Per serving: Calories: 168Kcal; Protein: 10g; Carbohydrate: 35g; Fat: 4g

264. LOADED BAKED SWEET POTATOES

Preparation time: 15 minutes
Cooking time: 20 minutes
Servings: 4
Ingredients:

- 4 sweet potatoes
- ½ cup non-fat: or low-fat plain Greek yogurt
- Freshly ground black pepper
- 1 tsp. olive oil
- 1 red bell pepper, cored and diced
- ½ red onion, diced
- 1 tsp. ground cumin
- 1 (15-ounce) can chickpeas, drained and rinsed

Directions:

1. Prick the potatoes using a fork and cook on your microwave's potato setting until potatoes are soft and cooked through, about 8 to 10 minutes for 4 potatoes. If you don't have a microwave, bake at 400°F for about 45 minutes.
2. Combine the yogurt and black pepper in a small bowl and mix well. Heat the oil in a medium pot over medium heat. Add bell pepper, onion, cumin, and additional black pepper to taste.
3. Add the chickpeas, stir to combine, and heat through, about 5 minutes. Slice the potatoes lengthwise down the middle and top each half with a portion of the bean mixture followed by 1 to 2 tbsp. of the yogurt. Serve immediately.

Per serving: Calories: 264Kcal; Protein: 11g; Carbohydrate: 51g; Fat: 2g

265. WHITE BEANS WITH SPINACH AND PAN-ROASTED TOMATOES

Preparation time: 15 minutes
Cooking time: 10 minutes
Servings: 2
Ingredients:

- 1 tbs. olive oil
- 4 small plum tomatoes, halved lengthwise
- 10 ounces frozen spinach, defrosted and squeezed of excess water
- 2 garlic cloves, thinly sliced
- 2 tbsp. water
- ¼ tsp. freshly ground black pepper
- 1 can white beans, drained
- Juice of 1 lemon

Directions:

1. Heat-up the oil in your large skillet over medium-high heat. Put the tomatoes, cut-side down, and cook within 3 to 5 minutes; turn and cook within 1 minute more. Transfer to a plate.
2. Reduce heat to medium and add the spinach, garlic, water, and pepper to the skillet. Cook, tossing until the

spinach is heated through, 2 to 3 minutes.

3. Return the tomatoes to the skillet, add the white beans and lemon juice, and toss until heated through 1 to 2 minutes.

Per serving: Calories: 293Kcal; Protein: 15g; Carbohydrate: 43g; Fat: 9g

266. ROASTED BRUSSELS SPROUTS

Preparation time: 5 minutes

Cooking time: 20 minutes

Servings: 4

Ingredients:

- 1½ pounds Brussels sprouts, trimmed and halved
- 2 tbsp. olive oil
- ¼ tsp. salt
- ½ tsp. freshly ground black pepper

Directions:

1. Preheat the oven to 400 °F. Combine the Brussels sprouts and olive oil in a large mixing bowl and toss until they are evenly coated.
2. Turn the Brussels sprouts out onto a large baking sheet and flip them over, so they are cut-side down with the flat part touching the baking sheet. Sprinkle with salt and pepper.
3. Bake within 20 to 30 minutes or until the Brussels sprouts are crisp and lightly charred on the outside and toasted on the bottom. The outer leaves will be extra dark, too. Serve immediately.

Per serving: Calories: 134Kcal; Protein: 6g; Carbohydrate: 15g; Fat: 8g

267. BROCCOLI WITH GARLIC AND LEMON

Preparation time: 2 minutes

Cooking time: 4 minutes

Servings: 4

Ingredients:

- 1 cup of water
- 4 cups broccoli florets
- 1 tsp. olive oil
- 1 tbs. minced garlic
- 1 tsp. lemon zest
- Salt
- Freshly ground black pepper

Directions:

1. Put the broccoli in the boiling water in a small saucepan and cook within 2 to 3 minutes. The broccoli should retain its bright-green color. Drain the water from the broccoli.
2. Put the olive oil in a small sauté pan over medium-high heat. Add the

garlic and sauté for 30 seconds. Put the broccoli, lemon zest, salt, plus pepper. Combine well and serve.

Per serving: Calories: 38Kcal; Protein: 3g; Carbohydrate: 5g; Fat: 1g

268. STUFFED EGGPLANT SHELLS

Preparation time: 10 minutes

Cooking time: 25 minutes

Servings: 2

Ingredients:

- 1 medium eggplant
- 1 cup of water
- 1 tbs. olive oil
- 4 oz. cooked white beans
- 1/4 cup onion, chopped
- 1/2 cup green, red, or yellow bell peppers, chopped
- 1 cup canned unsalted tomatoes
- 1/4 cup tomatoes liquid
- 1/4 cup celery, chopped
- 1 cup fresh mushrooms, sliced
- 3/4 cup whole-wheat breadcrumbs
- Freshly ground black pepper, to taste

Directions:

1. Prepare the oven to 350 degrees F to preheat. Grease a baking dish with cooking spray and set it aside. Trim and cut the eggplant into half, lengthwise. Scoop out the pulp using a spoon and leave the shell about ¼ inch thick.
2. Place the shells in the baking dish with their cut side up. Add water to the bottom of the dish. Dice the eggplant pulp into cubes and set them aside. Add oil to an iron skillet and heat it over medium heat. Stir in onions, peppers, chopped eggplant, tomatoes, celery, mushrooms, and tomato juice.
3. Cook for 10 minutes on simmering heat, then stir in beans, black pepper, and breadcrumbs. Put this mixture into separate eggplant shells. Cover the shells with a foil sheet and bake for 15 minutes. Serve warm.

Per serving: Calories: 334Kcal; Protein: 2g; Carbohydrates: 3g; Fat: 1g

269. BUCKWHEAT LEMON TABBOULEH

Preparation time: 15 minutes

Cooking time: 10 minutes

Servings: 4

Ingredients:

- 1 tbsp. olive oil
- 2 tsps. bottled minced garlic

- ½ cup chopped red onion
- Juice of 1 lemon (3 tbsps.)
- 2 cups cooked buckwheat
- Zest of 1 lemon (optional)
- ¼ cup chopped fresh mint
- ½ cup chopped fresh parsley
- Sea salt

Directions:

1. Heat the olive oil in your large skillet over medium-high heat.
2. Stir in the garlic and red onion. Sauté until translucent, about 3 minutes.
3. Add the lemon juice, buckwheat, and lemon zest (if using). Sauté until heated through, about 5 minutes.
4. Add the mint and parsley, stir well and sauté for another 1 minute.
5. Remove from the heat and with sea salt to season.

Per serving: Calories: 184 Kcal; Protein: 6g; Carbohydrates: 34g; Fat: 5 g

270. ASPARAGUS CHEESE VERMICELLI

Preparation time: 10 minutes

Cooking time: 15 minutes

Servings: 4

Ingredients:

- 2 tsp. olive oil, divided
- 6 asparagus spears, cut into pieces
- 4 oz. dried whole-grain vermicelli
- 1 medium tomato, chopped
- 1 tbs. garlic, minced
- 2 tbsp. fresh basil, chopped
- 4 tbsp. Parmesan, freshly grated, divided
- 1/8 tsp. black pepper, ground

Directions:

1. Add 1 tsp oil to a skillet and heat it. Stir in asparagus and sauté until golden brown.
2. Cut the sautéed asparagus into 1-inch pieces. Fill a sauce pot with water up to ¾ full. After boiling the water, add pasta and cook for 10 minutes until it is all done.
3. Drain and rinse the pasta under tap water. Add pasta to a large bowl, then toss in olive oil, tomato, garlic, asparagus, basil, garlic, and parmesan. Serve with black pepper on top.

Per serving: Calories: 325Kcal; Protein: 7.3g; Carbohydrates: 48g; Fat: 8 g

271. CHICKPEA BUTTERNUT SQUASH

Preparation time: 10 minutes
Cooking time: 15 minutes
Servings: 2
Ingredients:

- 15 oz. chickpeas, cooked
- 1 ½ section of a butternut squash
- ¼ plum tomato
- ¼ C. coconut milk
- 1 C. water (add more water to make thinner soup)
- Pinch dill
- Pinch allspice
- Pinch cayenne pepper
- ⅛ tsp. sea salt

Directions:

1. Add all the ingredients to a blender and blend to your desired consistency.
2. Add the blended ingredients to a saucepan over a medium/high flame until it starts to boil or air bubbles rise. Adjust it to low heat and cook for 30 minutes.

Per serving: Calories: 110Kcal; Protein: 11g; Carbohydrates: 6g; Fat: 2g

272. SWEET LIFE BOWL

Preparation time: 15 minutes
Cooking time: 5 minutes
Servings: 2
Ingredients:

- 1 red onion
- 2 baby spinach
- 1 C. cherry tomatoes, sliced in half
- 4 carrots, peeled and thinly sliced
- 3 stalks celery, thinly sliced
- 3 tbsp. olive oil or coconut oil
- 2 C. brown rice /quinoa, cooked
- 1 C. chickpeas, cooked, rinsed and drained
- 1 C. curry and turmeric cauliflower, roasted
- ¼ C. pecans, toasted, chopped
- 1 bunch kale
- ½ C. fresh parsley
- Fresh pepper and sea salt, for taste

For the dressing:

- ¼ C. olive oil
- 1 tsp. Dijon mustard
- 1 tsp. maple syrup or raw honey
- 2 tbsp. lemon juice, freshly squeezed
- ¼ tsp. red pepper flakes
- ½- inch fresh ginger

Directions:

1. Start off by reheating the brown rice or quinoa and share into 2 different bowls. Get a large pan and heat over medium-high heat and add coconut or olive oil.
2. Stir in carrots, onion, and celery. Sauté veggies for 3–4 minutes until they become soft and turn brownish. In the fourth minute, add chickpeas and roasted cauliflower.
3. Add sliced kale and allow it to wilt for about a minute. Take off the pan from heat. Add tomatoes and baby spinach and stir so that the vegetable heat cooks the tomatoes and spinach.
4. Now pour the sautéed mix over the quinoa and brown rice. Sprinkle pepper and sea salt and supplement it with dried fruit.

Making Curry and Turmeric Roasted Cauliflower:

5. Preheat oven to 400°F. Get a roasting pan and oil lightly. Get a mixing bowl, add cauliflower alongside turmeric, curry powder, pepper, salt, and olive oil
6. Set the bowl on the roasting pan and roast for 20–25 minutes until the edges change to a golden brown

Making the dressing:

7. In a mixing bowl, mix the mustard, honey, lemon juice, red pepper flakes, and ginger.
8. Gently whisk in the olive oil, the idea is to form an emulsion.
9. Sprinkle the dressing over the bowls.
10. Toss gently. The toppings should be fresh parsley and toasted pecans.

Per serving: Calories: 158Kcal; Protein: 28g; Carbohydrates: 20g; Fat: 21g

273. CORIANDER AND MINT WITH TURMERIC ROASTED CAULIFLOWER

Preparation time: 15 minutes
Cooking time: 15 minutes
Servings: 4
Ingredients:

- 1 tbsp. cumin, ground
- ¼ C. pine nuts
- 2 tsp. turmeric, ground
- ½ C. coconut oil
- 2 tbsp. cilantro/coriander, roughly chopped
- 1 tbsp. mint, chopped roughly
- 1 large cauliflower, broken down into bite-sized florets
- Himalayan salt to taste

Directions:

1. Pre-heat oven to 220°C. Get a clean, large bowl and combine the turmeric, coconut oil, and ½ tsp. salt with your hands. Add the cauliflower florets and mix them in properly.
2. Take off the cauliflower and spread it on a big baking tray. Slot the tray straight into the preheated oven for between 15–20 minutes until it softens and turns brown. Get a smaller baking trail, pour the pine on it and place it in the oven for about a minute.
3. Lastly, move the cauliflower to a serving bowl, sprinkle some pine nuts, mint, and cilantro/coriander. Then serve.

Per serving: Calories: 150Kcal; Protein: 21g; Carbohydrates: 19g; Fat: 15g

274. QUINOA WITH AVOCADO, GREEN ASPARAGUS, FRESH KELP, AND SPIRALIZED BEETROOT

Preparation time: 1 hour
Cooking time: 20 minutes
Servings: 4
Ingredients:

- 1 large avocado, ripe
- 4 tbsp. raw seed mix
- 4 tsp. sesame seed oil
- 4 tsp. fresh ginger
- 4 C. raw beetroot, spiralized
- 4 C. fresh kelp
- 1 tsp. organic sea salt
- 2 C. boiling water
- 4 C. fresh green asparagus spears
- 4 tsp. fresh red chili
- 4 tsp. fresh garlic
- 1 C. raw quinoa

Directions:

For the quinoa:

1. Get a saucepan over medium heat, add water, and add the raw quinoa and sea salt. Let it boil, reduce heat and allow simmering. Allow it to simmer for 50 minutes, but make sure the quinoa has absorbed enough water and is fluffy. Set it aside and allow to cool.

For the main dish:

1. Get four serving bowls and pour a ½ C. (125ml) of the cooked quinoa in each of them.
2. Add 1 C. of the fresh kale in each bowl. Add 1 C. of the chopped fresh green asparagus in each bowl. Add 1 C. of the spiralized raw beetroot in each bowl. Add 1 tsp. of the chopped ginger in each bowl.
3. Add 1 tsp. of the chopped garlic in each bowl. Add 1 tsp. of the chopped chili in the bowl. Cut the

avocado into four quarters, peel and pit it. Slice ¼ of the avocado over the ingredients in each bowl.

4. Sprinkle 1 tbsp. of sesame oil over each bowl. Stir together all ingredients in each bowl. Spray 1 tbsp. of the raw seed mix over each bowl.

Per serving: Calories: 301Kcal; Protein: 34g; Carbohydrates: 13g; Fat: 11g

275. OLIVES AND LENTILS SALAD

Preparation time: 10 minutes
Cooking time: 0 minutes
Servings: 2
Ingredients:

- ⅓ C. green lentils canned
- 1 tbsp. olive oil
- 2 C. baby spinach
- 1 C. black olives
- 2 tbsp. sunflower seeds
- 1 tbsp. Dijon mustard
- 2 tbsp. balsamic vinegar
- 2 tbsp. olive oil

Directions:

1. Mix the lentils with the spinach, olives, and the rest of the ingredients in a salad bowl, toss and serve cold.

Per serving: Calories: 279Kcal; Protein: 12g; Carbohydrates: 6.9g; Fat: 5.5g

276. MINTY OLIVES AND TOMATOES SALAD

Preparation time: 10 minutes
Cooking time: 0 minutes
Servings: 4
Ingredients:

- 1 C. Kalamata olives
- 1 C. black olives
- 1 C. cherry tomatoes
- 4 tomatoes
- 1 red onion, chopped
- 2 tbsp. oregano, chopped
- 1 tbsp. mint, chopped
- 2 tbsp. balsamic vinegar
- ¼ C. olive oil
- 2 tsp. Italian herbs, dried

Directions:

1. In a salad bowl, mix the olives with the tomatoes and the rest of the ingredients, toss, and serve cold.

Per serving: Calories: 190Kcal; Protein: 4.6g; Carbohydrates: 9g; Fat: 8.1g

277.   BEANS AND CUCUMBER SALAD

Preparation time: 10 minutes
Cooking time: 0 minutes
Servings: 4
Ingredients:

- 15 oz. great northern beans. canned
- 2 tbsp. olive oil
- ½ C. baby arugula
- 1 C. cucumber
- 1 tbsp. parsley
- 2 tomatoes, cubed
- 2 tbsp. balsamic vinegar

Directions:

1. Mix the beans with the cucumber and the rest of the ingredients in a large bowl, toss and serve cold.

Per serving: Calories: 233Kcal; Protein: 8g; Carbohydrates: 13g; Fat: 9g

278. TOMATO AND AVOCADO SALAD

Preparation time: 10 minutes
Cooking time: 0 minutes
Servings: 4
Ingredients:

- 1-lb. cherry tomatoes
- 2 avocados
- 1 sweet onion, chopped
- 2 tbsp. lemon juice
- 1 and ½ tbsp. olive oil
- Handful basil, chopped

Directions:

1. Mix the tomatoes with the avocados and the rest of the ingredients in a serving bowl, toss and serve right away.

Per serving: Calories: 148Kcal; Protein: 5.5g; Carbohydrates: 9g; Fat: 7.8g

279. ARUGULA SALAD

Preparation time: 5 minutes
Cooking time: 0 minutes
Servings: 4
Ingredients:

- 4 C. arugula leaves
- 1 C. cherry tomatoes
- ¼ C. pine nuts
- 1 tbsp. rice vinegar
- 2 tbsp. olive/grapeseed oil
- ¼ C. parmesan cheese, grated
- Black pepper and salt, as desired
- 1 large avocado, sliced

Directions:

1. Peel and slice the avocado. Rinse and dry the arugula leaves, grate the cheese, and slice the cherry tomatoes into halves.

2. Combine the arugula, pine nuts, tomatoes, oil, vinegar, salt, pepper, and cheese.

3. Toss the salad to mix and portion it onto plates with the avocado slices to serve.

Per serving: Calories: 257Kcal; Protein: 6.1g; Carbohydrates: 6g; Fat: 5g

280. CHICKPEA SALAD

Preparation time: 15 minutes
Cooking time: 0 minutes
Servings: 4
Ingredients:

- 15 oz. chickpeas, cooked
- 1 Roma tomato, diced
- ½ of 1 green medium bell pepper, diced
- 1 tbsp. fresh parsley
- 1 small white onion
- .5 tsp. garlic, minced
- 1 lemon, juiced

Directions:

1. Chop the tomato, green pepper, and onion. Mince the garlic. Combine each of the fixings into a salad bowl and toss well.

2. Cover the salad to chill for at least 15 minutes in the fridge. Serve when ready.

Per serving: Calories: 163Kcal; Protein: 4g; Carbohydrates: 6g; Fat: 2g

281. CHOPPED ISRAELI MEDITERRANEAN PASTA SALAD

Preparation time: 15 minutes
Cooking time: 2 minutes
Servings: 8

- **Ingredients:**
- ½ lb. small bow tie or other small pasta
- ⅓ C. cucumber
- ⅓ C. radish
- ⅓ C. tomato
- ⅓ C. yellow bell pepper
- ⅓ C. orange bell pepper
- ⅓ C. black olives
- ⅓ C. green olives
- ⅓ C. red onions
- ⅓ C. pepperoncini
- ⅓ C. feta cheese
- ⅓ C. fresh thyme leaves
- 1 tsp. oregano, dried

Dressing:

- ¼ C. + more, olive oil
- juice of 1 lemon

Directions:

1. Slice the green olives into halves. Dice the feta and pepperoncini. Finely dice the remainder of the veggies.
2. Prepare a pot of water with the salt, and simmer the pasta until it is al dente (checking at 2 minutes under the listed time). Rinse and drain in cold water.
3. Combine a small amount of oil with the pasta. Add the salt, pepper, oregano, thyme, and veggies. Pour in the rest of the oil, lemon juice, mix and fold in the grated feta.
4. Pop it into the fridge within 2 hours, best if overnight. Taste test and adjust the seasonings to your liking; add fresh thyme.

Per serving: Calories: 65Kcal; Protein: 0.8g; Carbohydrates: 6g; Fat: 1g

282. FETA TOMATO SALAD

Preparation time: 5 minutes

Cooking time: 0 minutes

Servings: 4

Ingredients:

- 2 tbsp. balsamic vinegar
- 1.5 tsp. basil, freshly minced, or .5 tsp, dried .5 tsp. salt
- ½ C. sweet onion, coarsely chopped
- 2 tbsp. olive oil
- 1 lb. cherry or grape tomatoes
- ¼ C. feta cheese, crumbled

Directions:

1. Whisk the salt, basil, and vinegar. Toss the onion into the vinegar mixture for 5 minutes
2. Slice the tomatoes into halves and stir in the tomatoes, feta cheese, and oil to serve.

Per serving: Calories: 121Kcal; Protein: 3g; Carbohydrates: 10g; Fat: 2g

283. TOFU SALAD

Preparation time: 10 minutes

Cooking time: 15 minutes

Servings: 2

Ingredients:

- ½ pack firm tofu
- ½ a red onion
- 2 spelt tortillas
- 1 avocado
- 4 handfuls baby spinach
- 1 handful almonds
- 2 tomatoes
- 1 pink grapefruit
- ½ lemon

Directions:

1. Heat up the tortillas in an oven and once warm, bake for 8–10 minutes in the oven.
2. Chop up the onions, tomatoes, and tofu and combine them.
3. Put it in the fridge and let it cool.
4. Now chop up the almonds, avocado, and grapefruit. Mix everything well and place nicely around the bowl you had put in the fridge.
5. Squeeze a lemon on top all over the salad and enjoy!

Per serving: Calories: 110Kcal; Protein: 36g; Carbohydrates: 19g; Fat: 15g

284. TOFU AND TOMATO

Preparation time: 15 minutes

Cooking time: 15 minutes

Servings: 2

Ingredients:

- 1 tbsp. coconut oil
- A little coriander/cilantro
- 10 oz. regular firm tofu
- 2 big handfuls of baby spinach
- ½ brown onion (or red if you fancy)
- 1 handful arugula/rocket
- Black pepper, freshly ground
- 2 tomatoes
- Himalayan/Sea salt
- Pinch turmeric
- A little basil
- ½ small red pepper
- A pinch cayenne pepper

Directions:

1. Use your hands to scramble the tofu into a bowl, then chop and fry the onion quickly in a pan. Dice the peppers and do the same thing.
2. Dice the tomatoes and throw them into the pan. Toss in a pinch of turmeric, and add the spinach. Add salt and grind in the pepper. Cook until the tofu is warm and cooked.
3. Throw in basil leaves, coriander, the rocket just when the meal is about to be done. Serve with a pinch of some hot cayenne pepper.
4. You can serve on some toasted sprouted bread and some baby spinach.

Per serving: Calories: 174Kcal; Protein: 27g; Carbohydrates: 16g; Fat: 12g

285. LENTIL-STUFFED POTATO CAKES

Preparation time: 15 minutes

Cooking time: 30 minutes

Servings: 4

Ingredients:

For the cakes:

- Salt
- 1 bay leaf
- 10 medium gold potatoes
- 1 C. potato starch- add more for dusting

For the stuffing:

- Coconut oil for pan-frying
- Salt and black pepper, freshly ground
- 1 medium onion, chopped
- 4 oz. mushrooms
- 2 tbsp. olive oil
- ¾ C. green lentils, dried and cooked (preferably French lentils)

Directions:

1. Combine the 7 C. of water, potatoes, and bay leaf in a large pot and boil until the potatoes are tender. Poke with a fork to ensure they are cooked.
2. Rinse the potatoes under cold water when done; the skins will peel off easily. Now mash the potatoes until smooth and add the potato starch, stir to make the dough. Add more potato starch if the dough feels too sticky.
3. For the stuffing, add olive oil to a sauté pan and place over medium-high heat. Add in onions and cook as you stir for 5 minutes. Add in the lentils together with pepper and salt (to taste) and cook for 2 minutes. Set aside.
4. To make the cakes, scoop about 3 tbsp. of the dough in your hand and press it into your palm. Add a spoonful of stuffing on top of the dough and fold it over to close it. Shape it into a round disk.
5. Now add coconut oil to a skillet and heat over medium heat. Cook the potato cakes on both sides until golden, roughly 4 minutes per side.

Per serving: Calories: 227Kcal; Protein: 41g; Carbohydrates: 19g; Fat: 1g

286. SESAME GINGER CAULIFLOWER RICE

Preparation time: 10 minutes

Cooking time: 15 minutes

Servings: 4

Ingredients:

- 2 tbsp. wheat-free tamari plus more to taste
- 4 C. mushrooms, finely chopped
- 1 large head cauliflower
- 2 tbsp. sesame oil, toasted
- 2 tbsp. grapeseed oil

- ½ tsp. Celtic Sea salt, plus more to taste
- 6 green onions, chopped
- 1 bunch cilantro, finely chopped (½ C.)
- 2 tbsp. fresh ginger, minced
- 2 tsp. fresh lime juice, plus more to taste
- 1 small green chili, ribbed, seeded, and minced
- 4 tsp. garlic cloves, minced

Directions:

1. For the cauliflower rice, roughly cut the cauliflower into florets and get rid of the tough middle core.
2. Fit a food processor with an S blade and add the florets to pulse. Pulse for a few seconds until the florets achieve a rice-like consistency. You should have 5–6 C. of rice in the end.
3. Heat oil in a large skillet or wok over medium-high heat and fry the ginger, green onions, chili, garlic, and mushroom seasoned with ¼ tsp. of salt for 5 minutes. Once combined well and soft, add in the tamari and cauliflower rice and cook for 5 more minutes until soft.
4. Add in remaining salt, cilantro, and lime juice and adjust the flavors as desired.
5. Serve and enjoy!

Per serving: Calories: 113Kcal; Protein: 12g; Carbohydrates: 9g; Fat: 7g

287. SPINACH WITH CHICKPEAS AND LEMON

Preparation time: 10 minutes
Cooking time: 15 minutes
Servings: 2
Ingredients:

- 3 tbsp. extra virgin olive oil
- Sea salt, to taste (i.e., Celtic Grey, Himalayan, or Redmond Real Salt)
- ½ container grape tomatoes
- 1 large can chickpeas, rinse well
- 1 large onion, thinly sliced
- 1 tbsp. ginger, grated
- 1 large lemon, zested and freshly juiced
- 1 tsp. red pepper flakes, crushed
- 4 garlic cloves, minced

Directions:

1. Pour the olive oil into a large skillet and add in the onion. Cook for about 5 minutes until the onion starts to brown.
2. Add in the ginger, lemon zest, garlic, tomatoes, and red pepper flakes and cook for 3–4 minutes.

3. Toss in the chickpeas (rinsed and drained) and cook for an additional 3–4 minutes. Now add the spinach in 2 batches and once it starts to wilt, season with some sea salt and lemon juice.
4. Cook for 2 minutes.

Per serving: Calories: 239Kcal; Protein: 28g; Carbohydrates: 69g; Fat: 5g

288. KALE WRAPS WITH CHILI AND GREEN BEANS

Preparation time: 30 minutes
Cooking time: 0 minute
Servings: 2
Ingredients:

- 1 tbsp. fresh lime juice
- 1 tbsp. raw seed mix
- 2 large kale leaves
- 2 tsp. fresh garlic, finely chopped
- ½ ripe avocado, pitted and sliced
- 1 tsp. fresh red chili, seeded and finely chopped
- 1 C. fresh cucumber sticks
- Fresh coriander leaves, finely chopped
- 1 C. green beans

Directions:

1. Spread kale leaves on a clean kitchen work surface.
2. Spread each chopped coriander leaves on each leaf, position them around the end of the leaf, perpendicular to the edge.
3. Spread green beans equally on each leaf, at the edge of each leaf, same as the coriander leaves.
4. Do the same with the cucumber sticks.
5. Cut the divided chopped garlic across each leaf, sprinkling it all over the green beans.
6. Cut and share the chopped chili across each leaf and sprinkle it over the garlic.
7. Now, divide the avocado across each leaf, and spread it over chili, garlic, coriander, and green beans.
8. Share the raw seed mix among each leaf, and sprinkle them over other ingredients.
9. Divide the lime juice across each leaf and drizzle it over all other ingredients.
10. Now fold or roll up the kale leaves and wrap up all the ingredients within them.
11. You can serve with soy sauce!

Per serving: Calories: 328Kcal; Protein: 42g; Carbohydrates: 30g; Fat: 15g

289. CABBAGE WRAPS WITH AVOCADO AND STRAWBERRIES

Preparation time: 30 minutes
Cooking time: 0 minute
Servings: 1–2
Ingredients:

- ½ C. raw pecan nuts, roughly chopped
- ½ C. fresh strawberries, sliced
- 2 large cabbage leaves
- Half ripe avocado
- 1 C. green asparagus spears

Directions:

1. Spread out the cabbage sheets on a clean kitchen work surface.
2. Share the asparagus shear among each cabbage leaf and place them on the edge of the leaf.
3. Share the avocado slices on each leaf and put them on top of the asparagus spears.
4. Share the strawberries over each leaf and spread them on top of the avocado slices.
5. Share the pecan nuts between each leaf and spread it on the strawberries.
6. Wrap the leaves with all ingredients inside them.
7. Serve with soy sauce (optional).

Per serving: Calories: 176Kcal; Protein: 34g; Carbohydrates: 19g; Fat: 15g

290. MILLET TABBOULEH, LIME AND CILANTRO

Preparation time: 10 minutes
Cooking time: 30 minutes
Servings: 6
Ingredients:

- ½ C. lime juice
- ½ C. cilantro
- 6 drops hot sauce
- ¼ C. and 2 tsp. olive oil
- 2 tomatoes
- 2 green onions
- 2 cucumbers
- 1 C. millet

Directions:

1. Heat olive oil in a saucepan over medium heat. Add the millet and fry until it begins to smell fragrant (this takes between 3–4 minutes). Add about 6 C. water and bring to boil.
2. Wait for about 15 minutes. Turn off the heat, wash and rinse under cold water. Drain the millet and transfer it to a large bowl.

3. Add cucumbers, tomatoes, lime juice, cilantro, green onions, ¼ C. oil, and hot sauce. Season with pepper and salt to taste.

Per serving: Calories: 211Kcal; Protein: 30g; Carbohydrates: 16g; Fat: 12g

CHAPTER 6: Fish and Seafood

291. WHITEFISH CURRY

Preparation time: 15 minutes
Cooking time: 15 minutes
Servings: 4-6
Ingredients:

- 2 tbsp. coconut oil
- 1 onion, chopped
- 2 garlic cloves, minced
- 1 tbs. minced fresh ginger
- 2 tsp. curry powder
- 1 tsp. salt
- ¼ tsp. freshly ground black pepper
- 1 (4-inch) piece lemongrass (white part only), bruised with the back of a knife
- 2 cups cubed butternut squash
- 2 cups chopped broccoli
- 1 (13½-ounce / 383-g) can coconut milk
- 1 cup vegetable broth, or chicken broth
- 1 pound (45g;) firm whitefish fillets
- ¼ cup chopped fresh cilantro
- 1 scallion, sliced thinly
- Lemon wedges, for garnish

Directions:

1. In a huge pot over medium-high heat, melt the coconut oil. Add the onion, garlic, ginger, curry powder, salt, and pepper. Sauté for 5 minutes.
2. Add the lemongrass, butternut squash, and broccoli. Sauté for 2 minutes more.
3. Stir in the vegetable broth and coconut milk and bring to a boil. Reduce the heat to simmer then add the fish. Cover the pot then simmer for 5 minutes, or until the fish is cooked through. Remove and discard the lemongrass.
4. Ladle the curry into a serving bowl. Garnish with the cilantro and scallion and serve with the lemon wedges.

Per serving: Calories: 553Kcal; Protein: 34g; Carbohydrates: 22g; Fat: 39g

292. COCONUT-CRUSTED SHRIMP

Preparation time: 10 minutes
Cooking time: 6 minutes
Servings: 4
Ingredients:

- 2 eggs
- 1 cup unsweetened dried coconut
- ¼ cup coconut flour
- ½ tsp. salt
- ¼ tsp. paprika
- Dash cayenne pepper
- Dash freshly grounds black pepper
- ¼ cup coconut oil
- 1 pound (45g;) raw shrimp, peeled and deveined

Directions:

1. In a small shallow bowl, whisk the eggs.
2. In another small shallow bowl, mix the coconut, coconut flour, salt, paprika, cayenne pepper, and black pepper.
3. In a huge skillet over medium-high heat, heat the coconut oil.
4. Pat the shrimp dry with a paper towel.
5. Working one at a time, hold each shrimp by the tail, dip it first into the egg mixture, then into the coconut mixture until coated. Place into the hot skillet. Cook for 1 to 3 minutes per side. Transfer to a paper towel-lined plate to drain excess oil.
6. Serve immediately.

Per serving: Calories121Kcal; Protein: 21g; Carbohydrates: 5g; Fat: 3g

293. LIME-SALMON PATTIES

Preparation time: 20 minutes
Cooking time: 10 minutes
Servings: 4
Ingredients:

- ½ pound (22g;) cooked boneless salmon fillet, flaked
- 2 eggs
- ¾ cup almond flour, plus more as needed
- 1 scallion, white and green parts, chopped
- 4 tbs. lemon juice
- Zest of 2 limes (optional)
- 1 tbs. chopped fresh dill
- Pinch sea salt
- 1 tbs. olive oil
- 1 lime, cut into wedges

Directions:

1. In a huge bowl, mix together the salmon, eggs, almond flour, scallion, lime juice, lime zest (if using), dill, and sea salt until the mixture holds together when pressed. If the mixture is too dry, add more lime juice; if it is too wet, add more almond flour.
2. Divide the salmon mixture into 4 equal portions, and press them into patties about ½ inch thick.
3. Refrigerate them for about 30 minutes to firm up.
4. Place a large skillet over medium-high heat and add the olive oil.
5. Add the salmon patties and brown for about 5 minutes per side, turning once.
6. Serve the patties with lime wedges.

Per serving: Calories: 243Kcal; Protein: 18g; Carbohydrates: 5g; Fat: 18g

294. COCONUT MILK-BAKED SOLE

Preparation time: 20 minutes
Cooking time: 20 minutes
Servings: 4
Ingredients:

- 2 tbsp. warm water
- Pinch saffron threads
- 2 pounds (90g;) sole fillets
- Sea salt, to taste
- 2 tbsp. freshly squeezed lemon juice
- 1 tbs. coconut oil
- 1 sweet onion, chopped, or about 1 cup precut packaged onion
- 2 tsp. bottled minced garlic
- 1 tsp. grated fresh ginger
- 1 cup canned full-fat: coconut milk
- 2 tbsp. chopped fresh cilantro

Directions:

1. Place the water in a mini bowl and sprinkle the saffron threads on top. Let it stand for 10 minutes.
2. Preheat the oven to 350 deg. (180°C).
3. Rub the fish with sea salt and the lemon juice, and place the fillets in a 9-by-9-inch baking dish. Roast the fish for 10 minutes.
4. While the fish is roasting, place a large skillet over medium-high heat and add the coconut oil.
5. Add the onion, garlic, and ginger. Sauté for about 3 minutes, or until softened.
6. Stir in the coconut milk and the saffron water. Bring to a boil. Place the heat to low then simmer the sauce for 5 minutes. Remove the skillet from the heat.
7. Pour the sauce over the fish. Cover and bake for about 10 minutes, or until the fish flakes easily with a fork.

8. Serve the fish topped with the cilantro.

Per serving: Calories: 449Kcal; Protein: 56g; Carbohydrates: 7g; Fat: 21g

295. WHITE FISH SOUP WITH MUSHROOM

Preparation time: 15 minutes
Cooking time: 18 minutes
Servings: 4
Ingredients:

- 1 leek, thinly sliced
- 1 tsp. minced fresh ginger root
- 1 garlic clove, minced
- ½ cup sliced shiitake mushrooms
- ½ cup dry white wine
- 1 tbs. toasted sesame oil
- 4 (6 oz.) white fish fillets (such as cod, haddock, or pollock)
- 1 tsp. salt
- 1teaspoon freshly ground black pepper

Directions:

1. Preheat the oven to 375°F.
2. Combine the leek, ginger root, garlic, mushrooms, wine, and sesame oil in a 9-by-13-inch baking pan. Toss well to combine.
3. Bake for 10 minutes.
4. Set the fish on top of the mushrooms. Add the salt and pepper, cover with aluminum foil, and bake until the fish is firm, 5 to 8 minutes. Serve.

RECIPE TIP: Salmon and swordfish also work well in this recipe. As with most cooked fish, eat within 3 days of making.

Per serving: Calories: 210Kcal; Protein: 31g; Carbohydrates: 5g; Fat: 5g

296. PAN FRIED SALMON AND BOK CHOY IN MISO VINAIGRETTE

Preparation time: 10 minutes
Cooking time: 30 minutes
Servings: 4
Ingredients:

- ¼ cup miso paste
- 2 tbsp. rice wine vinegar
- 6 tbsp. toasted sesame oil, divided
- 2 tsp. ground ginger
- 1 tsp. red pepper flakes
- 2 garlic cloves, minced
- 1 pound wild-caught salmon fillet, skin removed
- ½ cup avocado or extra-virgin olive oil, divided
- 8 heads baby Bok choy, quartered
- 2 tbsp. tamari or water

- 2 tbsp. sesame seeds

Directions:

1. In a mini bowl, combine the miso, vinegar, 2 tbsp. of sesame oil, ginger, red pepper flakes, and garlic and whisk until smooth.
2. In a glass baking dish or resealable storage bag, place the salmon and pour the marinade over it. Refrigerate for around 30 minutes or up to overnight.
3. To cook the fish, in a large skillet heat 4 tbsp. of avocado oil over medium-high heat. Remove the salmon from the marinade, reserving the liquid, and fry for 3 to 5 minutes per side, until the fish is crispy and golden brown. The time depends on your desired doneness and the thickness of the fish.
4. Transfer the fish to a huge platter and keep warm.
5. In the same skillet, add the remaining 4 tbsp. of avocado oil over medium-high heat. Add the Bok choy and fry for about 7 minutes, until it is crispy and just tender. Transfer it to the platter with the salmon.
6. Reduce the heat to low. Add the reserved miso marinade and tamari to the oil in the skillet and whisk to combine well. Simmer, uncovered, for 4 to 5 minutes, until slightly thickened. Whisk in the remaining 4 tbsp. of sesame oil until smooth.
7. Serve the salmon and Bok choy drizzled with the warm miso vinaigrette and sprinkled with the sesame seeds.

Per serving: Calories: 631Kcal; Protein: 27g; Carbohydrates: 8g; Fat: 56g

297. SEARED COD WITH COCONUT-MUSHROOM SAUCE

Preparation time: 10 minutes
Cooking time: 20 minutes
Servings: 4
Ingredients:

- 1 pound cod fillet
- ½ tsp. salt
- ¼ tsp. freshly ground black pepper
- ½ cup coconut oil, divided
- Grated zest and juice of 1 lime (separated)
- 4 ounces shiitake mushrooms, thinly sliced
- 2 garlic cloves, minced
- 1 (13.5-ounce) can full-Fat: coconut milk
- 1 tsp. ground ginger

- 1 tsp. red pepper flakes
- 2 tbsp. tamari (or 1 tbs. miso paste and 1 tbs. water)
- 2 tbsp. toasted sesame oil

Directions:

1. Cut the cod into four equal pieces and season with salt and pepper.
2. In a huge skillet, heat 4 tbsp. of coconut oil over high heat until just before smoking.
3. Add the cod, skin-side up, cover to prevent splattering and sear for 4 to 5 minutes, until it is golden brown. Remove the fish from the skillet, drizzle with the juice of ½ lime, and let rest.
4. In the same skillet, add the remaining 4 tbsp. of coconut oil and heat over medium. Add the mushrooms and sauté for 5 to 6 minutes, until they are just tender. Add the garlic and sauté for 1 minute, until fragrant.
5. Whisk in the coconut milk, ginger, red pepper flakes, tamari, and remaining lime zest and juice and reduce the heat to low. Return the cod to the skillet, skin-side down, cover and simmer for 3 to 4 minutes, until the fish is cooked through.
6. To serve, place the cod on rimmed plates or in shallow bowls and spoon the sauce over the fish. Drizzle with the sesame oil.

Per serving: Calories: 572Kcal; Protein: 23g; Carbohydrates: 9g; Fat: 51g

298. NEW ENGLAND CLAM CHOWDER

Preparation time: 10 minutes
Cooking time: 10 minutes
Servings:
Ingredients:

- 3 (6.5-ounce) cans clams, drained, juice reserved, and chopped
- ½ cup water
- 2 tbsp. ghee
- 2 garlic cloves, minced
- 2 celery stalks, chopped
- 1 yellow onion, diced
- 1 tsp. sea salt
- ¼ tsp. freshly ground black pepper
- 1½ pounds Yukon Gold potatoes, diced
- ¼ tsp. dried thyme
- 11/3 cups coconut milk

Directions:

1. In a glass measuring cup, combine the reserved clam juice and water,

adding more water as needed to equal 2 cups total. Set aside.

2. Press 'Sauté' on the Instant Pot and let the pot preheat.

3. Place the ghee in the pot to melt and add the garlic, celery, onion, salt, and pepper. Cook for 3 minutes.

4. Add the clam juice-water mixture and the potatoes and stir to combine. Select 'Cancel'. Lock the lid.

5. Select 'Pressure Cook' and cook at high pressure for 5 minutes.

6. When cooking is complete, use a quick release.

7. Remove the lid then stir in the clams, thyme, and coconut milk. Cook for 2 minutes with the residual heat from the pot to warm, then serve.

Per serving: Calories: 494Kcal; Protein: 30g; Carbohydrates: 43g; Fat: 24g

299. BUCKWHEAT RAMEN WITH COD AND SOFT-BOILED EGG

Preparation time: 15 minutes
Cooking time: 5 minutes
Servings:
Ingredients:

- 6 ounces buckwheat ramen
- 5 ounces shiitake or cremini mushrooms, sliced
- 2 garlic cloves, minced
- 1 yellow onion, diced
- 4 cups low-sodium vegetable broth
- ¼ cup tamari
- 2 tbsp. apple cider vinegar
- 3 cups chopped cod fillet
- 4 Soft-boiled eggs
- 2 tsp. toasted sesame seeds

Directions:

1. TO MAKE THE RAMEN: In the Instant Pot, combine the noodles, mushrooms, garlic, onion, broth, tamari, and vinegar. Lock the lid.

2. Select 'Pressure Cook' and cook at high pressure for 2 minutes.

3. When cooking is complete, use a natural release for 4 minutes, then quick release any remaining pressure.

4. Remove the lid and add the cod. Cook, stirring, for 2 minutes in 'Keep Warm' mode, or until the fish is cooked to your desired doneness.

5. TO SERVE: Divide the noodles, fish, and broth into serving bowls. Top each with a soft-boiled and a sprinkle of the sesame seeds.

Per serving: Calories: 415Kcal; Protein: 43g; Carbohydrates: 42g; Fat: 7g

300. MANHATTAN-STYLE SALMON CHOWDER

Preparation time: 10 minutes
Cooking time: 15 minutes
Servings: 4
Ingredients:

- ¼ cup extra-virgin olive oil
- 1 red bell pepper, chopped
- 1-pound skinless salmon, pin bones removed, chopped into ½-inch pieces
- 2 (28-ounce) cans crushed tomatoes, 1 drained and 1 undrained
- 6 cups no-salt-added chicken broth
- 2 cups diced (½ inch) sweet potatoes
- 1 tsp. onion powder
- ½ tsp. sea salt
- ¼ tsp. freshly ground black pepper

Directions:

1. In a large pot, over medium-high heat, heat the olive oil until it shimmers.

2. Add the red bell pepper and salmon.

3. Cook for around 5 minutes, stirring occasionally, until the fish is opaque and the bell pepper is soft.

4. Stir in the tomatoes, chicken broth, sweet potatoes, onion powder, salt, and pepper.

5. Bring to a simmer and reduce the heat to medium. Cook for around 10 mins. stirring occasionally, until the sweet potatoes are soft.

Per serving: Calories: 570Kcal; Protein: 16g; Carbohydrates: 55g; Fat: 42g

301. SALMON CEVICHE

Preparation time: 10 minutes
Cooking time: 20 minutes
Servings: 4
Ingredients:

- 1 pound salmon, skin and pin bones removed, cut into bite-size pieces (remove any gray flesh)
- ½ cup freshly squeezed lime juice
- 2 tomatoes, diced
- ¼ cup fresh cilantro leaves, chopped
- 1 jalapeño pepper, seeded and diced
- 2 tbsp. extra-virgin olive oil
- ½ tsp. sea salt

Directions:

1. In a medium-sized bowl, mix together the salmon and lime juice. Let it marinate for 20 minutes.

2. Stir in the tomatoes, cilantro, jalapeño, olive oil, and salt.

Per serving: Calories: 222Kcal; Protein: 23g; Carbohydrates: 3g; Fat: 14g

302. SEARED SCALLOPS WITH GREENS

Preparation time: 20 minutes
Cooking time: 15 minutes
Servings: 4
Ingredients:

- 1½ pounds (68g;) sea scallops, cleaned and patted dry
- Sea salt, to taste
- Freshly ground black pepper, to taste
- 2 tbsp. olive oil, divided
- 2 garlic cloves, thinly sliced
- 2 cups chopped kale leaves
- 2 cups fresh spinach

Directions:

1. Lightly season the scallops all over with sea salt and pepper.

2. Place a large skillet over medium-high heat and add 1 tbs. of olive oil.

3. Pan-sear the scallops for about 2 minutes per side, or until opaque and just cook through.

4. Transfer to a plate then cover loosely with aluminum foil to keep them warm. Wipe the skillet with a paper towel and place it back on the heat.

5. Place the remaining 1 tbs. of olive oil to the skillet and sauté the garlic for about 4 minutes, or until caramelized.

6. Stir in the kale and spinach. Cook, tossing with tongs, for about 6 minutes, or until the greens are tender and wilted.

7. Divide the greens with any juices equally among four plates and top each with the scallops.

Per serving: Calories: 232Kcal; Protein: 30g; Carbohydrates: 9g; Fat: 8g

303. MEDITERRANEAN TUNA-SPINACH SALAD

Preparation time: 10 minutes
Cooking time: 0 minutes
Servings: 1
Ingredients:

- 1 ½ tbsp. tahini
- 1 ½ tbsp. lemon juice
- 1 ½ tbsp. water
- 1 5-oz. can chunk light tuna in water, drained
- 4 Kalamata olives, pitted and chopped
- 2 tbsp. feta cheese
- 2 tbsp. parsley

- 2 cups baby spinach
- 1 medium orange, peeled or sliced

Directions:

1. Mix tahini, citrus juice, and water in the bowl. Add olives, tuna, feta, and parsley and stir until everything is well-mixed. Serving the salad of tuna with 2 cups of spinach with the orange to serve on the side.

Per serving: Calories: 376Kcal; Protein: 37g; Carbohydrates: 26.2g; Fat: 21g

304. MISO-GLAZED SALMON

Preparation time: 5 minutes

Cooking time: 10 minutes

Servings: 4

Ingredients:

- 4 (4-ounce / 113-g) salmon fillets
- 3 tbsp. miso paste
- 2 tbsp. raw honey
- 1 tsp. coconut aminos
- 1 tsp. rice vinegar

Directions:

1. Preheat the broiler.
2. Line a baking dish with aluminum foil and place the salmon fillets in it.
3. In a mini bowl, stir together the miso, honey, coconut aminos, and vinegar.
4. Brush the glaze evenly over the top of each fillet. Broil for about 5 minutes. The fish is done when it flakes easily. The exact cooking time depends on its thickness.
5. Brush any remaining glaze over the fish, and continue to broil for 5 minutes, if needed.

Per serving: Calories: 264Kcal; Protein: 30g; Carbohydrates: 13g; Fat: 9g

305. BAKED SALMON PATTIES WITH GREENS

Preparation time: 15 minutes

Cooking time: 38 minutes

Servings: 4

Ingredients:

- 2 cups sweet potatooes, cooked (about 2 large sweet potatoes)
- 2 (6-ounce / 170-g) cans wild salmon, drained
- ¼ cup almond flour
- ¼ tsp. ground turmeric
- 2 tbsp. coconut oil
- 2 kale bunches, thoroughly washed, stemmed, and cut into ribbons
- ¼ tsp. salt

Directions:

1. Preheat the oven to 350 deg. (180°C).
2. Line a baking sheet with parchment paper.
3. In a huge bowl, stir together the mashed sweet potatoes and salmon.
4. Blend in the almond flour and turmeric.
5. Using a 1/3-cup measure, scoop the salmon mixture onto the baking sheet. Flatten slightly with the bottom of the measuring cup. Repeat with the remaining mixture.
6. Place the sheet in the pre-heated oven and bake for 30 minutes, flipping the patties halfway through.
7. In a large saucepan set over medium heat, heat the coconut oil.
8. Add the kale. Sauté for around 5 to 8 minutes, or until the kale is bright and wilted. Sprinkle with the salt and serve with the salmon patties.

Per serving: Calories: 320Kcal; Protein: 21g; Carbohydrates: 32g; Fat: 13g

306. FRESH TUNA STEAK AND FENNEL SALAD

Preparation time: 15 minutes

Cooking time: 25 minutes

Servings: 4

Ingredients:

- 2 (1 inch) tuna steaks
- 2 tbsp. olive oil, 1 tbs. olive oil for brushing
- 1 tsp. crushed black peppercorns
- 1 tsp. crushed fennel seeds
- 1 fennel bulb, trimmed and sliced
- ½ cup water
- 1 lemon, juiced
- 1 tsp. fresh parsley, chopped

Directions:

1. Coat the fish with oil and then season with peppercorns and fennel seeds.
2. Heat the oil on a medium heat and sauté the fennel bulb slices for 5 minutes or until light brown.
3. Add the water to the pan and cook for 10 minutes until fennel is tender.
4. Stir in the lemon juice and lower heat to a simmer.
5. Meanwhile, heat another skillet and sauté the tuna steaks for about 2 to 3 minutes each side for medium-rare. (Add 1 minute each side for medium and 2 minutes each side for medium well).
6. Serve the fennel mix with the tuna steaks on top and garnish with the fresh parsley.

Per serving: Calories: 288Kcal; Protein: 44g; Carbohydrates: 6g; Fat: 9g

307. PAN-SEARED HADDOCK WITH BEETS

Preparation time: 20 minutes

Cooking time: 30 minutes

Servings: 4

Ingredients:

- 8 beets, peeled and cut into eighths
- 2 shallots, thinly sliced
- 1 tsp. bottled minced garlic
- 2 tbsp. olive oil, divided
- 2 tbsp. apple cider vinegar
- 1 tsp. chopped fresh thyme
- Pinch sea salt
- 4 (5-ounce / 142-g) haddock fillets, patted dry

Directions:

1. Preheat the oven to 400 degrees (205°C).
2. In a medium bowl, toss together the beets, shallots, garlic, and 1 tbs. of olive oil until well coated. Spread the beet mixture in a 9-by-13-inch baking dish. Roast for about 30 minutes, or until the vegetables are caramelized and tender.
3. Remove the beets from the oven and stir in the cider vinegar, thyme, and sea salt.
4. While the beets are roasting, place a large skillet over medium-high heat and add the remaining 1 tbs. of olive oil.
5. Panfry the fish for about 15 minutes, turning once, until it flakes when pressed with a fork.
6. Serve the fish with a generous scoop of roasted beets.

Storage: Store in an airtight container in the fridge for up to 4 days or in the freezer for up to 1 month.

Reheat: Microwave, covered, until the desired temperature is reached.

Per serving: Calories: 314Kcal; Protein: 38g; Carbohydrates: 21g; Fat: 9g

308. FISH TACO SALAD WITH STRAWBERRY AVOCADO SALSA

Preparation time: 20 minutes

Cooking time: 10 minutes

Servings: 2

Ingredients:

For the salsa:

- Two hulled and diced strawberries
- Half diced small shallot
- Two tbsp. of finely chopped fresh cilantro
- Two tbsp. of freshly squeezed lime juice

- 1 tsp. of cayenne pepper
- Half diced avocado
- Two tbsp. of canned black beans, rinsed and drained
- One thinly sliced green onions
- Half tsp. of finely chopped peeled ginger
- A quarter tsp. of sea salt

For the fish:

- One tsp. of agave nectar
- Two cups of arugula
- One tbs. of extra-virgin olive oil or avocado oil
- Half tbs. of freshly squeezed lime juice
- One pound of light fish (halibut, cod, or red snapper), cut into two fillets
- A quarter tsp. of freshly ground black pepper
- Half tsp. of sea salt

Directions:

1. Preheat the grill, whether it is gas or charcoal.
2. To create the salsa, add the avocado, beans, strawberries, shallot, cilantro, green onions, salt, cayenne pepper, ginger, and lime juice in a medium mixing cup. Put aside after mixing until all of the components are well combined.
3. To render the salad, whisk together the agave, oil, and lime juice in a small bowl. Toss the arugula with the vinaigrette in a big mixing bowl.
4. Season the fish fillets with pepper and salt. Grill the fish for around 7 to 9 minutes over direct high heat, flipping once during cooking. The fish should be translucent and flake quickly.
5. Place one cup of arugula salad on each plate to eat. Cover each salad with a fillet and a heaping spoonful of salsa.

Per serving: Calories: 878Kcal; Protein: 26g; Carbohydrates: 53g; Fat: 26g

309. SHRIMP MUSHROOM SQUASH

Preparation time: 10 minutes
Cooking time: 20 minutes
Servings: 4
Ingredients:

- 2 tbsp. hemp seeds
- 2 tbsp. olive oil
- 1 pound shrimp, peeled and deveined
- ¼ cup coconut aminos
- 2 tbsp. raw honey
- 2 tsp. sesame oil

- 1 yellow onion, chopped
- 4 ounces shiitake mushrooms, (cut into slices)
- 2 garlic cloves, minced
- 1 red bell pepper, (cut into slices)
- 1 yellow squash, peeled and cubed
- 2 cups chard, chopped

Directions:

1. In a bowl (medium size), mix the aminos, honey, sesame oil and hemp seeds.
2. In a skillet (you can also use a saucepan); heat the oil over medium stove flame.
3. Add the onions, stir the mixture and cook while stirring for about 2-3 minutes until softened.
4. Add the bell pepper, squash, mushrooms and garlic, stir-cook for 5 minutes.
5. Add the shrimp and aminos mix; stir-cook for 4 minutes more.
6. Add the chard, toss; add into serving bowls and serve.

Per serving: Calories: 236Kcal; Protein: 9g; Carbohydrates: 11g; Fat: 8g

310. SPINACH SEA BASS LUNCH

Preparation time: 10 minutes
Cooking time: 30 minutes
Servings: 2
Ingredients:

- 2 sea bass fillets, boneless
- 2 shallots, chopped
- Juice of ½ lemon
- 1 garlic clove, minced
- 5 cherry tomatoes, halved
- 1 tbs. parsley, chopped
- 1 tbs. olive oil
- 8 ounces baby spinach

Directions:

1. Pre-heat oven to 450°F. Grease a baking dish with cooking spray.
2. Add the fish, tomatoes, parsley and garlic, drizzle the lemon juice.
3. Cover the dish and bake for 12-15 minutes and add in serving plates.
4. In a skillet (you can also use a saucepan); heat the oil over medium stove flame.
5. Add the shallots, stir the mixture and cook while stirring for about 1-2 minutes until softened.
6. Add the spinach, stir, and cook for 4-5 minutes more. Add with the fish and serve warm.

Per serving: Calories: 218Kcal; Protein: 24g; Carbohydrates: 10g Fat: 11g

311. GARLIC COD MEAL

Preparation time: 5 minutes
Cooking time: 35 minutes
Servings: 4
Ingredients:

- 2 tbsp. olive oil
- 2 tbsp. tarragon, chopped
- ¼ cup parsley, chopped
- 4 cod fillets, skinless
- 2 garliccloves, minced
- 1 yellow onion, chopped
- (ground) black pepper and salt to the taste
- Juice of 1 lemon
- 1 lemon, (cut into slices)
- 1 tbs. thyme, chopped
- 4 cups water

Directions:

1. In a skillet (you can also use a saucepan); heat the oil over medium stove flame.
2. Add the onions, garlic, stir the mixture and cook while stirring for about 2-3 minutes until softened.
3. Add the salt, pepper, tarragon, parsley, thyme, water, lemon juice and lemon slices.
4. Boil the mix; add the cod, cook for 12-15 minutes, drain the liquid.
5. Serve with a side salad.

Per serving: Calories: 181Kcal; Protein: 12g; Carbohydrates: 9g; Fat: 3g

312. COD CUCUMBER DELIGHT

Preparation time: 10 minutes
Cooking time: 25 minutes
Servings: 4
Ingredients:

- 1 tbs. capers, drained
- 4 tbsp. + 1 tsp. olive oil
- 4 cod fillets, skinless and boneless
- 2 tbsp. mustard
- 1 tbs. tarragon, chopped
- (ground) black pepper and salt to the taste
- 2 cups lettuce leaves, torn
- 1 small red onion, (cut into slices)
- 1 small cucumber, (cut into slices)
- 2 tbsp. lemon juice
- 2 tbsp. water

Directions:

1. In a bowl (medium size), mix the mustard with 2 tbsp. olive oil, tarragon, capers and water, whisk well and set aside.
2. In a skillet (you can also use a saucepan); heat 1 tsp. oil over medium stove flame.

3. Add the fish, pepper, salt and cook, while stirring, until cooked well and turn softened on both sides.
4. In a bowl (medium size), mix the cucumber, onion, lettuce, lemon juice, 2 tbsp. olive oil, salt and pepper.
5. Arrange the cod in serving plates, top with the tarragon sauce.
6. Serve with the cucumber salad.

Per serving: Calories: 284Kcal; Protein: 14g; Carbohydrates: 9g; Fat: 8g

313. OREGANO LETTUCE SHRIMP

Preparation time: 5 minutes
Cooking time: 25 minutes
Servings: 4
Ingredients:

- 3 tbsp. dill, chopped
- 1 tbs. oregano, chopped
- 2 garlic cloves, chopped
- 1 pound shrimp, deveined and peeled
- 2 tsp. olive oil
- 6 tbsp. lemon juice
- (ground) black pepper and salt to taste
- 2 cucumbers, (cut into slices)
- 1 red onion, (cut into slices)
- ¾ cup coconut cream
- ½ pounds cherry tomatoes
- 8 lettuce leaves

Directions:

1. In a bowl (medium size), combine the shrimp, 1 tbs. oregano, 2 tbsp. lemon juice, 1 tbs. dill, and 1 tsp. oil. Set aside for 10 minutes.
2. In another bowl, mix 1 tbs. dill, half of the garlic, ¼ cup coconut cream, 2 tbsp. lemon juice, cucumber, salt and pepper. Combine well.
3. In another bowl, mix rest of the lemon juice, ½ cup cream, the rest of the garlic and the rest of the dill.
4. In a bowl (medium size), mix the tomatoes with onion and 1 tsp. olive oil.
5. Heat a grill over medium-high heat, grill tomato mix and shrimp mix for 5 minutes,
6. Add them in serving plates, add the cucumber salad, lettuce leaves and other ingredients on top.

Per serving: Calories: 268Kcal; Protein: 11g; Carbohydrates: 12g; Fat: 5g

314. MEXICAN PEPPER SALMON

Preparation time: 5 minutes
Cooking time: 25 minutes
Servings: 4

Ingredients:

- 1 garlic clove, minced
- 1 tsp. sweet paprika
- 4 medium salmon fillets, boneless
- 2 tsp. olive oil
- 4 tsp. lemon juice
- Pinch of ground black pepper and salt
- 4 tsp. oregano, chopped
- 1 small habanero pepper, chopped
- ¼ cup green onions, chopped
- 1 cup red bell pepper, chopped
- 1 garlic clove, minced
- ¼ cup lemon juice

Directions:

1. In a bowl (medium size), combine the green onion, ¼ cup lemon juice, bell pepper, habanero, garlic clove, oregano, black pepper and salt.
2. In another bowl, mix the paprika, 4 tsp. lemon juice, olive oil, and garlic clove.
3. Stir the mix, coat the fish with this mix; set aside for 10 minutes.
4. Add the fish on the pre-heated grill over medium-high heat setting.
5. Season the fish with black pepper and salt, cook for 5 minutes on each side.
6. Place in separate serving plates, top with the salsa and serve.

Per serving: Calories: 198Kcal; Protein: 8g; Carbohydrates: 14g; Fat: g

315. FISH CURRY DINNER

Preparation time: 4 minutes
Cooking time: 30 minutes
Servings: 4
Ingredients:

- 1 tbs. red curry paste
- 1½ cups chicken broth
- 1 (14-ounce) can coconut milk
- 1 tbs. avocado oil
- ½ cup diced white onion
- 2 garlic cloves, minced
- ½ tsp. coconut sugar
- 1 tsp. salt
- ½ tsp. ground black pepper
- 4 (4-ounce) halibut fillets

Directions:

1. In a skillet (you can also use a saucepan); heat the oil over medium stove flame.
2. Add the onions, garlic, stir the mixture and cook while stirring for about 2-3 minutes until softened.
3. Stir in the paste. Add the broth, coconut milk, coconut sugar, salt, and pepper; combine well.

4. Place the heat to low then simmer for 8-10 minutes.
5. Add the fillets; cover and cook for 8-10 minutes, until flakes easily.
6. Serve the fillets with the curried broth.

Per serving: Calories: 326Kcal; Protein: 27g; Carbohydrates: 13g; Fat: 21g

316. SALMON BROCCOLI BOWL

Preparation time: 5 minutes
Cooking time: 20 minutes
Servings: 4
Ingredients:

- 3 tbsp. avocado oil
- 2 garlic cloves, minced
- 1 broccoli head, separate florets
- 1 ½ pounds salmon fillets, boneless
- Pinch of ground black pepper and salt
- Juice of ½ lemon

Directions:

1. Pre-heat an oven to 450°F. Line a baking sheet with a foil.
2. Spread the broccoli; add the salmon, oil, garlic, salt, pepper and the lemon juice, toss gently.
3. Bake for 15 minutes.
4. Divide in serving plates and serve warm.

Per serving: Calories: 207Kcal; Protein: 9g; Carbohydrates: 14g; Fat: 6g

317. FENNEL BAKED COD

Preparation time: 10 minutes
Cooking time: 25 minutes
Servings: 4
Ingredients:

- 3 sun-dried tomatoes, chopped
- 1 small red onion, (cut into slices)
- ½ fennel bulb, (cut into slices)
- 2 cod fillets, boneless
- 1 garlic clove, minced
- 1 tsp. olive oil
- Black pepper to the taste
- 4 black olives, pitted and sliced
- 2 rosemary springs
- ¼ tsp. red pepper flakes

Directions:

1. Pre-heat an oven to 400°F. Grease a baking dish with a cooking spray.
2. Add the cod, garlic, black pepper, tomatoes, onion, fennel, olives, rosemary and pepper flakes; mix gently.
3. Bake for 14-15 minutes.
4. Divide the fish mix between plates and serve.

Per serving: Calories: 255Kcal; Protein: 16g; Carbohydrates: 11g; Fat: 4g

318. BEET HADDOCK DINNER

Preparation time: 10 minutes

Cooking time: 40-45 minutes

Servings: 4

Ingredients:

- 2 tbsp. olive oil
- 2 tbsp. apple cider vinegar
- 1 tsp. chopped fresh thyme
- 10 beets, peeled and chopped
- 2 shallots, (cut into slices)
- 1 tsp. minced garlic
- Pinch sea salt to taste
- 4 (5-ounce) haddock fillets, patted dry

Directions:

1. Preheat an oven to 400°F. Grease a baking dish with a cooking spray.
2. In a bowl (medium size), mix the beets, shallots, garlic, and 1 tbs. olive oil.
3. Add the beet mixture in the baking dish.
4. Bake for about 25-30 minutes, or until the vegetables are caramelized.
5. Remove from oven and stir in the cider vinegar, thyme, and sea salt.
6. In a skillet (you can also use a saucepan); heat the remaining oil over medium stove flame.
7. Add the fish, stir the mixture and cook while stirring for 12-15 minutes until cooked well.
8. Flake the fish and serve with roasted beets.

Per serving: Calories: 324Kcal; Protein: 37g; Carbohydrates: 22g; Fat: 8g

319. HONEY SCALLOPS

Preparation time: 5 minutes

Cooking time: 25 minutes

Servings: 4

Ingredients:

- 1-pound large scallops, rinsed
- Dash of ground black pepper and salt to taste
- 3 tbsp. coconut aminos
- 2 garlic cloves, minced
- 2 tbsp. avocado oil
- ¼ cup raw honey
- 1 tbs. apple cider vinegar

Directions:

1. Sprinkle the scallops with the salt and pepper.
2. In a skillet (you can also use a saucepan); heat the oil over medium stove flame.

3. Add the scallops, stir the mixture and cook while stirring for about 2-3 minutes until softened and golden.
4. Transfer to a plate, and set aside.
5. In the same skillet or pan, heat the honey, coconut aminos, garlic, and vinegar.
6. Cook for 6-7 minutes; add the scallops and coat well. Serve warm.

Per serving: Calories: 346Kcal; Protein: 21g; Carbohydrates: 27g; Fat: 17g

320. KALE COD SECRET

Preparation time: 10 minutes

Cooking time: 30 minutes

Servings: 4

Ingredients:

- 4 cod fillets, skinless and boneless
- 1 tbs. ginger, (shredded or grated)
- 4 tsp. lemon zest
- Pinch of ground black pepper and salt
- 3 leeks, chopped
- 2 cups veggie stock
- 2 tbsp. lemon juice
- 2 tbsp. olive oil
- 1 pound kale, chopped
- ½ tsp. sesame oil

Directions:

1. In a bowl (medium size), mix the zest with salt and pepper. Coat the fish with this mix.
2. In a skillet (you can also use a saucepan); heat the leeks, ginger and lemon juice over medium stove flame.
3. Heat for a few minutes; add the fish fillets.
4. Cover and cook for 8-10 minutes, transfer it to a plate.
5. Strain the liquid and reserve the leeks. Add the fish in serving plates.
6. In a skillet (you can also use a saucepan); heat the oil over medium stove flame.
7. Add the kale, stir the mixture and cook while stirring for about 3-4 minutes until softened.
8. Add the soup liquid and cook for 4-5 minutes more.
9. Add the reserved leeks; cook for 2 minutes.
10. Divide into fish bowls, drizzle the sesame oil all over and serve.

Per serving: Calories: 238Kcal; Protein: 16g; Carbohydrates: 12g; Fat: 3g

321. SCRUMPTIOUS COCONUT SHRIMPS

Preparation time: 5 minutes

Cooking time: 15-20 minutes

Servings: 4

Ingredients:

- 2 eggs
- 1 cup dried shredded coconut, unsweetened
- ¼ tsp. paprika
- Dash cayenne pepper
- ¼ cup coconut flour
- ½ tsp. salt
- Dash freshly grounds black pepper
- ¼ cup coconut oil
- 1-pound raw shrimp, peeled and deveined

Directions:

1. In a bowl, whisk the eggs.
2. In another bowl, mix the coconut, flour, salt, paprika, cayenne pepper, and black pepper.
3. Coat the shrimp into the egg mixture, and then into the coconut mix.
4. In a skillet (you can also use a saucepan); heat the oil over medium stove flame.
5. Add the shrimps then cook for 2-3 minutes per side. Serve warm.

Per serving: Calories: 246Kcal; Protein: 19g; Carbohydrates: 8g; Fat: 18g

322. HERBED MUSSELS TREAT

Preparation time: 5 minutes

Cooking time: 30 minutes

Servings: 4

Ingredients:

- 1 tbs. olive oil
- 2 tsp. minced garlic
- 1 cup coconut milk
- ½ cup chicken bone broth
- 2 tsp. chopped fresh thyme
- 1 tsp. chopped fresh oregano
- 1½ pounds mussels, scrubbed and debearded
- 1 scallion, sliced white and green parts

Directions:

1. In a skillet (you can also use a saucepan); heat the oil over medium stove flame.
2. Add the garlic, stir the mixture and cook while stirring for about 2-3 minutes until softened.
3. Add the coconut milk, broth, thyme, and oregano.
4. Boil the mix and add the mussels. Cover then cook for about 8

minutes, or until the shells opened up.

5. Remove any unopened shells and add in the scallion; serve warm.

Per serving: Calories: 318Kcal; Protein: 23g; Carbohydrates: 12g; Fat: 21g

323. COCONUT CHILI SALMON

Preparation time: 10 minutes
Cooking time: 25 minutes
Servings: 6
Ingredients:

- 1 ¼ cups coconut, shredded
- 2 tbsp. olive oil
- ¼ cup water
- 1 pound salmon, cubed
- 1/3 cup coconut flour
- Pinch of ground black pepper and salt
- 1 egg
- 4 red chilies, chopped
- 2 garlic cloves, minced
- ¼ cup balsamic vinegar
- ½ cup raw honey

Directions:

1. In a bowl (medium size), mix the flour with a pinch of salt.
2. In another bowl, whisk the egg and black pepper.
3. Add the shredded coconut in another bowl.
4. Coat the salmon cubes in flour, egg and coconut mix one by one.
5. In a skillet (you can also use a saucepan); heat the oil over medium stove flame.
6. Add the salmon, stir-fry them for 2-3 minutes on each side. Place in serving plates.
7. Heat water over medium-high heat in the pan, add the chilies, cloves, vinegar and honey, stir gently.
8. Boil the mix and simmer for 4 minutes; top over the salmon and serve.

Per serving: Calories: 218Kcal; Protein: 17g; Carbohydrates: 14g; Fat: 5g

324. SPICY BRAISED COD WITH VEGETABLES

Preparation time: 10 minutes
Cooking time: 18 minutes
Servings: 2
Ingredients:

- 1 tbs. olive oil
- ½ medium onion, minced
- 2 garlic cloves, minced
- 1 tsp. oregano

- 1 (15-ounce) can artichoke hearts in water, drained and halved
- 1 (15-ounce) can diced tomatoes with basil
- ¼ cup pitted Greek olives, drained
- 10 ounces (28g;) wild cod
- Salt and ground black pepper, to taste.

Directions:

1. In a skillet, heat the olive oil over medium-high heat.
2. Sauté the onion for about 5 minutes, stirring occasionally, or until tender.
3. Stir in the garlic and oregano. Let them cook for 30 seconds more until fragrant.
4. Add the artichoke hearts, tomatoes, and olives and stir to combine. Top with the cod.
5. Cover and cook for about 10-15 minutes, or until the fish flakes easily with a fork and juices run clean.
6. Sprinkle with the salt and pepper. Serve warm.

Per serving: Calories: 332Kcal; Protein: 29g; Carbohydrates: 30g; Fat: 10g

325. SWORDFISH WITH LEMONY PARSLEY

Preparation time: 10 minutes
Cooking time: 17-20 minutes
Servings: 4
Ingredients:

- 1 cup fresh Italian parsley
- ¼ cup lemon juice
- ¼ cup extra-virgin olive oil
- ¼ cup fresh thyme
- 2 cloves garlic
- ½ tsp. salt
- 4 swordfish steaks
- Olive oil spray

Directions:

1. Pre-heat the oven to 450 degrees (235°C). Grease a large baking dish generously with olive oil spray.
2. Place the parsley, lemon juice, olive oil, thyme, garlic, and salt in a food processor and pulse until smoothly blended.
3. Arrange the swordfish steaks in the greased baking dish and spoon the parsley mixture over the top.
4. Bake in the pre-heated oven for 15 to 18 minutes until flaky.
5. Divide the fish among four plates and serve hot.

Per serving: Calories: 396Kcal; Protein: 44g; Carbohydrates: 2.9g; Fat: 21g

326. HONEYED BROILED SALMON

Preparation time: 5 minutes
Cooking time: 5-10 minutes
Servings: 4
Ingredients:

- (4-ounce / 113-g) salmon fillets
- 3 tbsp. miso paste
- 2 tbsp. raw honey
- 1 tsp. coconut aminos
- 1 tsp. rice vinegar

Directions:

1. Preheat the broiler to High. Line a baking dish with aluminum foil and add the salmon fillets.
2. Whisk together the miso paste, honey, coconut aminos, and vinegar in a small bowl. Pour the glaze over the fillets and spread it evenly with a brush.
3. Broil for about 5 minutes, or until the salmon is browned on top and opaque. Brush any remaining glaze over the salmon and broil for an additional 5 minutes if needed. The cooking time depends on the breadth of the salmon.
4. Let the salmon cool for 5 minutes before serving.

Per serving: Calories: 263Kcal; Protein: 30.2g; Carbohydrates: 12.8g; Fat: 8.9g

327. MUSTARDY ROASTED SALMON WITH HONEY

Preparation time: 5 minutes
Cooking time: 15-20 minutes
Servings: 4
Ingredients:

- 2 tbsp. whole-grain mustard
- 2 garlic cloves, minced
- 1 tbs. honey
- ¼ tsp. salt
- ¼ tsp. freshly ground black pepper
- 1 pound (45g;) salmon fillet
- Nonstick cooking spray

Directions:

1. Preheat the oven to 425 deg. (220 °F). Coat a baking sheet with nonstick cooking spray.
2. Stir together the mustard, garlic, honey, salt, and pepper in a small bowl.
3. Arrange the salmon fillet, skin-side down, on the coated baking sheet. Spread the mustard mixture evenly over the salmon fillet.
4. Roast in the preheated oven for 15 to 20 minutes, or until it flakes apart

easily and the internal temperature is 145 deg. (63 °F).

5. Serve hot.

Per serving: Calories: 185Kcal; Protein: 23g; Carbohydrates: 5g; Fat: 7g

328. SALMON WITH PESTO AND MUSHROOM HASH

Preparation time: 15 minutes
Cooking time: 20 minutes
Servings: 6
Ingredients:
Pesto:

- ¼ cup extra-virgin olive oil
- 1 bunch fresh basil
- Juice and zest of 1 lemon
- 1 cup water
- ¼ tsp. salt, plus additional as needed

Hash:

- 2 tbsp. extra-virgin olive oil
- 6 cups mixed mushrooms (brown, white, shiitake, cremini, portobello, etc.), sliced
- 1 pound (45g;) wild salmon, cubed

Directions:

1. Make the pesto: Pulse the olive oil, basil, juice and zest, water, and salt in a blender or food processor until smoothly blended. Set aside.
2. Heat the olive oil in a huge skillet over medium heat.
3. Stir-fry the mushrooms for 6 to 8 minutes, or until they begin to exude their juices.
4. Place the salmon and cook each side for 5 to 6 minutes until cooked through.
5. Fold in the prepared pesto and stir well. Taste and add additional salt as needed.
6. Serve warm.

Per serving: Calories: 264Kcal; Protein: 7g; Carbohydrates: 30g; Fat: 14g

329. BUTTERED TUNA LETTUCE WRAPS

Preparation time: 10 minutes
Cooking time: 0 minutes
Servings: 2
Ingredients:

- 1 cup almond butter
- 1 tbs. freshly squeezed lemon juice
- 1 tsp. low-sodium soy sauce
- 1 tsp. curry powder
- ½ tsp. sriracha, or to taste
- ½ cup canned water chestnuts, drained and chopped
- 2 (2.6-ounce / 74-g) package tuna packed in water, drained
- 2 large butter lettuce leaves

Directions:

1. Stir together the almond butter, lemon juice, soy sauce, curry powder, sriracha in a medium bowl until well mixed. Add the water chestnuts and tuna and stir until well incorporated.
2. Place 2 butter lettuce leaves on a flat work surface, spoon half of the tuna mixture onto each leaf and roll up into a wrap. Serve immediately.

Per serving: Calories: 270Kcal; Protein: 19g; Carbohydrates: 18g; Fat: 13g

330. TILAPIA WITH LIMEY CILANTRO SALSA

Preparation time: 5 minutes
Cooking time: 10 minutes
Servings: 2
Ingredients:
Salsa:

- 1 cup chopped mango
- 2 tbsp. chopped fresh cilantro
- 2 tbsp. chopped red onion
- 2 tbsp. freshly squeezed lime juice
- ½ jalapeño pepper, seeded and minced
- Pinch salt

Tilapia:

- 1 tbs. paprika
- 1 tsp. onion powder
- ½ tsp. dried thyme
- ½ tsp. freshly ground black pepper
- ¼ tsp. cayenne pepper
- ½ tsp. garlic powder
- ¼ tsp. salt
- ½ pound (22g;) boneless tilapia fillets
- 2 tsp. extra-virgin olive oil
- 1 lime, cut into wedges, for serving

Directions:

1. Make the salsa: Place the mango, cilantro, onion, lime juice, jalapeño, and salt in a medium bowl and toss to combine. Set aside.
2. Make the tilapia: Stir together the paprika, onion powder, thyme, black pepper, cayenne pepper, garlic powder, and salt in a mini bowl until well mixed. Rub both sides of fillets generously with the mixture.
3. Heat the olive oil in a huge skillet over medium heat.
4. Add the fish fillets and cook each side for 3 to 5 minutes until golden brown and cooked through.
5. Divide the fillets among two plates and spoon half of the prepared salsa

onto each fillet. Serve the fish alongside the lime wedges.

Per serving: Calories: 239Kcal; Protein: 25g; Carbohydrates: 21g; Fat: 7.8g

331. PEPPERED PAPRIKA WITH GRILLED SEA BASS

Preparation time: 20 minutes
Cooking time: 20 minutes
Servings: 6
Ingredients:

- ¼ tsp. onion powder
- ¼ tsp. garlic powder
- ¼ tsp. paprika
- Lemon pepper and sea salt to taste
- 2 pounds (90g;) sea bass
- 3 tbsp. extra-virgin olive oil, divided
- 2 large cloves garlic, chopped
- 1 tbs. chopped Italian flat leaf parsley

Directions:

1. Pre-heat the grill to high heat.
2. Place the onion powder, garlic powder, paprika, lemon pepper, and sea salt in a large bowl and stir to combine.
3. Dredge the fish in the spice mixture, turning until well coated.
4. Heat 2 tbs. of olive oil in a small skillet. Add the parsley and garlic and cook for 1 to 2 minutes, stirring occasionally. Remove the skillet from the heat and set aside.
5. Brush the grill grates lightly with remaining 1 tbs. olive oil.
6. Grill the fish for about 7 minutes. Flip the fish and drizzle with the garlic mixture and cook for an additional 7 minutes, or until the fish flakes when pressed lightly with a fork.
7. Serve hot.

Per serving: Calories: 200Kcal; Protein: 26g; Carbohydrates: 0.6g; Fat: 10.3g

332. PEPPER-INFUSED TUNA STEAKS

Preparation time: 5 minutes
Cooking time: 10 minutes
Servings: 2
Ingredients:

- 2 (5-ounce / 142-g) ahi tuna steaks
- 1 tsp. kosher salt
- ¼ tsp. cayenne pepper
- 2 tbsp. olive oil
- 1 tsp. whole peppercorns

Directions:

1. On a plate, season the tuna steaks on both sides with salt and cayenne pepper.
2. In your skillet, heat the olive oil over medium-high heat until it shimmers.
3. Add the peppercorns and cook for about 5 minutes, or until they soften and pop.
4. Carefully put the tuna steaks in the skillet and sear for 1 to 2 minutes per side, depending on the breadth of the tuna steaks, or until the fish is cooked to the desired level of doneness.
5. Cool for 5 minutes before serving.

Per serving: Calories: 260Kcal; Protein: 33g; Carbohydrates: 0.2g; Fat: 14g

333. SALMON CAKES WITH BELL PEPPER PLUS LEMON YOGURT

Preparation time: 15 minutes

Cooking time: 15 minutes

Servings: 4

Ingredients:

- ¼ cup whole-wheat bread crumbs
- ¼ cup mayonnaise
- 1 large egg, beaten
- 1 tbs. chives, chopped
- 1 tbs. fresh parsley, chopped
- Zest of 1 lemon
- ¾ tsp. kosher salt, divided
- ¼ tsp. freshly ground black pepper
- 2 (5- to 6-ounce) cans no-salt boneless/skinless salmon, drained and finely flaked
- ½ bell pepper, diced small
- 2 tbsp. extra-virgin olive oil, divided
- 1 cup plain Greek yogurt
- Juice of 1 lemon

Directions:

1. Mix the bread crumbs, mayonnaise, egg, chives, parsley, lemon zest, ½ tsp. of salt, and black pepper in a large bowl. Add the salmon and the bell pepper and stir gently until well combined. Shape the mixture into 8 patties.
2. Heat-up 1 tbs. of the olive oil in a large skillet over medium-high heat. Cook half the cakes until the bottoms are golden brown, 4 to 5 minutes. Adjust the heat to medium if the bottoms start to burn.
3. Flip the cakes and cook until golden brown, an additional 4 to 5 minutes. Repeat process with the remaining 1 tbs. olive oil and the rest of the cakes.
4. Mix the yogurt, lemon juice, and the remaining ¼ tsp. salt in a small bowl. Serve with the salmon cakes.

Per serving: Calories: 330Kcal; Protein: 21g; Carbohydrates: 9g; Fat: 23g

334. HALIBUT IN PARCHMENT WITH ZUCCHINI, SHALLOTS, AND HERBS

Preparation time: 15 minutes

Cooking time: 15 minutes

Servings: 4

Ingredients:

- ½ cup zucchini, diced small
- 1 shallot, minced
- 4 (5-ounce) halibut fillets (about 1 inch thick)
- 4 tsp. extra-virgin olive oil
- ¼ tsp. kosher salt
- 1/8 tsp. freshly ground black pepper
- 1 lemon, sliced into 1/8 -inch-thick rounds
- 8 sprigs of thyme

Directions:

1. Pre-heat the oven to 450°F. Combine the zucchini and shallots in a medium bowl. Cut 4 (15-by-24-inch) pieces of parchment paper. Fold each sheet in half horizontally.
2. Draw a large half heart on one side of each folded sheet, with the fold along the heart center. Cut out the heart, open the parchment, and lay it flat on a table.
3. Place a fillet near the center of each parchment heart. Drizzle 1 tsp. olive oil on each fillet. Sprinkle with salt and pepper. Top each fillet with lemon slices and 2 sprigs of thyme. Sprinkle each fillet with one-quarter of the zucchini and shallot mixture. Fold the parchment over.
4. Starting at the top, fold the parchment edges over, and continue all the way around to make a packet. Twist the end tightly to secure. Arrange the 4 packets on a baking sheet. Bake for about 15 minutes. Place on plates; cut open. Serve immediately.

Per serving: Calories: 190Kcal; Protein: 27g; Carbohydrates: 5g; Fat: 7g

335. FLOUNDER WITH TOMATOES AND BASIL

Preparation time: 15 minutes

Cooking time: 20 minutes

Servings: 4

Ingredients:

- 1-pound cherry tomatoes
- 4 garlic cloves, sliced
- 2 tbsp. extra-virgin olive oil
- 2 tbsp. lemon juice
- 2 tbsp. basil, cut into ribbons
- ½ tsp. kosher salt
- ¼ tsp. freshly ground black pepper
- 4 (5- to 6-ounce) flounder fillets

Directions:

1. Preheat the oven to 425°F.
2. Mix the tomatoes, garlic, olive oil, lemon juice, basil, salt, and black pepper in a baking dish. Bake for 5 minutes.
3. Remove, then arrange the flounder fillets on top of the tomato mixture. Bake until the fish is cooked and begins to flake, around 10 to 15 minutes, depending on thickness.

Per serving: Calories: 215Kcal; Protein: 28g; Carbohydrates: 6g; Fat: 9g

336. GRILLED MAHI-MAHI WITH ARTICHOKE CAPONATA

Preparation time: 15 minutes

Cooking time: 30 minutes

Servings: 4

Ingredients:

- 2 tbsp. extra-virgin olive oil
- 2 celery stalks, diced
- 1 onion, diced
- 2 garlic cloves, minced
- ½ cup cherry tomatoes, chopped
- ¼ cup white wine
- 2 tbsp. white wine vinegar
- 1 can artichoke hearts, drained and chopped
- ¼ cup green olives, pitted and chopped
- 1 tbs. capers, chopped
- ¼ tsp. red pepper flakes
- 2 tbsp. fresh basil, chopped
- 4 (5- to 6-ounces each) skinless mahi-mahi fillets
- ½ tsp. kosher salt
- ¼ tsp. freshly ground black pepper
- Olive oil cooking spray

Directions:

1. Warm-up olive oil in a skillet over medium heat, then put in the celery and onion, and sauté 4 to 5 minutes. Add the garlic and sauté 30 seconds. Add the tomatoes and cook within 2 to 3 minutes. Add the wine and vinegar to deglaze the pan, increasing the heat to medium-high.
2. Add the artichokes, olives, capers, and red pepper flakes and simmer, reducing the liquid by half, about 10 minutes. Mix in the basil.

3. Season the mahi-mahi with salt and pepper. Heat a grill skillet or grill pan over medium-high heat and coat with olive oil cooking spray. Add the fish and cook within 4 to 5 minutes per side. Serve topped with the artichoke caponata.

Per serving: Calories: 245Kcal; Protein: 28g; Carbohydrates: 10g; Fat: 9g

337. COD AND CAULIFLOWER CHOWDER

Preparation time: 15 minutes
Cooking time: 40 minutes
Servings: 4
Ingredients:

- 2 tbsp. extra-virgin olive oil
- 1 leek, sliced thinly
- 4 garlic cloves, sliced
- 1 medium head cauliflower, coarsely chopped
- 1 tsp. kosher salt
- ¼ tsp. freshly ground black pepper
- 2 pints cherry tomatoes
- 2 cups no-salt-added vegetable stock
- ¼ cup green olives, pitted and chopped
- 1 to 1½ pounds cod
- ¼ cup fresh parsley, minced

Directions:

1. Heat-up the olive oil in a Dutch oven or large pot over medium heat. Add the leek and sauté until lightly golden brown, about 5 minutes.
2. Add the garlic and sauté within 30 seconds. Add the cauliflower, salt, and black pepper and sauté 2 to 3 minutes.
3. Add the tomatoes and vegetable stock, increase the heat to high and boil, then turn the heat to low and simmer within 10 minutes.
4. Add the olives and mix. Add the fish, cover, and simmer for 20 minutes or until fish is opaque and flakes easily. Gently mix in the parsley.

Per serving: Calories: 270Kcal; Protein: 30g; Carbohydrates: 19g; Fat: 9g;

338. SARDINE BRUSCHETTA WITH FENNEL AND LEMON CREMA

Preparation time: 15 minutes
Cooking time: 0 minutes
Servings: 4
Ingredients:

- 1/3 cup plain Greek yogurt
- 2 tbsp. mayonnaise
- 2 tbsp. lemon juice, divided
- 2 tsp. lemon zest
- ¾ tsp. kosher salt, divided
- 1 fennel bulb, cored and thinly sliced
- ¼ cup parsley, chopped, plus more for garnish
- ¼ cup fresh mint, chopped2 tsp. extra-virgin olive oil
- 1/8 tsp. freshly ground black pepper
- 8 slices multigrain bread, toasted
- 2 (4.4-ounce) cans of smoked sardines

Directions:

1. Mix the yogurt, mayonnaise, 1 tbs. of the lemon juice, the lemon zest, and ¼ tsp. of the salt in a small bowl.
2. Mix the remaining ½ tsp. salt, the remaining 1 tbs. lemon juice, the fennel, parsley, mint, olive oil, and black pepper in a separate small bowl.
3. Spoon 1 tbsp. of the yogurt mixture on each piece of toast. Divide the fennel mixture evenly on top of the yogurt mixture. Divide the sardines among the toasts, placing them on top of the fennel mixture. Garnish with more herbs, if desired.

Per serving: Calories: 400Kcal; Protein: 16g; Carbohydrates: 51g; Fat: 16g

339. CHOPPED TUNA SALAD

Preparation time: 15 minutes
Cooking time: 0 minutes
Servings: 4
Ingredients:

- 2 tbsp. extra-virgin olive oil
- 2 tbsp. lemon juice
- 2 tsp. Dijon mustard
- ½ tsp. kosher salt
- ¼ tsp. freshly ground black pepper
- 12 olives, pitted and chopped
- ½ cup celery, diced
- ½ cup red onion, diced
- ½ cup red bell pepper, diced
- ½ cup fresh parsley, chopped
- 2 (6-ounce) cans no-salt-added tuna packed in water, drained
- 6 cups baby spinach

Directions:

1. Mix the olive oil, lemon juice, mustard, salt, and black pepper in a medium bowl.
2. Add in the olives, celery, onion, bell pepper, and parsley and mix well. Add the tuna and gently incorporate.
3. Divide the spinach evenly among 4 plates or bowls. Spoon the tuna salad evenly on top of the spinach.

Per serving: Calories: 220Kcal; Protein: 25g; Carbohydrates: 7g; Fat: 11g

340. MONKFISH WITH SAUTÉED LEEKS, FENNEL, AND TOMATOES

Preparation time: 15 minutes
Cooking time: 35 minutes
Servings: 4
Ingredients:

- 1 to 1½ pounds monkfish
- 3 tbsp. lemon juice, divided
- 1 tsp. kosher salt, divided
- 1/8 tsp. freshly ground black pepper
- 2 tbsp. extra-virgin olive oil
- 1 leek, sliced in half lengthwise and thinly sliced
- ½ onion, julienned
- 3 garlic cloves, minced
- 2 bulbs fennel, cored and thinly sliced, plus ¼ cup fronds for garnish
- 1 (14.5-ounce) can no-salt-added diced tomatoes
- 2 tbsp. fresh parsley, chopped
- 2 tbsp. fresh oregano, chopped
- ¼ tsp. red pepper flakes

Directions:

1. Place the fish in a medium baking dish and add 2 tbsp. of the lemon juice, ¼ tsp. of the salt, plus the black pepper. Place in the refrigerator.
2. Warm-up olive oil in a large skillet over medium heat, then put the leek and onion and sauté until translucent, about 3 minutes. Add the garlic and sauté within 30 seconds. Add the fennel and sauté 4 to 5 minutes. Add the tomatoes and simmer for 2 to 3 minutes.
3. Stir in the parsley, oregano, red pepper flakes, the remaining ¾ tsp. salt, and the remaining 1 tbs. lemon juice. Put the fish over the leek mixture, cover, and simmer for 20 to 25 minutes. Garnish with the fennel fronds.

Per serving: Calories: 220Kcal; Protein: 22g; Carbohydrates: 11g; Fat: 9g

341. CARAMELIZED FENNEL AND SARDINES WITH PENNE

Preparation time: 15 minutes
Cooking time: 30 minutes
Servings: 4
Ingredients:

- 8 ounces whole-wheat penne
- 2 tbsp. extra-virgin olive oil
- 1 bulb fennel, cored and thinly sliced, plus ¼ cup fronds
- 2 celery stalks, thinly sliced, plus ½ cup leaves
- 4 garlic cloves, sliced

- ¾ tsp. kosher salt
- ¼ tsp. freshly ground black pepper
- Zest of 1 lemon
- Juice of 1 lemon
- 2 (4.4-ounce) cans boneless/skinless sardines packed in olive oil, undrained

Directions:

1. Cook the penne, as stated in the package directions. Drain, reserving 1 cup of pasta water. Warm-up olive oil in a large skillet over medium heat, then put the fennel and celery and cook within 10 to 12 minutes. Add the garlic and cook within 1 minute.
2. Add the penne, reserved pasta water, salt, and black pepper. Adjust the heat to medium-high and cook for 1 to 2 minutes.
3. Remove, then stir in the lemon zest, lemon juice, fennel fronds, and celery leaves. Break the sardines into bite-size pieces and gently mix in, along with the oil they were packed in.

Per serving: Calories: 400Kcal; Protein: 22g; Carbohydrates: 46g; Fat: 15g

342. GREEN GODDESS CRAB SALAD WITH ENDIVE

Preparation time: 15 minutes
Cooking time: 10 minutes
Servings: 4
Ingredients:

- 1-pound lump crabmeat
- 2/3 cup plain Greek yogurt
- 3 tbsp. mayonnaise
- 3 tbsp. fresh chives, chopped, plus additional for garnish
- 3 tbsp. fresh parsley, chopped, plus extra for garnish
- 3 tbsp. fresh basil, chopped, plus extra for garnish
- Zest of 1 lemon
- Juice of 1 lemon
- ½ tsp. kosher salt
- ¼ tsp. freshly ground black pepper
- 4 endives, ends cut off and leaves separated

Directions:

1. In a medium bowl, combine the crab, yogurt, mayonnaise, chives, parsley, basil, lemon zest, lemon juice, salt, plus black pepper and mix until well combined.
2. Place the endive leaves on 4 salad plates. Divide the crab mixture evenly on top of the endive. Garnish with additional herbs, if desired.

Per serving: Calories: 200Kcal; Protein: 25g; Carbohydrates: 44g; Fat: 9g

343. SEARED SCALLOPS WITH BLOOD ORANGE GLAZE

Preparation time: 15 minutes
Cooking time: 20 minutes
Servings: 4
Ingredients:

- 3 tbsp. extra-virgin olive oil, divided
- 3 garlic cloves, minced
- ½ tsp. kosher salt, divided
- 4 blood oranges, juiced
- 1 tsp. blood orange zest
- ½ tsp. red pepper flakes
- 1-pound scallops, small side muscle removed
- ¼ tsp. freshly ground black pepper
- ¼ cup fresh chives, chopped

Directions:

1. Heat-up 1 tbs. of the olive oil in a small saucepan over medium-high heat. Add the garlic and ¼ tsp. of the salt and sauté for 30 seconds.
2. Add the orange juice and zest, bring to a boil, reduce the heat to medium-low, and cook within 20 minutes, or until the liquid reduces by half and becomes a thicker syrup consistency. Remove and mix in the red pepper flakes.
3. Pat the scallops dry with a paper towel and season with the remaining ¼ tsp. salt and the black pepper. Heat-up the remaining 2 tbsp. of olive oil in a large skillet on medium-high heat. Add the scallops gently and sear.
4. Cook on each side within 2 minutes. If cooking in 2 batches, use 1 tbs. of oil per batch. Serve the scallops with the blood orange glaze and garnish with the chives.

Per serving: Calories: 140Kcal; Protein: 15g; Carbohydrates: 12g; Fat: 4g

344. LEMON GARLIC SHRIMP

Preparation time: 15 minutes
Cooking time: 10 minutes
Servings: 4
Ingredients:

- 2 tbsp. extra-virgin olive oil
- 3 garlic cloves, sliced
- ½ tsp. kosher salt
- ¼ tsp. red pepper flakes
- 1-pound large shrimp, peeled and deveined
- ½ cup white wine
- 3 tbsp. fresh parsley, minced
- Zest of ½ lemon
- Juice of ½ lemon

Directions:

1. Heat-up the olive oil in a wok or large skillet over medium-high heat. Add the garlic, salt, and red pepper flakes and sauté until the garlic starts to brown, 30 seconds to 1 minute.
2. Add the shrimp and cook within 2 to 3 minutes on each side. Pour in the wine and deglaze the wok, scraping up any flavorful brown bits, for 1 to 2 minutes. Turn off the heat; mix in the parsley, lemon zest, and lemon juice.

Per serving: Calories: 200Kcal; Protein: 23g; Carbohydrates: 3g; Fat: 9g

345. TUNA WITH VEGETABLE MIX

Preparation time: 8 minutes
Cooking time: 16 minutes
Servings: 4
Ingredients:

- ¼ C. extra-virgin olive oil, divided
- 1 tbsp. rice vinegar
- 1 tsp. kosher salt, divided
- ¾ tsp. Dijon mustard
- ¾ tsp. honey
- 4 oz. baby gold beets, thinly sliced
- 4 oz. fennel bulb, trimmed and thinly sliced
- 4 oz. baby turnips, thinly sliced
- 6 oz. Granny Smith apple, very thinly sliced
- 2 tsp. sesame seeds, toasted
- 6 oz. tuna steaks
- ½ tsp. black pepper
- 1 tbsp. fennel fronds, torn

Directions:

1. Scourge 2 tbsp. of oil, ½ a tsp. of salt, honey, vinegar, and mustard.
2. Give the mixture a nice mix.
3. Add fennel, beets, apple, and turnips; mix and toss until everything is evenly coated.
4. Sprinkle with sesame seeds and toss well.
5. Using a cast-iron skillet, heat 2 tbsp. of oil over high heat.
6. Carefully season the tuna with ½ a tsp. of salt and pepper
7. Situate the tuna in the skillet and cook for 4 minutes, giving 1½ minutes per side.
8. Remove the tuna and slice it up.
9. Place in containers with the vegetable mix.
10. Serve with the fennel mix, and enjoy!

Per serving: Calories: 443Kcal; Protein: 16.5g; Carbohydrates: 19g; Fat: 17.1g

346. TUNA BOWL WITH KALE

Preparation time: 4 minutes

Cooking time: 18 minutes

Servings: 6

Ingredients:

- 3 tbsp. extra virgin olive oil
- 1 ½ tsp. garlic, minced
- ¼ C. capers
- 2 tsp. sugar
- 15 oz. can great northern beans, drained and rinsed
- 1-lb. kale, chopped with the center ribs removed
- ½ tsp. black pepper, ground
- 1 C. onion, chopped
- 2 ½ oz. olives, drained and sliced
- ¼ tsp. sea salt
- ¼ tsp. red pepper, crushed
- 6 oz. tuna in olive oil, do not drain

Directions:

1. Place a large pot, like a stockpot, on the stove and turn the burner to high heat.
2. Fill the pot about ¾ of the way full with water and let it come to a boil.
3. Cook the kale for 2 minutes.
4. Drain the kale and set it aside.
5. Set the heat to medium and place the empty pot back on the burner.
6. Add the oil and onion. Sauté for 3–4 minutes.
7. Combine the garlic into the oil mixture and sauté for another minute.
8. Add the capers, olives, and red pepper.
9. Cook the ingredients for another minute while stirring.
10. Pour in the sugar and stir while you toss in the kale. Mix all the ingredients thoroughly and ensure the kale is thoroughly coated.
11. Cover the pot and set the timer for 8 minutes.
12. Turn off the heat and stir in the tuna, pepper, beans, salt, and any other herbs that will make this one of the best Mediterranean dishes you've ever made.

Per serving: Calories: 265Kcal; Protein: 16g; Carbohydrates: 16g; Fat: 15g

347. GREEK BAKED COD

Preparation time: 9 minutes

Cooking time: 13 minutes

Servings: 4

Ingredients:

- 1 ½ lb. Cod fillet pieces (4–6 pieces)
- 5 garlic cloves, peeled and minced
- ¼ C. fresh parsley leaves, chopped
- Lemon Juice Mixture:
- 5 tbsp. fresh lemon juice
- 5 tbsp. extra virgin olive oil
- 2 tbsp. vegan butter, melted
- For coating:
- ⅓ C. all-purpose flour
- 1 tsp. coriander, ground
- ¾ tsp. sweet Spanish paprika
- ¾ tsp. cumin, ground
- ¾ tsp. salt
- ½ tsp. black pepper

Directions:

1. Pre-heat oven to 400°F.
2. Scourge lemon juice, olive oil, and melted butter, set aside.
3. In another shallow bowl, mix all-purpose flour, spices, salt, and pepper, set next to the lemon bowl to create a station.
4. Pat the fish fillet dry, then dip the fish in the lemon juice mixture then dip it in the flour mixture, brush off extra flour.
5. In a cast-iron skillet over medium-high heat, add 2 tbsp. olive oil.
6. Once heated, add in the fish and sear on each side for color, but do not thoroughly cook, remove from heat.
7. With the remaining lemon juice mixture, add the minced garlic and mix.
8. Drizzle all over the fish fillets.
9. Bake for 10 minutes, until it begins to flake easily with a fork.
10. Allow the dish to cool completely.
11. Distribute among the containers, store for 2–3 days.
12. To Serve: Reheat in the microwave for 1–2 minutes or until heated through. Sprinkle chopped parsley. Enjoy!

Per serving: Calories: 321Kcal; Protein: 23g; Carbohydrates: 14g; Fat: 13g

348. PISTACHIO SOLE FISH

Preparation time: 4 minutes

Cooking time: 11 minutes

Servings: 4

Ingredients:

- 4 (5 oz.) sole fillets, boneless
- Salt and pepper, as needed
- ½ C. pistachios, finely chopped
- Zest of 1 lemon
- Juice of 1 lemon
- 1 tsp. extra virgin olive oil

Directions:

1. Pre-heat your oven to 350°F.
2. Prep a baking sheet using parchment paper then keep side.
3. Pat fish dry with kitchen towels and lightly season with salt and pepper.
4. Take a small bowl and stir in pistachios and lemon zest.
5. Place sole fillets on the prepped sheet and press 2 tbsp. of pistachio mixture on top of each fillet.
6. Rub fish with lemon juice and olive oil.
7. Bake for 10 minutes until the top is golden and fish flakes with a fork.
8. Serve and enjoy!
9. Meal Prep/Storage options: Store in airtight containers in your fridge for 1–2 days.

Per serving: Calories: 166Kcal; Protein: 26g; Carbohydrates: 16g; Fat: 12g

349. BAKED TILAPIA

Preparation time: 9 minutes

Cooking time: 16 minutes

Servings: 4

Ingredients:

- 1 lb. tilapia fillets (about 8 fillets)
- 1 tsp. olive oil
- 1 tbsp. vegan butter
- 2 shallots, finely chopped
- 3 garlic cloves, minced
- 1 ½ tsp. cumin, ground
- 1 ½ tsp. paprika
- ¼ C. capers
- ¼ C. fresh dill, finely chopped
- Juice from 1 lemon
- Salt and Pepper, to taste

Directions:

1. Pre-heat oven to 375°F.
2. Prep a rimmed baking sheet using parchment paper or foil.
3. Lightly mist with cooking spray, arrange the fish fillets evenly on the baking sheet.
4. Mix the cumin, paprika, salt, and pepper.
5. Rub the fish fillets with the spice mixture.
6. Scourge the melted butter, lemon juice, shallots, olive oil, and garlic, and brush evenly over fish fillets.
7. Top with the capers.
8. Bake for 13 minutes.
9. Pull out from the oven and allow the dish to cool completely.
10. Distribute among the containers, store for 2–3 days.

11. To Serve: Reheat in the microwave for 1–2 minutes or until heated through. Top with fresh dill. Serve!

Per serving: Calories: 410Kcal; Protein: 21g; Carbohydrates: 18g; Fat: 11g

350. CATFISH FILLETS AND RICE

Preparation time: 10 minutes

Cooking time: 55 minutes

Servings: 2

Ingredients:

- 2 catfish fillets, boneless
- 2 tbsp. Italian seasoning
- 2 tbsp. olive oil

For the rice:

- 1 C. brown rice
- 2 tbsp. olive oil
- 1 and ½ C. water
- ½ C. green bell pepper, chopped
- 2 garlic cloves, minced
- ½ C. white onion, chopped
- 2 tsp. Cajun seasoning
- ½ tsp. garlic powder
- Salt and black pepper to the taste

Directions:

1. Heat a pot with 2 tbsp. oil over medium heat, then add the onion, garlic, garlic powder, salt, and pepper and sauté for 5 minutes.
2. Add the rice, water, bell pepper, and the seasoning, bring to a simmer, and cook over medium heat for 40 minutes.
3. Heat a pan with 2 tbsp. oil over medium heat, add the fish and the Italian seasoning, and cook for 5 minutes on each side.
4. Divide the rice between plates, add the fish on top and serve.

Per serving: Calories: 261Kcal; Protein: 12.5g; Carbohydrates: 24.8g; Fat: 17.6g

CHAPTER 7: Meat Recipes: Beef, Pork, Lamb, Poultry

351. CHICKEN WITH ASIAN VEGETABLES

Preparation time: 10 minutes
Cooking time: 20 minutes
Servings: 8
Ingredients:

- 2 - tablespoons canola oil
- 6 - boneless chicken breasts
- 1 - cup low-sodium chicken broth
- 3 - tablespoons reduced-sodium soy sauce
- ¼ - tsp. crushed red pepper flakes
- 1 - garlic clove, crushed
- 1 - can (8ounces) water chestnuts, sliced and rinsed (optional)
- ½ - cup sliced green onions
- 1 - cup chopped red or green bell pepper
- 1 - cup chopped celery
- ¼ - cup cornstarch
- 1/3 - cup water
- 3 - cups cooked white rice
- ½ - large chicken breast for one chicken thigh

Directions:

1. Warm oil in a skillet and dark-colored chicken on all sides.
2. Add chicken to a slow cooker with the remainder of the fixings aside from cornstarch and water.
3. Spread and cook on low for 6 to 8 hours.
4. Following 6-8 hours, independently blend cornstarch and cold water until smooth. Gradually include into the slow cooker.
5. At that point, turn on high for about 15mins until thickened. Don't close the top on the slow cooker to enable steam to leave.
6. Serve.

Per serving: Calories: 415Kcal; Protein: 20g; Carbohydrates: 36g; Fat: 20g

352. CHICKEN AND VEGGIE SOUP

Preparation time: 15 minutes
Cooking time: 25 minutes
Servings: 8
Ingredients:

- 4 - cups cooked and chopped chicken
- 7 - cups reduced-sodium chicken broth
- 1 - pound froze white corn
- 1 - medium onion diced
- 4 - cloves garlic minced
- 2 - carrots peeled and diced
- 2 - celery stalks chopped
- 2 - tsp. oregano
- 2 - tsp. curry powder
- ½ - tsp. black pepper

Directions:

1. Put all fixings into the slow cooker.
2. Cook on LOW for 8 hours
3. Serve over cooked white rice.

Per serving: Calories: 220Kcal; Protein: 24g; Carbohydrates: 19g; Fat: 7g

353. TURKEY SAUSAGES

Preparation time: 10 minutes
Cooking time: 10 minutes
Servings: 2
Ingredients:

- 1/4 tsp. salt
- 1/8 tsp. garlic powder
- 1/8 tsp. onion powder
- One tsp. fennel seed
- 1 pound 7% Fat: ground turkey

Directions:

1. Press the fennel seed and put together turkey with fennel seed, garlic, onion powder, and salt in a small cup.
2. Cover the bowl and refrigerate overnight.
3. Prepare the turkey with seasoning into different portions with a circle form and press them into patties ready to be cooked.
4. Cook at medium heat until browned.
5. Cook it for 1 to 2 minutes per side and serve them hot. Enjoy!

Per serving: Calories: 55Kcal; Protein: 3g; Carbohydrates: 5g; Fat: 7g

354. ROSEMARY CHICKEN

Preparation time: 10 minutes
Cooking time: 10 minutes
Servings: 2
Ingredients:

- Two zucchinis
- One carrot
- One tsp. dried rosemary
- Four chicken breasts
- 1/2 bell pepper
- 1/2 red onion
- Eight garlic cloves
- Olive oil
- 1/4 tbs. ground pepper

Directions:

1. Prepare the oven and preheat it at 375 °F (or 200°C).
2. Slice both zucchini and carrots and add bell pepper, onion, garlic, and put everything adding oil in a 13" x 9" pan.
3. Spread the pepper over everything and roast for about 10 minutes.
4. Meanwhile, lift the chicken skin and spread black pepper and rosemary on the flesh.
5. Remove the vegetable pan from the oven and add the chicken, returning it to the oven for about 30 more minutes. Serve and enjoy!

Per serving: Calories: 215 Protein: 2g; Carbohydrates: 4g; Fat: 6.3g

355. SMOKEY TURKEY CHILI

Preparation time: 5 minutes
Cooking time: 45 minutes
Servings: 8
Ingredients:

- 12ounce lean ground turkey
- 1/2 red onion, chopped
- Two cloves garlic, crushed and chopped
- ½ tsp. of smoked paprika
- ½ tsp. of chili powder
- ½ tsp. of dried thyme
- ¼ cup reduced-sodium beef stock
- ½ cup of water
- 1 ½ cups baby spinach leaves, washed
- Three wheat tortillas

Directions:

1. Brown the ground beef in a dry skillet over medium-high heat.
2. Add in the red onion and garlic.
3. Sauté the onion until it goes clear.
4. Transfer the contents of the skillet to the slow cooker.
5. Add the remaining ingredients and simmer on low for 30–45 minutes.
6. Stir through the spinach for the last few minutes to wilt.
7. Slice tortillas and gently toast under the broiler until slightly crispy.
8. Serve on top of the turkey chili.

Per serving: Calories: 93.5Kcal; Protein: 8g; Carbohydrates: 3g; Fat: 5.5g

356. AVOCADO-ORANGE GRILLED CHICKEN

Preparation time: 20 minutes
Cooking time: 60 minutes
Servings: 4
Ingredients:

- ¼ cup fresh lime juice
- ¼ cup minced red onion
- One avocado
- 1 cup low-fatyogurt
- One small red onion, sliced thinly
- One tbs. honey
- Two oranges, peeled and cut
- Two tablespoons. chopped cilantro
- Four pieces of 4-6ounce boneless, skinless chicken breasts
- Pepper and salt to taste

Directions:

1. In a large bowl, mix honey, cilantro, minced red onion, and yogurt.
2. Submerge chicken into mixture and marinate for at least 30 minutes.
3. Grease and pre-heat grill to medium-high fire.
4. Remove chicken from marinade and season with pepper and salt.
5. Grill for around 6 minutes per side or until chicken is cooked and juices run clear.
6. Meanwhile, peel the avocado and discard the seed—chop avocados and place in a bowl. Quickly add lime juice and toss avocado to coat well with liquid.
7. Add cilantro, thinly sliced onions, and oranges into the bowl of avocado, mix well.
8. Serve grilled chicken and avocado dressing on the side.

Per serving: Calories: 209Kcal; Protein: 8g; Carbohydrates: 26g; Fats: 10g

357. HERBS AND LEMONY ROASTED CHICKEN

Preparation time: 15 minutes
Cooking time: 1 Hour and 30 minutes
Servings: 8
Ingredients:

- ½ tsp. ground black pepper
- ½ tsp. mustard powder
- ½ tsp. salt
- One 3-lb whole chicken
- One tsp. garlic powder
- Two lemons
- Two tablespoons. olive oil
- Two teaspoons. Italian seasoning

Directions:

1. In a small bowl, mix well black pepper, garlic powder, mustard powder, and salt.
2. Rinse chicken well and slice off giblets.
3. In a greased 9 x 13 baking dish, place chicken and add 1 ½ tsp. of seasoning made earlier inside the chicken and rub the remaining seasoning around the chicken.
4. In a small bowl, blend olive oil and juice from 2 lemons. Drizzle over chicken.
5. Bake chicken in a pre-heated 350oF oven until juices run exact, around 1 ½ hour. Every once in a while, baste the chicken with its juices.

Per serving: Calories: 190Kcal; Protein: 35g; Carbohydrates: 2g; Fats: 9g

358. GROUND CHICKEN AND PEAS CURRY

Preparation time: 15 minutes
Cooking time: 6 to 10 minutes
Servings: 3-4
Ingredients:

- Three tbsp. essential olive oil
- Two bay leaves
- Two onions, ground to some paste
- ½ tbs. garlic paste
- ½ tbs. ginger paste
- Two tomatoes, chopped finely
- One tbs. ground cumin
- One tbs. ground coriander
- One tsp. ground turmeric
- One tsp. red chili powder
- Salt, to taste
- 1-pound lean ground chicken
- 2 cups frozen peas
- 1½ cups water
- 1-2 tsp. garam masala powder

Directions:

1. In a deep skillet, heat-up oil on moderate heat.
2. Add bay leaves and sauté for approximately half a minute.
3. Add onion paste and sauté for approximately 3-4 minutes.
4. Add garlic and ginger paste and sauté for around 1-1½ minutes.
5. Add tomatoes and spices and cook, occasionally stirring, for about 3-4 minutes.
6. Stir in chicken then cook for about 4-5 minutes.
7. Stir in peas and water and bring to a boil on high heat.
8. Place the heat to low then simmer approximately 5-8 minutes or till the desired doneness.
9. Stir in garam masala and remove from heat.
10. Serve hot.

Per serving: Calories: 450Kcal; Protein: 38g; Carbohydrates: 19g; Fat: 10g

359. CHICKEN MEATBALLS CURRY

Preparation time: 20 minutes
Cooking time: 25 minutes
Servings: 3-4
Ingredients:
For Meatballs:

- 1-pound lean ground chicken
- One tbs. onion paste
- One tsp. fresh ginger paste
- One tsp. garlic paste
- One green chili, chopped finely
- One tbs. fresh cilantro leaf, chopped
- One tsp. ground coriander
- ½ tsp. cumin seeds
- ½ tsp. red chili powder
- ½ tsp. ground turmeric
- Salt, to taste

For Curry:

- Three tbsp. extra-virgin olive oil
- ½ tsp. cumin seeds
- 1 (1-inch) cinnamon stick
- Three whole cloves
- Three whole green cardamoms
- One whole black cardamom
- Two onions, chopped
- One tsp. fresh ginger, minced
- One tsp. garlic, minced
- Four whole tomatoes, chopped finely
- Two tsp. ground coriander
- One tsp. garam masala powder
- ½ tsp. ground nutmeg
- ½ tsp. red chili powder
- ½ tsp. ground turmeric
- Salt, to taste
- 1 cup of water
- Chopped fresh cilantro for garnishing

Directions:

1. For meatballs: in a large bowl, add all ingredients and mix till well combined.
2. Make small equal-sized meatballs from the mixture.
3. In a big deep skillet, heat oil on medium heat

4. Add meatballs and fry approximately 3-5 minutes or till browned from all sides.

5. Transfer the meatballs to a bowl.

6. In the same skillet, add cumin seeds, cinnamon stick, cloves, green cardamom, and black cardamom and sauté for approximately 1 minute.

7. Add onions and sauté for around 4-5 minutes.

8. Add ginger and garlic paste, then sauté for approximately 1 minute.

9. Add tomato and spices and cook, crushing with the back of the spoon, for approximately 2-3 minutes.

10. Add water and meatballs and provide to a boil.

11. Reduce heat to low.

12. Simmer for approximately 10 minutes.

13. Serve hot with all the garnishing of cilantro.

Per serving: Calories: 421Kcal; Protein: 34g; Carbohydrates: 18g; Fat: 8g

360. PERSIAN CHICKEN

Preparation time: 10 minutes
Cooking time: 20 minutes
Servings: 5
Ingredients:

- Sweet onion – ½, chopped
- Lemon juice – ¼ cup
- Dried oregano – 1 Tbsp.
- Minced Garlic – 1 tsp.
- Sweet paprika – 1 tsp.
- Ground cumin – ½ tsp.
- Olive oil – ½ cup
- Boneless, skinless chicken thighs – 5

Directions:

1. Put the cumin, paprika, garlic, oregano, lemon juice, and onion in a food processor and pulse to mix the ingredients.

2. Retain the motor running and add the olive oil until the mixture is even.

3. Put the chicken thighs in a large sealable freezer container and pour the sauce into the bag.

4. Seal the container and place it in the fridge, turning the bag two times for 2 hours.

5. Get rid of the thighs from the marinade and discard the extra marinade.

6. Pre-heat the barbecue to medium.

7. Cook the chicken for 20 minutes on the grill, flipping once, until it reaches 165 °F.

Per serving: Calories: 321Kcal; Protein: 22g; Carbohydrates: 3g; Fat: 21g

361. CREAMY CHICKEN WITH CIDER

Preparation time: 5 minutes
Cooking time: 25 minutes
Servings: 8
Ingredients:

- Four bone-in chicken breasts
- 2 tbsp. of lightly salted butter
- ¾ cup of apple cider vinegar
- 2/3 cup of creamy unsweetened coconut milk or cream
- Kosher pepper

Directions:

1. Thaw the butter in a skillet over medium heat.

2. Season the chicken with the pepper and add to the skillet. Cook over low heat for approx. 20 minutes.

3. Remove the chicken from the heat then set aside in a dish.

4. In a same skillet, add the cider and bring to a boil until most of it has evaporated.

5. Add the coconut cream and let cook for 1 minute until slightly thickened.

6. Pour the cider cream over the cooked chicken and serve.

Per serving: Calories: 86.76Kcal; Protein: 1.5g; Carbohydrate: 1.88g; Fat: 8.21g

362. HERBED CHICKEN

Preparation time: 20 minutes
Cooking time: 15 minutes
Servings: 4
Ingredients:

- Boneless, skinless chicken breast – 12 ounces, cut into eight strips
- Egg white – 1
- Water – 2 Tbsps. divided
- Breadcrumbs – ½ cup
- Unsalted butter – ¼ cup, divided
- Juice of 1 lemon
- Zest of 1 lemon
- Fresh chopped basil – 1 Tbsp.
- Fresh chopped thyme – 1 tsp.
- Lemon slices, for garnish

Directions:

1. Put the chicken strips between 2 sheets of plastic wrap and pound each flat with a rolling pin.

2. In a bowl, stick together the egg and 1 tbsp water.

3. Put the breadcrumbs in another bowl.

4. Comb the chicken strips, one at a time, in the egg, then the

breadcrumbs, and set the breaded strips aside on a plate.

5. In a large frying pan over medium heat, thaw 2 tbsps. of the butter.

6. Cook the butter's strips for 3 minutes, turning once, or until they are golden and cooked through. Transfer the chicken to a plate.

7. Add the lemon zest, lemon juice, basil, thyme, and remaining 1 tbsp water to the skillet and stir until the mixture simmers.

8. Remove the sauce from the heat then mix in the remaining 2 tbsps. butter

9. Serve the chicken with the lemon sauce drizzled over the top and garnish with lemon slices.

Per serving: Calories: 255Kcal; Protein: 20g; Carbohydrates: 11g; Fat: 14g

363. SPICY LAMB CURRY

Preparation time: 15 minutes
Cooking time: 15 minutes
Servings: 6-8
Ingredients:

For Spice Mixture:

- Four tsp. ground coriander
- Four tsp. ground coriander
- Four tsp. ground cumin
- ¾ tsp. ground ginger
- Two tsp. ground cinnamon
- ½ tsp. ground cloves
- ½ tsp. ground cardamom
- Two tbsp. sweet paprika
- ½ tbs. cayenne pepper
- Two tsp. chili powder
- Two tsp. salt

For Curry:

- One tbs. coconut oil
- 2 pounds boneless lamb, trimmed and cubed into 1-inch size
- Salt and freshly ground black pepper
- 2 cups onions, chopped
- 1¼ cups water
- 1 cup of coconut milk

Directions:

1. For spice mixture: In a bowl, mix all spices. Keep aside.

2. Season the lamb with salt and black pepper.

3. In a large Dutch oven, heat oil on medium-high heat

4. Add lamb and stir fry for around 5 minutes.

5. Add onion and cook for approximately 4-5 minutes.

6. Stir in the spice mixture and cook for approximately 1 minute.

7. Add water and coconut milk and bring to aboil on high heat.
8. Reduce the heat to low and boil, covered for approximately 1-120 minutes or until the lamb's desired doneness.
9. Uncover and simmer for approximately 3-4 minutes.
10. Serve hot.

Per serving: Calories: 466Kcal; Protein: 36g; Carbohydrates: 23g; Fat: 10g

364. LAMB WITH PRUNES

Preparation time: 15 minutes
Cooking time: 2 to 3 hours
Servings: 4-6
Ingredients:

- Three tbsp. coconut oil
- Two onions, chopped finely
- 1 (1-inch) piece fresh ginger, minced
- Three garlic cloves, minced
- ½ tsp. ground turmeric
- 2 ½ pound lamb shoulder, trimmed and cubed into 3-inch size
- Salt and freshly ground black pepper
- ½ tsp. saffron threads, crumbled
- One cinnamon stick
- 3 cups of water
- 1 cup prunes, pitted and halved

Directions:

1. In a big pan, melt coconut oil on medium heat.
2. Add onions, ginger, garlic cloves, and turmeric and sauté for about 3-5 minutes.
3. Sprinkling the lamb with salt and black pepper evenly.
4. In the pan, add lamb and saffron threads and cook for approximately 4-5 minutes.
5. Add cinnamon stick and water and bring to a boil on high heat.
6. Reduce the temperature to low and simmer, covered for around 1½-120 minutes or until the lamb's desired doneness.
7. Stir in prunes and simmer for approximately 20-a half-hour.
8. Remove cinnamon stick and serve hot.

Per serving: Calories: 393Kcal; Protein: 36g; Carbohydrates: 10g; Fat: 12g

365. LAMB WITH ZUCCHINI AND COUSCOUS

Preparation time: 15 minutes
Cooking time: 8 minutes
Servings: 2

Ingredients:

- ¾ cup couscous
- ¾ cup boiling water
- ¼ cup fresh cilantro, chopped
- 1 tbsp olive oil
- 5-ounces lamb leg steak, cubed into ¾-inch size
- One medium zucchini, sliced thinly
- One medium red onion, cut into wedges
- One tsp. ground cumin
- One tsp. ground coriander
- ¼ tsp. red pepper flakes, crushed
- Salt, to taste
- ¼ cup plain Greek yogurt
- One garlic herb, minced

Directions:

1. In a bowl, add couscous and boiling water and stir to combine.
2. Cover while aside, approximately 5 minutes.
3. Add cilantro, and with a fork, fluff entirely.
4. Meanwhile, in a substantial skillet, heat oil on high heat.
5. Add lamb and stir fry for about 2-3 minutes.
6. Add zucchini and onion and stir fry for about 2 minutes.
7. Stir in spices and stir fry for about 1 minute
8. Add couscous and stir fry for approximately 2 minutes.
9. In a bowl, mix yogurt and garlic.
10. Divide lamb mixture in serving plates evenly.
11. Serve using the topping of yogurt.

Per serving: Calories: 392Kcal; Protein: 35g; Carbohydrates: 2g; Fat: 5g

366. BAKED LAMB WITH SPINACH

Preparation time: 15 minutes
Cooking time: 2-3 hours
Servings: 6
Ingredients:

- Two tbsp. coconut oil
- 2-pound lamb necks, trimmed and cut into 2-inch pieces crosswise
- Salt, to taste
- Two medium onions, chopped
- Three tbsp. fresh ginger, minced
- Four garlic cloves, minced
- Two tbsp. ground coriander
- One tbs. ground cumin
- One tsp. ground turmeric
- ¼ cup of coconut milk
- ½ cup tomatoes, chopped
- 2 cups boiling water

- 30-ounce frozen spinach, thawed and squeezed
- 1½ tbsp. garam masala
- One tbs. fresh lemon juice
- Freshly ground black pepper, to taste

Directions:

1. Pre-heat the oven to 300 degrees F.
2. In a largel Dutch oven, melt coconut oil on medium-high heat.
3. Add lamb necks and sprinkle with salt.
4. Stir fry approximately 4-5 minutes or till browned completely.
5. Transfer the lamb into a plate and lower the heat to medium.
6. In the same pan, add onion and sauté for about 10 minutes.
7. Add ginger, garlic, and spices and sauté for around 1 minute.
8. Add coconut milk and tomatoes and cook for approximately 3-4 minutes.
9. With an immersion blender, blend the mixture till smooth.
10. Add lamb, boiling water, and salt and bring to a boil.
11. Cover the pan and transfer it into the oven.
12. Bake for approximately 2½ hours.
13. Now, take away the pan from the oven and place it on medium heat.
14. Stir in spinach and garam masala and cook for about 3-5 minutes.
15. Stir in fresh lemon juice, salt, and black pepper and take off from the heat.
16. Serve hot.

Per serving: Calories: 423Kcal; Protein: 33g; Carbohydrates: 26g; Fat: 15g

367. GROUND LAMB WITH HARISSA

Preparation time: 15 minutes
Cooking time: 1 Hour and 11 minutes
Servings: 4
Ingredients:

- One tbs. extra-virgin olive oil
- Two red peppers, seeded and chopped finely
- One yellow onion, chopped finely
- Two garlic cloves, chopped finely
- One tsp. ground cumin
- ½ tsp. ground turmeric
- ¼ tsp. ground cinnamon
- ¼ tsp. ground ginger
- 1½ pound lean ground lamb
- Salt, to taste
- 1 (14½-ounce) can diced tomatoes

- Two tbsp. harissa
- 1 cup of water
- Chopped fresh cilantro for garnishing

Directions:

1. In a sizable pan, heat oil on medium-high heat.
2. Add bell pepper, onion, and garlic and sauté for around 5 minutes.
3. Add spices and sauté for around 1 minute.
4. Add lamb and salt and cook for approximately 5 minutes.
5. Stir in tomatoes, harissa, and water and bring to a boil.
6. Reduce the warmth to low and simmer, covered for about 1 hour.
7. Serve hot. Useharissa garnishing..

Per serving: Calories: 441Kcal; Protein: 36g; Carbohydrates: 24g; Fat: 12g

368. GROUND LAMB WITH PEAS

Preparation time: 15 minutes

Cooking time: 55 minutes

Servings: 4

Ingredients:

- One tbs. coconut oil
- Three dried red chilies
- 1 (2-inch) cinnamon stick
- Three green cardamom pods
- ½ tsp. cumin seeds
- One medium red onion, chopped
- 1 (¾-inch) piece fresh ginger, minced
- Four garlic cloves, minced
- 1½ tsp. ground coriander
- ½ tsp. garam masala
- ½ tsp. ground cumin
- ½ tsp. ground turmeric
- ¼ tsp. ground nutmeg
- Two bay leaves
- 1-pound lean ground lamb
- ½ cup Roma tomatoes, chopped
- 1-1½ cups water
- 1 cup fresh green peas, shelled
- Two tbsp. plain Greek yogurt, whipped
- ¼ cup fresh cilantro, sliced
- Salt and freshly ground black pepper

Directions:

1. In a Dutch oven, melt coconut oil on medium-high heat.
2. Add red chilies, cinnamon sticks, cardamom pods, and cumin seeds and sauté for around thirty seconds.
3. Add onion and sauté for about 3-4 minutes.
4. Add ginger, garlic cloves, and spices and sauté for around thirty seconds.

5. Add lamb and cook for approximately 5 minutes.
6. Add tomatoes and cook for approximately 10 min.
7. Stir in water and green peas and cook, covered, for approximately 25-thirty minutes.
8. Stir in yogurt, cilantro, salt, and black pepper and cook for around 4-5 minutes.
9. Serve hot.

Per serving: Calories: 430Kcal; Protein: 26g; Carbohydrates: 22g; Fat: 10g

369. STEAK AND ONION SANDWICH

Preparation time: 5 minutes

Cooking time: 8 minutes

Servings: 4

Ingredients:

- Four flank steaks (around 4 oz. each)
- One medium red onion, sliced
- 1 tbsp. of lemon juice
- 1 tbsp. of Italian seasoning
- 1 tsp. of black pepper
- 1 tbsp. of vegetable oil
- Four sandwich/burger buns

Directions:

1. Rub the steak with the lemon juice, the Italian seasoning, and pepper to taste. Cut into four pieces.
2. Heat the vegetable oil in a medium skillet over medium heat.
3. Cook steaks for around 3 minutes on each side until you get a medium to well-done result. Remove and transfer onto a dish with absorbing paper.
4. In the same skillet, sauté the onions until tender and transparent (around 3 minutes).
5. Cut the sandwich bun into half and place one piece of steak in each topped with the onions. Serve or wrap with paper or foil and keep in the fridge for the next day.

Per serving: Calories: 315.26Kcal; Protein: 38.33g; Carbohydrate: 8.47g; Fat: 13.22g

370. PESTO PORK CHOPS

Preparation time: 20 minutes

Cooking time: 20 minutes

Servings: 4

Ingredients:

- Pork top-loin chops – 4 (3-ounce) boneless, Fat: trimmed
- Herb pesto – 8 tsp.
- Breadcrumbs – ½ cup

- Olive oil – 1 Tbsp.

Directions:

1. Pre-heat the oven to 450F.
2. Line a baking sheet with foil. Set aside.
3. Rub 1 tsp. of pesto evenly over both sides of each pork chop.
4. Lightly dredge each pork chop in the breadcrumbs.
5. Heat the oil in a skillet.
6. Brown the pork chops on each side for 5 minutes.
7. Place the pork chops on the baking sheet.
8. Bake for 10 minutes or until pork reaches 145F in the center.

Per serving: Calories: 210Kcal; Protein: 24g; Carbohydrates: 10g; Fat: 7g

371. GRILLED STEAK WITH SALSA

Preparation time: 20 minutes

Cooking time: 15 minutes

Servings: 4

Ingredients:

For the salsa

- Chopped English cucumber - 1 cup
- Boiled and diced red bell pepper – ¼ cup
- Scallion – 1, both green and white parts, chopped
- Chopped fresh cilantro – 2 tbsps.
- Juice of 1 lime

For the steak

- Beef tenderloin steaks – 4 (3-ounce), room temperature
- Olive oil
- Freshly ground black pepper

Directions:

1. In a bowl, to make the salsa, combine the lime juice, cilantro, scallion, bell pepper, and cucumber. Set aside.
2. To make the steak: Pre-heat a barbecue to medium heat.
3. Rub the steaks all roundwith oil and season with pepper.
4. Grill the steaks for around 5 minutes on each side for medium-rare, or until the desired doneness.
5. Serve the steaks topped with salsa.

Per serving: Calories: 130Kcal; Protein: 19g; Carbohydrates: 1g; Fat: 6g

372. BEEF WITH CARROT AND BROCCOLI

Preparation time: 15 minutes

Cooking time: 14 minutes

Servings: 4

Ingredients:

- 2 tbsp. coconut oil, divided
- 2 medium garlic cloves, minced
- 1 lb. beef sirloin steak (sliced into thin strips)
- Salt, to taste
- ¼ cup chicken broth
- 2 tsp. fresh ginger, grated
- 1 tbsp. Ground flax seeds
- ½ tsp. Red pepper flakes, crushed
- ¼ tsp. freshly ground black pepper
- 1 large carrot, peeled and sliced thinly
- 2 cups broccoli florets
- 1 medium scallion, sliced thinly

Directions:

1. In a skillet, heat 1 tbsp. of oil on medium-high heat.
2. Put garlic and sauté, approximately 1 minute.
3. Add beef and salt and cook for at least 4-5 minutes or till browned.
4. Using a slotted spoon, put the beef into a bowl.
5. Remove the liquid from the skillet.
6. In a bowl, put together broth, ginger, flax seeds, red pepper flakes, and black pepper then mix.
7. In the same skillet, heat remaining oil on medium heat.
8. Put the carrot, broccoli, and ginger mixture then cook for at least 3-4 minutes or till desired doneness.
9. Mix in beef and scallion then cook for around 3-4 minutes.

Per serving: Calories: 412Kcal; Protein: 35g; Carbohydrates: 28g; Fat: 13g

373. OREGANO PORK

Preparation time: 10 minutes
Cooking time: 8 hours
Servings: 4
Ingredients:

- 2 pounds pork roast, sliced
- 2 tbsp. oregano, chopped
- ¼ cup balsamic vinegar
- 1 cup tomato paste
- 1 tbs. sweet paprika
- 1 tsp. onion powder
- 2 tbsp. chili powder
- 2 garlic cloves, minced
- A pinch of salt and black pepper

Directions:

1. In a slow cooker, combine the roast with the oregano, the vinegar, and the other ingredients, toss, put the lid on, then cook on low for 8 hours.

2. Divide everything between plates and serve.

Per serving: Calories: 300Kcal; Protein: 24g; Carbohydrates: 12g; Fat: 5g

374. CREAMY PORK AND TOMATOES

Preparation time: 10 minutes
Cooking time: 35 minutes
Servings: 4
Ingredients:

- 2 pounds pork stew meat, cubed
- 2 tbsp. avocado oil
- 1 cup tomatoes, cubed
- 1 cup coconut cream
- 1 tbs. mint, chopped
- 1 jalapeno pepper, chopped
- Pinch of sea salt
- Pinch of black pepper
- 1 tbs. hot pepper
- 2 tbsp. lemon juice

Directions:

1. Heat a pan with the oil over medium heat, add the meat and brown for 5 minutes.
2. Add the rest of the ingredients, toss, then cook over medium heat for 30 minutes more, divide between plates and serve.

Per serving: Calories: 230Kcal; Protein: 14g; Carbohydrates: 9g; Fat: 4g

375. LIME CHICKEN WITH BLACK BEANS

Preparation time: 15 minutes
Cooking time: 30 minutes
Servings: 8
Ingredients:

- 8 chicken thighs, boneless and skinless
- 3 tbsp. lime juice
- 1 C. black beans
- 1 C. tomatoes, canned
- 4 tsp. garlic powder

Directions:

1. Marinate the chicken in a mixture of lime juice and garlic powder.
2. Add the chicken to the Instant Pot.
3. Place the tomatoes on top of the chicken.
4. Seal the pot.
5. Set it to manual.
6. Cook at high pressure for 10 minutes.
7. Release the pressure naturally.
8. Stir in the black beans.
9. Press sauté to simmer until black beans are cooked.

Per serving: Calories: 370Kcal; Protein: 47.9g; Carbohydrates: 17.5g; Fat: 11.2g

376. ZERO-FUSSING PORK MEAL

Preparation time: 20 minutes
Cooking time: 6 hours
Servings: 4
Ingredients:

- 1 lb. lean pork, cut into bite-sized cubes
- 2 potatoes, peeled and quartered
- 1 lb. fresh green beans
- 2 carrots, peeled and sliced thinly
- 2 celery stalks, sliced thinly
- 1 large onion, chopped
- 3 fresh tomatoes, grated
- ½ C. extra-virgin olive oil
- 1 tsp. thyme, dried
- Salt and black pepper, freshly ground, to taste

Directions:

1. In a slow cooker, place all the ingredients and stir to combine.
2. Set the slow cooker on "High" and cook, covered for about 6 hours.
3. Serve hot.

Per serving: Calories: 533Kcal; Protein: 35.1g; Carbohydrates: 35.3g; Fat: 29.7g

377. GRILLED STEAK

Preparation time: 10 minutes
Cooking time: 20 minutes
Servings: 2
Ingredients:

- 2 steaks
- 1 C. spinach, chopped
- 1 tbsp. olive oil
- 2 tbsp. red onions, diced
- 2 tbsp. feta cheese, crumbled
- 2 tbsp. panko breadcrumbs
- 1 tbsp. tomato, diced and sun-dried
- Salt and pepper

Directions:

1. Pre-heat grill to medium-high heat.
2. Use a skillet to sauté the onions in olive oil for 5 minutes.
3. Add the remaining ingredients, except the steaks, and stir for 2 minutes. Take off the stove and let sit.
4. Grill the steaks to the desired doneness.
5. Top each steak with the spinach mix. Cook in the broiler until the top turns brown.

Per serving: Calories: 531Kcal; Protein: 22.7g; Carbohydrates: 37.8g; Fat: 33.2g

378. SPICY ROASTED LEG OF LAMB

Preparation time: 30 minutes
Cooking time: 2 hours
Servings: 4
Ingredients:
For the lamb:

- 1 lb./450 g. leg of lamb, bone-in
- Salt and pepper
- 3 tbsp. olive oil
- 5 garlic cloves, sliced
- 2 C. water
- 4 potatoes, cubed
- 1 onion, chopped
- 1 tsp. garlic powder

For the lamb spice rub:

- 15 garlic cloves, peeled
- 3 tbsp. oregano
- 2 tbsp. mint
- 1 tbsp. paprika
- ½ C. olive oil
- ¼ C. lemon juice

Directions:

1. Allow the lamb to rest for 1 hour at room temperature.
2. While you wait, put all of the spice rub ingredients in a food processor and blend. Refrigerate the rub.
3. Make a few cuts in the lamb using a knife. Season with salt and pepper.
4. Place on a roasting pan.
5. Heat the broiler and broil for 5 minutes on each side so the whole thing is seared.
6. Place the lamb on the counter and preheat the oven to 375 degrees Fahrenheit/190 degrees Celsius.
7. Allow the lamb to cool before stuffing the chops with garlic slices and sprinkling the spice rub on top. Place it into the roasting pan, and pour in 2 cups of water.
8. Add garlic powder, salt, and pepper to the potatoes and onions. Arrange the vegetables around the lamb leg.
9. Add oil to the top of lamb and vegetables.
10. Use aluminum foil to cover the roasting pan and place it back in the oven.
11. Roast the lamb for 1 hour.
12. Discard the foil and roast for 15 more minutes.
13. Let the leg of lamb sit for 20 minutes before serving.

Per serving: Calories: 504Kcal; Protein: 37.6g; Carbohydrates: 45.2g; Fat: 19.9g

379. DIJON AND HERB PORK TENDERLOIN

Preparation time: 1hour
Cooking time: 30 minutes
Servings: 6
Ingredients:

- ½ C. Italian parsley leaves, freshly chopped
- 3 tbsp. fresh rosemary leaves, chopped
- 3 tbsp. fresh thyme leaves, chopped
- 3 tbsp. Dijon mustard
- 1 tbsp. extra-virgin olive oil
- 4 garlic cloves, minced
- ½ tsp. sea salt
- ¼ tsp. black pepper, freshly ground
- 1½ lbs./680 g. pork tenderloin

Directions:

1. Pre-heat the oven to 400°F.
2. In a blender or food processor, combine the parsley, rosemary, thyme, mustard, olive oil, garlic, sea salt, and pepper. Process for about 30 seconds until smooth.
3. Spread the mixture evenly over the pork and place it on a rimmed baking sheet.
4. Bake for about 20 minutes, or until the meat reaches an internal temperature of 140°F/60°C.
5. Allow resting for 10 minutes before slicing and serving.

Per serving: Calories: 393Kcal; Protein: 74g; Carbohydrates: 5g; Fat: 12g

380. GRILLED LAMB GYRO BURGER

Preparation time: 15 minutes
Cooking time: 12 minutes
Servings: 2
Ingredients:

- 4 oz./115 g. lean ground lamb
- 4 naan flatbread or pita
- 2 tbsp. olive oil
- 2 tbsp. tzatziki sauce
- 1 red onion, thinly sliced
- 1 tomato, sliced
- 1 bunch lettuce, separated

Directions:

6. Grill meat for 10 minutes.
7. Toast naan bread, and drizzle with olive oil.
8. Top 2 of the halves of naan bread with meat and the remaining ingredients.
9. Cover with other halves and enjoy!

Per serving: Calories: 470Kcal; Protein: 20g; Carbohydrates: 44g; Fat: 28g

381. PORK LOIN AND ORZO

Preparation time: 20 minutes
Cooking time: 30 minutes
Servings: 4
Ingredients:

- 1 lb./450 g. pork tenderloin
- 1 tsp. pepper, coarsely ground
- 1 tsp. kosher salt
- 2 tbsp. olive oil
- 1 C. orzo pasta, uncooked
- Water as needed
- 2 C. spinach
- 1 C. cherry tomatoes
- ¾ C. feta cheese, crumbled

Directions:

1. Coat the pork loin with kosher salt and black pepper and massage it into the meat. Then cut the meat into 1-inch cubes.
2. Heat the olive oil in a cast-iron skillet over medium heat until sizzling hot. Cook the pork for about 8 minutes until there's no pink left.
3. Cook the orzo in water according to package directions (adding a pinch of salt to the water).
4. Stir in the spinach and tomatoes and add the cooked pork.
5. Top with feta and serve.

Per serving: Calories: 372Kcal; Protein: 31g; Carbohydrates: 34g; Fat: 11g

382. LAMB CHOPS

Preparation time: 10 minutes
Cooking time: 20 minutes
Servings: 4
Ingredients:

- 4 oz./115 g lamb rib chops, trimmed
- 4 tbsp. olive oil
- 1 tbsp. kosher salt
- ½ tsp. black pepper
- 3 tbsp. balsamic vinegar
- Non-stick cooking spray

Directions:

1. Mix 1 tbsp. of oil with the rind and juice into a Ziploc-type bag. Add the chops and coat well. Marinate at room temperature for 10 minutes.
2. Remove it from the bag and season with pepper and salt.
3. Using the med-high heat setting; coat a pan with the spray. Add the lamb and cook 2 minutes per side until it is the way you like it.
4. Using a saucepan, pour in the vinegar (med-high) and cook until it is syrupy or for about 3 minutes.

5. Drizzle the vinegar and the rest of the oil (1 tsp) over the lamb.
6. Serve with your favorite sides.

Per serving: Calories: 226Kcal; Protein: 15.86g; Carbohydrates: 0g; Fat: 17.55g

383. BEAN BEEF CHILI

Preparation time: 10 minutes
Cooking time: 40 minutes
Servings: 4
Ingredients:

- 1 lb. beef, ground
- ½ onion, diced
- 1 tsp. chili powder
- 1 tsp. garlic, chopped
- 14 oz. can black beans, rinsed and drained
- 14 oz. can red beans, rinsed and drained
- ½ jalapeno pepper, minced
- ½ bell pepper, chopped
- 1 C. chicken broth
- Pepper
- Salt

Directions:

1. Set instant pot on sauté mode.
2. Add meat and sauté until brown.
3. Add remaining ingredients and stir well.
4. Seal pot with lid then cook on high for 35 minutes.
5. Once done, release pressure using quick release. Remove lid.
6. Stir well and serve.

Per serving: Calories: 409Kcal; Protein: 46.6g; Carbohydrates: 36.3g; Fat: 8.3g

384. CAULIFLOWER TOMATO BEEF

Preparation time: 10 minutes
Cooking time: 25 minutes
Servings: 2
Ingredients:

- ½ lb. beef stew meat, chopped
- 1 tsp. paprika
- 1 celery stalk, chopped
- 1 tbsp. balsamic vinegar
- ¼ C. grape tomatoes, chopped

- 1 onion, chopped
- ¼ C. cauliflower, chopped
- 1 tbsp. olive oil
- Salt
- Pepper

Directions:

1. Put oil into the instant pot and set the pot on sauté mode.
2. Add meat and sauté for 5 minutes.

3. Add remaining ingredients and stir well.
4. Cover pot with lid and cook on high for 20 minutes.
5. Once done, allow to release pressure naturally. Remove lid.
6. Stir and serve.

Per serving: Calories: 306Kcal; Protein: 35.7g; Carbohydrates: 7.6g; Fat: 14.3g

385. SUNDAY DINNER BRISKET

Preparation time: 10 minutes
Cooking time: 8 hours 10 minutes
Servings: 6
Ingredients:

- 2 ½ lb. beef brisket, trimmed
- Salt and black pepper, freshly ground, to taste
- 2 tsp. olive oil
- 2 medium onions, chopped
- 2 large garlic cloves, sliced
- 1 tbsp. Herbs de Provence
- 1 (15-oz.) can tomatoes, diced and drained
- 2 tsp. Dijon mustard
- 1 C. dry red wine

Directions:

1. Season the brisket with salt and black pepper evenly.
2. In a non-stick skillet, heat the oil over medium heat and cook the brisket for about 4–5 minutes per side.
3. Transfer the brisket into a slow cooker.
4. Add the remaining ingredients and stir to combine.
5. Set the slow cooker on "Low" and cook, covered for about 8 hours.
6. Uncover the slow cooker and with a slotted spoon, transfer the brisket onto a platter.
7. Cut the brisket into desired-sized slices and serve with the topping of the pan sauce.

Per serving: Calories: 427Kcal; Protein: 58.5g; Carbohydrates: 7.7g; Fat: 193.6g

386. DELICIOUSLY SIMPLE BEEF

Preparation time: 10 minutes
Cooking time: 10 hours
Servings: 4
Ingredients:

- 1 large onion, sliced thinly
- ¼ C. extra-virgin olive oil
- 1 tbsp. garlic, minced
- 1 tsp. oregano, dried
- Salt and black pepper, freshly ground, to taste

- 2 tbsp. fresh lemon juice
- 2 lb. beef chuck roast, cut into bite-sized pieces

Directions:

1. In a slow cooker, place all the ingredients except for beef cubes and stir to combine.
2. Add the beef cubes and stir to combine.
3. Set the slow cooker on "Low" and cook, covered for about 8–10 hours.
4. Serve hot.

Per serving: Calories: 553Kcal; Protein: 62.8g; Carbohydrates: 4.6g; Fat: 30.3g

387. HOLIDAY FEAST LAMB SHANKS

Preparation time: 15 minutes
Cooking time: 8 hours 5 minutes
Servings: 4
Ingredients:

- 4 lamb shanks
- Salt and black pepper, freshly ground, to taste
- 1 tbsp. olive oil
- 1 lb. baby potatoes, halved
- 1 C. Kalamata olives
- 1 (3-oz.) jar tomatoes, sun-dried
- 1 C. chicken broth
- 3 tbsp. fresh lemon juice
- 2 ½ tsp. oregano, dried
- 1 tsp. rosemary, dried
- 1 tsp. basil, dried
- 1 tsp. onion powder

Directions:

1. Season the lamb shanks with salt and black pepper evenly.
2. In a large heavy-bottomed skillet, heat the olive oil over medium-high heat and sear the lamb shanks for about 4–5 minutes or until browned completely.
3. Remove from the heat.
4. In a slow cooker, place the potatoes, olives, sun-dried tomatoes, salt, place the lamb on top and sprinkle with dried herbs and onion powder.
5. Set the slow cooker on "Low" and cook, covered for about 8 hours.
6. Serve hot.

Per serving: Calories: 696Kcal; Protein: 83.5g; Carbohydrates: 22.5g; Fat: 28.6g

388. ZUCCHINI NOODLE BEEF LASAGNA

Preparation time: 30 minutes
Cooking time: 45minutes
Servings: 4

Ingredients:

- 2 tbsp. olive oil
- ½ red chili, chopped
- 1 lb. ground beef
- 3 large zucchinis, sliced lengthwise
- 2 garlic cloves, minced
- 1 shallot, chopped
- 1 cup tomato sauce
- Salt and black pepper to taste
- 2 tsp sweet paprika
- 1 tsp dried thyme
- 1 tsp dried basil
- 1 cup mozzarella cheese, shredded
- 1 cup chicken broth

Directions:

1. Warm the oil in a skillet and then cook the beef for 4 minutes while breaking any lumps as you stir. Top with shallot, garlic, chili, tomatoes, salt, paprika, and black pepper. Stir and cook for 5 more minutes.
2. Lay 1/3 of the zucchinis slices in a greased baking dish. Top off 1/3 of the beef mixture and repeat the layering process twice with the same quantities. Season with basil and thyme. Pour in the chicken broth. Sprinkle the mozzarella cheese on top and tuck the baking dish in the oven. Bake for 35 minutes at 380 F. Remove the lasagna and let it rest for 10 minutes before serving.

Per serving: Calories: 451Kcal; Protein: 42g; Carbohydrates: 6.8g; Fat: 22.8g

389. BEEF STEAKS WITH CREAMY BACON AND MUSHROOMS

Preparation time: 10 minutes

Cooking time: 40 minutes

Servings: 4

Ingredients:

- 2 oz. bacon, chopped
- 1 cup mushrooms, sliced
- 1 garlic clove, chopped
- 1 shallot, chopped
- 1 cup heavy cream
- 1 pound beef steaks
- 1 tsp ground nutmeg
- ¼ cup coconut oil
- Salt and black pepper to taste
- 1 tbsp. parsley, chopped

Directions:

1. Put a frying pan at medium heat, then cook the bacon for 2-3 minutes and set aside. In the same pan, warm the oil, add in the onions, garlic, and mushrooms, and cook for 4 minutes. Stir in the beef, season with salt, black pepper and nutmeg, and sear until browned, about 2 minutes per side.

2. Preheat oven to 360 F and insert the pan in the oven to bake for 25 minutes. Remove the beef steaks from the pan and put in a bowl and cover with foil.
3. Place the pan over medium heat, pour in the heavy cream over the mushroom mixture, add in the reserved bacon and cook for 5 minutes; remove from heat. Spread the bacon/mushroom sauce over beef steaks, sprinkle with parsley and serve.

Per serving:

Calories: 765Kcal; Protein 32g; Carbohydrates: 3.8g; Fat 71g

390. CILANTRO BEEF CURRY WITH CAULIFLOWER

Preparation time: 6 minutes

Cooking time: 15 minutes

Servings: 3

Ingredients:

- 1 tbsp. olive oil
- ½ lb. ground beef
- 1 garlic clove, minced
- 1 tsp turmeric
- 1 tbsp. cilantro, chopped
- 1 tbsp. ginger paste
- ½ tsp gram masala
- 5 oz. canned whole tomatoes
- 1 head cauliflower, cut into florets
- Salt and chili pepper to taste
- ¼ cup water

Directions:

1. Warm oil in a saucepan at medium heat, put the beef, garlic, ginger paste, and garam masala. Cook for 5 minutes while breaking any lumps.
2. Stir in the tomatoes and cauliflower, season with salt, turmeric, and chili pepper, and cook covered for 6 minutes. Add the water and bring to a boil over medium heat for 10 minutes or until the water has reduced by half. Scoop the curry into serving bowls and serve sprinkled with cilantro.

Per serving: Calories: 365Kcal; Protein 19.5g; Carbohydrates: 3.5g; Fat 31.6g

391. CRANBERRY PORK BBQ DISH

Preparation time: 10 minutes

Cooking time: 45 minutes

Servings: 4

Ingredients:

- 3-4 pounds pork shoulder, boneless, fat trimmed
- For Sauce
- 3 tbsp. of liquid smoke

- 2 tbsp. tomato paste
- 2 cups fresh cranberries
- ¼ cup hot sauce
- 1/3 cup blackstrap molasses
- ½ cup of water
- ½ cup apple cider vinegar
- 1 tsp. salt
- 1 tbs. adobo sauce
- 1 cup tomato puree
- 1 chipotle pepper in adobo sauce, diced

Directions:

1. Cut pork into halves/thirds and keep on the side
2. Set your Ninja Foodi to sauté mode and let it heat up. Add cranberries and water to the pot
3. Let them simmer for 4-5 minutes until cranberries start to pop, add the rest of the sauce ingredients and simmer for 5 minutes more. Add pork to the pot and lock lid
4. Cook on high pressure for 40 minutes. Quick-release pressure
5. Use a fork to shred the pork and serve on your favorite greens

Per serving: Calories: 250Kcal; Protein: 15g; Carbohydrates: 5g; Fat: 17g

392. ROPA VIEJA

Preparation time: 20 minutes

Cooking time: 6 hours and 10 minutes

Servings: 2

Ingredients:

- 3 lbs. roasted mandrel
- 1 Tbsp. ghee
- 1 diced onion
- garlic cloves, finely chopped
- 2 tsp cumin
- 2 tsp smoked pepper
- 2 tsp dried oregano
- 2 tsp salt
- 1 tsp ground pepper
- ½ tsp allspice
- ½ cup beef broth
- 1 can of tomato cubes (14.5 oz.)
- 1 can of tomato puree (6 oz.)
- 1 tbsp. white vinegar
- 2 Bay leaves
- 3 sliced peppers
- 1 can of drained green olives

Directions:

1. Cut the steak (against the grain) into 2-inch-wide strips.
2. In a large pan, heat ghee over medium heat. Pan sear half of the steak strips on the flank–leave on each side in the frying pan for 2-3 min. Continue with the other half of the pieces of the flank steak.

3. Put all ingredients on a slow cooker. Cook on low for 6 hours.
4. Shred the steak on the flank and mix it in.

Per serving: Calories: 400Kcal; Protein: 36.5g; Carbohydrates: 16.8g; Fat: 20g

393. TANDOORI LAMB TAIL

Preparation time: 10 minutes

Cooking time: 1hour and 10 minutes

Servings: 2-4

Ingredients:

Roast meat:

- 1 lb. minced lamb
- 1 diced onion
- 5 finely chopped garlic cloves
- 1 serrano pepper, chopped
- 5 tbsp. organic tomato puree
- 2 tsp bell pepper
- 1 tsp coriander powder
- 1 tsp turmeric
- 1 tsp salt
- ¼ tsp freshly ground black pepper
- ¼ tsp cumin powder
- ¼ tsp ground cloves
- ¼ tsp cinnamon (ground)
- A pinch freshly grated nutmeg
- 2 eggs
- A small hand of chopped mint

"Ketchup" filling:

- 5 tbsp. organic tomato puree
- ¼ cup water
- A pinch of salt and pepper
- A pinch of garlic powder

5. Directions:
1. Put all ingredients in a bowl, then mix and divide the mixture into a bowl with greased bread.
2. Bake the bread at 350° C for 1 hour.
3. While the bread is baking, prepare the tomato sauce by mixing the ingredients in a pan over low heat.
4. When the bread is ready, apply ketchup and put it in the oven for 10 minutes.
5. Remove from the oven, then let stand for a few minutes to cool the juice, remove the meatloaf from the pan, and serve.

Per serving: Calories: 506Kcal; Protein: 5.93g; Carbohydrates: 11.82g; Fat: 30.01g

394. SMOKED LAMB

Preparation time: 30 minutes + smoke time

Cooking time: 100 minutes

Servings: 4

Ingredients:

- 2.5kg boneless 5 lb. shoulder

- 3-4 sprigs fresh rosemary
- Himalayan salt
- Freshly ground black pepper
- About 6 cups of cherry wood chips

Directions:
1. Place 4 cups of wood chips to soak in water for at least an hour before smoking your lamb.
2. Remove the fillet around the shoulder of lamb, rinse it in cold water and dry it. Place the lamb on a cutting board (cut the thicker parts if necessary) and make several deep incisions along with the meat with a kitchen knife. Insert pieces of fresh rosemary into these incisions. Sprinkle generously with salt and pepper.
3. Pre-heat your outdoor grill to 225 ° F. lighting a single burner in the lowest setting should be the trick.
4. Make 8 bags of wood chips. Cut a piece of heavy-duty 12 "x 24" aluminum foil for each bag (double if you are using lighter weight paper) and place about half a cup of damp wood chips at 1 end of the paper. Add a handful of dried chips and fold the sheet over the wood chips. Fold the 4 edges in the center at least twice, then make holes in the top and bottom of the bag with a fork or other sharp object.
5. Lift the grill on the ignition element and place 2 bags directly on the heat source. Close and wait for the smoke to come out of the bags.
6. Place the roast lamb on the other side of the grill and close the lid.
7. Smoke the meat for about 6 hours and replace the bags with 2 new ones every 90 min If necessary, increase the heat under the new bag until the smoke comes out and lower the temperature.
8. Try to keep the temperature of your grill as stable as possible at around 225 ° F. *Please note that it is not necessary to get massive amounts of smoke to get a good taste however if you feel you don't have enough, no problem to add more dry chips to your foil pouches or place an aluminum container with a handful of baked chips next to your existing foil pouches.*
9. When the lamb has smoked for 6 hours, remove it from the grill and wrap it in aluminum foil. Use a double layer to make sure n1 of the cooking juices leak out. You want to preserve moisture at this time.
10. Place it back on the grill and crank up the heat to 350° F. Cook the

meat for another 90 min, or until the meat becomes very tender and can be easily removed with a fork.
11. Take off the roast from the grill, then let it sit for 10 min, then cut and serve sprinkled with the cooking juices.

Per serving: Calories: 797Kcal; Protein: 136.98g; Carbohydrates: 1.97g; Fat: 27.1g

395. CHICKEN MARSALA

Preparation time: 15 minutes

Cooking time: 15 minutes

Servings: 4

Ingredients:

- 4 chicken breast fillets
- 1/2 cup all-purpose flour
- 2 tbsp. olive oil
- 1/2 cup shallots, chopped
- 2 cups fresh mushrooms, sliced
- 5 tbsp. fresh parsley, chopped
- 1 tbs. butter mixed with 1 tbs. olive oil
- 1/4 cup dry Marsala wine
- 1/4 tsp. garlic powder
- 1/8 tsp. black pepper

Directions:
1. Coat both sides of chicken with flour.
2. Cook in hot oil in a pan over medium heat.
3. Cook until golden or for 5 minutes per side.
4. Put chicken on a platter and set aside.
5. Sauté mushrooms, parsley and shallots in olive oil butter blend for 3 minutes.
6. Add the rest of the ingredients.
7. Simmer for 2 minutes.
8. Pour sauce over chicken and serve with rice.

Per serving: Calories: 425Kcal; Protein: 32g; Carbohydrates: 40g; Fat: 15g

396. ZESTY CHICKEN

Preparation time: 40 minutes

Cooking time: 10 minutes

Servings: 2

Ingredients:

- 2 tbsp. olive oil
- 2 tbsp. balsamic vinegar
- 1/4 cup green onion, chopped
- 1 tsp. fresh oregano
- 1/2 tsp. garlic powder
- 1/4 tsp. black pepper
- 1/4 tsp. paprika
- 8 ounces chicken breast fillets

Directions:

1. Mix olive oil and vinegar.
2. Add green onion, herbs and seasonings.
3. Mix well.
4. Marinate chicken in the mixture for 30 minutes.
5. Cover and put inside the refrigerator.
6. Fry the chicken for 5 minutes per side.

Per serving: Calories: 280Kcal; Protein: 27g; Carbohydrates: 4g; Fat: 16g

397. ROASTED SPATCHCOCK CHICKEN

Preparation time: twenty or so minutes
Cooking time: 50 minutes
Servings: 4-6
Ingredients:

- 1 (4-pound) whole chicken
- 1 (1-inch) piece fresh ginger, sliced
- 4 garlic cloves, chopped
- 1 small bunch fresh thyme
- Pinch of cayenne
- Salt and freshly ground black pepper, to taste
- ¼ cup fresh lemon juice
- 3 tbsp. extra virgin olive oil

Directions:

1. Arrange chicken, breast side down onto a large cutting board.
2. With a kitchen shear, begin with thigh and cut along 1 side of backbone and turn chicken around.
3. Now, cut along sleep issues and discard the backbone.
4. Change the inside and open it like a book.
5. Flatten the backbone firmly to flatten.
6. In a food processor, add all ingredients except chicken and pulse till smooth.
7. In a big baking dish, add the marinade mixture.
8. Add chicken and coat with marinade generously.
9. With a plastic wrap, cover the baking dish and refrigerate to marinate overnight.
10. Pre-heat the oven to 450 deg. F. Arrange a rack in a roasting pan.
11. Remove the chicken from refrigerator and put on rack over roasting pan, skin side down.
12. Roast for about 50 minutes, turning once in midway.

Per serving: Calories: 419Kcal; Protein: 40g; Carbohydrates: 28g; Fat: 14g

398. TURMERIC BAKED CHICKEN BREAST

Preparation time: 5 minutes
Cooking time: 40 minutes
Servings: 2
Ingredients:

- 8 oz. chicken breast, skinless, boneless
- 2 tbsp. capers
- 1 tsp. olive oil
- ½ tsp. paprika
- ½ tsp. turmeric, ground
- ½ tsp. salt
- ½ tsp. garlic, minced

Directions:

1. Make the lengthwise cut in the chicken breast.
2. Rub the chicken with olive oil, paprika, capers, ground turmeric, salt, and minced garlic.
3. Then fill the chicken cut with capers and secure it with toothpicks.
4. Bake the chicken breast for 40 minutes at 350°F.
5. Remove the toothpicks from the chicken breast and slice it.

Per serving: Calories: 156Kcal; Protein: 24.4g; Carbohydrates: 1.3g; Fat: 5.4g

399. BALSAMIC CHICKEN

Preparation time: 10 minutes
Cooking time: 30 minutes
Servings: 4
Ingredients:

- 3 chicken breasts
- ¼ C. olive oil
- ¼ C. balsamic vinegar
- 1 clove garlic

Directions:

1. In a bowl, add all ingredients.
2. Add chicken and the marinade for 3–4 hours.
3. Grill and serve with vegetables.

Per serving: Calories: 200Kcal; Protein: 3g; Carbohydrates: 8g; Fat: 8g

400. LEMON CHICKEN MIX

Preparation time: 10 minutes
Cooking time: 10 minutes
Servings: 2
Ingredients:

- 8 oz. chicken breast, skinless, boneless
- 1 tsp. Cajun seasoning
- 1 tsp. balsamic vinegar
- 1 tsp. olive oil
- 1 tsp. lemon juice

Directions:

1. Cut the chicken breast on the halves and sprinkle with Cajun seasoning.
2. Sprinkle the poultry with olive oil and lemon juice.
3. Sprinkle the chicken breast with balsamic vinegar.
4. Pre-heat the grill to 385°F.
5. Grill the chicken breast halves for 5 minutes from each side.
6. Slice Cajun chicken and place it on the serving plate.

Per serving: Calories: 150Kcal; Protein: 24.1g; Carbohydrates: 0.1g; Fat: 5.2g

401. CHICKEN SHAWARMA

Preparation time: 15 minutes
Cooking time: 30 minutes
Servings: 8
Ingredients:

- 2 lb. chicken breast, sliced into strips
- 1 tsp. paprika
- 1 tsp. cumin, ground
- ¼ tsp. garlic, granulated
- ½ tsp. turmeric
- ¼ tsp. allspice, ground

Directions:

1. Season the chicken with spices, and a little salt and pepper.
2. Pour 1 C. chicken broth into the pot.
3. Seal the pot.
4. Choose a poultry setting.
5. Cook for 15 minutes.
6. Release the pressure naturally.

Per serving: Calories: 132Kcal; Protein: 24.2g; Carbohydrates: 0.5g; Fat: 3g

402. GREEK CHICKEN BITES

Preparation time: 10 minutes
Cooking time: 20 minutes
Servings: 6
Ingredients:

- 1-lb. chicken fillet
- 1 tbsp. Greek seasoning
- 1 tsp. sesame oil
- ½ tsp. salt
- 1 tsp. balsamic vinegar

Directions:

1. Cut the chicken fingers on small tenders (fingers) and sprinkle them with Greek seasoning, salt, and balsamic vinegar. Mix well with the help of the fingertips.
2. Sprinkle chicken with sesame oil and shake gently.
3. Line the baking tray with parchment.

4. Place the marinated chicken fingers in the tray in one layer.
5. Bake the chicken fingers for 20 minutes at 355°F. Flip them onto another side after 10 minutes of cooking.

Per serving: Calories: 154Kcal; Protein: 22g; Carbohydrates: 0.8g; Fat: 6.4g

403. TURKEY VERDE WITH BROWN RICE

Preparation time: 15 minutes
Cooking time: 30 minutes
Servings: 5
Ingredients:

- ⅔ C. chicken broth
- 1 ¼ C. brown rice
- 1 ½ lb. turkey tenderloins
- 1 onion, sliced
- ½ C. salsa verde

Directions:

1. Put the chicken broth and rice to the Instant Pot.
2. Top with the turkey, onion, and salsa.
3. Cover the pot.
4. Set it to manual.
5. Cook at high pressure for 18 minutes.
6. Release the pressure naturally.
7. Wait for 8 minutes before opening the pot.

Per serving: Calories: 336Kcal; Protein: 38.5g; Carbohydrates: 39.4g; Fat: 3.3g

404. CHICKEN TACOS

Preparation time: 10 minutes
Cooking time: 20 minutes
Servings: 4
Ingredients:

- 2 bread tortillas
- 1 tsp. butter
- 2 tsp. olive oil
- 1 tsp. Taco seasoning
- 6 oz. chicken breast, skinless, boneless, sliced
- ⅓ C. Cheddar cheese, shredded
- 1 bell pepper, cut on the wedges

Directions:

1. Pour 1 tsp. of olive oil in the skillet then add chicken.
2. Sprinkle the meat with Taco seasoning and mix up well.
3. Roast chicken for 10 minutes over medium heat. Stir it from time to time.
4. Transfer the cooked chicken to the plate.

5. Add remaining olive oil to the skillet.
6. Add bell pepper and roast it for 5 minutes. Stir it all the time.
7. Mix together bell pepper with chicken.
8. Toss butter in the skillet and melt it.
9. Put 1 tortilla in the skillet.
10. Put Cheddar cheese on the tortilla and flatten it.
11. add a chicken-pepper mixture and cover it with the second tortilla.
12. Roast the quesadilla for 2 minutes from each side.
13. Cut the cooked meal on the halves and transfer it to the serving plates.

Per serving: Calories: 194Kcal; Protein: 13.2g; Carbohydrates: 16.4g; Fat: 8.3g

405. CHICKEN AND BUTTER SAUCE

Preparation time: 5 minutes
Cooking time: 30 minutes
Servings: 5
Ingredients:

- 1-lb. chicken fillet
- ⅓ C. butter, softened
- 1 tbsp. rosemary
- ½ tsp. thyme
- 1 tsp. salt
- ½ lemon

Directions:

1. Churn together thyme, salt, and rosemary.
2. Chop the chicken fillet roughly and mix it up with churned butter mixture.
3. Place the prepared chicken in the baking dish.
4. Squeeze the lemon over the chicken.
5. Chop the squeezed lemon and add it to the baking dish.
6. Cover the chicken with foil and bake it for 20 minutes at 365°F.
7. Discard the foil and bake the chicken for 10 minutes more.

Per serving: Calories: 285Kcal; Protein: 26.5g; Carbohydrates: 1g; Fat: 19.1g

406. PORK AND CHESTNUTS MIX

Preparation time: 30 minutes
Cooking time: 0 minutes
Servings: 6
Ingredients:

- 1 and ½ C. brown rice, already cooked
- 2 C. pork roast, already cooked and shredded

- 3 oz. water chestnuts, drained and sliced
- ½ C. sour cream
- A pinch salt and white pepper

Directions:

1. In a bowl, mix the rice with the roast and the other ingredients, toss and keep in the fridge for 2 hours before serving.

Per serving: Calories: 294Kcal; Protein: 23.5g; Carbohydrates: 16g; Fat: 17g

407. STEAK WITH OLIVES AND MUSHROOMS

Preparation time: 20 minutes
Cooking time: 9 minutes
Servings: 6
Ingredients:

- 1 lb. beef sirloin steak, boneless
- 1 large onion, sliced
- 5–6 white button mushrooms
- ½ C. green olives, coarsely chopped
- 4 tbsp. extra virgin olive oil

Directions:

1. Heat-up olive oil in a heavy-bottomed skillet over medium-high heat. Brown the steaks on both sides then put aside.
2. Gently sauté the onion in the same skillet, for 2–3 minutes, stirring rarely. Sauté in the mushrooms and olives.
3. Return the steaks to the skillet, cover, cook for 5–6 minutes and serve.

Per serving: Calories: 299Kcal; Protein: 16g; Carbohydrates: 12g; Fat: 56g

408. GREEK PORK

Preparation time: 10 minutes
Cooking time: 1 Hour and 10 minutes
Servings: 8
Ingredients:

- 3 lb. pork roast, sliced into cubes
- ¼ C. chicken broth
- ¼ C. lemon juice
- 2 tsp. oregano, dried
- 2 tsp. garlic powder

Directions:

1. Put the pork in the Instant Pot.
2. In a bowl, mix all the remaining ingredients.
3. Pour the mixture over the pork.
4. Toss to coat evenly.
5. Secure the pot.
6. Choose a manual mode.
7. Cook at high pressure for 50 minutes.

8. Release the pressure naturally.

Per serving: Calories: 478Kcal; Protein: 65.1g; Carbohydrates: 1.2g; Fat: 21.6g

409. PORK RIND SALMON CAKES

Preparation time: 10 minutes

Cooking time: 10 minutes

Servings: 2

Ingredients:

- 6 oz. Alaska wild salmon, canned and drained
- 2 tbsp. pork rinds, crushed
- 1 egg, lightly beaten
- 1 tbsp. ghee
- ½ tbsp. Dijon mustard

Directions:

1. In a medium bowl, incorporate salmon, pork rinds, egg, and 1½ tbsp. of mayonnaise, and season with pink Himalayan salt and pepper.

2. With the salmon mixture, form patties the size of hockey pucks or smaller. Keep patting the patties until they keep together.

3. Put the medium skillet over medium-high heat, melt the ghee. When the ghee sizzles, place the salmon patties in the pan. Cook for 6 minutes on both sides. Transfer the patties to a paper towel-lined plate.

4. In a small bowl, mix together the remaining 1½ tbsp. of mayonnaise and the mustard.

5. Serve the salmon cakes with the mayo-mustard dipping sauce.

Per serving: Calories: 362Kcal; Protein: 24g; Carbohydrates: 12g; Fat: 31g

410. ROSEMARY PORK CHOPS

Preparation time: 30 minutes

Cooking time: 35 minutes

Servings: 4

Ingredients:

- 4 pork loin chops, boneless
- Salt and black pepper, to taste
- 4 garlic cloves, minced
- 1 tbsp. rosemary, chopped
- 1 tbsp. olive oil

Directions:

1. In a roasting pan, combine the pork chops with the rest of the ingredients, toss, and bake at 425°F for 10 minutes.

2. Reduce the heat to 350°F then cook the chops for 25 minutes more.

3. Divide the chops between plates and serve with a side salad.

Per serving: Calories: 161Kcal; Protein: 25g; Carbohydrates: 1g; Fat: 5g

CHAPTER 8: Stews and Soups

411. BROCCOLI SOUP

Preparation time: 15 minutes

Cooking time: 3 hours

Servings: 2

- **Ingredients:**
- 4 cups chopped broccoli
- ½ cup chopped onion (white)
- 1 ½ cup Chicken Broth (low sodium)
- 1/8 tsp. Black Pepper (cracked)
- 1 tbsp. Olive Oil
- 1 garlic Clove
- 1/16 tsp. Pepper Flakes (chili)
- ¼ cup Milk (low fat)

Directions:

1. In the slow cooker, cover the broccoli with water and cook for an hour on "high." Set aside after draining. Sauté onion and garlic in oil and transfer them to slow cooker when done. Add the broth.
2. Cook on "low" for 2 hrs. Transfer the mixture to a blender and make a smooth puree. Add black pepper, milk, and pepper flakes to the puree. Boil briefly. Serve the soup in heated bowls.

Per serving: Calories: 291Kcal; Protein: 1g; Carbohydrates: 28g; Fats: 1g

412. ROASTED GARLIC SOUP

Preparation time: 15 minutes

Cooking time: 60 minutes

Servings: 10

Ingredients:

- 1 tbs. olive oil
- 2 bulbs garlic, peeled
- 3 shallots, chopped
- 1 large head cauliflower, chopped
- 6 cups vegetable broth
- Sunflower seeds and pepper to taste

Directions:

1. Warm your oven to 400 degrees F. Slice ¼ inch top of the garlic bulb and place it in aluminum foil. Oil it using olive oil and roast in the oven for 35 minutes. Squeeze flesh out of the roasted garlic.
2. Heat-up oil in a saucepan and add shallots, sauté for 6 minutes. Add garlic and remaining ingredients. Adjust heat to low. Let it cook for 15-20 minutes.
3. Puree the mixture using an immersion blender. Season soup

with sunflower seeds and pepper. Serve and enjoy!

Per serving: Calories: 142Kcal; Protein: 4g; Carbohydrates: 3.4g; Fat: 8g

413. ROASTED CARROT SOUP

Preparation time: 15 minutes

Cooking time: 50 minutes

Servings: 4

- **Ingredients:**
- 8 large carrots, washed and peeled
- 6 tbsp. olive oil
- 1-quart broth
- Cayenne pepper to taste
- Sunflower seeds and pepper to taste

Directions:

1. Warm your oven to 425 degrees F. Take a baking sheet, add carrots, drizzle olive oil, and roast for 30-45 minutes.
2. Put roasted carrots into a blender and add broth, puree.
3. Pour into saucepan and heat soup. Season with sunflower seeds, pepper and cayenne. Drizzle olive oil.
4. Serve and enjoy!

Per serving: Calories: 222Kcal; Protein: 5g; Carbohydrates: 7g; Fat: 18g

414. GARLIC AND PUMPKIN SOUP

Preparation time: 15 minutes

Cooking time: 5 hours

Servings: 4

Ingredients:

- 1-pound pumpkin chunks
- 1 onion, diced
- 2 cups vegetable stock
- 1 2/3 cups coconut cream
- ½ stick almond butter
- 1 tsp. garlic, crushed
- 1 tsp. ginger, crushed
- Pepper to taste

Directions:

1. Add all the fixing into your Slow Cooker.
2. Cook for 4-6 hours on high. Puree the soup by using your immersion blender.
3. Serve and enjoy!

Per serving: Calories: 235Kcal; Protein: 2g; Carbohydrates: 11g; Fat: 21g

415. GOLDEN MUSHROOM SOUP

Preparation time: 15 minutes

Cooking time: 8 hours

Servings: 6

Ingredients:

- 1 onion, finely chopped
- 1 carrot, peeled and finely chopped
- 1 fennel bulb, finely chopped
- 1-pound fresh mushrooms, quartered
- 8 cups Vegetable Broth, Poultry Broth, or store-bought
- ¼ cup dry sherry
- 1 tsp. dried thyme
- 1 tsp. garlic powder
- ½ tsp. of sea salt
- 1/8 tsp. freshly ground black pepper

Directions:

1. In your slow cooker, combine all the ingredients, mixing to combine.
2. Cover and set on low. Cook for 8 hours.

Per serving: Calories: 71Kcal; Protein: 3g; Carbohydrates: 15g; Fat: 0g

416. MINESTRONE

Preparation time: 15 minutes

Cooking time: 9 hours

Servings: 6

Ingredients:

- 2 carrots, peeled and sliced
- 2 celery stalks, sliced
- 1 onion, chopped
- 2 cups green beans, chopped
- 1 (16-ounce) can crushed tomatoes
- 2 cups cooked kidney beans, rinsed
- 6 cups Poultry Broth, Vegetable Broth, or store-bought
- 1 tsp. garlic powder
- 1 tsp. dried Italian seasoning
- ¼ tsp. of sea salt
- ¼ tsp. freshly ground black pepper
- 1½ cups cooked whole-wheat elbow macaroni (or pasta shape of your choice)

1 zucchini, chopped

Directions:

1. In your slow cooker, combine the carrots, celery, onion, green beans, tomatoes, kidney beans, broth, garlic powder, salt, Italian seasoning, and pepper in the slow cooker.
2. Cook on low within 8 hours. Stir in the macaroni and zucchini.

3. Cook on low within 1 hour more.

Per serving: Calories: 193Kcal; Protein: 10g; Carbohydrates: 39g; Fat: 0g

417. SQUASH GREEN PEA SOUP

Preparation time: 5 minutes

Cooking time: 50 minutes

Servings: 7

Ingredients:

- 5 cups butternut squash, skinned, seeded, and cubed
- 5 cups low-sodium chicken broth
- Topping:
- 2 cups fresh green peas
- Two tbsp. fresh lime juice
- Black pepper, to taste

Directions:

1. Begin by warming the broth and squash in a saucepan on moderate heat.
2. Let it simmer for approximately 45 minutes, then add the black pepper, lime juice, and green peas.
3. Cook for another 5 minutes, then allow it to cool.
4. Puree the soup using the handheld blender until smooth.
5. Serve.

Per serving: Calories: 152Kcal; Protein: 4.2g; Carbohydrates: 31g; Fat: 3.7g

418. HOMINY POSOLE

Preparation time: 5 minutes

Cooking time: 53 minutes

Servings: 6

Ingredients:

- Two garlic cloves, peeled
- 1 cup boneless pork, diced
- One tbs. cumin powder
- One onion, chopped
- Two garlic cloves, chopped
- Two tbsp. oil
- 1/2 tsp. black pepper
- 1/2 tsp. cayenne
- Two tbsp. chili powder
- 1/4 tsp. oregano
- 1 (29 oz.) can of White Hominy, drained
- 5 cups pork broth
- 1 cup canned diced green chilis
- Two jalapeños, chopped

Directions:

1. Set a suitable sized cooking pot over moderate heat and add the oil to heat.
2. Toss in the pork pieces and sauté for 4 minutes.

3. Stir in the garlic and onion, then stir-fry for 4 minutes until the onion is soft.
4. Add the remaining ingredients, then cover the pork soup.
5. Cook for 45 minutes until the pork is tender.
6. Serve warm.

Per serving: Calories: 128Kcal; Protein: 5.3g; Carbohydrates: 11.7g; Fat: 6.7g

419. CRAB CORN CHOWDER

Preparation time: 5 minutes

Cooking time: 12 minutes

Servings: 6

Ingredients:

- Six bacon slices
- Two celery ribs, diced
- One green bell pepper, diced
- One onion, diced
- One jalapeño pepper, seeded and diced
- 1 (32-oz.) container chicken broth
- Three tbsp. flour
- 3 cups corn kernels
- 1 lb. crabmeat, drained
- 1 cup whipping cream
- 1/4 tsp. pepper

Directions:

1. Add the bacon to a wok and sear it until golden brown, then transfer to a plate.
2. Stir in the onion, celery, and bell pepper, then sauté until soft.
3. Add the corn, broth, crabmeat, cream, black pepper, and flour.
4. Mix well and cook, stirring slowly for 10 minutes.
5. Serve warm.

Per serving: Calories: 330Kcal; Protein: 16.7g; Carbohydrates: 33.5g; Fat: 15.5g

420. CREAM OF CORN SOUP

Preparation time: 5 minutes

Cooking time: 10 minutes

Servings: 3

Ingredients:

- Two tbsp. butter
- Two tbsp. flour
- 1/8 tsp. black pepper
- 1 cup of water
- 1 cup liquid non-dairy creamer
- Two jars (4.5 oz. non-dairy creamer) strained baby corn

Directions:

1. Thaw the butter in a saucepan, then add the black pepper and flour.

2. Stir well until smooth, then add the water and creamer.
3. Mix well and cook until the soup bubbles.
4. Add the baby corn and mix well.
5. Serve.

Per serving: Calories: 128Kcal; Protein: 0.6g; Carbohydrates: 8.1g; Fat: 9.1g

421. CABBAGE BEEF BORSCHT

Preparation time: 5 minutes

Cooking time: 2 hours

Servings: 12

Ingredients:

- Two tbsp. vegetable oil
- 3 lbs. beef short ribs
- 1/2 cup dry red wine
- 8 cups low-sodium chicken broth
- 1/2 tbs. berries
- 1/2 tbs. whole black peppercorns
- 1/2 tbs. coriander seeds
- Two dill sprigs
- Two oregano sprigs
- Two parsley sprigs
- Two tbsp. unsalted butter
- Three beets (1 1/2 lbs.), peeled and diced
- One small rutabaga (1/2 lb.), peeled and diced
- One leek, diced
- One small onion, diced (1 cup)
- 1/2 lb. carrots, diced
- Two celery ribs, diced
- 1/2 head savoy cabbage (1 lb.), cored and shredded
- 7 oz. chopped tomatoes, canned
- 1/2 cup dry red wine
- Two tbsp. red wine vinegar
- Freshly ground pepper
- 1/2 cup sour cream
- 1/4 cup chopped dill
- Horseradish, grated, for serving

Directions:

1. Start by placing the ribs in a large cooking pot and pour enough water to cover it.
2. Cover the beef pot and let simmer until it is tender, then shred it using a fork.
3. Add the olive oil, rutabaga, carrots, shredded cabbage, and the remaining ingredients to the cooking mixture in the pot.
4. Cover the cabbage soup and cook on low heat for 1 ½ hour.
5. Serve warm.

Per serving: Calories: 537Kcal; Protein: 18.7g; Carbohydrates: 10g; Fat: 45.5g

422. LEMON PEPPER BEEF SOUP

Preparation time: 5 minutes
Cooking time: 35 minutes
Servings: 6
Ingredients:

- 1 lb. lean ground beef
- 1/2 cup onion, chopped
- Two tsp. lemon-pepper seasoning blend
- 1 cup beef broth
- 2 cups of water
- 1/3 cup white rice, uncooked
- 3 cups of frozen mixed vegetables
- One tbs. sour cream
- Cooking oil

Directions:

1. Spray a saucepan with cooking oil and place it over moderate heat.
2. Toss in the onion and ground beef, and sauté until brown.
3. Stir in the broth, and the rest of the ingredients, then boil.
4. Reduce the heat to a simmer, then cover the soup to cook for another 30 minutes.
5. Garnish with sour cream.
6. Enjoy.

Per serving: Calories: 252Kcal; Protein: 27.2g; Carbohydrates: 21.3g; Fat: 5.6g

423. CREAM OF CRAB SOUP

Preparation time: 5 minutes
Cooking time: 20 minutes
Servings: 4
Ingredients:

- One tbs. unsalted butter
- 1/2 medium onion, chopped
- 1/2 lb. imitation crab meat, shredded
- 1/4 low-sodium chicken broth
- 1 cup coffee creamer
- Two tbsp. cornstarch
- 1/8 tsp. dillweed

Directions:

1. Add the butter to a cooking pan and melt it over moderate heat.
2. Toss in the onion and sauté until soft, then stir in the crab meat.
3. Stir-fry for 3 minutes then add the broth.
4. Cook up to a boil, then reduce the heat to low.
5. Whisk the coffee creamer with the cornstarch in a bowl until smooth.
6. Place this cornstarch slurry to the soup and cook until it thickens.
7. Stir in the dillweed and mix gently.
8. Serve warm.

Per serving: Calories: 232Kcal; Protein: 8.1g; Carbohydrates: 16.7g; Fat: 14.7g

424. CRAB AND SHRIMP GUMBO

Preparation time: 5 minutes
Cooking time: 25 minutes
Servings: 8
Ingredients:

- 1 cup bell pepper, chopped
- 1 1/2 cups onion, chopped
- One garlic clove, chopped
- 1/4 cup celery leaves, chopped
- 1 cup green onion tops
- 1/4 cup parsley, chopped
- Four tbsp. olive oil
- Six tbsp. flour
- 3 cups of water
- 4 cups chicken broth
- 8 oz. shrimp, uncooked
- 6 oz. crab meat
- 1/4 tsp. black pepper
- One tsp. hot sauce
- 3 cups rice, cooked

Directions:

1. First, prepare the roux in a suitable pan by heating oil in it.
2. Stir in the flour and sauté until it changes its color.
3. Pour in 1 cup of water, then add the onion, garlic, celery leaves, and bell pepper.
4. Cover the roux mixture and cook on low heat until the veggies turn soft.
5. Add two more cups of water and the chicken broth, then mix again.
6. Cook for 5 minutes, then add the crab meat and shrimp.
7. Cook for 10 minutes, then add the parsley and green onion.
8. Continue cooking for 5 minutes, then garnish with black pepper and hot sauce.
9. Serve warm with rice.

Per serving: Calories: 423Kcal; Protein: 17.8g; Carbohydrates: 47g; Fat: 9.2g

425. BEEF & VEGETABLE SOUP

Preparation time: 5 minutes
Cooking time: 55 minutes
Servings: 4
Ingredients:

- 1 lb. beef stew
- 3 ½ cups water
- 1 cup raw sliced onions
- ½ cup of frozen green peas
- One tsp. black pepper
- ½ cup frozen okra
- ½ tsp. basil
- ½ cup frozen carrots, diced
- ½ tsp. thyme
- ½ cup of frozen corn

Directions:

1. Put a large pot over moderate heat, then add the beef, water, thyme, basil, and black pepper.
2. Cook the beef for 45 minutes on a simmer.
3. Stir in the okra and other vegetables and cook until the meat is al dente.
4. Serve warm.

Per serving: Calories: 163Kcal; Protein: 8g; Carbohydrates: 19.3g; Fat: 6.5g

426. CHICKEN NOODLE SOUP

Preparation time: 5 minutes
Cooking time: 45 minutes
Servings: 6
Ingredients:

- 1 lb. chicken, cut into parts
- One tsp. red pepper
- ¼ cup lemon juice
- One tsp. caraway seed
- 3 ½ cups water
- One tsp. oregano
- One tbs. poultry seasoning
- 1/8 tsp. stevia
- One tsp. garlic powder
- ½ cup celery
- One tsp. onion powder
- ½ cup green pepper
- Two tbsp. vegetable oil
- 1 cup egg noodles
- One tsp. black pepper

Directions:

1. First, rub the chicken with lemon juice and place it in a large pot.
2. Add water, vegetable oil, all the spices, herbs, and the red pepper.
3. Cover the chicken soup and cook for about 30 minutes.
4. Stir in the noodles along with the other ingredients and cook for 15 minutes.
5. Serve.

Per serving: Calories: 213Kcal; Protein: 23.9g; Carbohydrates: 10g; Fat: 7.7g

427. TRADITIONAL CHICKEN-VEGETABLE SOUP

Preparation time: 20 minutes
Cooking time: 35 minutes
Servings: 6
Ingredients:

- One tbs. unsalted butter
- ½ sweet onion, diced
- Two tsp. minced garlic

- Two celery stalks, chopped
- One carrot, diced
- 2 cups chopped cooked chicken breast
- 1 cup Easy Chicken Stock
- 4 cups of water
- One tsp. chopped fresh thyme
- Freshly ground black pepper
- Two tbsp. chopped fresh parsley

Directions:

1. In a large pot over medium temperature, melt the butter.
2. Sauté the onion and garlic until softened, about 3 minutes.
3. Add the celery, carrot, chicken, chicken stock, and water.
4. Bring the soup to a boil, decrease the heat, and simmer for about 30 minutes or until the vegetables are tender.
5. Add the thyme; boil the soup for 2 minutes.
6. Season with pepper and serve topped with parsley.

Per serving: Calories: 121Kcal; Protein: 15g; Carbohydrates: 2g; Fat: 6g

428. GROUND BEEF AND RICE SOUP

Preparation time: 15 minutes
Cooking time: 40 minutes
Servings: 6
Ingredients:

- ½ pound extra-lean ground beef
- ½ small sweet onion, chopped
- One tsp. minced garlic
- 2 cups of water
- 1 cup homemade low-sodium beef broth
- ½ cup long-grain white rice, uncooked
- One celery stalk, chopped
- ½ cup fresh green beans, cut into 1-inch bits
- One tsp. chopped fresh thyme
- Freshly ground black pepper

Directions:

1. Place a huge saucepan over medium-high heat and add the ground beef.
2. Sauté, often stirring, for about 6 minutes or until the beef is completely browned.
3. Drain off the excess fat then add the onion and garlic to the saucepan.
4. Sauté the vegetables for about 3 minutes or until they are softened.
5. Add the water, beef broth, rice, and celery.

6. Bring the soup to a boil, decrease the heat to low, and simmer for about 30 minutes or until the rice is tender.
7. Add the green beans and thyme and simmer for 3 minutes.
8. Remove the soup from the heat and season with pepper.

Per serving: Calories: 154Kcal; Protein: 9g; Carbohydrates: 14g; Protein: 9g

429. HERBED CABBAGE STEW

Preparation time: 20 minutes
Cooking time: 35 minutes
Servings: 6
Ingredients:

- One tsp. unsalted butter
- ½ large sweet onion, chopped
- One tsp. minced garlic
- 6 cups shredded green cabbage
- Three celery stalks, chopped with the leafy tops
- One scallion, both green and white parts, chopped
- Two tbsp. chopped fresh parsley
- Two tbsp. freshly squeezed lemon juice
- One tbs. chopped fresh thyme
- One tsp. chopped savory
- One tsp. chopped fresh oregano
- Water
- 1 cup fresh green beans, sliced into 1-inch pieces
- Freshly ground black pepper

Directions:

1. In a medium stockpot over medium-high temperature, melt the butter.
2. Sauté the onion and garlic in the melted butter for about 3 minutes or until the vegetables are softened.
3. Add the cabbage, celery, scallion, parsley, lemon juice, thyme, savory, and oregano to the pot, and add sufficient water to cover the vegetables by about 4 inches.
4. Bring the soup to a boil, lessen the temperature to low, and simmer the soup for around 25 minutes or 'til the vegetables are tender.
5. Add the green beans then simmer for 3 minutes.
6. Season with pepper.

Per serving: Calories: 33kcal; Protein: 1g; Carbohydrates: 6g; Fat: 1g

430. WINTER CHICKEN STEW

Preparation time: 20 minutes
Cooking time: 50 minutes
Servings: 6

Ingredients:

- One tbs. olive oil
- 1-pound boneless, skinless chicken thighs, cut into 1-inch cubes
- ½ sweet onion, chopped
- One tbs. minced garlic
- 2 cups easy chicken stock
- 1 cup plus two tbsp. water
- One carrot, sliced
- Two celery stalks, sliced
- One turnip, sliced thin
- One tbs. chopped fresh thyme
- One tsp. finely chopped fresh rosemary
- Two tsp. cornstarch
- Freshly ground black pepper

Directions:

1. Place a large saucepan on medium-high temperature and add the olive oil.
2. Sauté the chicken for about 6 minutes or until it is lightly browned, stirring often.
3. Add the onion and garlic then sauté for 3 minutes.
4. Add the chicken stock, 1 cup water, carrot, celery, and turnip, and bring the stew to a boil.
5. Lessen the temperature to low and simmer for about 30 minutes or until the chicken is cooked through and tender.
6. Add the thyme and rosemary and simmer for three more minutes.
7. In a small bowl, stir together the two tbsp. water and the cornstarch, and add it to the stew.
8. Stir to incorporate the cornstarch mixture and cook for 3 to 4 minutes or until the stew thickens.
9. Remove from the heat then season with pepper.

Per serving: Calories: 141Kcal; Protein: 9g; Carbohydrates: 5g; Fat: 8g

431. CAULIFLOWER SOUP

Preparation time: 20 minutes
Cooking time: 30 minutes
Servings: 6
Ingredients:

- Unsalted butter – 1 tsp.
- Sweet onion – 1 small, chopped
- Minced Garlic – 2 tsp.
- Small head cauliflower – 1, cut into small florets
- Curry powder – 2 tsp.
- Water to cover the cauliflower
- Light sour cream – ½ cup
- Chopped fresh cilantro – 3 tbsps.

Directions:

1. In a huge saucepan, heat the butter over medium-high heat and sauté the onion-garlic for about 3 minutes or until softened.
2. Add the cauliflower, water, and curry powder.
3. Bring the solution to a boil, then lessen the heat to low and simmer for 20 minutes or until the cauliflower is tender.
4. Puree the soup until creamy and smooth with a hand mixer.
5. Transfer the soup back into a pan and stir in the sour cream and cilantro.
6. Heat the soup on medium heat for around 5 minutes or until warmed through.

Per serving: Calories: 33Kcal; Protein: 1g; Carbohydrates: 4g; Fat: 2g

432. CABBAGE STEW

Preparation time: 20 minutes
Cooking time: 35 minutes
Servings: 6
Ingredients:

- Unsalted butter – 1 tsp.
- Large sweet onion - ½, chopped
- Minced Garlic – 1 tsp.
- Shredded green cabbage – 6 cups
- Celery stalks - 3, chopped with leafy tops
- Scallion – 1, both green and white parts, chopped
- Chopped fresh parsley – 2 Tbsps.
- Freshly squeezed lemon juice – 2 Tbsps.
- Chopped fresh thyme – 1 Tbsp.
- Chopped savory – 1 tsp
- Chopped fresh oregano – 1 tsp.
- Water as needed
- Fresh green beans – 1 cup, cut into 1-inch pieces
- Ground black pepper

Directions:

1. Melt the butter in a pot.
2. Sauté the onion and garlic in the melted butter for 3 minutes, or until the vegetables are softened.
3. Add the celery, cabbage, scallion, parsley, lemon juice, thyme, savory, and oregano to the pot, add enough water to cover the vegetables by 4 inches.
4. Bring the soup to a boil. Change the heat to low and simmer the soup for 25 minutes or until the vegetables are tender.
5. Add the green beans then simmer for 3 minutes.

6. Season with pepper.

Per serving: Calories: 33Kcal; Protein: 1g; Carbohydrates: 6g; Fat: 1g

433. CHICKEN AND TORTILLA SOUP

Preparation time: 15 minutes
Cooking time: 6 hours
Servings: 12

- **Ingredients:**
- 3 chicken breasts (boneless and skinless)
- 15 ounces diced tomatoes
- 10 ounces enchilada sauce
- 1 chopped onion (med.)
- 4 ounces chopped chili pepper (green)
- 3 minced cloves garlic
- 2 cups water
- 14.5-ounces chicken broth (fat-free)
- 1 tbsp. cumin
- 1 tbs. chile powder
- 1 tsp. salt
- ¼ tsp. black pepper
- bay leaf as desired
- 1 tbsp. cilantro (chopped)
- 10 ounces frozen corn
- 3 tortillas, cut into thin slices

Directions:

1. Put all the listed fixings in the slow cooker. Stir well to mix. Cook on low heat within 8 hrs. or high heat for 6 hrs. Shred the chicken breasts into a plate. Add chicken to other ingredients. Serve hot, garnished with tortilla slices.

Per serving: Calories: 93.4Kcal; Protein: 8.1g; Carbohydrates: 11.5g; Fat: 1.6g

434. CHICKEN AND RICE SOUP

Preparation time: 15 minutes
Cooking time: 8 hours
Servings: 6
Ingredients:

- 1-pound boneless, skinless chicken thighs, cut into 1-inch pieces
- 1 onion, chopped
- 3 carrots, peeled and sliced
- 2 celery stalks, sliced
- 6 cups Poultry Broth or store-bought
- 1 tsp. garlic powder
- 1 tsp. dried rosemary
- ¼ tsp. of sea salt
- ¼ tsp. freshly ground black pepper
- 3 cups cooked Brown Rice

Directions:

1. In your slow cooker, combine the chicken, onion, carrots, celery,

broth, garlic powder, rosemary, salt, and pepper.
2. Cover and cook on low within 8 hours. Stir in the rice about 10 minutes before serving, and allow the broth to warm it.

Per serving: Calories: 354Kcal; Protein: 28g; Carbohydrates: 43g; Fat: 7g

435. TOM KHA GAI

Preparation time: 15 minutes
Cooking time: 8 hours
Servings: 6

- **Ingredients:**
- 1-pound boneless, skinless chicken thighs, cut into 1-inch pieces
- 1-pound fresh shiitake mushrooms halved
- 2 tbsp. grated fresh ginger
- 3 cups canned light coconut milk
- 3 cups Poultry Broth or store-bought
- 1 tbs. Asian fish sauce
- 1 tsp. garlic powder
- ¼ tsp. freshly ground black pepper
- Juice of 1 lime
- 2 tbsp. chopped fresh cilantro

Directions:

1. In your slow cooker, combine the chicken thighs, mushrooms, ginger, coconut milk, broth, fish sauce, garlic powder, and pepper.
2. Cover and cook on low within 8 hours. Stir in the lime juice and cilantro just before serving.

Per serving: Calories: 481Kcal; Protein: 28g; Carbohydrates: 19g; Fat: 35g

436. CHICKEN CORN CHOWDER

Preparation time: 15 minutes
Cooking time: 8 hours
Servings: 6
Ingredients:

- 1-pound boneless, skinless chicken thighs, cut into 1-inch pieces
- 2 onions, chopped
- 3 jalapeño peppers, seeded and minced
- 2 red bell peppers, seeded and chopped
- 1½ cups fresh or frozen corn
- 6 cups Poultry Broth or store-bought
- 1 tsp. garlic powder
- ½ tsp. of sea salt
- ¼ tsp. freshly ground black pepper
- 1 cup skim milk

Directions:

1. In your slow cooker, combine the chicken, onions, jalapeños, red bell peppers, corn, broth, garlic powder, salt, and pepper.
2. Cover and cook on low within 8 hours. Stir in the skim milk just before serving.

Per serving: Calories: 236Kcal; Protein: 28g; Carbohydrates: 17g; Fat: 6g

437. TURKEY GINGER SOUP

Preparation time: 15 minutes

Cooking time: 8 hours

Servings: 6

Ingredients:

- 1-pound boneless, skinless turkey thighs, cut into 1-inch pieces
- 1-pound fresh shiitake mushrooms halved
- 3 carrots, peeled and sliced
- 2 cups frozen peas
- 1 tbs. grated fresh ginger
- 6 cups Poultry Broth or store-bought
- 1 tbs. low-sodium soy sauce
- 1 tsp. toasted sesame oil
- 2 tsp. garlic powder
- 1½ cups cooked Brown Rice

Directions:

1. In your slow cooker, combine the turkey, mushrooms, carrots, peas, ginger, broth, soy sauce, sesame oil, and garlic powder.
2. Cover and cook on low within 8 hours. About 30 minutes before serving, stir in the rice to warm it through.

Per serving: Calories: 318Kcal; Protein: 24g; Carbohydrates: 42g; Fat: 7g

438. ITALIAN WEDDING SOUP

Preparation time: 15 minutes

Cooking time: 7 hours

Servings: 6

Ingredients:

- 1-pound ground turkey breast
- 1½ cups cooked Brown Rice
- 1 onion, grated
- ¼ cup chopped fresh parsley
- 1 egg, beaten
- 1 tsp. garlic powder
- 1 tsp. sea salt, divided
- 6 cups Poultry Broth or store-bought
- 1/8 tsp. freshly ground black pepper
- Pinch red pepper flakes
- 1-pound kale, tough stems removed, leaves chopped

Directions:

1. In a small bowl, combine the turkey breast, rice, onion, parsley, egg, garlic powder, and ½ tsp. of sea salt. Roll the mixture into ½-inch meatballs and put them in the slow cooker.
2. Add the broth, black pepper, red pepper flakes, and the remaining ½ tsp. of sea salt. Cover and cook on low for 7 to 8 hours. Before serving, stir in the kale. Cover and cook until the kale wilts.

Per serving: Calories: 302Kcal; Protein: 29g; Carbohydrates: 29g; Fat: 7g

439. TACO SOUP

Preparation time: 15 minutes

Cooking time: 8 hours

Servings: 6

Ingredients:

- 1-pound ground turkey breast
- 1 onion, chopped
- 1 can tomatoes and green chilis, with their juice
- 6 cups Poultry Broth or store-bought
- 1 tsp. chili powder
- 1 tsp. ground cumin
- ½ tsp. of sea salt
- ¼ cup chopped fresh cilantro
- Juice of 1 lime
- ½ cup grated low-fatCheddar cheese

Directions:

1. Crumble the turkey into the slow cooker. Add the onion, tomatoes, green chilis (with their juice), broth, chili powder, cumin, and salt.
2. Cover and cook on low within 8 hours. Stir in the cilantro and lime juice. Serve garnished with the cheese.

Per serving: Calories: 281Kcal; Protein: 30g; Carbohydrates: 20g; Fat: 10g

440. ITALIAN SAUSAGE AND FENNEL SOUP

Preparation time: 15 minutes

Cooking time: 8 hours

Servings: 6

Ingredients:

- 1-pound Italian chicken or turkey sausage, cut into ½-inch slices
- 2 onions, chopped
- 1 fennel bulb, chopped
- 6 cups Poultry Broth or store-bought
- ¼ cup dry sherry
- 1½ tsp. garlic powder
- 1 tsp. dried thyme

- ½ tsp. of sea salt
- ¼ tsp. freshly ground black pepper
- Pinch red pepper flakes

Directions:

1. In your slow cooker, combine all the ingredients.
2. Cover and cook on low within 8 hours.

Per serving: Calories: 311Kcal; Protein: 18g; Carbohydrates: 8g; Fat: 22g

441. STUFFED PEPPER SOUP

Preparation time: 15 minutes

Cooking time: 8 hours and 10 minutes

Servings: 6

Ingredients:

- 1 lb. ground Beef (drained)
- 1 chopped onion (large)
- 2 cups Tomatoes (diced)
- 2 chopped Green Peppers
- 2 cups Tomato Sauce
- 1 tbs. Beef Bouillon
- 3 cups of water
- Pepper
- 1 tsp. of Salt
- 1 cup of cooked rice (white)

Directions:

1. Place all ingredients in a cooker. Cook for 8 hours on "low." Serve hot.

Per serving: Calories: 216.1Kcal; Protein: 18.3g; Carbohydrates: 21.8g; Fat: 5.2g

442. HAM AND PEA SOUP

Preparation time: 15 minutes

Cooking time: 8 hours

Servings: 8

Ingredients:

- 1 lb. Split Peas (dried)
- 1 cup sliced Celery
- 1 cup sliced Carrots
- 1 cup sliced Onion
- 2 cups chopped ham (cooked)
- 8 cups of water

Directions:

1. Place all the listed fixings in the slow cooker. Cook on "high" within 4 hrs. Serve hot.

Per serving: Calories: 118.6Kcal; Protein: 11.6g; Carbohydrates: 14.5g; Fat: 1.3g

443. CHIPOTLE SQUASH SOUP

Preparation time: 15 minutes

Cooking time: 4 hours and 20 minutes

Servings: 6

Ingredients:

- 6 cups butternut squash (cubed)

- ½ cup chopped onion
- 2 tsp. adobo chipotle
- 2 cups chicken broth
- 1 tbsp. brown sugar
- ¼ cup tart apple (chopped)
- 1 cup yogurt (greek style)
- 2 tbsp. chives (chopped)

Directions:

1. Except for yogurt, chives, and apple, place all the ingredients in the slow cooker. Cook on "low" for 4 hrs. Now, in a blender or food processor, puree the cooked ingredients. Transfer puree to slow cooker.
2. Put the yogurt and cook on "Low" within 20 more mins. Garnish with chives and apples. Serve hot in heated bowls.

Per serving: Calories: 102Kcal; Protein: 2g; Carbohydrates: 22g; Fat: 1g

444. CHICKEN SQUASH SOUP

Preparation time: 15 minutes

Cooking time: 5 hours & 30 minutes

Servings: 3

Ingredients:

- ½ Butternut Squash (large)
- 1 clove garlic
- 1 ¼ quarts broth (vegetable or chicken)
- 1/8 tsp. pepper (white)
- ½ tbsp. chopped parsley
- 2 minced sage leaves
- 1 tbsp. olive oil
- ¼ chopped onion (white)
- 1/16 tsp. black pepper (cracked)
- 1/2 tbsp. of pepper flakes (chili)
- ½ tsp. chopped rosemary

Directions:

1. Pre-heat oven to 400 degrees. Grease a baking sheet. Roast the squash in a preheated oven for 30 mins. Transfer it to a plate and let it cool. Sauté onion and garlic in the oil.
2. Now, scoop out the flesh from the roasted squash and add to the sautéed onion and garlic. Mash all of it well. Pour ½ quart of the broth into the slow cooker. Add the squash mixture. Cook on "low" for 4 hrs. Using a blender, make a smooth puree.
3. Transfer the puree to the slow cooker. Add in the rest of the broth and other ingredients. Cook again for 1 hr. on "high". Serve in heated soup bowls.

Per serving: Calories: 158Kcal; Protein: 3g; Carbohydrates: 24g; Fats: 3g

445. VEGGIE AND BEEF SOUP

Preparation time: 15 minutes

Cooking time: 4 hours

Servings: 4

Ingredients:

- 1 chopped Carrot
- 1 chopped Celery Rib
- ¾ l. Sirloin (ground)
- 1 cup Water
- ½ butternut squash (large)
- 1 clove garlic
- ½ quart beef broth
- 7 ounces diced tomatoes (unsalted)
- ½ tsp. kosher salt
- 1 tbsp. chopped parsley
- ¼ tsp. thyme (dried)
- ¼ tsp. black pepper (ground)
- ½ bay leaf

Directions:

1. Sauté all the vegetables in oil. Put the vegetables to the side, then place sirloin in the center. Sauté, using a spoon to crumble the meat. When cooked, combine with the vegetables on the sides of the pan.
2. Now, pour the rest of the ingredients into the slow cooker. Add cooked meat and vegetables. Stir well. Cook on "low" for 3 hrs. Serve in soup bowls.

Per serving: Calories: 217Kcal; Protein: 2g; Carbohydrates: 17g; Fats: 2g

446. COLLARD, SWEET POTATO AND PEA SOUP

Preparation time: 15 minutes

Cooking time: 4 hours

Servings: 4

Ingredients:

- 3 1/2 oz. Ham Steak, chopped
- ½ chopped Yellow Onion
- ½ lb. sliced Sweet Potatoes
- ¼ tsp. Red Pepper (hot and crushed)
- ½ cup frozen Peas (black-eyed)
- ½ tbsp. Canola Oil
- 1 minced clove of Garlic
- 1 ½ cup Water
- ¼ tsp. Salt
- 2 cups Collard Greens (julienned and without stems)

Directions:

1. Sauté ham with garlic and onion in oil. In a slow cooker, place other ingredients except for collard greens and peas.
2. Add in the ham mixture. Cook on "low" for 3 hrs. Now, add collard green and peas and cook again for

an hour on "low." Serve in soup bowls.

Per serving: Calories: 172Kcal; Protein: 1g; Carbohydrates: 24g; Fats: 1g

447. BEAN SOUP

Preparation time: 15 minutes

Cooking time: 5 hours

Servings: 4

Ingredients:

- ½ cup Pinto Beans (dried)
- ½ Bay Leaf
- 1 clove Garlic
- ½ onion (white)
- 2 cups Water
- 2 tbsp. Cilantro (chopped)
- 1 cubed Avocado
- 1/8 cup White Onion (chopped)
- ¼ cup Roma Tomatoes (chopped)
- 2 tbsp. Pepper Sauce (chipotle)
- ¼ tsp. Kosher Salt
- 2 tbsp. chopped Cilantro
- 2 tbsp. Low Fat: Monterrey Jack Cheese, shredded

Directions:

1. Place water, salt, onion, pepper, garlic, bay leaf, and beans in the slow cooker.
2. Cook on high for 5-6 hours. Discard the Bay leaf. Serve in heated bowls.

Per serving: Calories: 258Kcal; Protein: 3g; Carbohydrates: 25g; Fats: 1g

448. BROWN RICE AND CHICKEN SOUP

Preparation time: 15 minutes

Cooking time: 4 hours

Servings: 4

Ingredients:

- 1/3 cups Brown Rice
- 1 chopped Leek
- 1 sliced Celery Rib
- 1 ½ cups water
- ½ tsp. Kosher Salt
- ½ Bay Leaf
- 1/8 tsp. Thyme (dried)
- ¼ tsp. Black Pepper (ground)
- 1 tbsp. chopped parsley
- ½ quart Chicken Broth (low sodium)
- 1 sliced Carrot
- ¾ lb. of Chicken Thighs (skin and boneless)

Directions:

1. Boil 1 cup of water with ½ tsp. of salt in a saucepan. Add the rice. Cook for 30 mins on medium flame. Brown chicken pieces in the oil.

1. Transfer the chicken to a plate when done.
2. In the same pan, sauté the vegetables for 3 mins. Now, place the chicken pieces in the slow cooker. Add water and broth. Cook on "low" for 3 hrs. Put the rest of the fixing, the rice last. Cook again for 10 mins on "high." After discarding Bay leaf, serve in soup bowls.

Per serving: Calories: 208Kcal; Protein: 2g; Carbohydrates: 18g; Fats: 1g

449. BUTTERNUT SQUASH SOUP

Preparation time: 15 minutes
Cooking time: 8 hours
Servings: 6
Ingredients:

- 1 butternut squash, peeled, seeded, and diced
- 1 onion, chopped
- 1 sweet-tart apple (such as Braeburn), peeled, cored, and chopped
- 3 cups Vegetable Broth or store-bought
- 1 tsp. garlic powder
- ½ tsp. ground sage
- ¼ tsp. of sea salt
- ¼ tsp. freshly ground black pepper
- Pinch cayenne pepper
- Pinch nutmeg
- ½ cup fat-free half-and-half

Directions:

1. In your slow cooker, combine the squash, onion, apple, broth, garlic powder, sage, salt, black pepper, cayenne, and nutmeg. Cook on low within 8 hours.
2. Using an immersion blender, counter-top blender, or food processor, purée the soup, adding the half-and-half as you do. Stir to combine, and serve.

Per serving: Calories: 106Kcal; Protein: 3g; Carbohydrates: 26g; Fat: 0g

450. CHICKPEA AND KALE SOUP

Preparation time: 15 minutes
Cooking time: 9 hours
Servings: 6
Ingredients:

- 1 summer squash, quartered lengthwise and sliced crosswise
- 1 zucchini, quartered lengthwise and sliced crosswise
- 2 cups cooked chickpeas, rinsed
- 1 cup uncooked quinoa

- 2 cans diced tomatoes, with their juice
- 5 cups vegetable broth, poultry broth, or store-bought
- 1 tsp. garlic powder
- 1 tsp. onion powder
- 1 tsp. dried thyme
- ½ tsp. of sea salt
- 2 cups chopped kale leaves

Directions:

1. In your slow cooker, combine the summer squash, zucchini, chickpeas, quinoa, tomatoes (with their juice), broth, garlic powder, onion powder, thyme, and salt.
2. Cover and cook on low within 8 hours. Stir in the kale.
3. Cover and cook on low for 1 more hour.

Per serving: Calories: 221Kcal; Protein: 10g; Carbohydrates: 40g; Fat: 3g

451. CLAM CHOWDER

Preparation time: 15 minutes
Cooking time: 8 hours
Servings: 6
Ingredients:

- 1 red onion, chopped
- 3 carrots, peeled and chopped
- 1 fennel bulb and fronds, chopped
- 1 (10-ounce) can chopped clams, with their juice
- 1-pound baby red potatoes, quartered
- 4 cups poultry broth or store-bought
- ½ tsp. of sea salt
- 1/8 tsp. freshly ground black pepper
- 2 cups skim milk
- ¼ pound turkey bacon, browned and crumbled, for garnish

Directions:

1. In your slow cooker, combine the onion, carrots, fennel bulb and fronds, clams (with their juice), potatoes, broth, salt, and pepper.
2. Cover and cook on low within 8 hours. Stir in the milk and serve garnished with the crumbled bacon.

Per serving: Calories: 172Kcal; Protein: 10g; Carbohydrates: 29g; Fat: 1g

452. BEEF AND BARLEY SOUP

Preparation time: 15 minutes
Cooking time: 8 hours
Servings: 6
Ingredients:

- 1-pound extra-lean ground beef
- 2 onions, chopped
- 3 carrots, peeled and sliced

- 1-pound fresh mushrooms, quartered
- 1½ cups dried barley
- 6 cups Beef Broth or store-bought
- 1 tsp. ground mustard
- 1 tsp. dried thyme
- 1 tsp. garlic powder
- ¼ tsp. of sea salt
- 1/8 tsp. freshly ground black pepper

Directions:

3. In your slow cooker, crumble the ground beef into small pieces.
1. Add the remaining ingredients.
2. Cover and cook on low within 8 hours.

Per serving: Calories: 319Kcal; Protein: 28g; Carbohydrates: 44g; Fat: 5g

453. LEEK AND CAULIFLOWER SOUP

Preparation time: 20 minutes
Cooking time: 20 minutes
Servings: 6
Ingredients:

- 1 tbs. olive oil
- 1 leek, trimmed & sliced thin
- 1 yellow onion, peeled & diced
- 1 head cauliflower, chopped into florets
- 3 cloves garlic, minced
- 2 tbsp. thyme, fresh & chopped
- 1 tsp. smoked paprika
- 1 ¼ tsp. sea salt, fine
- 1/4teaspoon ground cayenne pepper
- 1 tbs. heavy cream
- 3 cups vegetable stock, unsalted
- ½ lemon, juiced & zested

Directions:

1. Heat your oil in a stockpot over medium heat, and add in your leek, onion, and cauliflower. Cook for around 5 minutes or 'til the onion begins to soften. Add in your garlic, thyme, smoked paprika, salt, pepper and cayenne. Pour in your vegetable stock and bring it to a simmer, cooking for fifteen minutes. Your cauliflower should be very tender.
2. Remove from heat then stir in your lemon juice, lemon zest and cream. Use an immersion blender to puree, and serve warm.

Per serving: Calories: 92Kcal; Protein: 5 g; Carbohydrates: 13g; Fat: 4g

454. CHICKEN WILD RICE SOUP

Preparation time: 10 minutes
Cooking time: 15 minutes

Servings: 6

Ingredients:

- 2/3 cup wild rice, uncooked
- 1 tbs. onion, chopped finely
- 1 tbs. fresh parsley, chopped
- 1 cup carrots, chopped
- 8-ounces chicken breast, cooked
- 2 tbs. butter
- 1/4 cup all-purpose white flour
- 5 cups low-sodium chicken broth
- 1 tbs. slivered almonds

Directions:

1. Start by adding rice and 2 cups broth along with ½ cup water to a cooking pot. Cook the chicken until the rice is al dente and set it aside. Add butter to a saucepan and melt it.
2. Stir in onion and sauté until soft then add the flour and the remaining broth.
3. Stir it and then cook for about 1 minute then add the chicken, cooked rice, and carrots. Cook for 5 minutes on simmer. Garnish with almonds. Serve fresh.

Per serving: Calories: 287Kcal; Protein: 21g; Carbohydrates: 30g; Fat: 35g

455. CLASSIC CHICKEN SOUP

Preparation time: 10 minutes

Cooking time: 25 minutes

Servings: 2

Ingredients:

- 1 1/2 cups low-sodium vegetable broth
- 1 cup of water
- 1/4 tsp. poultry seasoning
- 1/4 tsp. black pepper
- 1 cup chicken strips
- 1/4 cup carrot
- 2-ounces egg noodles, uncooked

Directions:

1. Gather all the ingredients into a slow cooker and toss it.
2. Cook soup on high heat for 25 minutes.
3. Serve warm.

Per serving: Calories: 103Kcal; Protein: 8g; Carbohydrates: 18g; Fat: 11g

456. CUCUMBER SOUP

Preparation time: 10 minutes

Cooking time: 0 minute

Servings: 4

Ingredients:

- 2 medium cucumbers
- 1/3 cup sweet white onion

- 1 green onion
- 1/4 cup fresh mint
- 2 tbsp. fresh dill
- 2 tbsp. lemon juice
- 2/3 cup water
- 1/2 cup half and half cream
- 1/3 cup sour cream
- 1/2 tsp. pepper
- Fresh dill sprigs for garnish

Directions:

1. Situate all of the ingredients into a food processor and toss.
2. Puree the mixture and refrigerate for 2 hours. Garnish with dill sprigs. Enjoy fresh.

Per serving: Calories: 77Kcal; Protein: 2g; Carbohydrates: 8g; Fat: 6g

457. SQUASH AND TURMERIC SOUP

Preparation time: 10 minutes

Cooking time: 30 minutes

Servings: 4

Ingredients:

- 4 cups low-sodium vegetable broth
- 2 medium zucchini squash
- 2 medium yellow crookneck squash
- 1 small onion
- 1/2 cup frozen green peas
- 2 tbsp. olive oil
- 1/2 cup plain nonfat Greek yogurt
- 2 tsp. turmeric

Directions:

1. Warm the broth in a saucepan on medium heat. Toss in onion, squash, and zucchini. Let it simmer for approximately 25 minutes then add oil and green peas.
2. Cook for another 5 minutes then allow it to cool. Puree the soup using a handheld blender then add Greek yogurt and turmeric. Refrigerate it overnight and serve fresh.

Per serving: Calories: 100Kcal; Protein: 4g; Carbohydrates: 16g; Fat: 10g

458. LEEK, POTATO, AND CARROT SOUP

Preparation time: 15 minutes

Cooking time: 25 minutes

Servings: 4

Ingredients:

- 1 - leek
- ¾ - cup diced and boiled potatoes
- ¾ - cup diced and boiled carrots
- 1 - garlic clove
- 1 - tbs. oil
- Crushed pepper to taste

- 3 - cups low sodium chicken stock
- Chopped parsley for garnish
- 1 - bay leaf
- ¼ - tsp. ground cumin

Directions:

1. Trim off and remove a portion of the coarse portions of the leek. Warm the oil in an extensively based pot. Add the leek and garlic, and sear over low warmth for 2-3 minutes, till sensitive.
2. Include the inventory, inlet leaf, cumin, and pepper. Heat the mixture, mix constantly. Add the bubbled potatoes and carrots and stew for 10-15minutes Modify the flavoring, eliminate the inlet leaf, and serve sprinkled generously with slashed parsley.
3. To make a pureed soup, mix the soup in a blender or processor till smooth Return to the pan. Add ½ field milk. Bring to a bubble and stew for 2-3minutes.

Per serving: Calories: 315Kcal; Protein: 15g; Carbohydrates: 25g; Fat: 8g

459. KALE CHICKEN SOUP

Preparation time: 12 minutes.

Cooking time: 18 minutes.

Servings: 6.

Ingredients:

- 1 tbs. Olive Oil.
- 3 Cups Kale, Chopped.
- 1 Cup Carrot, Minced.
- 2 Cloves Garlic, Minced.
- 8 Cups Chicken Broth, Low Sodium.
- Sea Salt & Black Pepper to Taste.
- ¾ Cup Patina Pasta, Uncooked.
- 2 Cups Chicken, Cooked & Shredded.
- 3 Tablespoons Parmesan Cheese, Grated.

Directions:

1. Start by getting out a stockpot over medium heat and heat your oil. Add in your garlic, cooking for half a minute. Stir frequently and add in the kale and carrots. Cook for an additional five minutes, and make sure to stir so it doesn't burn.
2. Add in salt, pepper, and broth, turning the heat to high. Boil before adding in your pasta.
3. Set the heat to medium then cook for an extra ten minutes. Your pasta should be cooked all the way through, but make sure to stir occasionally so it doesn't stick to the bottom. Add in the chicken, and cook for two minutes.

4. Ladle the soup and serve topped with cheese.

Per serving: Calories: 187Kcal; Protein: 15g; Carbohydrates: 228g; Fat: 5g

460. ROASTED ROOT VEGETABLE SOUP

Preparation time: 10 minutes

Cooking time: 35 minutes

Servings: 6

Ingredients:
- 2 parsnips, peeled and sliced
- 2 carrots, peeled and sliced
- 2 sweet potatoes, peeled and sliced
- 1 tsp. chopped fresh rosemary
- 1 tsp. chopped fresh thyme
- 1 tsp. sea salt
- ½ tsp. freshly ground black pepper
- 2 tbsp. extra-virgin olive oil
- 4 cups low-sodium vegetable soup
- ½ cup grated Parmesan cheese, for garnish (optional)

Directions:
1. Pre-heat the oven to 400 deg. F (205°C). Line a baking sheet with aluminum foil.
2. Combine the parsnips, carrots, and sweet potatoes in a large bowl, then sprinkle with rosemary, thyme, salt, and pepper, and drizzle with olive oil. Toss to coat the vegetables well.
3. Arrange the vegetables on the baking sheet, then roast in the pre-heated oven for 30 minutes or until lightly browned and soft. Flip the vegetables halfway through the roasting.
4. Pour the roasted vegetables with vegetable broth in a food processor, then pulse until creamy and smooth.
5. Pour the puréed vegetables in a saucepan, then warm over low heat until heated through.
6. Spoon the soup in a large serving bowl, then scatter with Parmesan cheese. Serve immediately.
7. Tip: If you don't have vegetable soup, just use the same amount of water to replace it.

Per serving: Calories: 192Kcal; Protein: 4.8g; Carbohydrates: 31.5g; Fat: 5.7g

CHAPTER 9: Snacks and Appetizers

461. CABBAGE APPLE STIR-FRY

Preparation time: 15 minutes

Cooking time: 10 minutes

Servings: 4

Ingredients:

- Two tbsp. extra-virgin olive oil
- 3 cups chopped red cabbage
- Two tbsp. water
- 1 granny smith apple, chopped
- three scallions, both white and green parts, chopped
- One tbs. freshly squeezed lemon juice
- One tsp. caraway seed
- Pinch salt

Directions:

1. In a big skillet or frying pan, heat the olive oil over medium-high temperature.
2. Add the cabbage and stir-fry for 2 minutes. Add the water, cover, and cook for 2 minutes.
3. Uncover and stir in the apple and scallions and sprinkle with the lemon juice, caraway seeds, and salt—Stir-fry for 4 to 6 minutes longer, or until the cabbage is crisp-tender. Serve.

Per serving: Calories: 106Kcal; Protein: 1g; Carbohydrates: 11g; Fat: 7g

462. PARMESAN ROASTED CAULIFLOWER

Preparation time: 15 minutes

Cooking time: 25 minutes

Servings: 4

Ingredients:

- 4 cups cauliflower florets
- ½ cup grated Parmesan cheese
- Two tbsp. extra-virgin olive oil
- Four garlic cloves, minced
- ½ tsp. dried thyme leaves
- ¼ tsp. freshly ground black pepper
- 1/8 tsp. salt

Directions:

1. Preheat the oven to 400°F.
2. Combine the cauliflower, Parmesan cheese, olive oil, garlic, thyme, pepper, salt on a baking sheet, and toss to coat.
3. Bake for 25 to 30 minutes, stirring once during the cooking time until the cauliflower has light golden-brown edges and is tender. Serve.

Per serving: Calories: 144Kcal; Protein: 6g; Carbohydrates: 4g; Fat: 11g

463. CELERY AND FENNEL SALAD WITH CRANBERRIES

Preparation time: 15 minutes

Cooking time: 0 minutes

Servings: 6

Ingredients:

- ¼ cup extra-virgin olive oil
- Two tbsp. freshly squeezed lemon juice
- One tbs. Dijon mustard
- 2 cups sliced celery
- ½ cup chopped fennel
- ½ cup dried cranberries
- Two tbsp. minced celery leaves

Directions:

1. In a serving bowl, paddle the olive oil, lemon juice, and mustard.
2. Add the celery, fennel, and cranberries to the dressing and toss to coat. Sprinkle with the celery leaves and serve.

Per serving: Calories: 130Kcal; Protein: 1g; Carbohydrates: 13g; Fat: 9g

464. KALE WITH CARAMELIZED ONIONS

Preparation time: 15 minutes

Cooking time: 20 minutes

Servings: 4

Ingredients:

- One yellow onion, chopped
- Two tbsp. butter
- One tbs. extra-virgin olive oil
- One bunch kale, rinsed and torn into pieces
- Two tbsp. water
- One tbs. freshly squeezed lemon juice
- One tsp. maple syrup
- Salt
- Freshly ground black pepper

Directions:

1. In a heavy saucepan, combine the onion, butter, and olive oil over medium heat. Cook for about 3 minutes, until the onion starts to become translucent, stirring frequently.
2. Reduce the heat to low and continue cooking for 10 to 15 minutes longer, frequently stirring, until the onion starts to brown.
3. Surge the heat to medium and add the kale and water. Cover the pan and cook for about 2 minutes, shaking the pan occasionally, until the kale starts to soften.
4. Add the lemon juice and maple syrup and season with salt and pepper. Cook for 3 to 4 minutes longer, frequently stirring, until the kale is tender. Serve.

Per serving: Calories: 115Kcal; Protein: 2g; Carbohydrates: 6g; Fat: 10g

465. BAKED JICAMA FRIES

Preparation time: 20 minutes

Cooking time: 50 minutes

Servings: 4

Ingredients:

- 1-pound jicama root
- Two tbsp. butter
- One tbs. extra-virgin olive oil
- One tsp. chili powder
- One tsp. paprika
- ¼ tsp. salt
- 1/8 tsp. freshly ground black pepper
- Two tbsp. grated Parmesan cheese

Directions:

1. Peel the jicama and cut into ½-inch slices. Cut the slices into strips, each about 4 inches long.
2. In a large saucepan, place the jicama strips and cover with water. Bring to a boil, then boil for 9 minutes. Drain the jicama well and transfer to a rimmed baking sheet. Pat the strips with a paper towel while waiting for them to dry so that the stripes will crisp in the oven.
3. Pre-heat the oven to 400°F.
4. In a mini saucepan, melt the butter with the olive oil. Drizzle over the jicama on the baking sheet. Sprinkle with the chili powder, paprika, salt, and pepper and toss to coat. Spread the strips into a single layer.
5. Bake the jicama fries for 40 to 45 minutes or until they are browned and crisp, turning once with a spatula halfway through the cooking time.
6. Sprinkle with the Parmesan cheese and serve.

Per serving: Calories: 140Kcal; Protein: 2g; Carbohydrates: 11g; Fat: 10g

466. DOUBLE-BOILED SWEET POTATOES

Preparation time: 20 minutes
Cooking time: 25 minutes
Servings: 4
Ingredients:

- Two large sweet potatoes, peeled and cut into 1-inch cubes
- Two tbsp. extra-virgin olive oil
- Two tbsp. butter
- One red onion, chopped
- ¼ cup half-and-half
- One tbs. honey
- ¼ tsp. salt
- 1/8 tsp. freshly ground black pepper

Directions:

1. In a large saucepan, fill the pot with water to about an inch above the potatoes. Add the sweet potato cubes and bring to a boil. Boil for 10 minutes.
2. Drain the sweet potatoes, discarding the water.
3. In the same saucepan, fill the pot to the same level again. Add the sweet potato cubes and bring to a boil for 10 to 15 minutes, or until the potatoes are tender.
4. In the meantime, in a huge frying pan, heat the olive oil and butter. Add the red onion and cook for 3 to 5 minutes, stirring, until the onion is very tender.
5. Drain the sweet potatoes once more, discarding the water again. Add the sweet potatoes in your skillet along with the half-and-half, honey, salt, and pepper.
6. Pound the potatoes, using an immersion blender or a potato masher, until the desired consistency. Serve.

Per serving: Calories: 246Kcal; Protein: 2g; Carbohydrates: 29g; Fat: 14g

467. EDAMAME GUACAMOLE

Preparation time: 10 minutes
Cooking time: 0 minutes
Servings: 4
Ingredients:

- 1 cup frozen shelled edamame, thawed
- ¼ cup of water
- Juice and zest of 1 lemon
- Two tbsp. chopped fresh cilantro
- One tbs. olive oil
- One tsp. minced garlic

Directions:

1. In your food processor or blender, blend the edamame, water, lemon juice, lemon zest, cilantro, olive oil, and garlic, and pulse until blended but still a bit chunky.
2. Serve fresh.

Per serving: Calories: 63Kcal; Protein: 3g; Carbohydrates: 1g; Fat: 5g

468. TOASTED PEAR CHIPS

Preparation time: 15 minutes
Cooking time: 3 to 4 hours
Servings: 4
Ingredients:

- Olive oil cooking spray
- Four firm pears, cored and cut into 1/8-inch-thick slices
- Two tsp. ground cinnamon
- One tbs. sugar

Directions:

1. Pre-heat the oven to 200°F.
2. Line a baking sheet with parchment paper, then lightly coat with cooking spray.
3. Spread the pear slices on the baking sheet with no overlap.
4. Sprinkle with the cinnamon and sugar.
5. Bake until the chips are dry, 3 to 4 hours. Cool completely.
6. Store in a sealed container for up to 4 days in a cool, dark place.

Per serving: Calories: 101Kcal; Protein: 1g; Carbohydrates: 27g; Fat: 0g

469. CITRUS SESAME COOKIES

Preparation time: 15 minutes
Cooking time: 10 minutes
Servings: 18
Ingredients:

- ¾ cup unsalted butter, at room temperature
- ½ cup of sugar
- One egg
- One tsp. vanilla extract
- 2 cups all-purpose flour
- Two tbsp. toasted sesame seeds
- ½ tsp. baking soda
- One tsp. freshly grated lemon zest
- One tsp. freshly grated orange zest

Directions:

1. Pulse together the margarine and sugar on high speed up until thick and fluffy, around 3 minutes.
2. Add the egg and vanilla, then beat to mix carefully, grinding down the sides of the bowl.
3. In a small container, stir together the flour, sesame seeds, baking soda, lemon zest, and orange zest.
4. Put the flour mix into the butter mixture, and stir until well blended.
5. Roll the dough into a long cylinder around 2 inches in diameter, and wrap in plastic wrap. Chill for an hour.
6. Turn on the oven to 350°F.
7. Line a baking sheet with parchment paper.
8. Cut the firm cookie dough into ½-inch-thick rounds, and place them on the prepared baking sheet.
9. Bake for around 10 to 12 minutes until lightly golden. Cool completely on wire racks.
10. Place in a sealed container and store in the refrigerator for up to 1 week. You can also store it in the freezer for up to 2 months.

Per serving: Calories: 150Kcal; Protein: 2g; Carbohydrates: 16g; Fat: 9g

470. CRUNCHY CHICKEN SALAD WRAPS

Preparation time: 15 minutes
Cooking time: 0 minutes
Servings: 4
Ingredients:

- 8 ounces cooked shredded chicken
- One scallion, white and green parts, chopped
- ½ cup halved seedless red grapes
- One celery stalk, chopped
- ¼ cup Low-Sodium Mayonnaise or store-bought mayonnaise
- Pinch freshly ground black pepper
- Four large lettuce leaves, butter or red leaf

Directions:

1. In your medium-sized bowl, stir together the chicken, scallion, grapes, celery, and mayonnaise until mixed.
2. Season the mixture with pepper.
3. Spoon the chicken salad onto the lettuce leaves and serve.

Per serving: Calories: 110Kcal; Protein: 13g; Carbohydrates: 6g; Fat: 3g

471. WILD MUSHROOM COUSCOUS

Preparation time: 15 minutes
Cooking time: 10 minutes
Servings: 5

Ingredients:

- One tbs. olive oil
- 1 cup mixed wild mushrooms (shiitake, cremini, portobello, oyster, enoki)
- ¼ sweet onion, finely chopped
- One tsp. minced garlic
- One tbs. chopped fresh oregano
- 3½ cups water
- 10 ounces couscous

Directions:

1. In a large frying pan over medium-high heat, put the olive oil.
2. Add the mushrooms, onion, and garlic, and sauté until tender, about 6 minutes.
3. Stir in the oregano and water, and bring the mixture to a boil.
4. Remove the saucepan from the heat, and stir in the couscous.
5. Cover the pan and allow it to stand for 5 minutes.
6. Fluff the couscous with a fork, and serve.

Per serving: Calories: 237Kcal; Protein: 8g; Carbohydrates: 44g; Fat: 3g

472. SAUTÉED BUTTERNUT SQUASH

Preparation time: 10 minutes
Cooking time: 20 minutes
Servings: 8
Ingredients:

- One tbs. olive oil
- 4 cups peeled, seeded, 1-inch cubes butternut squash
- ½ sweet onion, chopped
- One tsp. chopped fresh thyme
- Pinch freshly ground black pepper

Directions:

1. In a huge frying pan over medium-high heat, put the olive oil.
2. Add the butternut squash and sauté until tender, about 15 minutes.
3. Add the onion and thyme, and sauté for 5 minutes.
4. Season with pepper, and serve hot.

Per serving: Calories: 45Kcal; Protein: 1g; Carbohydrates: 7g; Fat: 1g

473. HERB ROASTED CAULIFLOWER

Preparation time: 10 minutes
Cooking time: 20 minutes
Servings: 4
Ingredients:

- One tbs. olive oil, plus more for the pan

- One head cauliflower, cut in half and then into ½-inch-thick slices
- One tsp. chopped fresh thyme
- One tsp. chopped fresh chives
- ¼ tsp. freshly ground black pepper

Directions:

1. Pre-heat the oven to 400°F.
2. Lightly coat a baking sheet with olive oil.
3. Toss the cauliflower, one tbs. of olive oil, the thyme, chives, and pepper until well coated.
4. Spread the cauliflower on the prepared baking sheet.
5. Roast, turning once, until both sides are golden, about 20 minutes.

Per serving: Calories: 82Kcal; Protein: 1g; Carbohydrates: 4g; Fat: 7g

474. TASTY CHICKEN MEATBALLS

Preparation time: 10 minutes
Cooking time: 25 minutes
Servings: 6
Ingredients:

- ½ pound lean ground chicken
- ¼ cup bread crumbs
- One scallion, white and green parts, chopped
- One egg, beaten
- One tsp. minced garlic
- ¼ tsp. freshly ground black pepper
- Pinch red pepper flakes

Directions:

1. Pre-heat the oven to 400°F.
2. In a large bowl, blend the chicken, bread crumbs, scallion, egg, garlic, black pepper, and red pepper flakes.
3. Form the chicken mixture into 18 meatballs, and place them on a baking sheet.
4. Bake the meatballs for about 25 minutes, turning several times, until golden brown.
5. Serve hot.

Per serving: Calories: 85Kcal; Protein: 8g; Carbohydrates: 4g; Fat: 4g

475. MARINATED FETA AND ARTICHOKES

Preparation time: 10 minutes + 4 hours
Cooking time: 0 minute
Servings: 3
Ingredients:

- 4 ounces traditional Greek feta, cut into ½-inch cubes
- 4 ounces drained artichoke hearts, quartered lengthwise
- 1/3 cup extra-virgin olive oil
- Zest and juice of 1 lemon

- 2 tbsp. roughly chopped fresh rosemary
- 2 tbsp. roughly chopped fresh parsley
- ½ tsp. black peppercorns

Directions:

1. In a glass bowl, combine the feta and artichoke hearts. Add the olive oil, lemon zest and juice, rosemary, parsley, and peppercorns and toss gently to coat, being sure not to crumble the feta.
2. Cover and chill for 4 hours before serving.

Per serving: Calories: 235Kcal; Protein: 4g; Carbohydrates: 11g; Fat: 23g

476. CITRUS-MARINATED OLIVES

Preparation time: 10 minutes + 4 hours
Cooking time: 0 minute
Servings: 4
Ingredients:

- 2 cups mixed green olives with pits
- ¼ cup red wine vinegar
- ¼ cup extra-virgin olive oil
- 2 garlic cloves, finely minced
- Zest and juice orange
- 1 tsp. red pepper flakes
- 2 bay leaves
- ½ tsp. ground cumin
- ½ tsp. ground allspice

Directions:

1. In a jar, mix olives, vinegar, oil, garlic, orange zest and juice, red pepper flakes, bay leaves, cumin, and allspice.
2. Cover and chill for 4 hours, tossing again before serving.

Per serving: Calories: 133Kcal; Protein: 1g; Carbohydrates: 4g; Fat: 14g

477. BALSAMIC ARTICHOKE ANTIPASTO

Preparation time: 5 minutes
Cooking time: 0 minutes
Servings: 4
Ingredients:

- 1 (12-ounce / 340-g) jar roasted red peppers, stemmed, drained and seeded
- 1 (16-ounce / 454-g) can garbanzo beans, drained
- 8 artichoke hearts, either jarred (drained) or frozen (thawed)
- 1 cup whole Kalamata olives, drained
- ¼ cup balsamic vinegar
- ½ tsp. salt

Directions:

1. Slice the peppers into ½-inch slices and place them into a huge bowl.
2. Slice the artichoke hearts into quarters, and add them to the bowl.
3. Add the olives, garbanzo beans, salt and balsamic vinegar.
4. Toss all the ingredients together. Serve chilled.

Per serving: Calories: 281Kcal; Protein: 7g; Carbohydrates: 30g; Fat: 15g

478. MASCARPONE PECANS STUFFED DATES

Preparation time: 5 minutes
Cooking time: 5 minutes
Servings: 12 to 15
Ingredients:

- 1 cup pecans, shells removed
- 1 (8-ounce) container Mascarpone cheese
- 20 medjool dates

Directions:

1. Let the oven heat to 350°F (180°C). Place the pecans on a baking sheet and bake for about 5 to 6 minutes, until aromatic and lightly toasted. Get the pecans out of the oven and cool them for 5 minutes.
2. Once chilled, place the pecans in a food processor fitted with a chopping blade and chop until they bear a resemblance to the texture of coarse sugar or bulgur wheat.
3. Reserve ¼ cup of ground pecans in a mini bowl. Pour the remaining chopped pecans into a bigger bowl and put the Mascarpone cheese.
4. Mix the cheese with the pecans until evenly combined using a spatula.
5. Ladle the cheese mixture into a piping bag.
6. Cut one side of the date lengthwise, from the stem to the bottom using a knife. Slightly open and remove the pit.
7. Squeeze a substantial amount of the cheese mixture into the date where the pit used to be using the piping bag. Close up the date and repeat with the rest of the dates.
8. Dip any visible cheese from the stuffed dates into the reserved chopped pecans to cover it up.
9. Put the dates on a serving plate; serve immediately or chill in the fridge until you are ready to serve.

Per serving: Calories: 253Kcal; Protein: 2g; Carbohydrates: 31g; Fat: 15g

479. PEPPERY POTATOES

Preparation time: 10 minutes
Cooking time: 18 minutes
Servings: 4
Ingredients:

- 4-pcs large potatoes, cubed
- 4-tbsp extra-virgin olive oil (divided)
- 3-tbsp garlic, minced
- ½-cup coriander or cilantro, finely chopped
- 2-tbsp fresh lemon juice
- 1¾-tbsp paprika
- 2-tbsp parsley, minced

Directions:

1. Place the potatoes in a microwave-safe dish. Pour over a tbs. of olive oil. Cover the dish tightly with plastic wrap. Heat the potatoes for seven minutes in your microwave to par-cook them.
2. Cook 2 tbsp. of olive oil in a pan placed over medium-low heat. Add the garlic and cover. Cook for 3 minutes. Add the coriander, and cook for 2 minutes. Transfer the garlic-coriander sauce into a bowl, and set aside.
3. In the same pan placed over medium heat, heat 1 tbs. of olive oil. Add the par-cooked potatoes. Do not stir! Cook for 3 minutes until browned, flipping once with a spatula. Continue cooking until browned all the sides.
4. Take the potatoes and place them on a dish. Pour over the garlic-coriander sauce and lemon juice. Add the paprika, parsley, and salt. Toss gently to coat evenly.

Per serving: Calories: 316.2Kcal; Protein: 4.5g; Carbohydrates: 20g; Fat: 14.2g

480. SALTED POTATO CHIPS

Preparation time: 10 minutes.
Cooking time: 5 minutes.
Servings: 4
Ingredients:

- 1 tbsp. vegetable oil
- 1 potato, sliced paper-thin
- Sea salt, to taste

Directions:

1. Toss potato with oil and sea salt. Spread the slices in a baking dish in a single layer.
2. Cook in a microwave for 5 minutes until golden brown. Serve.

Per serving: Calories: 80Kcal; Protein: 1.2g; Carbohydrates: 11.6g; Fat: 3.5g

481. ZUCCHINI PEPPER CHIPS

Preparation time: 10 minutes.
Cooking time: 15 minutes.
Servings: 4
Ingredients:

- 1-⅔ C. vegetable oil
- 1 tsp. onion powder
- ½ tsp. black pepper
- 3 tbsp. red pepper flakes, crushed
- 2 zucchinis, thinly sliced

Directions:

1. Mix oil with all the spices in a bowl. Add zucchini slices and mix well.
2. Transfer the mixture into a Ziplock bag and seal it. Refrigerate for 10 minutes.
3. Spread the zucchini slices on a greased baking sheet. Bake for 15 minutes Serve.

Per serving: Calories: 172Kcal; Protein: 13.5g; Carbohydrates: 19.9g; Fat: 11.1g

482. SUPER SEED SPELT PANCAKES

Preparation time: 15 minutes
Cooking time: 10 minutes
Servings: 3
Ingredients:

- 5 oz. buckwheat groats
- 1 ½ tsp. cinnamon, ground
- 1 ½ oz. flax seeds
- 1 ½ oz. sesame seeds
- oz. chia seeds
- 1 oz. pumpkin seeds
- 1 tbsp. almond milk
- ½ tsp. stevia extract
- 1 tsp. coconut oil
- 1 tsp. baking soda
- ½ tsp. baking powder
- ¼ tsp. fine sea salt

Directions:

1. Grind the pumpkin seeds, sesame seeds, flax seeds, chia seeds and buckwheat groats into flour and keep ¼ of the seed flour for later use (not for this recipe).
2. Add 2 C. of seed flour to a medium bowl.
3. Add in the rest of the ingredients but not the coconut oil. Pour in more milk if needed to attain the right consistency.
4. Add coconut oil to a non-stick pan and place overheat.
5. Once heated, pour thin layers of the batter and flip once you see bubbles form on top.
6. Cook until all the batter is used up.

Per serving: Calories: 140Kcal; Protein: 34g; Carbohydrates: 15g; Fat: 8g

483. SCRAMBLED TOFU

Preparation time: 10 minutes
Cooking time: 15 minutes
Servings: 1
Ingredients:

- 3 cloves
- 1 onion
- ½ tsp. turmeric
- Salt for taste
- 2 oz. firm tofu
- ½ tsp. paprika
- 1 handful baby spinach
- 3 tomatoes
- ½ C. yeast
- ½ tsp. cumin

Directions:

1. Mince the garlic and dice up the onion.
2. Toss the onions into a pan and let them cook over medium heat for about 7 minutes. Add in the garlic and cook for 1 minute.
3. Toss in the tofu and tomatoes and cook for 10 more minutes. Add in some water, cumin, and paprika and stir well. Continue cooking.
4. When the dish is about to cook, add in spinach, stir and once wilted, turn off the heat and serve.

Per serving: Calories: 151Kcal; Protein: 29g; Carbohydrates: 15g; Fat: 10g

484. SPROUTED BUCKWHEAT CREPES

Preparation time: 15 minutes
Cooking time: 10 minutes
Servings: 4
Ingredients:

- 1 tbsp. pure 100% vanilla extract
- ¾ C. pure water
- 1 C. buckwheat groats—soaked overnight
- 1 tbsp. chia seeds

Directions:

1. Rinse buckwheat thoroughly and soak it in 1:2 parts water overnight.
2. Rinse, then drain well the following morning.
3. Add all your ingredients to a blender and process until smooth.
4. Add coconut oil to a nonstick pan over high medium heat and pour in a thin layer to the center of your pan. Swirl the pan to make sure the batter spreads out. The texture

should be thick enough to hold the shape for flipping.
5. Once the top is not liquid, flip and cook the other side until browned.
6. Do this with the rest of the batter.
7. Serve with some sprouted nut butter, fresh lemon juice, hemp seeds, or whatever you like.

Per serving: Calories: 232Kcal; Protein: 18g; Carbohydrates: 22g; Fat: 8g

485. POACHED APPLES WITH GREEK YOGURT AND GRANOLA

Preparation time: 5 minutes
Cooking time: 15 minutes
Servings: 4
Ingredients:

- 4 medium-sized apples, peeled
- ½ C. brown sugar
- 1 vanilla bean
- 1 cinnamon stick
- ½ C. cranberry juice
- 1 C. water
- ½ C. 2% Greek yogurt
- ½ C. granola

Directions:

1. Add the apples, brown sugar, water, cranberry juice, vanilla bean, and cinnamon stick to the inner pot of your Instant Pot.
2. Secure the lid. Choose the "Manual" mode and cook for 5 minutes at High pressure. Once cooking is complete, use a natural pressure release for 5 minutes; carefully remove the lid. Reserve poached apples.
3. Press the "Sauté" button and let the sauce simmer on "Less" mode until it has thickened.
4. Place the apples in serving bowls. Add the syrup and top each apple with granola and Greek yogurt. Enjoy!

Per serving: Calories: 247Kcal; Protein: 3.5g; Carbohydrates: 52.6g; Fat: 3.1g

486. JASMINE RICE PUDDING WITH CRANBERRIES

Preparation time: 5 minutes
Cooking time: 15 minutes
Servings: 4
Ingredients:

- 1 C. apple juice
- 1 heaping tbsp. honey
- ⅓ C. sugar, granulated
- 1 ½ C. jasmine rice
- 1 C. water

- ¼ tsp. cinnamon, ground
- ¼ tsp. cloves, ground
- ⅓ tsp. cardamom, ground
- 1 tsp. vanilla extract
- 3 eggs, well-beaten
- ½ C. cranberries

Directions:

1. Thoroughly combine the apple juice, honey, sugar, jasmine rice, water, and spices in the inner pot of your Instant Pot.
2. Secure the lid. Choose the "Manual" mode and cook for 4 minutes at high pressure. Once cooking is complete, use a natural pressure release for 5 minutes; carefully remove the lid.
3. Press the "Sauté" button and fold in the eggs. Cook on "Less" mode until heated through.
4. Ladle into individual bowls and top with dried cranberries. Enjoy!

Per serving: Calories: 402Kcal; Protein: 8.9g; Carbohydrates: 81.1g; Fat: 3.6g

487. ORANGE AND ALMOND CUPCAKES

Preparation time: 5 minutes
Cooking time: 20 minutes
Servings: 9
Ingredients:

Cupcakes:

- 1 orange extract
- 2 tbsp. olive oil
- 2 tbsp. ghee, at room temperature
- 3 eggs, beaten
- 2 oz. Greek yogurt
- 2 C. cake flour
- A pinch salt
- 1 tbsp. orange rind, grated
- ½ C. brown sugar
- ½ C. almonds, chopped

Cream cheese frosting:

- 2 oz. cream cheese
- 1 tbsp. whipping cream
- ½ C. butter, at room temperature
- 1 ½ C. confectioners' sugar, sifted
- ⅓ tsp. vanilla
- A pinch salt

Directions:

1. Mix the orange extract, olive oil, ghee, eggs, and Greek yogurt until well combined.
2. Thoroughly combine the cake flour, salt, orange rind, and brown sugar in a separate mixing bowl. Add the egg/yogurt mixture to the flour mixture. Stir in the chopped almonds and mix again.

3. Place parchment baking liners on the bottom of a muffin tin. Pour the batter into the muffin tin.

4. Place 1 C. of water and metal trivet in the inner pot of your Instant Pot. Lower the prepared muffin tin onto the trivet.

5. Secure the lid. Choose the "Manual" mode and cook for 11 minutes at high pressure. Once cooking is complete, use a quick pressure release; carefully remove the lid. Transfer to wire racks.

6. Meanwhile, make the frosting by mixing all ingredients until creamy. Frost your cupcakes, and enjoy!

Per serving: Calories: 392Kcal; Protein: 5.9g; Carbohydrates: 50.1g; Fat: 18.7g

488. BREAD PUDDING

Preparation time: 5 minutes
Cooking time: 25 minutes
Servings: 4
Ingredients:

- 4 egg yolks
- 3 C. brioche, cubed
- 2 C. half and half
- ½ tsp. vanilla extract
- 1 C. sugar
- 2 tbsp. butter, softened
- 1 C. cranberries
- 2 C. warm water
- ½ C. raisins
- 1 lime zest

Directions:

1. Grease a baking dish with some butter and set the dish aside. In a bowl, mix the egg yolks with the half and half, cubed brioche, vanilla extract, sugar, cranberries, raisins, and lime zest, and stir well.

2. Pour this into a greased dish, cover with some aluminum foil, and set aside for 10 minutes. Put the dish in the steamer basket of the Instant Pot, add the warm water to the Instant Pot, cover, and cook on the 'Manual' setting for 20 minutes.

3. Release the pressure naturally, uncover the Instant Pot, take the bread pudding out, set it aside to cool down, slice, and serve.

Per serving: Calories: 300Kcal; Protein: 11g; Carbohydrates: 46g; Fat: 7g

489. RUBY PEARS

Preparation time: 10 minutes
Cooking time: 10 minutes
Servings: 4
Ingredients:

- 4 pears
- Juice and zest of 1 lemon
- 26 oz. grape juice
- 11 oz. currant jelly
- 4 garlic cloves, peeled
- ½ vanilla bean
- 4 peppercorns
- 2 rosemary sprigs

Directions:

1. Pour the jelly and grape juice into the Instant Pot and mix with lemon zest and lemon juice. Dip each pear in this mix, wrap them in aluminum foil and arrange them in the steamer basket of the Instant Pot.

2. Add the garlic cloves, peppercorns, rosemary, and vanilla bean to the juice mixture, cover the Instant Pot and cook on the Manual setting for 10 minutes.

3. Release the pressure, uncover the Instant Pot, take the pears out, unwrap them, arrange them on plates, and serve cold with cooking juice poured on top.

Per serving: Calories: 145Kcal; Protein: 12g; Carbohydrates: 12g; Fat: 5.6g

490. CHOCOLATE PUDDING IN A MUG

Preparation time: 10 minutes
Cooking time: 70 seconds
Servings: 2
Ingredients:

- 2 eggs
- 2 oz. almond
- 1 cup Flour
- 1 Tbsp. xylitol
- 1 Tbsp. cocoa powder, unsweetened
- 1 oz. almond milk
- 1 Tbsp. olive oil
- ½ tsp. baking powder
- Cream, whipped, for topping as desired

Directions:

1. Mix almond flour, xylitol, cocoa powder, espresso powder, eggs, coconut milk, olive oil, and baking powder in a bowl.

2. Pour the mix into mugs ¾ way up and cook in a microwave for 70 seconds.

3. Remove and swirl a generous amount of whipping cream on the cakes and serve.

Per serving: Calories: 200Kcal; Protein: 14g; Carbohydrates: 20g; Fat: 3g

491. HEALTHY FRUIT SALAD WITH YOGURT CREAM

Preparation time: 10 minutes
Cooking time: 0 minutes
Servings: 4
Ingredients:

- 1 ½ C. grapes halved
- 2 plums, chopped
- 1 peach, chopped
- 1 C. cantaloupe, chopped
- ½ C. fresh blueberries
- 1 C. plain non-fat Greek yogurt, unsweetened
- ½ tsp. cinnamon, ground
- 2 tbsp. honey

Directions:

1. In a large bowl, combine the grapes, plums, peach, cantaloupe, and blueberries. Toss to mix. Divide among 4 dessert dishes.

2. In a small bowl, whisk the yogurt, cinnamon, and honey. Spoon over the fruit.

3. Sprinkle yogurt with sugar, and drizzle with honey. Serve fruit with yogurt mixture.

Per serving: Calories: 74Kcal; Protein: 2g; Carbohydrates: 16g; Fat: 0.7g

492. SUMMERTIME FRUIT SALAD

Cooking time: 0 minutes
Preparation time: 30 minutes
Servings: 6

- **Ingredients:**
- 1-lb. strawberries, hulled and sliced thinly
- 3 medium peaches, sliced thinly
- 6 oz. blueberries
- 1 tbsp. fresh mint, chopped
- 2 tbsp. lemon juice
- 1 tbsp. honey
- 2 tsp. balsamic vinegar

Directions:

1. In a salad bowl, combine all ingredients.

2. Gently toss to coat all ingredients.

3. Chill for at least 20-30 minutes before serving.

Per serving: Calories: 146Kcal; Protein: 8.1g; Carbohydrates: 22.8g; Fat: 3.4g

493. STRAWBERRY MUFFINS

Preparation time: 5 minutes
Cooking time: 25 minutes
Servings: 8
Ingredients:

- 2 C. wheat flour

- 1 C. strawberry
- ½ C. milk
- 2 fl. oz. olive oil
- 1 egg
- 2 tsp. baking powder
- Sugar and salt, to taste

Directions:

1. In a bowl, mix the baking powder, sugar, and flour. In another bowl, beat the egg with milk and olive oil.
2. Mix both mixtures and mix well. Add a glass of sliced strawberries and mix gently, without damaging the berries.
3. Grease the muffin pan with butter or put a paper mold in each hole. Fill ⅔ dough, and bake for 20–25 minutes in an oven preheated to 375°F until cooked.
4. Allow to cool in shape, then shift to a platter.

Per serving: Calories: 284Kcal; Protein: 5.3g; Carbohydrates: 48g; Fat: 8g

494. COMPOTE DIPPED BERRIES MIX

Preparation time: 10 minutes

Cooking time: 10 minutes

Servings: 8

Ingredients:

- 2 C. fresh strawberries, hulled and halved lengthwise
- 4 sprigs fresh mint
- 2 C. fresh blackberries
- 1 C. pomegranate juice
- 2 tsp. vanilla
- 6 orange pekoe tea bags
- 2 C. fresh red raspberries
- 1 C. water
- 2 C. fresh golden raspberries
- 2 C. fresh sweet cherries, pitted and halved
- 2 C. fresh blueberries
- 2 ml bottle Sauvignon Blanc

Directions:

1. Pre-heat the oven to 290°F and lightly grease a baking dish.
2. Soak mint sprigs and tea bags in boiled water for about 10 minutes in a covered bowl.
3. Mix together all the berries and cherries in another bowl and keep aside.
4. Cook wine with pomegranate juice in a saucepan and add strained tea liquid.
5. Toss in the mixed berries to serve and enjoy.

Per serving: Calories: 356Kcal; Protein: 2.2g; Carbohydrates: 89.9g; Fat: 0.8g

495. POPPED QUINOA BARS

Preparation time: 10 minutes

Cooking time: 10 minutes

Servings: 3

Ingredients:

- 2 (4 oz.) semi-sweet chocolate bars, chopped
- ½ tbsp. peanut butter
- ½ C. dry quinoa
- ¼ tsp. vanilla

Directions:

1. Toast dry quinoa in a pan until golden and stir in chocolate, vanilla, and peanut butter.
2. Spread this mixture in a baking sheet evenly and refrigerate for about 4 hours.
3. Break it into small pieces and serve chilled.

Per serving: Calories: 278Kcal; Protein: 6.9g; Carbohydrates: 36.2g; Fat: 11.8g

496. ALMOND ORANGE PANDORO

Preparation time: 10 minutes

Cooking time: 0 minutes

Servings: 12

Ingredients:

- 2 large oranges, zested
- 2½ C. mascarpone
- ½ C. almonds, whole
- 2 ½ C. coconut cream
- ½ pandoro, diced
- 2 tbsp. sherry

Directions:

1. Whisk cream with mascarpone, icing sugar, ¾ zest, and half sherry in a bowl.
2. Dice the pandoro into equal-sized horizontal slices.
3. Place the bottom slice in a plate and top with the remaining sherry.
4. Spoon the mascarpone mixture over the slice.
5. Top with almonds and place another pandoro slice over.
6. Continue adding layers of pandoro slices and cream mixture.
7. Dish out / serve.

Per serving: Calories: 346Kcal; Protein: 7.7g; Carbohydrates: 8.5g; Fat: 10.4g

497. BLUEBERRY MUFFINS

Preparation time: 5 minutes

Cooking time: 20 minutes

Servings: 24

Ingredients:

- 2 C. all-purpose flour
- 2 C. whole wheat flour
- ⅔ C. sugar
- 6 tsp. baking powder
- 1 tsp. salt
- 2 C. blueberries
- 2 free-range eggs
- ⅔ C. olive oil
- 2 C. milk

Directions:

1. Pre-heat your oven to 400°F and line a muffin tin with paper cases.
2. Grab a large bowl and add the dry ingredients. Stir well to combine.
3. Add the blueberries and stir through.
4. Take a medium bowl and add the wet ingredients. Stir well, then pour into the dry ingredients.
5. Pour the muffin batter into the muffin cases and pop it into the oven.
6. Bake for 18 minutes.
7. Remove from the oven and allow to cool slightly before enjoying.

Per serving: Calories: 179Kcal; Protein: 4g; Carbohydrates: 24g; Fat: 7g

498. MINT CHOCOLATE CHIP NICE CREAM

Preparation time: 5 minutes

Cooking time: 0minutes

Servings: 1–2

Ingredients:

- 2 overripe bananas, frozen
- Pinch salt
- ⅛ tsp. pure peppermint extract
- Pinch spirulina, or natural food coloring (optional)
- ½ C. coconut cream
- 2–3 tbsp. chocolate chips

Directions:

1. Pop all the ingredients into your blender and whizz until smooth.
2. Serve and enjoy.

Per serving: Calories: 601Kcal; Protein: 8g; Carbohydrates: 130g; Fat: 12g

499. CREAMY BERRY CRUNCH

Preparation time: 10 minutes

Cooking time: 0 minutes

Servings: 2

Ingredients:

- 2 C. heavy cream for whipping
- 3 oz. berries, fresh if possible
- The zest of half a lemon
- ¼ tsp. vanilla extract

- 2 oz. pecan nuts, chopped

Directions:

1. Into a large bowl, whip the cream until stiff.
2. Add the vanilla and the lemon zest and whip for a few seconds more.
3. Add the nuts and the berries and stir in gently.
4. Place plastic cling film over the top of the bowl.
5. Serve!

Per serving: Calories: 260Kcal; Protein: 3g; Carbohydrates: 3g; Fat: 27g

500. BUTTON MUSHROOM SAUCE

Preparation time: 5 minutes
Cooking time: 5 minutes
Servings: 4
Ingredients:

- 2 C. button mushrooms, sliced
- 1 C. heavy cream
- 3 tbsp. sour cream
- 3 tbsp. gorgonzola cheese
- 2 tbsp. soy sauce
- 2 tbsp. butter
- 1 tbsp. sesame oil
- 2 tbsp. Parmesan cheese, freshly grated
- 1 tsp. agar powder

Spices:

- 1 tsp. salt
- ⅓ tsp. black pepper
- 1 tsp. dried celery

Directions:

1. Melt the butter on the "Sauté" mode, then put in the mushrooms. Season with salt and pepper.
2. Mix and cook until the liquid from the mushrooms evaporates.
3. Now add sour cream, gorgonzola cheese, and heavy cream. Sprinkle with dried celery and cook until cheese melts.
4. Finally, pour in the soy sauce and add sesame oil. Stir in agar powder and briefly cook, for another minute.
5. Press the "Cancel" button and remove the sauce from the pot.
6. Serve immediately.

Per serving: Calories: 265Kcal; Protein: 6.6g; Carbohydrates: 3.1g; Fat: 26g

501. CRÈME BRÛLÉE WITH A GINGERBREAD TWIST

Preparation time: 5 minutes
Cooking time: 5 minutes
Servings: 4

Ingredients:

- 1 C. heavy cream for whipping
- 2 tbsp. erythritol
- 4 egg yolks
- 2 tsp. pumpkin spice
- ¼ tsp. vanilla extract
- 4 ramekin glasses

Directions:

1. Pre-heat the oven to 180°C.
2. Separate the eggs, with the whites in one bowl and the yolks in the other. You can save the whites for something else.
3. Cook the cream in a pan and allow to boil lightly, before adding the pumpkin spice, vanilla extract, and erythritol.
4. Pour the mixture a little at a time into the egg yolks and whisk continuously.
5. Take small oven-proof bowl (ramekins) and place them into a large dish with sides to hold everything in place.
6. Add water into the larger dish.
7. Add the mixture evenly to each small ramekin.
8. Cook in the oven for around half an hour.
9. Once finished, remove the ramekins and place them to one side to cool.
10. Serve warm or cold.

Per serving: Calories: 274Kcal; Protein: 4g; Carbohydrates: 3g; Fat: 28g

502. LEMON MARMALADE

Preparation time: 10 minutes
Cooking time: 15 minutes
Servings: 8
Ingredients:

- 2 lb. lemons, washed, sliced, and cut into quarters
- 4 lb. sugar
- 2 C. water

Directions:

1. Put the lemon pieces into the Instant Pot, add the water, cover, and cook on the Manual setting for 10 minutes. Release the pressure naturally, uncover the Instant Pot, add the sugar, stir, set the Instant Pot on Manual mode, and cook for 6 minutes, stirring all the time.
2. Divide into jars, and serve when needed.

Per serving: Calories: 100Kcal; Protein: 8g; Carbohydrates: 4g; Fat: 2g

503. PEACH JAM

Preparation time: 10 minutes
Cooking time: 5 minutes
Servings: 6
Ingredients:

- 4 ½ C. peaches, peeled and cubed
- 6 C. sugar
- ¼ C. ginger, crystallized and chopped
- 1 box fruit pectin

Directions:

1. Set the Instant Pot on Manual mode, add the peaches, ginger, and pectin, stir and bring to a boil.
2. Add the sugar, stir, cover, and cook on the Manual setting for 5 minutes. Release the pressure, uncover the Instant Pot, divide the jam into jars, and serve.

Per serving: Calories: 50Kcal; Protein: 0g; Carbohydrates: 3g; Fat: 0g

504. KEY LIME PIE

Preparation time: 10 minutes
Cooking time: 15 minutes
Servings: 6
Ingredients:

For the crust:

- 1 tbsp. sugar
- 3 tbsp. butter, melted
- 5 graham crackers, crumbled

For the filling:

- 4 egg yolks
- 14 oz. milk, canned and condensed
- ½ C. key lime juice
- ⅓ C. sour cream
- Vegetable oil cooking spray
- 1 C. water
- 2 tbsp. key lime zest, grated

Directions:

1. In a bowl, whisk the egg yolks well.
2. Add the milk gradually and stir again.
3. Add the lime juice, sour cream, and lime zest and stir again. In another bowl, whisk the butter with the graham crackers and sugar, stir well, and spread on the bottom of a springform greased with some cooking spray. Cover the pan with some aluminum foil and place it in the steamer basket of the Instant Pot.
4. Add water into the Instant Pot, cover, and cook on the Manual setting for 15 minutes.
5. Release the pressure for 10 minutes, uncover the Instant Pot, take the pie out, set aside to cool down, and

keep it in the refrigerator for 4 hours before slicing and serving it.

Per serving: Calories: 400Kcal; Protein: 7g; Carbohydrates: 34g; Fat: 21g

505. FRUIT COBBLER

Preparation time: 10 minutes

Cooking time: 12 minutes

Servings: 4

Ingredients:

- 3 apples, cored and cut into chunks
- 2 pears, cored and cut into chunks
- 1½ C. hot water
- ¼ C. honey
- 1 C. steel-cut oats
- 1 tsp. cinnamon, ground
- ice cream, for serving

Directions:

1. Put the apples and pears into the Instant Pot and mix with hot water, honey, oats, and cinnamon. Stir, cover, and cook on the Manual setting for 12 minutes.
2. Release the pressure naturally, transfer.

Per serving: Calories: 170Kcal; Protein: 3g; Carbohydrates: 10g; Fat: 4g

506. STUFFED PEACHES

Preparation time: 10 minutes

Cooking time: 4 minutes

Servings: 6

Ingredients:

- 6 peaches, pits, and flesh removed
- Salt
- ¼ C. coconut flour
- ¼ C. maple syrup
- 2 tbsp. coconut butter
- ½ tsp. cinnamon, ground
- 1 tsp. almond extract
- 1 C. water

Directions:

1. In a bowl, mix the flour with the salt, syrup, butter, cinnamon, and half of the almond extract and stir well. Fill the peaches with this mix, place them in the steamer basket of the Instant Pot, add the water and the rest of the almond extract to the Instant Pot, cover, and cook on the Steam setting for 4 minutes.
2. Release the pressure naturally, divide the stuffed peaches on serving plates, and serve warm.

Per serving: Calories: 160Kcal; Protein: 4g; Carbohydrates: 12g; Fat: 6.7g

507. PEACH COMPOTE

Preparation time: 10 minutes

Cooking time: 3 minutes

Servings: 6

Ingredients:

- 8 peaches, pitted and chopped
- 6 tbsp. sugar
- 1 tsp. cinnamon, ground
- 1 tsp. vanilla extract
- 1 vanilla bean, scraped
- 2 tbsp. Grape Nuts cereal

Directions:

1. Put the peaches into the Instant Pot and mix with the sugar, cinnamon, vanilla bean, and vanilla extract. Stir well, cover the Instant Pot and cook on the Manual setting for 3 minutes.
2. Release the pressure for 10 minutes, add the cereal, stir well, transfer the compote to bowls, and serve.

Per serving: Calories: 100Kcal; Protein: 1g; Carbohydrates: 11g; Fat: 2g

508. PISTACHIO AND FRUITS

Preparation time: 5 minutes

Cooking time: 7 minutes

Servings: 12

Ingredients:

- ½ C. apricots, dried and chopped
- ¼ C. cranberries, dried
- ½ tsp. cinnamon
- ¼ tsp. allspice
- ¼ tsp. nutmeg, ground
- 1 ¼ C. pistachios, unsalted and roasted
- 2 tsp. sugar

Directions:

1. Start by heating the oven to a temperature of around 345°F.
2. Using a tray, place the pistachios and bake for seven minutes. Allow the pistachio to cool afterward.
3. Combine all ingredients in a container.
4. Once everything is combined well, it is ready to be served.

Per serving: Calories: 377Kcal; Protein: 16g; Carbohydrates: 24.5g; Fat: 5g

509. AVOCADO SORBET

Preparation time: 5 minutes

Cooking time: 10 minutes

Servings: 4

Ingredients:

- ¼ C. sugar

- 1 C. water
- 1 tsp. lime zest, grated
- 1 tbsp. honey
- 2 ripe avocados, pitted and skin removed
- 2 tbsp. lime juice

Directions:

1. Combine together the sugar and water in a small pan over medium flame. Continue until the sugar dissolves completely, and then remove from the flame.
2. Place the avocados in the food processor. Add the sugar and water, mix along with the honey, lime zest, and lime juice into the food processor.
3. Process until you reach a smooth consistency.
4. Place the mix into a baking pan and cover with foil. Place the mix into the freezer until completely frozen.
5. Upon serving, process the food in the food processor until you reach a smooth consistency.

Per serving: Calories: 390.3Kcal; Protein: 10g; Carbohydrates: 19g; Fat: 6g

510. CIOCCOLATA CALDA

Preparation time: 5 minutes

Cooking time: 10 minutes

Servings: 2

Ingredients:

- 1 ½ tbsp. sugar
- 1 tbsp. cornstarch
- 3 tbsp. cocoa powder, unsweetened
- 1½ C. plus 2 tbsp. milk

Directions:

1. Mix together the cocoa powder and sugar in a little frying pan. Add one and a half C. of milk while mixing. Start with medium heat and gradually lower until the sugar is fully dissolved. The entire mixture should simmer.
2. In a separate container, mix the cornstarch and the remaining two tbsp. of milk. After it is well mixed, add to the cocoa mix on the frying pan.
3. Continue mixing until the entire mixture reaches a thick consistency. Serve while hot.

Per serving: Calories: 427Kcal; Protein: 12g; Carbohydrates: 22g; Fat: 4g

CHAPTER 10: Desserts

511. INSTANT BANANA PUDDING

Preparation time: 10 minutes

Cooking time: 10 minutes

Servings: 12

Ingredients:

- 14g; box Jell-O vanilla instant pudding
- 600 ml lactose-free milk
- 15g; pack gluten-free cookies
- 3 whole bananas, peeled

Directions:

1. Whisk the pudding mix and milk together for 2 minutes until the pudding begins to thicken.
2. Place in the refrigerator to continue thickening.
3. Slice the bananas and divide them into 2 piles.
4. Break up the cookies and spread half of them over the base of an 8 x 8 pan.
5. Place half of the bananas over the top and follow with half of the pudding mix.
6. Repeat with the rest of the ingredients.

Per serving: Calories: 110Kcal; Protein: 4g; Carbohydrates: 10g; Fat: 1g

512. CARROT CAKE BITES

Preparation time: 10 minutes

Cooking time: 0 minutes

Servings: 4

Ingredients:

- 4 baby carrots, peeled and chopped
- ⅛ tsp. pure vanilla extract, sugar-free
- ⅓ C. coconut, shredded and unsweetened
- 2 tbsp. almond butter, unsalted
- ⅛ tsp. cinnamon, ground
- 1 tbsp. pure maple syrup
- ⅓ C. gluten-free oats, rolled
- ⅛ tsp. salt, iodized

Directions:

1. Thoroughly clean carrots and remove the skins. Chop into big chunks and transfer to a food blender.
2. Pulse for approximately 2 minutes until consistency is slightly chunky. Transfer to a glass dish.

3. Combine coconut and oats in a food blender and pulse for an additional 2 minutes.
4. Empty carrots, almond butter, maple syrup, salt, vanilla extract, and cinnamon in a food blender and pulse for a total of 2 minutes until the batter thickens. Divide into 4 pieces and hand roll into spheres.
5. Serve immediately and enjoy!

Per serving: Calories: 160Kcal; Protein: 9g; Carbohydrates: 12g; Fat: 4g

513. PUMPKIN PEANUT PUDDING

Preparation time: 10 minutes

Cooking time: 0 minutes

Servings: 4

Ingredients:

- ⅛ tsp. nutmeg, ground
- ½ C. peanuts, raw and unsalted
- ⅛ tsp. salt, iodized
- ⅓ C. pumpkin puree
- ¼ tsp. cinnamon, ground
- ⅛ C. pure maple syrup
- ¼ C. almond milk, unsweetened
- ½ tbsp. coconut oil, melted
- ⅛ cloves, ground

Directions:

1. Pulse nutmeg, peanuts, salt, pumpkin puree, cinnamon, maple syrup, almond milk, coconut oil, and cloves for approximately 3 minutes.
2. Make sure all ingredients are incorporated. Divide equally into individual glasses or a dish.
3. Serve immediately and enjoy!

Per serving: Calories: 140Kcal; Protein:6 g; Carbohydrates: 18g; Fat: 5g

514. RICE PUDDING

Preparation time: 5 minutes

Cooking time: 20 minutes

Servings: 4

Ingredients:

- 4 ⅓ C. almond milk, unsweetened
- 3½ oz. brown rice
- 1 tbsp. brown sugar, packed
- 2 tbsp. pure maple syrup, separated

Directions:

1. Empty milk in a saucepan on the highest heat setting. As it starts to bubble, turn heat to medium/low, then transfer the rice into the pot.
2. Toss to cover the rice completely. Blend sugar and integrate fully. Toss

frequently for 20 minutes or until it reaches the desired thickness.

3. Transfer to serving dishes and drizzle with ½ tbsp. each with maple syrup.

Per serving: Calories: 100Kcal; Protein:21g; Carbohydrates: 9g; Fat: 10g

515. PUDDING GLASS WITH BANANA AND WHIPPED CREAM

Preparation time: 10 minutes

Cooking time: 8 minutes

Servings: 2

Ingredients:

- Two portions of banana cream pudding mix
- 2 1/2 cups of rice milk
- 8 oz. of dairy whipped cream
- 12 oz. of vanilla wafers

Directions:

1. Put vanilla wafers in a pan, and in another bowl, mix banana cream pudding and rice milk.
2. Boil the ingredients, blending them slowly.
3. Pour the mixture over the wafers and make 2 or 3 layers.
4. Put the pan in the fridge for one hour and afterward spread the whipped topping over the dessert.
5. Put it back in the fridge for 2 hours and serve it cold in transparent glasses. Serve and enjoy!

Per serving: Calories: 255Kcal; Protein: 3g; Carbohydrates: 13g; Fat: 8g

516. CHOCOLATE BEET CAKE

Preparation time: 10 minutes

Cooking time: 50 minutes

Servings: 12

Ingredients:

- 3 cups of grated beets
- 1/4 cup of canola oil
- Four eggs
- 4 oz. of unsweetened chocolate
- 2 tsp. of Phosphorus-free baking powder
- 2 cups of all-purpose flour
- 1 cup of sugar

Directions:

1. Set your oven to 325°F. Grease two 8-inch cake pans.
2. Mix the baking powder, flour, and sugar. Set aside.

3. Slice up the chocolate as excellently as you can and melt using a double boiler. A microwave can also be used, but don't let it burn.

4. Allow it to cool, and then mix in the oil and eggs.

5. Mix all of the wet ingredients into the flour mixture and combine everything until well mixed.

6. Fold the beets in and pour the batter into the cake pans.

7. Let them bake for 40 to 50 minutes. To know it iss done, a toothpick should come out clean when inserted into the cake.

8. Remove from the oven and allow them to cool.

9. Once cool, invert over a plate to remove.

10. It is great when served with whipped cream and fresh berries. Enjoy!

Per serving: Calories: 270Kcal; Protein: 6g; Carbohydrates: 21g; Fat: 6g

517. STRAWBERRY PIE

Preparation time: 25 minutes
Cooking time: 3 hours
Servings: 8
Ingredients:
For the Crust:

- 1 1/2 cups of Graham cracker crumbs
- 5 tbsp. of unsalted butter
- 2 tbsp. of sugar

For the Pie:

- 1 1/2 tsp. of gelatin powder
- 3 tbsp. of cornstarch
- 3/4 cup of sugar
- 5 cups of sliced strawberries, divided
- 1 cup of water

Directions:
For the crust:

1. Heat your oven to 375°F. Grease a pie pan.

2. Combine the butter, crumbs, and sugar and then press them into your pie pan.

3. Bake the crust for around 10 to 15 minutes, until lightly browned.

4. Take out of the oven and let it cool completely.

For the pie:

1. Crush up a cup of strawberries.

2. Using a small pot, combine the sugar, water, gelatin, and cornstarch.

3. Bring the mixture in the pot up to a boil, lower the heat, and simmer until it has thickened.

4. Add in the crushed strawberries in the pot and let it simmer for another

5 minutes until the sauce has thickened up again.

5. Set it off the heat and pour it into a bowl.

6. Cool until it comes to room temperature.

7. Toss the remaining berries with the sauce to be well distributed, pour into the pie crust, and spread it into an even layer.

8. Refrigerate the pie until cold. It will take about 3 hours. Serve and enjoy!

Per serving: Calories: 265Kcal; Protein: 3g; Carbohydrates: 10g; Fat: 8g

518. GRAPE SKILLET GALETTE

Preparation time: 20 minutes
Cooking time: 2 hours
Servings: 6
Ingredients:
For the Crust:

- 1/2 cup of unsweetened rice milk
- 4 tbsp. of cold butter
- 1 tbsp. of sugar
- 1 cup of all-purpose flour
- For the Galette:
- 1 tbsp. of cornstarch
- 1/3 cup of sugar
- One egg white
- 2 cups of halved seedless grapes

Directions:
For the crust:

1. Add the sugar and the flour to a food processor and mix for a few seconds.

2. Place in the butter and pulse until it looks like a coarse meal.

3. Add in the rice milk and combine until the dough forms.

4. Put the dough on a clean surface and form it into a disc.

5. Wrap it with plastic wrap and place it in the fridge for 2 hours.

For the galette:

1. Set your oven to 425°F.

2. Mix the cornstarch and sugar and toss the grapes in.

3. Unwrap the dough and roll out on a floured surface.

4. Press it into a 14-inch circle and place it in a cast-iron skillet.

5. Add the grape filling in the center and spread out to fill, leaving a 2-inch crust. Fold the edge over.

6. Brush the crust with egg white and cook for 20 to 25 minutes. The crust should be golden.

7. Allow to rest for around 20 minutes before you serve. Enjoy!

Per serving: Calories: 172Kcal; Protein: 2g; Carbohydrates: 8g; Fat: 3g

519. PUMPKIN CHEESECAKE

Preparation time: 20 minutes
Cooking time: 50 minutes
Servings: 2
Ingredients:

- One egg white
- One wafer crumb, 9-inch pie crust
- 1/2 small bowl of granular sugar
- 1 tsp. of vanilla extract
- 1 tsp. of pumpkin pie flavoring
- 1/2 bowl of pumpkin cream
- 1/2 small bowl of liquid egg substitute
- 8 tbsp. of frozen topping for desserts
- 16 oz. of cream cheese

Directions:

1. Brush pie crust with egg white and cook for 5 minutes in a Pre-heated oven from 375°F from 375°F now down to 350°F.

2. Put together sugar, vanilla, and cream cheese in a large cup, beating with a mixer until smooth.

3. Beat the egg substitute and add pumpkin cream with pie flavoring: blend everything until softened.

4. Put the pumpkin mixture in a pie shell and bake for 50 minutes to set the center.

5. Let the pie cool down and then put it in the fridge. When you wish to, serve it in 8 slices, putting some topping on it. Serve and enjoy!

Per serving: Calories: 364Kcal; Protein: 5g; Carbohydrates: 11g; Fat: 3g

520. CREAMY BUTTERNUT PORRIDGE

Preparation time: 10 minutes
Cooking time: 25 minutes
Servings: 3
Ingredients:

- 2 C. butternut squash, peeled and cubed
- 4 tbsp. coconut kefir
- ¼ tsp. sea salt

Directions:

1. Cook butternut squash in water until tender.

2. Add cooked butternut squash, salt and kefir in a blender and blend until creamy.

3. Serve and enjoy.

Per serving: Calories: 270Kcal; Protein: 2g; Carbohydrates: 4 g; Fat: 1g

521. AVOCADO AND SAUERKRAUT

Preparation time: 5 minutes
Cooking time: 0 minutes
Servings: 1
Ingredients:

- ¼ avocado, pitted and mashed
- 1 tsp. homemade sauerkraut
- 1 pinch Celtic Sea salt

Directions:

1. Slice the avocado and mash with the sauerkraut.
2. Season with salt and enjoy right away.

Per serving: Calories: 298Kcal; Protein: 6g; Carbohydrates: 2g; Fat: 1g

522. DELICIOUS COCONUT MACAROONS

Preparation time: 5 minutes
Cooking time: 30 minutes
Servings: 6
Ingredients:

- 1 tbsp. raw cocoa powder
- 3 dates, pitted
- 2 tsp. vanilla extract
- ¼ C. raisins
- 6 egg whites
- 2 C. coconut, unsweetened and shredded
- ⅛ tsp. sea salt

Directions:

1. Preheat the oven at 350°F/176°C.
2. Combine all ingredients together in the bowl.
3. Line the baking tray with parchment paper.
4. Place 1 tbsp. of dough on the baking tray. Press down to flatten.
5. Bake in preheated oven for around 15 minutes or until golden.
6. Serve and enjoy.

Per serving: Calories: 200Kcal; Protein: 6g; Carbohydrates: 10g; Fat: 3g

523. HEALTHY BROCCOLI MUFFINS

Preparation time: 5 minutes
Cooking time: 30 minutes
Servings: 6
Ingredients:

- 12 eggs, whisked
- Coconut oil
- 1 C. broccoli, chopped
- 1 small onion, chopped
- Pepper
- Sea salt

Directions:

1. Grease muffin tray with coconut oil.
2. Divide broccoli and onion evenly in the muffin tray.
3. Now divide evenly eggs in the muffin tray.
4. Season with pepper and salt.
5. Bake at 400°F/204°C for 15 minutes.

Per serving: Calories: 283Kcal; Protein: 4g; Carbohydrates: 8g; Fat: 3g

524. SIMPLE ZUCCHINI MUFFINS

Preparation time: 5 minutes
Cooking time: 40 minutes
Servings: 5
Ingredients:

- Coconut oil as needed
- 1 C. zucchini, shredded
- 3 eggs
- 1 C. almond flour
- ¼ tsp. sea salt

Directions:

1. Grease muffin tray with coconut oil.
2. Add all ingredients in your blender, and blend until mixed well.
3. Pour into grease muffin tray and bake at 350°F/176°C for 25 minutes.
4. Serve warm and enjoy.

Per serving: Calories: 354Kcal; Protein: 2g; Carbohydrates: 1g; Fat: 1g

525. WHITE BEAN BASIL HUMMUS

Preparation time: 10 minutes
Cooking time: 0 minutes
Servings: 4
Ingredients:

- 2 ½ C. white beans, soaked and cooked
- 1 clove garlic
- 2 C. fresh basil
- 2 tbsp. homemade tahini
- 2 tbsp. lemon juice
- ½ tsp. mineral salt
- ¼ C. olive oil, cold-pressed

Directions:

1. In your food processor or high-speed blender, add all of the ingredients and blend until smooth. If it is too thick, add a splash of water.
2. Serve with chopped, fresh vegetables (cucumbers, peppers, carrots, or celery).

Per serving: Calories: 298Kcal; Protein: 9g; Carbohydrates: 2g; Fat: 1g

526. ORANGE BUTTERSCOTCH PUDDING

Preparation time: 10 minutes
Cooking time: 15 minutes
Servings: 4
Ingredients:

- 4 caramels
- 2 eggs, well-beaten
- ¼ C. orange juice, freshly squeezed
- ⅓ C. sugar
- 1 C. cake flour
- ½ tsp. baking powder
- ¼ C. milk
- 1 stick butter, melted
- ½ tsp. vanilla essence
- Sauce:
- ½ C. golden syrup
- 2 tsp. corn flour
- 1 C. boiling water

Directions:

1. Melt the butter and milk in the microwave. Whisk in the eggs, vanilla, and sugar. After that, stir in the flour, baking powder, and orange juice.
2. Lastly, add the caramels and stir until everything is well combined and melted.
3. Divide into the 4 jars. Add 1 ½ C. of water and a metal trivet to the bottom of the Instant Pot. Lower the jars onto the trivet.
4. To make the sauce, whisk the boiling water, corn flour, and golden syrup until everything is well combined. Pour the sauce into each jar.
5. Secure the lid. Choose the "Steam" mode and cook for 15 minutes under High pressure. Once cooking is complete, use a natural pressure release; carefully remove the lid. Enjoy!

Per serving: Calories: 565Kcal; Protein: 6g; Carbohydrates: 79g; Fat: 25g

527. RUBY PEARS DELIGHT

Preparation time: 10 minutes
Cooking time: 10 minutes
Servings: 4
Ingredients:

- 4 pears
- 26 oz. grape juice
- 11 oz. currant jelly
- 2 garlic cloves
- Juice and zest of 1 lemon
- 4 peppercorns
- 2 rosemary springs
- ½ vanilla bean

Directions:

1. Pour the jelly and grape juice in your instant pot and mix with lemon zest and juice.
2. In the mix, dip each pear and wrap them in a clean tin foil and place them orderly in the steamer basket of your instant pot.
3. Combine peppercorns, rosemary, garlic cloves, and vanilla bean to the juice mixture.
4. Seal the lid and cook at High for 10 minutes.
5. Release the pressure quickly, and carefully open the lid; bring out the pears, remove wrappers and arrange them on plates. Serve when cold with toppings of cooking juice.

Per serving: Calories: 145Kcal; Protein: 1g; Carbohydrates: 1g; Fat: 5g

528. MIXED BERRY AND ORANGE COMPOTE

Preparation time: 15 minutes
Cooking time: 15 minutes
Servings: 4
Ingredients:

- ½-lb. strawberries
- 1 tbsp. orange juice
- ¼ tsp. cloves, ground
- ½ C. brown sugar
- 1 vanilla bean
- 1-lb. blueberries
- ½-lb. blackberries

Directions:

1. Place the berries in the inner pot. Add the sugar and let sit for 15 minutes. Add in the orange juice, ground cloves, and vanilla bean.
2. Secure the lid. Choose the "Manual" mode and cook for 2 minutes at high pressure. Once cooking is complete, use a natural pressure release for 10 minutes; carefully remove the lid.
3. As your compote cools, it will thicken. Bon appétit!

Per serving: Calories: 224Kcal; Protein: 2g; Carbohydrates: 56g; Fat: 0g

529. STREUSELKUCHEN WITH PEACHES

Preparation time: 10 minutes
Cooking time: 20 minutes
Servings: 6
Ingredients:

- 1 C. oats, rolled
- 1 tsp. vanilla extract
- ⅓ C. orange juice
- 4 tbsp. raisins
- 2 tbsp. honey
- 4 tbsp. butter
- 4 tbsp. all-purpose flour
- A pinch nutmeg, grated
- ½ tsp. cardamom, ground
- A pinch salt
- 1 tsp. cinnamon, ground
- 6 peaches, pitted and chopped
- ⅓ C. brown sugar

Directions:

1. Place the peaches at the bottom of the inner pot. Sprinkle with cardamom, cinnamon, and vanilla. Top with orange juice, honey, and raisins.
2. In a mixing bowl, whisk together the butter, oats, flour, brown sugar, nutmeg, and salt. Drop by a spoonful on top of the peaches.
3. Secure the lid. Choose the "Manual" mode and cook for 8 minutes at high pressure. Once cooking is complete, use a natural pressure release for 10 minutes; carefully remove the lid. Bon appétit!

Per serving: Calories: 329Kcal; Protein: 6g; Carbohydrates: 5g; Fat:1g

530. FIG AND HOMEY BUCKWHEAT PUDDING

Preparation time: 10 minutes
Cooking time: 10 minutes
Servings: 4
Ingredients:

- ½ tsp. cinnamon, ground
- ½ C. figs, dried and chopped
- ⅓ C. honey
- 1 tsp. pure vanilla extract
- 3 ½ C. milk
- ½ tsp. pure almond extract
- 1 ½ C. buckwheat

Directions:

1. Add all the above ingredients to your Instant Pot.
2. Secure the lid. Choose the "Multigrain" mode and cook for 10 minutes under high pressure. Once cooking is complete, use a natural pressure release; carefully remove the lid.
3. Serve topped with fresh fruits, nuts, or whipped topping. Bon appétit!

Per serving: Calories: 320Kcal; Protein: 9g; Carbohydrates: 57g; Fat: 7g

531. ZINGY BLUEBERRY SAUCE

Preparation time: 5 minutes
Cooking time: 20 minutes
Servings: 10
Ingredients:

- ¼ C. fresh lemon juice
- 1-lb. sugar, granulated
- 1 tbsp. lemon zest, freshly grated
- ½ tsp. vanilla extract
- 2 lb. fresh blueberries

Directions:

1. Place the blueberries, sugar, and vanilla in the inner pot of your Instant Pot.
2. Secure the lid. Choose the "Manual" mode and cook for 2 minutes at high pressure. Once cooking is complete, use a natural pressure release for 15 minutes; carefully remove the lid.
3. Stir in the lemon zest and juice. Puree in a food processor; then, strain and push the mixture through a sieve before storing. Enjoy!

Per serving: Calories: 230Kcal; Protein: 2g; Carbohydrates: 5g; Fat: 2g

532. SMALL PUMPKIN PASTRY CREAM

Preparation time: 5 minutes
Cooking time: 10 minutes
Servings: 8
Ingredients:

- 1 can (16 oz.) pumpkin, prepared
- 1 (14-oz.) can milk, sweetened and condensed
- 3 eggs, beaten
- 1 tsp. polished ginger, finely chopped (optional)
- 1 tsp. cinnamon, ground
- ¼ tsp. cloves, ground
- 1 C. water

Directions:

1. Mix the pumpkin, milk, eggs, cinnamon, ginger, and cloves. Pour into individual cups for custard.
2. Cover each cup firmly with the foil. Pour the water into the pot. Position the cups on the rack of the pot. Close and secure the lid.
3. Put the pressure regulator on the vent tube and cook for 10 minutes once the pressure regulator begins to rock slowly. Cool the pot quickly. Let the cream cool well in the refrigerator. If desired, serve with whipped cream.

Per serving: Calories: 207Kcal; Protein: 8g; Carbohydrates: 32g; Fat: 7g

533. TAPIOCA PUDDING

Preparation time: 5 minutes

Cooking time: 20 minutes

Servings: 6

Ingredients:

- 2 C. low-Fat milk
- 2 tbsp. quick-cooking tapioca
- 2 eggs, lightly beaten
- ⅓ C. sugar
- ½ tsp. vanilla
- 1 C. water

Directions:

1. Heat the milk and tapioca. Remove from heat then let stand for 15 minutes.
2. Combine eggs, sugar, and vanilla. Add milk and tapioca, stirring constantly.
3. Pour them into individual custard cups. Cover each cup firmly with the foil. Pour the water into the pot.
4. Position the cups on the rack of the pot. Close and secure the lid.
5. Place the pressure regulator on the vent tube and cook for 5 minutes once the pressure regulator begins to rock slowly.
6. Cool the pot quickly. Let the pudding cool well in the refrigerator.

Per serving: Calories: 113Kcal; Protein: 12g; Carbohydrates: 21g; Fat: 8g

534. MANGO MUG CAKE

Preparation time: 5 minutes

Cooking time: 10 minutes

Servings: 2

Ingredients:

- 1 medium-sized mango, peeled and diced
- 2 eggs
- 1 tsp. vanilla
- ¼ tsp. nutmeg, grated
- 1 tbsp. cocoa powder
- 2 tbsp. honey
- ½ C. coconut flour

Directions:

1. Combine the coconut flour, eggs, honey, vanilla, nutmeg, and cocoa powder in 2 lightly greased mugs.
2. Add 1 C. of water and a metal trivet to the Instant Pot. Lower the uncovered mugs onto the trivet.
3. Secure the lid. Choose the "Manual" mode and High pressure; cook for 10 minutes. Once cooking is complete, use a quick pressure release; carefully remove the lid.
4. Top with diced mango and serve chilled. Enjoy!

Per serving: Calories: 268Kcal; Protein: 10g; Carbohydrates: 34g; Fat: 10g

535. HONEY STEWED APPLES

Preparation time: 5 minutes

Cooking time: 5 minutes

Servings: 4

Ingredients:

- 2 tbsp. honey
- 1 tsp. cinnamon, ground
- ½ tsp. cloves, ground
- 4 apples

Directions:

1. Add all ingredients to the inner pot. Now, pour in ⅓ C. of water.
2. Secure the lid. Choose the "Manual" mode and cook for 2 minutes at high pressure. Once cooking is complete, use a quick pressure release; carefully remove the lid.
3. Serve in individual bowls. Bon appétit!

Per serving: Calories: 128Kcal; Protein: 0g; Carbohydrates: 34g; Fat: 0g

536. GREEK-STYLE COMPOTE WITH YOGURT

Preparation time: 5 minutes

Cooking time: 15 minutes

Servings: 4

Ingredients:

- 1 C. Greek yogurt
- 1 C. pears
- 4 tbsp. honey
- 1 C. apples
- 1 vanilla bean
- 1 cinnamon stick
- ½ C. caster sugar
- 1 C. rhubarb
- 1 tsp. ginger, ground
- 1 C. plums

Directions:

1. Place the fruits, ginger, vanilla, cinnamon, and caster sugar in the inner pot of your Instant Pot.
2. Secure the lid. Choose the "Manual" mode and cook for 2 minutes at high pressure. Once cooking is complete, use a natural pressure release for 10 minutes; carefully remove the lid.
3. Meanwhile, whisk the yogurt with the honey.
4. Serve your compote in individual bowls with a dollop of honeyed Greek yogurt. Enjoy!

Per serving: Calories: 304Kcal; Protein: 5g; Carbohydrates: 75g; Fat: 0g

537. BUTTERSCOTCH LAVA CAKES

Preparation time: 5 minutes

Cooking time: 15 minutes

Servings: 6

Ingredients:

- 7 tbsp. all-purpose flour
- A pinch coarse salt
- 6 oz. butterscotch morsels
- ¾ C. sugar, powdered
- ½ tsp. vanilla extract
- 3 eggs, whisked
- 1 stick butter

Directions:

1. Add 1 ½ C. water and a metal rack to the Instant Pot. Line a standard-size muffin tin with muffin papers.
2. In a microwave-safe bowl, microwave butter and butterscotch morsels for about 40 seconds. Stir in the powdered sugar.
3. Add the remaining ingredients. Spoon the batter into the prepared muffin tin.
4. Secure the lid. Choose the "Manual" and cook at High pressure for 10 minutes. Once cooking is complete, use a quick release; carefully remove the lid.
5. To remove, let it cool for 5–6 minutes. Run a small knife around the sides of each cake and serve. Enjoy!

Per serving: Calories: 393Kcal; Protein: 5g; Carbohydrates: 45g; Fat: 21g;

538. VANILLA BREAD PUDDING WITH APRICOTS

Preparation time: 5 minutes

Cooking time: 15 minutes

Servings: 6

Ingredients:

- 2 tbsp. coconut oil
- 1 ⅓ C. heavy cream
- 4 eggs, whisked
- ½ C. apricots, dried, soaked and chopped
- 1 tsp. cinnamon, ground
- ½ tsp. star anise, ground
- A pinch nutmeg, grated
- A pinch salt
- ½ C. sugar, granulated
- 2 tbsp. molasses
- 2 C. milk
- 4 C. Italian bread, cubed
- 1 tsp. vanilla paste

Directions:

1. Add 1 ½ C. water and a metal rack to the Instant Pot.

2. Grease a baking dish with a nonstick cooking spray. Throw the bread cubes into the prepared baking dish.
3. In a mixing bowl, thoroughly combine the remaining ingredients. Pour the mixture over the bread cubes. Cover with a piece of foil, making a foil sling.
4. Secure the lid. Choose the "Porridge" mode and high pressure; cook for 15 minutes. Once cooking is complete, use a quick pressure release; carefully remove the lid. Enjoy!

Per serving: Calories: 410Kcal; Protein: 11.g; Carbohydrates: 37g; Fat: 24g

539. MEDITERRANEAN-STYLE CARROT PUDDING

Preparation time: 15 minutes
Cooking time: 15 minutes
Servings: 4
Ingredients:

- ⅓ C. almonds, ground
- ¼ C. figs, dried and chopped
- 2 large-sized carrots, shredded
- ½ C. water
- 1 ½ C. milk
- ½ tsp. star anise, ground
- ⅓ tsp. cardamom, ground
- ¼ tsp. kosher salt
- ⅓ C. sugar, granulated
- 2 eggs, beaten
- ½ tsp. pure almond extract
- ½ tsp. vanilla extract
- 1 ½ C. jasmine rice

Directions:

1. Place the jasmine rice, milk, water, carrots, and salt in your Instant Pot.
2. Stir to combine and secure the lid. Choose "Manual" and cook at High pressure for 10 minutes. Once cooking is complete, use a natural release for 15 minutes; carefully remove the lid.
3. Now, press the "Sauté" button and add the sugar, eggs, and almonds; stir to combine well. Bring to a boil; press the "Keep Warm/Cancel" button.
4. Add the remaining ingredients and stir; the pudding will thicken as it sits. Bon appétit!

Per serving: Calories: 331Kcal; Protein: 13g; Carbohydrates: 44g; Fat: 17g

540. OATMEAL CAKES WITH MANGO

Preparation time: 5 minutes
Cooking time: 17 minutes
Servings: 2
Ingredients:
Hotcakes:

- 2 C. oatmeal
- 3 eggs
- 1 tbsp. baking powder
- 1¼ C. natural yogurt
- 1 tsp. vanilla extract
- 1 C. apple, chopped into small cubes
- Oil spray

Mango honey (syrup):

- 2 C. mango, diced
- Orange juice
- 1 tbsp. maple honey
- 1 tbsp. vanilla extract
- 1 cinnamon stick

Directions:

1. In the pot, place all the ingredients of mango honey. Cover with the valve open then cook at medium-high temperature until it whistles (in about 5 minutes). Place the temperature to low, remove the lid and continue cooking for 4 more minutes. Let cool a little and blend for a few seconds until you get a homogeneous mixture.
2. Also, blend all the ingredients of the hotcakes (except apple and oil spray) at speed 6, for 1 minute (until you get a homogeneous consistency). Pour into the Mixing Bowl and stir with the apple pieces, using the Balloon Whisk.
3. Pre-heat at medium-high temperature for 2 minutes. Reduce the temperature to low and sprinkle some oil spray.
4. Cook 6–8 hotcakes, for 2 minutes per side. Repeat with the remaining mixture.

Per serving: Calories: 245Kcal; Protein: 8g; Carbohydrates: 51g; Fat: 4g;

541. RIPE BANANA PUDDING

Preparation time: 5 minutes
Cooking time: 25 minutes
Servings: 8
Ingredients:

- 1 lb. (½ kg) white/square white bread, in thick slices
- 1 can milk, condensed (14 oz./396 ml)
- 1 can milk, evaporated (12 oz./354 ml)
- 1 C. coconut milk
- 3 eggs, beaten
- ½ C. Marsala wine (optional)
- 2 ripe bananas, chopped into small pieces
- ½ C. pecan nuts (optional)
- 1 tsp. vanilla extract
- 1 tsp. cinnamon, ground
- ½ tsp. nutmeg powder
- 1 tsp. whole wheat flour (optional)
- Oil spray

Directions:

1. Chop the bread into medium cubes. Place it in the bowl, and pour half of the condensed milk, half of the evaporated milk, and half of the coconut milk. Stir well.
2. Add the beaten eggs, wine, bananas, nuts, vanilla extract, cinnamon, and nutmeg. Combine and let the bread absorb the mixture for about 15 minutes.
3. Meanwhile, in the pot, mix the remaining portions of the 3 types of milk (evaporated, condensed, and coconut), and cook for 8 minutes at medium temperature, or until they begin to thicken. Stir occasionally. If you need thickness, add whole wheat flour.
4. Preheat the skillet over medium heat for 2 minutes, sprinkle oil spray, and add the bread mixture.
5. Reduce the temperature to low, cover, and cook for 18 minutes.
6. Remove the pan from the pot and let stand for about 5 minutes.
7. Serve and pour a little of the milk mixture into each serving.

Per serving: Calories: 288Kcal; Protein: 2g; Carbohydrates: 4g; Fat: 1g

542. PICOSITOS BROWNIES

Preparation time: 5 minutes
Cooking time: 15 minutes;
Servings: 8
Ingredients:

- 3 C. brownies mix
- 2 eggs
- ⅓ C. milk
- ½ tsp. cayenne pepper
- 1 tsp. cinnamon
- 1 tsp. vanilla extract
- ¼ C. chocolate sprinkles
- Liquid candy, to taste (decoration)
- Chocolate sauce, to taste (decoration)
- Oil spray

Directions:

1. In a bowl, stir the following ingredients untila homogeneous mixture is obtained. Be sure to add them little by little, in the same order: mix for brownies, eggs, milk, cayenne pepper, cinnamon, vanilla, and chocolate sprinkles.
2. Pre-heat the skillet at medium-high temperature for 2 and a half minutes. Cover the pot with spray oil and reduce the temperature to low. Make sure the oil does not start to burn.
3. Add the previous mixture immediately, cover with the valve closed and cook for 15 minutes. Turn off the pot, remove the pan from the burner and let it sit for 3 minutes. Carefully invert the brownies on the Bamboo Cutting Board, slice it, and serve with caramel or chocolate sauce.

Per serving: Calories: 539Kcal; Protein: 1g; Carbohydrates: 5g; Fat: 3g

543. FRUIT CREPES

Preparation time: 5 minutes
Cooking time: 15 minutes
Servings: 4
Ingredients:
Crepes:

- 1 C. wheat flour
- 2 eggs
- 1¼ C. milk
- 1 tsp. vanilla extract
- 2 tbsp. butter, melted
- A pinch salt
- Sugar, powdered, to taste
- Olive oil spray

Filling:

- 2 C. strawberries, sliced
- ½ C. sour cream
- ¼ C. brown sugar
- 1 tsp. vanilla extract

Directions:

1. In a bowl, combine the flour and eggs. Add the milk gradually. Then add the vanilla extract, butter, salt, and icing sugar. Beat well until you get a homogeneous mixture.
2. In the other bowl, combine the filling ingredients well with the help of the Spatula.
3. Pre-heat the skillet at medium-high temperature for about 2 and a half minutes and immediately lower the temperature to low. Cover the pan with olive oil spray.
4. With the help of the ladle, add approximately ⅛ C. of the mixture

to the pan. Tilt the pan slightly to allow the mixture to spread evenly across the surface.
5. Cook the crepes for 40–45 seconds per side, or until lightly browned. Use the Silicone Spatula to flip them.
6. Repeat steps 4 and 5 with the remaining mixture. Add more spray oil, if necessary.
7. Fill the crepes and serve with syrup.

Per serving: Calories: 101Kcal; Protein: 3g; Carbohydrates: 1g; Fat: 1g

544. CHOCOLATE CUPS

Preparation time: 2 hours
Cooking time: 0 minutes
Servings: 6
Ingredients:

- ½ C. avocado oil
- 1 C., chocolate, melted
- 1 tsp. matcha powder
- 3 tbsp. stevia

Directions:

1. In a bowl, mix the chocolate with the oil and the rest of the ingredients, whisk really well, divide into cups and keep in the freezer for 2 hours before serving.

Per serving: Calories: 174Kcal; Protein: 2g; Carbohydrates: 3.g; Fat: 9g

545. MANGO BOWLS

Preparation time: 30 minutes
Cooking time: 0 minutes
Servings: 4
Ingredients:

- 3 C. mango, cut into medium chunks
- ½ C. coconut water
- ¼ C. stevia
- 1 tsp. vanilla extract

Directions:

1. In your blender, combine the mango with the rest of the ingredients, pulse well, divide into bowls and serve cold.

Per serving: Calories: 122Kcal; Protein: 4.g; Carbohydrates: 6. Fat: 2g

546. COCOA AND PEARS CREAM

Preparation time: 10 minutes
Cooking time: 0 minutes
Servings: 4
Ingredients:

- 2 C. heavy creamy
- ⅓ C. stevia
- ¾ C. cocoa powder

- 6 oz. dark chocolate, chopped
- Zest of 1 lemon
- 2 pears, chopped

Directions:

1. In a blender, combine the cream with the stevia and the rest of the ingredients, pulse well, divide into cups and serve cold.

Per serving: Calories: 172Kcal; Protein: 10g; Carbohydrates: 7g; Fat: 5g

547. PINEAPPLE PUDDING

Preparation time: 10 minutes
Cooking time: 40minutes
Servings: 4
Ingredients:

- 3 C. almond flour
- ¼ C. olive oil
- 1 tsp. vanilla extract
- 2 and ¼ C. stevia
- 3 eggs, whisked
- 1 and ¼ C. natural apple sauce
- 2 tsp. baking powder
- 1 and ¼ C. almond milk
- 2 C. pineapple, chopped
- Cooking spray

Directions:

1. In a bowl, combine the almond flour with the oil and the rest of the ingredients except the cooking spray and stir well.
2. Grease a cake pan with the cooking spray, pour the pudding mix inside, put it in the oven and bake at 370°F for 40 minutes.
3. Serve the pudding cold.

Per serving: Calories: 223Kcal; Protein: 4g; Carbohydrates: 7g; Fat: 8g

548. VANILLA CAKE

Preparation time: 5 minutes
Cooking time: 23 minutes
Servings: 12
Ingredients:
Flan:

- 1 C. milk, condensed
- 1 C. milk, evaporated
- 3 eggs
- 1 tsp. vanilla extract

Cake:

- 2 C. chocolate cake mix
- 2 eggs
- ¾ C. non-fat milk
- Oil spray

Directions:
Flan:

1. Blend condensed milk, evaporated milk, 3 eggs and vanilla extract for 2 minutes. Reserve this mix.

Cake:

2. In the bowl, combine the cake mix, eggs, and milk with the help of the Balloon Whisk. Reserve this preparation.
3. Pre-heat the pan at medium-high temperature for 3 minutes; Remove the pan from the stove for 1 minute and lightly spray the spray oil all over the surface, including the walls of the pan.
4. Add the cake mixture to the pan. With the help of a spoon, pour the flan mixture evenly. Put the pan back on the pot, reduce the temperature to low, cover with the valve closed, and cook for 23 minutes.
5. Let the pan rest for a few minutes. Turn it carefully, so that the cake falls on a plate or flat surface. Slice it and serve.

Per serving: Calories: 84.62Kcal; Protein: 3.7g; Carbohydrates: 5g; Fat: 7.0g

549. VANILLA PASTRY CREAM

Preparation time: 5 minutes
Cooking time: 5 minutes
Servings: 4
Ingredients:

- 2 C. low Fat milk
- 2 eggs, lightly beaten
- ¼ C. sugar
- ¼ tsp. salt
- ½ tsp. vanilla
- Nutmeg as desired
- 1 C. water

Directions:

1. Combine milk, eggs, sugar, salt, and vanilla and pour into individual custard cups. . Sprinkle with nutmeg.
2. Cover each cup firmly with the foil. Pour the water into the pot. Position the cups on the rack of the pot.
3. Close and secure the lid. Place the pressure regulator on the vent tube and cook for 5 minutes once the pressure regulator begins to rock slowly.
4. Cool the pot quickly. Let the cream cool well in the refrigerator.

Per serving: Calories: 137Kcal; Protein: 14g; Carbohydrates: 34g; Fat: 5g

550. CHOCOLATE COFFEE POTS DE CRÈME

Preparation time: 10 minutes
Cooking time: 15 minutes
Servings: 6
Ingredients:

- 1 tsp. instant coffee
- 9 oz. chocolate chips
- ½ C. whole milk
- ⅓ C. sugar
- A pinch pink salt
- 4 egg yolks
- 2 C. double cream

Directions:

1. Place a metal trivet and 1 C. of water in your Instant Pot.
2. In a saucepan, bring the cream and milk to a simmer.
3. Then, thoroughly combine the egg yolks, sugar, instant coffee, and salt. Slowly and gradually, whisk in the hot cream mixture.
4. Whisk in the chocolate chips and blend again. Pour the mixture into mason jars. Lower the jars onto the trivet.
5. Secure the lid. Choose the "Manual" mode and cook for 6 minutes at high pressure. Once cooking is complete, use a natural pressure release for 10 minutes; carefully remove the lid.
6. Serve well chilled, and enjoy!

Per serving: Calories: 351Kcal; Protein: 5g; Carbohydrates: 39g; Fat: 19g

551. CHOCOLATE PUDDING

Preparation time: 10 minutes
Cooking time: 20 minutes
Servings: 4
Ingredients:

- 6 oz. bittersweet chocolate, chopped
- ½ C. milk
- 1½ C. heavy cream
- 5 egg yolks
- ⅓ C. brown sugar
- 2 tsp. vanilla extract
- 1½ C. water
- ¼ tsp. cardamom
- Salt
- Crème fraiche, for serving
- Chocolate shavings, for serving

Directions:

1. Put the cream and milk in a pot, bring to a simmer over medium heat, take off the heat, add the chocolate and whisk well. In a bowl, mix the egg yolks with the vanilla, sugar, cardamom, and a pinch of

salt, stir, strain, and mix with chocolate mixture. Pour this into a soufflé dish, cover with aluminum foil, place in the steamer basket of the Instant Pot, add water to the Instant Pot, cover, and cook on Manual for 18 minutes, release the pressure naturally.
2. Take the pudding out of the Instant Pot, set aside to cool down, and keep it in the refrigerator for 3 hours before serving with crème Fraiche and chocolate shavings on top.

Per serving: Calories: 200Kcal; Protein: 14g; Carbohydrates: 20g; Fat: 3g

552. REFRESHING CURD

Preparation time: 10 minutes
Cooking time: 5 minutes
Servings: 4
Ingredients:

- 3 tbsp. stevia
- 12 oz. raspberries
- 2 egg yolks
- 2 tbsp. lemon juice
- 2 tbsp. ghee

Directions:

1. Put raspberries in your instant pot, add stevia and lemon juice, stir, cover, and cook on High for 2 minutes.
2. Strain this into a bowl, add egg yolks, stir well and return to your pot.
3. Set the pot on Simmer mode, cook for 2 minutes, add ghee, stir well, transfer to a container and serve cold.
4. Enjoy!

Per serving: Calories: 132Kcal; Protein: 4g; Carbohydrates: 2g; Fat: 1g

553. THE BEST JAM EVER

Preparation time: 10 minutes
Cooking time: 5 minutes
Servings: 6
Ingredients:

- 4 and ½ C. peaches, peeled and cubed
- 4 tbsp. stevia
- ¼ C. ginger, crystallized and chopped

Directions:

1. Set your instant pot on 'Simmer' mode, add peaches, ginger, and stevia, stir, bring to a boil, cover and cook on High for 5 minutes.
2. Divide into bowls and serve cold.
3. Enjoy!

Per serving: Calories: 53Kcal; Protein: 2g; Carbohydrates: 0g; Fat: 0g

554. RASPBERRY CURD

Preparation time: 10 minutes
Cooking time: 5 minutes
Servings: 4
Ingredients:

- 1 C. sugar
- 12 oz. raspberries
- 2 egg yolks
- 2 tbsp. lemon juice
- 2 tbsp. butter

Directions:

1. Put the raspberries into the Instant Pot. Add the sugar and lemon juice, stir, cover, and cook on the Manual setting for 2 minutes.
2. Release the pressure for 5 minutes, uncover the Instant Pot, strain the raspberries and discard the seeds.
3. In a bowl, mix the egg yolks with raspberries and stir well. Return this to the Instant Pot, set it on Sauté mode, simmer for 2 minutes, add the butter, stir, and transfer to a container. Serve cold.

Per serving: Calories: 110Kcal; Protein: 1g; Carbohydrates: 16g; Fat: 4g

555. PEAR JAM

Preparation time: 10 minutes
Cooking time: 4 minutes
Servings: 12
Ingredients:

- 8 pears, cored, and cut into quarters
- 2 apples, peeled, cored, and cut into quarters
- ¼ C. apple juice
- 1 tsp. cinnamon, ground

Directions:

1. In the Instant Pot, mix the pears with apples, cinnamon, and apple juice, stir, cover, and cook on the Manual setting for 4 minutes. Release the pressure naturally, uncover the Instant Pot, blend using an immersion blender, divide the jam into jars, and keep it in a cold place until you serve it.

Per serving: Calories: 90Kcal; Protein: 0g; Carbohydrates: 20g; Fat: 0g

556. BERRY COMPOTE

Preparation time: 10 minutes
Cooking time: 5 minutes
Servings: 8

Ingredients:

- 1 C. blueberries
- 2 C. strawberries, sliced
- 2 tbsp. lemon juice
- ¾ C. sugar
- 1 tbsp. cornstarch
- 1 tbsp. water

Directions:

1. In the Instant Pot, mix the blueberries with lemon juice and sugar, stir, cover, and cook on the Manual setting for 3 minutes. Release the pressure naturally for 10 minutes and uncover the Instant Pot. In a bowl, mix the cornstarch with water, stir well, and add to the Instant Pot.
2. Stir, set the Instant Pot on Sauté mode, and cook compote for 2 minutes. Divide into jars and keep in the refrigerator until you serve it.

Per serving: Calories: 260Kcal; Protein: 3g; Carbohydrates: 23g; Fat: 13g

557. APPLE COUSCOUS PUDDING

Preparation time: 10 minutes
Cooking time: 25 minutes
Servings: 4
Ingredients:

- ½ cup couscous
- ½ cups milk
- ¼ cup apple, cored and chopped
- 2 tbsps. stevia
- ½ tsp. rose water
- 1 tbsp. orange zest, grated

Directions:

1. Heat the milk in a saucepan over medium heat, then add the couscous and the remaining ingredients, whisking constantly. Simmer for 25 minutes, then divide into bowls and serve.

Per serving: Calories 150Kcal; Protein: 4g; Carbohydrates: 7.5g; Fat: 4.5g

558. RICOTTA RAMEKINS

Preparation time: 10 minutes
Cooking time: 1 hour
Servings: 4
Ingredients:

- 6 eggs, whisked
- ½ pounds ricotta cheese, soft
- ½ pound stevia
- 1 tsp. vanilla extract
- ½ tsp. baking powder
- Cooking spray as needed

Directions:

1. In a medium sized bowl, whisk together the eggs, and then add the

cottage cheese, and all other ingredients (except the cooking spray).
2. Spray 4 ramekins with cooking spray, spoon ricotta cream into each, and bake for 1 hour at 360 °F. Serve cold.

Per serving: Calories 180Kcal; Protein: 4g; Carbohydrates: 11.5g; Fat: 5.3g

559. PAPAYA CREAM

Preparation time: 10 minutes
Cooking time: 0 minutes
Servings: 2
Ingredients:

- 1 cup papaya, peeled and chopped
- 1 cup heavy cream
- 1 tbsp. stevia
- ½ tsp. vanilla extract

Directions:

1. In a blender, combine the cream with the papaya and the other ingredients, pulse well, divide into cups and serve cold.

Per serving: Calories 182Kcal; Protein: 2g; Carbohydrates: 3.5g; Fat: 3.1g

560. ORANGE CAKE

Preparation time: 20 minutes
Cooking time: 60 minutes
Servings: 8
Ingredients:

- 4 oranges
- 1/3 cup water
- ½ cup Erythritol
- ½ tsp. ground cinnamon
- 4 eggs, beaten
- 3 tbsps. stevia powder
- 10 oz. Phyllo pastry
- ½ tsp. baking powder
- ½ cup Plain yogurt
- 3 tbsps. olive oil

Directions:

1. Squeeze the juice from 1 orange and pour it in the saucepan.
2. Add water, squeezed orange, water, ground cinnamon, and Erythritol. Bring the liquid to boil.
3. Simmer the liquid for 5 minutes over medium heat. When the time is over, cool it.
4. Grease the baking mold with 1 tbsp. of olive oil. Chop the phyllo dough and place it in the baking mold.
5. Slice ½ of orange for decorating the cake. Slice it. Squeeze juice from remaining oranges.
6. Then mix up together, squeeze orange juice, plain yogurt, baking

powder, stevia powder, and eggs. Add remaining olive oil

7. Mix up the mixture with the help of a hand mixer.

8. Pour the liquid over the chopped Phyllo dough. Stir to distribute evenly.

9. Top the cake with sliced orange (left for decorating).

10. Bake the dessert for 50 minutes at 370F.

11. Pour the baked cake with cooled orange juice syrup. Leave it for 10 minutes to let the cake soaks the syrup.

12. Cut it into servings.

Per serving: Calories 237Kcal; Protein: 1.9g; Carbohydrates: 36.9g; Fat: 4.4 g

CHAPTER 11: Drinks and Smoothies

561. BLUEBERRY MATCHA SMOOTHIE

Preparation time: 5 minutes
Cooking time: 0 minutes
Servings: 2
Ingredients:

- 2 Cups Blueberries, Frozen
- 2 Cups Almond Milk
- 1 Banana
- 2 Tablespoons Protein: Powder, Optional
- ¼ tsp. Ground Cinnamon
- 1 tbs. Chia Seeds
- 1 tbs. Matcha Powder
- ¼ tsp. Ground Ginger
- A Pinch Sea Salt

Directions:

1. Blend everything until smooth.

Per serving: Calories: 208Kcal; Protein: 8g; Carbohydrates: 3g; Fat: 5.g

562. PUMPKIN PIE SMOOTHIE

Preparation time: 5 minutes
Cooking time: 0 minutes
Servings: 2
Ingredients:

- 1 Banana
- ½ Cup Pumpkin, Canned & Unsweetened
- 2-3 Ice Cubes
- 1 Cup Almond Milk
- 2 Tablespoons Almond Butter, Heaping
- 1 tsp. Ground Nutmeg
- 1 tsp. Ground Cinnamon
- 1 tsp. Vanilla Extract Pure
- 1 tsp. Maple Syrup, Pure

Directions:

1. Blend everything together until smooth.

Per serving: Calories: 235Kcal; Protein: 5g; Carbohydrates: 27g; Fat: 1g

563. RASPBERRY BANANA SMOOTHIE

Preparation time: 10 minutes
Cooking time: 0 minutes
Servings: 1
Ingredients:

- 1 banana
- 16 whole almonds
- 1/4 cup rolled oats
- 1 tbsp. flaxseed meal
- 1 cup frozen raspberries
- 1 cup raspberry yogurt
- 1/4 cup Concord grape juice
- 1 cup almond milk

Directions:

1. Add everything to a blender jug.
2. Cover the jug tightly.
3. Blend until smooth and then serve. Enjoy!

Per serving: Calories: 214Kcal; Protein: 5g; Carbohydrates: 4g; Fat: 0g

564. ALMOND BLUEBERRY SMOOTHIE

Preparation time: 10 minutes
Cooking time: 0 minutes
Servings: 1
Ingredients:

- 1 cup frozen blueberries
- 1 banana
- 1/2 cup almond milk
- 1 tbsp. almond butter
- Water, as needed

Directions:

1. Add everything to a blender jug.
2. Cover the jug tightly.
3. Blend until smooth. Serve and enjoy!

Per serving: Calories: 211Kcal; Protein: 5g; Carbohydrates: 3g; Fat: 0g

565. GREEN VANILLA SMOOTHIE

Preparation time: 10 minutes
Cooking time: 0 minutes
Servings: 1
Ingredients:

- 1 banana, cut in chunks
- 1 cup grapes
- 1 tub (6 oz.) vanilla yogurt
- 1/2 apple, cored and chopped
- 1 1/2 cups fresh spinach leaves

Directions:

1. Add everything to a blender jug.
2. Cover the jug tightly.
3. Blend until smooth. Serve and enjoy!

Per serving: Calories: 131Kcal; Protein: 2g; Carbohydrates: 9g; Fat: 0.g

566. PURPLE FRUIT SMOOTHIE

Preparation time: 10 minutes
Cooking time: 0 minutes
Servings: 1
Ingredients:

- 2 frozen bananas, cut in chunks
- 1/2 cup frozen blueberries
- 1 cup orange juice
- 1 tbsp. honey, optional
- 1 tsp. vanilla extract, optional

Directions:

1. Add everything to a blender jug.
2. Cover the jug tightly.
3. Blend until smooth. Serve and enjoy!

Per serving: Calories: 133Kcal; Protein: 3g; Carbohydrates: 7g; Fat: 1g

567. VANILLA AVOCADO SMOOTHIE

Preparation time: 10 minutes
Cooking time: 0 minutes
Servings: 1
Ingredients:

- 1 ripe avocado, halved and pitted
- 1 cup almond milk
- 1/2 cup vanilla yogurt
- 3 tbsp. honey
- 8 ice cubes

Directions:

1. Add everything to a blender jug.
2. Cover the jug tightly.
3. Blend until smooth. Serve and enjoy!

Per serving: Calories: 143Kcal; Protein: 4g; Carbohydrates: 2g; Fat: 1g

568. TRIPLE FRUIT SMOOTHIE

Preparation time: 10 minutes
Cooking time: 0 minutes
Servings: 1
Ingredients:

- 1 kiwi, sliced
- 1 banana, peeled and chopped
- 1/2 cup blueberries
- 1 cup strawberries
- 1 cup ice cubes
- 1/2 cup orange juice
- 1 container (8 oz.) peach yogurt

Directions:

1. Add everything to a blender jug.
2. Cover the jug tightly.
3. Blend until smooth. Serve and enjoy!

Per serving: Calories: 124Kcal; Protein: 5g; Carbohydrates: 3g; Fat: 0g

569. PEACH MAPLE SMOOTHIE

Preparation time: 10 minutes
Cooking time: 0 minutes
Servings: 1

Ingredients:

- 4 large peaches, peeled and chopped
- 2 tbsp. maple syrup
- 1 cup fat-free yogurt
- 1 cup ice

Directions:

1. Add everything to a blender jug.
2. Cover the jug tightly.
3. Blend until smooth. Serve and enjoy!

Per serving: Calories: 125Kcal; Protein: 5g; Carbohydrates: 5g; Fat: 0g;

570. PINK CALIFORNIA SMOOTHIE

Preparation time: 10 minutes
Cooking time: 0 minutes
Servings: 1
Ingredients:

- 7 large strawberries
- 1 container (8 oz.) lemon yogurt
- 1/3 cup orange juice

Directions:

1. Add everything to a blender jug.
2. Cover the jug tightly.
3. Blend until smooth. Serve and enjoy!

Per serving: Calories: 144Kcal; Protein: 5g; Carbohydrates: 3g; Fat: 0g

571. MANGO AND GINGER INFUSED WATER

Preparation time: 5 minutes
Cooking time: 5 minutes
Servings: 4
Ingredients:

- 1 cup fresh mango, chopped
- 2-inch piece ginger, peeled, cubed
- Water to cover ingredients

Directions:

1. Place ingredients in the mesh steamer basket.
2. Place basket in the instant pot.
3. Add water to cover contents.
4. Lock the lid. Cook on HIGH pressure 5 minutes.
5. Once done, release pressure quickly.
6. Remove steamer basket. Discard cooked produce.
7. Allow flavored water to cool. Chill completely. Serve.

Per serving: Calories: 209Kcal; Protein: 2g; Carbohydrates: 51g; Fat: 1g

72. PEACH AND RASPBERRY LEMONADE

Preparation time: 5 minutes
Cooking time: 5 minutes

Servings: 4
Ingredients:

- 1 cup fresh peaches, chopped
- ½ cup fresh raspberries
- Zest and juice of 1 lemon
- Water to cover ingredients

Directions:

1. Place ingredients in mesh basket for instant pot. Place in pot.
2. Add water to barely cover the fruit.
3. Lock the lid. Cook on HIGH pressure 5 minutes.
4. Once done, release pressure quickly.
5. Remove steamer basket. Discard cooked produce.
6. Allow flavored water to cool. Chill completely before serving.

Per serving: Calories: 77Kcal; Protein: 0g; Carbohydrates: 19g; Fat: 0g

573. SWEET CRANBERRY JUICE

Preparation time: 5 minutes
Cooking time: 8 minutes
Servings: 4
Ingredients:

- 4 cups fresh cranberries
- 1 cinnamon stick
- 1-gallon filtered water
- ½ cup honey
- Juice of 1 lemon

Directions:

1. Add cranberries, ½ of water, cinnamon stick to the instant pot.
2. Lock the lid. Cook on HIGH pressure 8 minutes.
3. Release pressure naturally.
4. Once cool, strain liquid. Add remaining water.
5. Stir in honey and lemon. Cool completely.
6. Chill before serving.

Per serving: Calories: 184Kcal; Protein: 1g; Carbohydrates: 49g; Fat: 0g

574. VANILLA TURMERIC ORANGE JUICE

Preparation time: 5 minutes
Cooking time: 0 minutes
Servings: 2
Ingredients:

- 6 oranges, peeled, separated into segments, deseeded
- 2 tsp. vanilla extract
- ½ tsp. turmeric powder
- 2 cups unsweetened almond milk
- 1 tsp. ground cinnamon
- Pepper to taste

Directions:

1. Juice the oranges. Add the rest of the ingredients.
2. Pour into glasses and serve.

Per serving: Calories: 223Kcal; Protein: 11.4g; Carbohydrates: 15.g; Fat: 11.7g

575. CUCUMBER KIWI GREEN SMOOTHIE

Preparation time: 5 minutes
Cooking time: 0 minutes
Servings: 2
Ingredients:

- 2 ripe kiwi fruit
- 1 cup of seedless cucumber, chopped
- 1 cup of coconut water
- 6 to 8 ice cubes
- ice cubes
- ¼ cup of canned coconut milk
- 2 tbsps. of fresh chopped cilantro

Directions:

1. Combine the smoothie ingredients in high-speed blender.
2. Pulse for a few times to cut them up.
3. Blend the mixture on the highest speed setting for 30 to 60 seconds.
4. Pour finished smoothie into glasses and drink.

Per serving: Calories: 140Kcal; Protein: 5g; Carbohydrates: 7g; Fat: 10.5g

576. TROPICAL PINEAPPLE KIWI SMOOTHIE

Preparation time: 5 minutes
Cooking time: 0 minutes
Servings: 2
Ingredients:

- 1 ½ cup of frozen pineapple
- 1 ripe kiwi; peeled and chopped
- 1 cup of canned full-Fat: coconut milk
- 6 to 8 ice cubes
- 1 tsp of spirulina powder
- 3 tsp of lime juice

Directions:

1. Combine the smoothie ingredients in r high-speed blender.
2. Pulse for a few times to cut them up.
3. Blend the mixture on the highest speed setting.
4. Pour finished smoothie into glasses and drink.

Per serving: Calories: 480Kcal; Protein: 7.3g; Carbohydrates: 48.3g; Fat: 31.9g

577. DREAMY YUMMY ORANGE CREAM SMOOTHIE

Preparation time: 5 minutes
Cooking time: 0 minutes
Servings: 2
Ingredients:

- 1 navel orange, peel removed
- 1 cup of almond milk
- 6 to 8 ice cubes
- ½ cup of canned full-Fat: coconut milk
- ¼ cup of fresh orange juice

Directions:

1. Combine the smoothie ingredients in your high-speed blender.
2. Pulse for a few times to cut them up.
3. Blend the mixture on the highest speed setting for 30 to 60 seconds.
4. Pour finished smoothie into glasses and drink.

Per serving: Calories: 269Kcal; Protein: 8.6g; Carbohydrates: 12.7g; Fat: 21.3g

578. PEACHY KEEN SMOOTHIE

Preparation time: 5 minutes
Cooking time: 0 minutes
Servings: 2
Ingredients:

- 1 ½ cups of frozen peaches
- 1 small frozen banana
- 1 cup of almond milk
- 6 to 8 ice cubes
- 2 tbsp. of raw hemp seeds
- Pinch of ground ginger

Directions:

1. Combine the smoothie ingredients in high-speed blender.
2. Pulse for a few times to cut them up.
3. Blend the mixture on the highest speed setting for 30 to 60 seconds.
4. Pour finished smoothie into glasses and drink.

Per serving: Calories: 388Kcal; Protein: 10.5g; Carbohydrates: 64.0g; Fat: 11.9g

579. CUCUMBER MELON SMOOTHIE

Preparation time: 5 minutes
Cooking time: 0 minutes
Servings: 2
Ingredients:

- 1 ½ cups of chopped honeydew
- 1 cup of seedless cucumber, diced
- 1 cup of chilled coconut water
- 6 to 8 ice cubes

- 2 tbsp. of fresh mint

Directions:

1. Combine the smoothie ingredients in high-speed blender.
2. Pulse for a few times to cut them up.
3. Blend the mixture on the highest speed setting for 30 to 60 seconds.
4. Pour finished smoothie into glasses and drink.

Per serving: Calories: 300Kcal; Protein: 5.8g; Carbohydrates: 51.2g; Fat: 8.5g

580. TROPICAL MANGO COCONUT SMOOTHIE

Preparation time: 5 minutes
Cooking time: 0 minutes
Servings: 2
Ingredients:

- 1 ½ cups of frozen mango
- 1 medium frozen banana
- ½ cup of fresh orange juice
- ½ cup of canned coconut milk
- 1 tbsp. of fresh lemon juice
- 1 ½ tsp of honey

Directions:

1. Combine the smoothie ingredients in yhigh-speed blender.
2. Pulse for a few times to cut them up.
3. Blend the mixture on the highest speed setting for 30 to 60 seconds.
4. Pour finished smoothie into glasses and drink.

Per serving: Calories: 354Kcal; Protein: 6.g; Carbohydrates: 47.4g; Fat: 18.0g

581. BLUEBERRY AND STRAWBERRY SMOOTHIE

Preparation time: 5 minutes
Cooking time: 0 minutes
Servings: 2
Ingredients:

- 6–7 strawberries, sliced
- ½ lb. blueberries
- ½ pint almond milk

Directions:

1. Add all ingredients to a blender jar. Blend until smooth. Add to serving glasses.
2. Serve and enjoy.

Per serving: Calories: 107Kcal; Protein: 4g; Carbohydrates: 7g; Fat: 7g

582. BLUEBERRY AND APPLE SMOOTHIE

Preparation time: 25 minutes
Cooking time: 15 minutes
Servings: 4
Ingredients:

- 1 Brae burn apple, or another kind of organic apple
- ½-1 lb. Brazil nuts
- ½ lb. homemade walnut milk
- ½ lb. blueberries
- ½ lb. approved greens (dandelion greens, turnip greens, watercress, etc.)
- ½ tbsp. date sugar or agave syrup

Directions:

1. Combine all the ingredients in a high-speed mixer. Add more water if the mixture is too concentrated.

Per serving: Calories: 181Kcal; Protein: 3.8g; Carbohydrates: 30.2g; Fat: 5.8g

583. BLUEBERRY PIE SMOOTHIE

Preparation time: 20 minutes
Cooking time: 0 minutes
Servings: 2
Ingredients:

- 1 oz. fresh blueberries
- 1 burro banana
- 1 glass coconut milk
- ½ lb. amaranth, cooked
- 1 tsp. Bromide Plus Powder
- 1 tbsp. homemade walnut butter
- 1 tbsp. date sugar

Directions:

1. Combine all the ingredients in a high-speed mixer. Add more water if the mixture is too concentrated.

Per serving: Calories: 413Kcal; Protein: 5.8g; Carbohydrates: 32g; Fat: 31.9g

584. CUCUMBER AND CARLEY GREEN SMOOTHIE

Preparation time: 10 minutes
Cooking time: 0 minutes
Servings: 4
Ingredients:

- 1 lb. soft jelly coconut water
- 4 cucumbers, seeded
- 2–3 key limes
- 1 bunch basil or sweet basil leaves
- ½ tsp. Bromide Plus Powder

Directions:

1. Mix cucumbers, basil, and lime. If you don't have a juicer, treat them in a grinder with sweet coconut jelly. Transfer into a tall glass and stir in

coconut water to make it smooth, and add powdered bromide. Mix well and enjoy.

Per serving: Calories: 141Kcal; Protein: 5g; Carbohydrates: 14.2g; Fat: 7.4g

585. KALE AND GINGER SMOOTHIE

Preparation time: 5 minutes
Cooking time: 0 minute
Servings: 2
Ingredients:

- 2 C. spring water
- 1 C. kale leaves, fresh
- ¼ C. key lime juice
- 1 medium fresh apple, cored
- 1-inch piece ginger, fresh
- 1 C. fresh cucumber, sliced
- 1 tbsp. sea moss gel

Directions:

1. Take a high-powered blender, switch it on, and then place all the ingredients inside, in order.
2. Close blender, then pulses at high speed for 1 minute.

Per serving: Calories: 65.5Kcal; Protein: 0.7g; Carbohydrates: 14.7g; Fat: 0.4g

586. ARUGULA AND CUCUMBER SMOOTHIE

Preparation time: 5 minutes
Cooking time: 0 minute
Servings: 2
Ingredients:

- 2 C. spring water
- 1 large bunch callaloo, fresh
- ¼ C. lime juice
- 1 C. fresh cucumber, diced
- 1 large bunch arugulas, fresh
- ¼ of a honeydew, fresh
- 1-inch piece ginger, fresh
- 1 pear, destemmed, diced
- 6 Medjool dates, pitted
- 1 tbsp. sea moss gel

Directions:

1. Take a high-powered blender, switch it on, and then place all the ingredients inside, in order.
2. Close blender, then pulses at high speed for 1 minute.

Per serving: Calories: 369Kcal; Protein: 5.5g; Carbohydrates: 85g; Fat: 0.8g

587. DANDELION AND WATERCRESS SMOOTHIE

Preparation time: 5 minutes
Cooking time: 0 minute
Servings: 2

Ingredients:

- 2 C. spring water
- 1 large bunch dandelion greens, fresh
- ¼ C. key lime juice
- 1 C. watercress, fresh
- 3 baby bananas, peeled
- ½ C. fresh blueberries
- 1-inch piece ginger, fresh
- 6 Medjool dates, pitted
- 1 tbsp. burdock root powder

Directions:

1. Take a high-powered blender, switch it on, and then place all the ingredients inside, in order.
2. Close blender, then pulses at high speed for 1 minute.

Per serving: Calories: 418.5Kcal; Protein: 5.2g; Carbohydrates: 96.3g; Fat: 1.4g

588. TRIPLE BERRY SMOOTHIE

Preparation time: 5 minutes
Cooking time: 0 minute
Servings: 2
Ingredients:

- 1 C. spring water
- 1 C. fresh whole strawberries
- 2 small bananas
- 1 C. fresh whole raspberries
- 2 tbsp. agave syrup
- 1 C. fresh whole blueberries

Directions:

1. Take a high-powered blender, switch it on, and then place all the ingredients inside, in order.
2. Close blender, then pulses at high speed for 1 minute.

Per serving: Calories: 281Kcal; Protein: 2.8g; Carbohydrates: 64.6g; Fat: 1.2g

589. WATERCRESS SMOOTHIE

Preparation time: 5 minutes
Cooking time: 0 minute
Servings: 2
Ingredients:

- 2 C. spring water
- 1 large bunch dandelion greens, fresh
- ¼ C. key lime juice
- 1 C. watercress, fresh
- 3 baby bananas, peeled
- ½ C. fresh blueberries
- 1-inch piece of ginger, fresh
- 6 Medjool dates, pitted
- 1 tbsp. burdock root powder

Directions:

1. Take a high-powered blender, switch it on, and then place all the ingredients inside, in order.
2. Cover the blender with its lid and then pulse at high speed for 1 minute.

Per serving: Calories: 102Kcal; Protein: 8g; Carbohydrates: 4g; Fat: 2g

590. PAPAYA LIME SMOOTHIE

Preparation time: 15 minutes
Cooking time: 0 minute
Servings: 1
Ingredients:

- 2 C. Papaya, chopped into square pieces
- 1 tbsp. papaya seeds
- Lime juice
- 1 C. water, filtered

Directions:

1. Place the ingredients into a high-speed blender, then process for about 1 minute until all the ingredients are finely blended. Serve and enjoy.

Per serving: Calories: 94Kcal; Protein: 2g; Carbohydrates: 6g; Fat: 1g

591. BANANA CITRUS SMOOTHIE

Preparation time: 15 minutes
Cooking time: 0 minute
Servings: 1
Ingredients:

- Spring water
- ¼ avocado, pitted
- 1 medium burro banana
- 1 Seville orange
- 2 C. fresh lettuce
- 1 tbsp. hemp seeds
- 1 C. berries (blueberries or an aggregate of blueberries, strawberries, and raspberries)

Directions:

1. Add the spring water to your blender. Put the fruits and veggies right inside the blender.
2. Blend all ingredients till smooth.

Per serving: Calories: 94Kcal; Protein: 17; Carbohydrates: 16g; Fat: 12g

592. APPLE LIME AND AMARANTH DETOXIFYING SMOOTHIE

Preparation time: 15 minutes
Cooking time: 0 minute
Servings: 1

Ingredients:

- ¼ avocado
- 1 key lime
- 2 apples, chopped
- 2 C. water
- 2 C. amaranth veggie

Directions:

1. Put all the ingredients collectively in a blender. Blend all the ingredients evenly. Enjoy this delicious smoothie.

Per serving: Calories: 104Kcal; Protein: 8g; Carbohydrates: 6g; Fat: 1g

593. ARUGULA REFRESHER SMOOTHIE

Preparation time: 15 minutes
Cooking time: 0 minute
Servings: 1
Ingredients:

- 2 C. spring water
- 1 large bunch of callaloo, fresh
- ¼ C. lime juice
- 1 C. fresh cucumber, diced
- 1 large bunch arugulas, fresh
- ¼ honeydew, fresh
- 1-inch piece ginger, fresh
- 1 pear, destemmed, diced
- 6 Medjool dates, pitted
- 1 tbsp. sea moss gel

Directions:

1. Take a high-powered blender, switch it on, and then place all the ingredients inside, in order.
2. Cover the blender with its lid and then pulse at high speed for 1 minute.

Per serving: Calories: 107Kcal; Protein: 18g; Carbohydrates: 16g; Fat: 12g

594. SWEET KALE SMOOTHIE

Preparation time: 10 minutes
Cooking time: 15 minutes
Servings: 2
Ingredients:

- 1 cup low-fat plain Greek yogurt
- ½ cup apple juice
- 1 apple, cored and quartered
- 4 Medjool dates
- 3 cups packed coarsely chopped kale
- Juice of ½ lemon
- 4 ice cubes

Directions:

1. In a blender, combine the yogurt, apple juice, apple, and dates and pulse until smooth.
2. Add the kale and lemon juice and pulse until blended. Add the ice

cubes and blend until smooth and thick. Pour into glasses and serve.

Per serving: Calories: 355Kcal; Protein: 11g; Carbohydrates: 77g; Fat: 2g

595. AVOCADO-BLUEBERRY SMOOTHIE

Preparation time: 5 minutes
Cooking time: 0 minutes
Servings: 2
Ingredients:

- ½ cup unsweetened vanilla almond milk
- ½ cup low-fat plain Greek yogurt
- 1 ripe avocado, peeled, pitted, and coarsely chopped
- 1 cup blueberries
- ¼ cup gluten-free rolled oats
- ½ tsp. vanilla extract
- 4 ice cubes

Directions:

1. In a blender, combine the almond milk, yogurt, avocado, blueberries, oats, and vanilla and pulse until well blended.
2. Add the ice cubes and blend until thick and smooth. Serve.

Per serving: Calories: 273Kcal; Protein: 10g; Carbohydrates: 28g; Fat: 15g

596. CRANBERRY-PUMPKIN SMOOTHIE

Preparation time: 5 minutes
Cooking time: 0 minutes
Servings: 2
Ingredients:

- 2 cups unsweetened almond milk
- 1 cup pure pumpkin purée
- ¼ cup gluten-free rolled oats
- ¼ cup pure cranberry juice (no sugar added)
- 1 tbs. honey
- ¼ tsp. ground cinnamon
- Pinch ground nutmeg

Directions:

1. In a blender, combine the almond milk, pumpkin, oats, cranberry juice, honey, cinnamon, and nutmeg and blend until smooth.
2. Pour into glasses and serve immediately.

Per serving: Calories: 190Kcal; Protein: 4g; Carbohydrates: 26g; Fat: 7g

597. SWEET CRANBERRY NECTAR

Preparation time: 8 minutes
Cooking time: 5 minutes
Servings: 4

Ingredients:

- 4 cups fresh cranberries
- 1 fresh lemon juice
- ½ cup agave nectar
- 1 piece of cinnamon stick
- 1-gallon water, filtered

Directions:

1. Add cranberries, ½ gallon water, and cinnamon into your pot
2. Close the lid.
3. Cook on HIGH pressure for 8 minutes
4. Release the pressure naturally
5. First, strain the liquid, then add remaining water
6. Cool, add agave nectar and lemon
7. Served chilled and enjoy!

Per serving: Calories: 184Kcal; Protein: 1g; Carbohydrates: 49g; Fat: 0g

598. HEARTY PEAR AND MANGO SMOOTHIE

Preparation time: 10 minutes
Cooking time: 0 minutes
Servings: 1
Ingredients:

- 1 ripe mango, cored and chopped
- ½ mango, peeled, pitted and chopped
- 1 cup kale, chopped
- ½ cup plain Greek yogurt
- 2 ice cubes

Directions:

1. Add pear, mango, yogurt, kale, and mango to a blender and puree.
2. Add ice and blend until you have a smooth texture.
3. Serve and enjoy!

Per serving: Calories: 293Kcal; Protein: 8g; Carbohydrates: 53g; Fat: 8g

599. BREAKFAST ALMOND MILK SHAKE

Preparation time: 4 minutes
Cooking time: 0 minutes
Servings: 2
Ingredients:

- 3 cups almond milk
- 4 tbsp heavy cream
- ½ tsp vanilla extract
- 4 tbsp flax meal
- 2 tbsp protein powder
- 4 drops of liquid stevia
- Ice cubes as desired (to serve)

Directions:

1. In the bowl of your food processor, add almond milk, heavy cream, flax

meal, vanilla extract, collagen peptides, and stevia.

2. Blitz until uniform and smooth, for about 30 seconds.
3. Add a bit more almond milk if it is very thick.
4. Pour in a smoothie glass, add the ice cubes and sprinkle with cinnamon.

Per serving: Calories 326Kcal; Protein: 19g; Carbohydrates: 6g; Fat: 27g

600. APPLE, BERRIES, AND KALE SMOOTHIE

Preparation time: 5 minutes
Cooking time: 0 minute
Servings: 2
Ingredients:
- 1 C. spring water
- 1 C. berries, mixed
- 2 C. kale leaves, fresh
- 1 large apple, cored

Directions:
1. Take a high-powered blender, switch it on, and then place all the ingredients inside, in order.
2. Cover the blender with its lid and then pulse at high speed for 1 minute or more until smooth.

Per serving: Calories: 112Kcal; Protein: 2g; Carbohydrates: 24.4g; Fat: 0.7g

LOW-SUGAR AND LOW-CARB

ANTI-INFLAMMATORY

RECIPES

CHAPTER 12: Breakfast Recipes

601. SAUSAGE ON SHEET PAN AND BREAKFAST EGG BAKE

Preparation time: 10 minutes
Cooking time: 35 minutes
Servings: 2
Ingredients:

- 16 halved cocktail tomatoes
- 1 tablespoon olive oil
- 2 cloves garlic, chopped
- 4 slices bacon
- ½ cup flat-leaf parsley, chopped
- 4 breakfast sausages, uncooked
- 4 large-sized eggs
- ¼ teaspoon Kosher salt
- ¼ teaspoon pepper
- A toast
- 8 ounces halved cremini mushrooms

Directions:

1. Pre-heat the oven to around 400⁰F.
2. Roast the sausages and bacon on a large rimmed baking sheet for around 15 minutes.
3. Toss the mushrooms, garlic and tomatoes with the oil and a sprinkle of salt and pepper in the medium mixing bowl.
4. Roast the veggies for 10 minutes on a sheet of baking.
5. Make some wells between the veggies and break 1 egg in every space.
6. Roast the mixture in the oven for another 10 minutes, or till the meat is thoroughly cooked and whites of the egg are completely opaque.
7. Garnish with fresh parsley and serving is done with toast.

Per serving: Calories: 290 Kcal; Fat: 21g; Carbs: 10g; Protein: 17g; sodium: 0.78g; sugar: ?g.

602. BERRY YOGURT BOWL

Preparation time: 5 minutes
Cooking time: 0 minutes
Servings: 1
Ingredients:

- ½ cup citrus and mint berries
- 2 ½ tablespoons walnuts, chopped
- ¾ cup plain type Greek yogurt
- 1 tablespoon mint, chopped

Directions:

1. Add the Greek yoghurt into a bowl.
2. Top with mint berries, walnuts, citrus and mint.
3. Serve and enjoy.

Per serving: Calories: 220Kcal; Fat: 9g; Carbs: 35g; Protein: 25g; Sodium: 0.1g; Sugar: 0.4g.

603. BERRY OATMEAL

Preparation time: 5 minutes
Cooking time: 0 minutes
Servings: 3
Ingredients:

- ½ cup easy and quick oatmeal
- 1 ½ tablespoon walnuts
- ½ cup mint and citrus berries

Directions:

1. Preheat the quick and easy oatmeal.
2. Add a topping of citrus with mint berries and walnuts.
3. Serve and enjoy.

Per serving: Calories: 229Kcal; Fat: 2.8g; Carbs: 23.4g; Protein: 5.8g; sodium: 0.42g; sugar: 11g.

604. SHAKSHUKA

Preparation time: 5 minutes
Cooking time: 29 minutes
Servings: 2
Ingredients:

- 8 large-sized eggs
- 2 tablespoons olive oil
- ½ teaspoon kosher salt
- ½ teaspoon pepper
- Toasted baguette, as needed
- 1 clove garlic, chopped
- 1 teaspoon ground cumin
- 1 yellow onion, chopped
- 1-pound tomatoes
- ¼ cup baby spinach, chopped

Directions:

1. Pre-heat the oven to 400⁰F.
2. In a big skillet, heat sufficient oil on medium-high heat.
3. Add onion and cook for 10 minutes, or until it becomes golden brown and soft.
4. Cook for 1 minute before adding cumin, baguette, garlic, and ½ teaspoon salt with black pepper.
5. Mix in the tomatoes, and then bake for 10 minutes in the oven.
6. Take the pan out of the oven, and create 8 tiny wells in the vegetable mix, gently cracking one egg in each.
7. Bake these eggs until done to your liking, around 8 minutes for runny type yolks.
8. Serve it with bread, if preferred, and a sprinkling of spinach.

Per serving: Calories: 479Kcal; Fat: 16.5g; Carbs: 8g; Protein: 14g; sodium: 1.493g; sugar: 14g.

605. PROTEIN PUMPKIN PANCAKES

Preparation time: 10 minutes
Cooking time: 6 minutes
Servings: 3
Ingredients:

- 1 ½ cups rolled oats, old-fashioned
- ¼ teaspoon salt
- ¼ cup cottage cheese
- 1 teaspoon spice pumpkin pie
- 2 tablespoons maple syrup
- 2/3 cup pumpkin puree
- 2 teaspoons baking powder
- 2 large-sized eggs

Directions:

1. Add each ingredient into a high-powered blender and mix until completely smooth.
2. Prepare a skillet on medium-low heat while the battery sits inside the blender.
3. Grease a sizable pan with oil or butter and set on medium-low heat.
4. Once the pan is heated, add 1/3 of the batter for preparing each pancake. To attain a spherical pancake, smooth the battery completely using the back of a spoon.
5. Cook the batter for 4 minutes, or till the bubbles develop around the edges and the pancakes are gently puffed up.
6. Cook for 2 additonal minutes on the opposite side until it becomes golden brown.
7. Serve hot with your favorite toppings.

Per serving: Calories: 213.3Kcal; Fat: 7g; Carbs: 41g; Protein: 16g; sodium: 0.25g; sugar: 4.4g.

606. BACON, SPINACH AND GRUYÈRE SCRAMBLED EGGS

Preparation time: 5 minutes
Cooking time 3 minutes
Servings: 2
Ingredients:

- 2 cups spinach, torn
- 2 ounces Gruyère cheese, shredded
- 1 tablespoon olive oil
- 8 large-sized eggs
- 2 slices thick cooked bacon
- ½ teaspoon salt
- ½ teaspoon pepper
- 1 teaspoon Dijon mustard
- 1 tablespoon water

Directions:

1. Heat a non-sticky pan with olive oil.
2. Mix the eggs with Dijon mustard, 1 tablespoon water, and half teaspoon salt with pepper inside a large mixing pan.
3. Cook and mix with a rubber spatula after every few minutes, until eggs are done to your liking. Cook for approximately 3 minutes for moderate eggs or until they become soft.
4. Wrap in the bacon, Gruyère cheese and the spinach.
5. Serve and enjoy.

Per serving: Calories: 240Kcal; Fat: 20 g; Carbs: 0.1 g; Protein: 49 g; sodium: 0.01g; sugar: 15g.

607. SMOOTHIE WITH GREEK YOGURT AND BERRIES FOR BREAKFAST

Preparation time: 5 minutes
Cooking time: 0 minutes
Servings: 1
Ingredients:

- 2 tablespoons milk, no fat
- 1 tablespoon sweetener, any
- 1 cup strained Greek yogurt, without fat
- 1 cup of mixed berries, frozen

Directions:

1. Transfer all the ingredients into a blender and blend the mixture until it gets smooth.
2. Serve and enjoy.

Per serving: Calories: 160kcal; Fat: 0g; Carbs: 30g; Protein: 22g; Sodium: 0.14g; Sugar: 20g.

608. AVOCADO TOAST

Preparation time: 10 minutes
Cooking time: 0 minutes
Servings: 1
Ingredients:

- 1/8 teaspoon black pepper
- ½ medium-sized avocado, peeled
- ¼ tsp. red pepper
- Juice ½ lime
- ⅛ tablespoon sea salt
- 2 slices bread

Directions:

1. Toast the bread slices till they become brownish golden.
2. Put the peeled avocado in a bowl and squeeze in the lime. Season with black pepper and sea salt.
3. Mash the avocado with a fork to attain the desired smoothness.
4. Uniformly spread the avocado on the toast.
5. Serve and enjoy.

Per serving: Calories: 195Kcal; Fat: 11g; Carbs: 20g; Protein: 3.8g; sodium: 0.15g; sugar: 1g.

609. CHICKEN BAKE FOR BRUNCH

Preparation time: 15 minutes
Cooking time: 60 minutes
Servings: 2
Ingredients:

- 4 cups cooked chicken, cubed
- 4 large-sized eggs
- ½ teaspoon salt
- ½ cup pimientos, diced
- 9 slices cubed bread, day-old
- 2 tablespoons parsley, minced
- ½ cup instant rice, uncooked
- 3 cups chicken broth

Directions:

1. Toss the bread cubes with broth in a big mixing bowl.
2. Mix the rice, chicken, pimientos, salt and parsley.
3. Transfer the mixture to a sizable buttered baking pot.
4. Pour the eggs over the mixture in the pot.
5. Heat up your oven to 325°F and bake uncovered for about one hour.
6. Set aside and serve.
7. Enjoy.

Per serving: Calories: 233Kcal; Fat: 6g; Carbs: 18g; Protein: 27g; Sodium: 0.5g; Sugar: 2g.

610. YOGURTY FRUITY PARFAIT

Preparation time: 5 minutes
Cooking time: 0 minutes
Servings: 1
Ingredients:

- ½ kiwi
- 1 teaspoon full vanilla extract
- 1 tablespoon flaxseed
- 1 cup mixed berries, frozen
- 1/4 cup blueberries
- 3 tablespoons grains fruit and nut clusters
- 1 cup Greek yogurt, non-fat

Directions:

1. In a processor, pulse the frozen mixed berries, flaxseed, yogurt, and vanilla extract to attain the desired smoothness.
2. Combine the processed mixture with blueberries, kiwis, fruits and nut clusters and put them in a bowl.
3. Serve and enjoy.

Per serving: Calories: 379Kcal; Fat: 1g; Carbs: 16g; Protein: 3.4g; sodium: 0.081g; sugar: 48g.

611. COTTAGE CHEESE BOWL

Preparation time: 5 minutes
Cooking time: 0 minutes
Servings: 1
Ingredients:

- 1 cup cottage cheese
- Handful walnuts
- Cinnamon, as desired
- Salt, as desired

Directions:

1. Fill a sizable bowl halfway with cheese, and top with walnuts.
2. Add a cinnamon topping before seasoning with salt.
3. Serve and enjoy.

Per serving: Calories: 159Kcal; Fat: 2.3g; Carbs: 6.2g; Protein: 28g; sodium: 0.7g; sugar: 12g.

612. BUCKWHEAT GROUTS BREAKFAST BOWL

Preparation time: 5 minutes
Cooking time: 12 minutes
Servings: 4
Ingredients:

- ½ cup unsalted pistachios
- ¼ cup cacao nibs
- 2 teaspoons vanilla extract
- ½ teaspoon ground cinnamon
- 1 cup water
- 2 cups sliced fresh strawberries

- ¼ cup chia seeds
- ¼ teaspoon salt
- 3 cups skim milk
- 1 cup buckwheat groats

Directions:

1. Stir together the milk, groats, chia seeds, vanilla, cinnamon, and salt in a large bowl. Cover and refrigerate overnight.
2. Transfer the wet mixture to a medium pot and add water the next morning.
3. Bring the mixture to a boil over medium-high heat. Lower the heat to attain a simmer, then cook for 12 minutes until the buckwheat becomes tender and thickened.
4. Transfer to bowls and serve, topped with the pistachios, strawberries, and cacao nibs.

Per serving: Calories: 340Kcal; Fat: 8g; Carbs: 52g; Protein: 15g; Sodium: 0.14g; Sugar: 14g.

513. HAWAIIAN HASH

Preparation time: 20 minutes
Cooking time: 17 minutes
Servings: 2
Ingredients:

- ½ teaspoon Sesame seeds, black
- 4 cups sweet potatoes, peeled & cubed
- ½ cup of red pepper, chopped and sweet
- 1 cup cooked ham, cubed
- 1 teaspoon sesame oil
- Fresh cilantro, chopped, as needed
- 2 teaspoon canola oil
- ¼ cup water
- 1 cup fresh pineapple, cubed
- 1 cup chopped onion
- 1 teaspoon soy sauce
- 1 teaspoon ginger root, minced
- ¼ cup salsa Verde

Directions:

1. Heat the oils in a big cast iron heavy skillet on medium to high-level heat.
2. Add the sweet potatoes, pepper, onion, and ginger root and stir for 5 minutes before filling with water.
3. Lower the heat and cook covered for 10 minutes until the potatoes are properly cooked. Keep turning occasionally until they become tender.
4. Add the remaining ingredients and cook for 2 minutes on medium-to-

high heat, or until the mixture is well heated.

5. Serve it with cilantro and enjoy.

Per serving: Calories: 201Kcal; Fat: 4g; Carbs: 26g; Protein: 7g; Sodium: 0.15g; Sugar: 0.2g

614. TASTY AVOCADO BREAD TOAST

Preparation time: 5 minutes
Cooking time: 0 minutes
Servings: 1
Ingredients

- 2 teaspoon olive oil, extra virgin
- 1 slice hearty toasted bread
- 1/8 teaspoon sea salt
- ¼ medium-sized sliced ripe avocado

Directions:

1. Spread the olive oil over the bread before topping with the avocado slices. If preferred, gently mash the avocado and sprinkle with more oil.
2. Season with salt before serving.
3. Enjoy.

Per serving: Calories: 145Kcal; Fat: 11g; Carbs: 15g; Protein: 3g; Sodium: 0.03g; Sugar: 1.2g

615. WHOLE-GRAIN BREAKFAST COOKIES

Preparation time: 20 minutes
Cooking time: 15 minutes
Servings: 18
Ingredients:

- 1 cup unsweetened applesauce
- 2 ounces dark chocolate, chopped
- 2 large eggs
- 2 tablespoons vegetable oil
- 2 teaspoons vanilla extract
- 2 cups rolled oats
- ½ cup whole-wheat flour
- 1 teaspoon baking powder
- 1 teaspoon ground cinnamon
- ¼ cup ground flaxseed
- ½ cup dried cherries
- ¼ cup unsweetened shredded coconut

Directions:

1. Pre-heat the oven to 350⁰F.
2. In a sizable bowl, combine the oats, flour, flaxseed, and baking powder. Stir properly.
3. Whisk the applesauce, eggs, vegetable oil, vanilla, and cinnamon in a medium bowl. Mix the wet and dry mixtures, and stir until just combined. Fold in cherries, coconut, and chocolate.

4. Drop tablespoon-size balls of dough onto a baking sheet and bake for 12 minutes, until browned and cooked through.
5. Let the cookies cool for around 3 minutes and remove them from the baking sheet.
6. Serve and enjoy.

Per serving: Calories: 136Kcal; Fat: 7g; Carbs: 14g; Protein: 4g; Sodium: 0.011g; Sugar: 4g.

616. PEACH MUESLI BAKE

Preparation time: 10 minutes
Cooking time: 40 minutes
Servings: 8
Ingredients:

- 1 ½ cups rolled oats
- ½ cup chopped walnuts
- 3 peaches, sliced
- 1 large egg
- 2 tablespoons maple syrup
- Non-stick cooking spray
- 1 teaspoon ground cinnamon
- ½ teaspoon salt
- 1 teaspoon baking powder
- 2 cups skim milk

Directions:

1. Preheat the oven to 375⁰F.
2. Spray a sizable pan with cooking spray and set aside.
3. Stir together milk, oats, walnuts, egg, maple syrup, cinnamon, baking powder, and salt in a large bowl. Spread half the mixture in the ready baking tray.
4. Place half the peaches in a single layer across the oat mixture.
5. Spread the remaining oat mixture over the top.
6. Add the remaining peaches in a thin layer over the oats and bake for 40 minutes, uncovered until thickened and browned.
7. Cut into 8 squares and serve warm.
8. Enjoy.

Per serving: Calories: 138Kcal; Fat: 1g; Carbs: 22g; Protein: 6g; Sodium: 0.191g; Sugar: 10g.

617. STEEL-CUT OATMEAL BOWL WITH FRUIT AND NUTS

Preparation time: 5 minutes
Cooking time: 20 minutes
Servings: 4
Ingredients:

- 2 cups chopped fresh fruit
- ¼ teaspoon salt
- 2 cups almond milk

- 1 teaspoon ground cinnamon
- ¾ cup water
- 1 cup steel-cut oats
- ½ cup chopped walnuts
- ¼ cup chia seeds

Directions:

1. Combine the oats, almond milk, water, cinnamon, and salt in a medium saucepan over medium-high heat.
2. Bring the mixture to a slight boil, then lower the heat and simmer for about 20 minutes and wait until the oats have softened and thickened.
3. Top each bowl with ½ cup of fresh fruit, 2 tablespoons of walnuts, and 1 tablespoon of chia seeds before serving.
4. Enjoy.

Per serving: Calories: 288Kcal; Fat: 11g; Carbs: 38g; Protein: 10g; Sodium: 0.32g; Sugar: 7g

618. FRUITED GRANOLA

Preparation time: 15 minutes
Cooking time: 35 minutes
Servings: 6
Ingredients:

- ½ cup dried cranberries
- 3 tablespoons butter
- 3 cups fast cooking oats
- 1 cup sliced almonds
- ½ cup wheat germ
- 1 teaspoon crushed cinnamon
- 3 cups whole-grain cereal flakes
- ½ cup raisin
- 1 cup honey

Directions:

1. Preheat the oven to 350⁰F.
2. Dispose the almonds in a single layer on a baking sheet.
3. Bake the almonds at 350°F for 15 minutes.
4. In a bowl, combine the wheat germ, butter, cinnamon, and honey.
5. Stir in the almonds and oats and combine thoroughly.
6. Spread evenly on the prepared baking sheet.
7. Bake at 350°F for 20 minutes.
8. Combine with the remaining ingredients.
9. Allow cooling before serving.
10. Enjoy.

Per serving: Calories: 210Kcal; Fat: 7 g; Carbs: 36 g; Protein: 2g; Sodium: 0.06; Sugar: 4g.

619. SCRAMBLED SPINACH

Preparation time: 5 minutes
Cooking time: 15 minutes
Servings: 2

- 13 ounces spinach, drained
- ¼ teaspoon salt
- ¼ teaspoon pepper
- 2 tablespoons crumbled bacon
- 14 cups liquid egg substitute
- 14 cups skim milk

Directions:

1. In a sizable mixing bowl, mix all of the ingredients.
2. Transfer the mixture to a sizable skillet coated with oil and set over medium heat.
3. Continue stirring until thoroughly cooked.
4. Serve and enjoy.

Per serving: Calories: 70Kcal; Fat: 2g; Carbs: 0.7g; Protein: 1g; Sodium: 0.025g; Sugar; 2g.

620. POTATOES, SAUSAGE, AND EGG

Preparation time: 15 minutes
Cooking time: 10 hours
Servings: 6
Ingredients:

- 2 red sweet peppers, sliced into strips
- 12 ounces sliced chicken sausage links
- 1 onion, chopped into wedges
- ½ teaspoon crushed dry thyme
- ½ cups low-sodium chicken broth
- 12 pounds sliced potatoes
- ¼ teaspoon black pepper
- 6 eggs
- ½ cup shredded low-fat cheddar cheese
- Cooking spray, as needed.

Directions:

1. Spray oil or cooking spray onto a hefty foil sheet.
2. Arrange the sausage, onion, cheese, sweet peppers, and potatoes in a single layer on the foil.
3. Drizzle chicken broth over the top.
4. Season with pepper and thyme to taste and seal with a fold.
5. Insert the packet into the cooker and cook on low heat for ten hours.
6. Boil the egg until fully cooked in the meantime.
7. Combine eggs and sausage mixture in a serving dish.

Per serving: Calories: 281Kcal; Fat: 12g; Carbs 0.485g; Protein: 3g; Sodium: 0.262g; Sugar: 3g.

621. YOGURT AND CUCUMBER

Preparation time: 5 minutes
Cooking time: 0 minutes
Servings: 1
Ingredients:

- ¼ teaspoon lemon zest
- ½ cups diced cucumber
- ¼ teaspoon fresh mint, chopped
- ¼ teaspoon lemon juice
- 1 cup low-fat yogurt

Directions:

1. In a jar, merge all ingredients.
2. Refrigerate until ready to serve.
3. Enjoy.

Per serving: Calories: 164Kcal; Fat: 4g; Carbs: 0.15g; Protein: 18g; Sodium: 0.318g; Sugar; 1g.

622. VEGETABLE OMELET

Preparation time: 5 minutes
Cooking time: 25 minutes
Servings: 4
Ingredients:

- ½ ripe avocado, pitted and chopped
- ½ cup cucumber, sliced
- 2 eggs
- ½ cup canned diced tomatoes with herbs, drained
- 2 tablespoons water
- 1 teaspoon dry basil, crushed
- ½ cups yellow summer squash, chopped
- ¼ teaspoon salt
- ¼ teaspoon pepper

Directions:

1. Combine the squash, tomatoes, avocado, and cucumber in a large bowl.
2. Whisk together the eggs, water, salt, pepper, and basil in a separate bowl.
3. Spray oil onto a skillet set over medium heat.
4. Pour the egg mixture into the prepared pan.
5. Scatter the veggie mixture over the egg.
6. Continue cooking until the egg is set.
7. Garnish with cheese and chives.
8. Serve and enjoy.

Per serving: Calories: 128Kcal; Fat: 6g; Carbs: 7g; Protein: 4g; Sodium: 0.357g; Sugar: 3g;

623. BREAKFAST PARFAIT

Preparation time: 5 minutes
Cooking time: 0 minutes
Servings: 2
Ingredients:

- 1 cup low-fat granola
- 6 ounces vanilla yogurt, non-fat and sugar-free
- ¼ teaspoon honey
- ¼ teaspoon pumpkin pie spice
- 4 ounces unsweetened applesauce

Directions:

1. Mix all ingredients (except the granola) in a bowl.
2. Layer the mixture with the granola in a cup.
3. Refrigerate before serving.
4. Enjoy.

Per serving: Calories: 286Kcal; Fat: 2.9g; Carbs: 56.8g; Protein: 8.1g; Sodium: 0.01g; Sugar: 2.1g:

624. BANANA CRÊPE CAKES

Preparation time: 5 minutes
Cooking time: 10 minutes
Servings: 4
Ingredients:

- 2 medium bananas
- 4 ounces reduced-fat plain cream cheese, softened
- ½ teaspoon vanilla extract
- 1/8 teaspoon salt
- 4 large eggs
- Avocado oil cooking spray

Directions:

1. Heat a large skillet over low heat.
2. Coat the cooking surface with cooking spray, and allow the pan to heat for another 2 to 3 minutes.
3. Meanwhile, in a medium bowl, mash the cream cheese and bananas together with a fork until combined. The bananas can be a little chunky.
4. Add vanilla, eggs, and salt, and mix well.
5. For each cake, drop 2 tablespoons of the batter onto the warmed skillet and use the bottom of a large spoon or ladle to spread it thin. Let it cook for 9 minutes.
6. Flip the cake over and cook briefly, about 1 minute.

Per serving: Calories: 175.8Kcal; Fat: 8.5g; Carbs: 14.6g; Protein: 9.6g; Sodium: 0.021g; Sugar: 7.6g.

625. CINNAMON AND COCONUT PORRIDGE

Preparation time: 5 minutes
Cooking time: 5 minutes
Servings: 4
Ingredients:

- ¼ cup blueberries
- 1 cup cream
- 1 tablespoon butter
- 2 tablespoons flaxseed meal
- 1 ½ teaspoon stevia
- 1 teaspoon cinnamon
- ½ cup unsweetened dried coconut, shredded
- ¼ teaspoon salt
- 2 cups water

Directions:

1. Add all the ingredients to a sizable pot and mix well.
2. Transfer pot to stove and place it over medium-low heat. Bring the ingredient mixture to a slight boil and stir well. Remove the mix from heat.
3. Divide the mix into equal servings and let them sit for 10 minutes.
4. Enjoy.

Per serving: Calories: 170.2Kcal; Fat: 15.3g; Carbs: 5.6g; Protein: 3.4g; Sodium: 0.07g; Sugar: 5g

626. COCONUT PANCAKES

Preparation time: 5 minutes
Cooking time: 4 minutes
Servings: 4
Ingredients:

- 3 tablespoons coconut oil
- 2 tablespoons arrowroot powder
- 1 cup coconut milk
- 1 teaspoon baking powder
- 1 cup coconut flour

Directions:

1. In a medium container, mix all the dry ingredients.
2. Add the coconut milk and 2 tablespoons of coconut oil and mix properly.
3. In a skillet, melt the remaining 1 tablespoon of coconut oil. Ladle the batter into the skillet, then swirl the pan to spread the batter evenly into a smooth pancake. Cook it for 2 minutes on medium heat until it becomes firm.
4. Turn the pancake to the other side, then cook it for an additional 2 minutes until it turns golden brown.
5. Cook the remaining pancakes in the same process.
6. Serve and enjoy.

Per serving: Calories: 376.2Kcal; Fat: 14.7g; Carbs: 53.7g; Protein: 6.6g; Sodium: 0.01g; Sugar: 3.5g

627. BANANA BARLEY PORRIDGE

Preparation time: 15 minutes
Cooking time: 5 minutes
Servings: 2
Ingredients:

- ½ cup coconuts, chopped
- ½ cup barley
- 3 drops liquid stevia
- 1 small banana, peeled and sliced
- 1 cup unsweetened coconut milk, divided

Directions:

1. In a bowl, mix barley with half the coconut milk and stevia.
2. Cover the blending bowl, then refrigerate for 6 hours.
3. In a saucepan, combine the mixture with the remaining coconut milk and cook for 5 minutes on moderate heat.
4. Top it with the chopped coconuts and, then, the banana slices.
5. Serve and enjoy.

Per serving: Calories: 158.7Kcal; Fat: 8.3g; Carbs: 19g; Protein: 4.1g; Sodium: 0.02g; Sugar: 1g.

628. PORRIDGE WITH WALNUTS

Preparation time: 5 minutes
Cooking time: 8 minutes
Servings: 1
Ingredients:

- ¼ teaspoon salt
- 50 g. raspberries
- ½ teaspoon cinnamon
- 50 g. blueberries
- 20 g. flaxseed, crushed
- 10 g. oatmeal
- 25 g. ground walnuts
- 1 tsp. agave syrup
- 200 ml. nut drink

Directions:

1. Warm the nut drink in a saucepan.
2. Add the flaxseed, walnuts, and oatmeal, stirring constantly.
3. Stir in the cinnamon and salt and simmer, stirring for 8 minutes. Sweeten with agave syrup.
4. Put the porridge in a bowl.

5. Wash all the berries and allow them to drain before adding them to the porridge.
6. Serve and enjoy.

Per serving: Calories: 377Kcal; Fat: 26.2g; Carbs: 10.8g; Protein: 19g; Sodium: 0.02g; Sugar: 3.3 g

629. HEALTHY AVOCADO TOAST

Preparation time: 5 minutes

Cooking time: 13 minutes

Servings: 4

Ingredients:

- 2 eggs fried, scrambled, optional
- ½ tablespoon red pepper flakes, optional
- Juice half a lime
- 2 tablespoons chopped cilantro
- ¼ teaspoon salt
- ¼ teaspoon pepper to taste
- 1 avocado, peeled and seeded
- 2 slices whole grain bread

Directions:

1. Toast whole grain bread slices in an oven until they are crispy and golden.
2. Mix and crush the avocado, lime, cilantro, salt, and pepper in a shallow bowl.
3. Spread on the toasted bread slices.
4. Top with fried, poached, or scrambled egg.

Per serving: Calories: 80.54Kcal; Fat: 4g; Carbs: 8.5g; Protein: 2.34g; Sodium: 0.24g; Sugar: 1g.

630. ZUCCHINI BREAD PANCAKES

Preparation time: 5 minutes

Cooking time: 5 minutes

Servings: 5

Ingredients:

- 2 tablespoons date sugar
- 1 cup finely shredded zucchini
- 2 cups homemade walnut milk
- ¼ cup mashed burro banana
- 2 cups spelt or kamut flour
- 1 tablespoon grapeseed oil
- ½ cup chopped walnuts

Directions:

1. Whisk flour in a large bowl with date sugar.
2. Mix in walnut milk and mashed banana burro. Stir untilwell blended, make sure the bowl's bottom is scraped so there are no dry mix pockets.
3. Stir in shredded walnuts and zucchini.
4. Heat the grape seed oil over medium-to-high heat in a griddle or skillet.
5. Add batter onto the griddle to make the pancakes. Cook on each side for 5 minutes.
6. Serve with a syrup of agave and enjoy!

Per serving: Calories: 101Kcal; Fat: 15g; Carbs: 44g; Protein: 27g; Sodium: 0.01g; Sugar: 0.02g.

CHAPTER 13: Grains, Beans and Legumes

631. BEAN HUMMUS

Preparation time: 10 minutes

Cooking time: 0 minutes

Servings: 6

Ingredients:

- ½ cup cannellini beans, canned
- 2 tablespoons olive oil
- 1 teaspoon garlic powder
- ¼ teaspoon ground cinnamon 1 cup
- 1 tablespoon tahini

Directions:

1. Blend the beans until smooth and transfer into a big bowl.
2. Add olive oil, garlic powder, ground cinnamon, and tahini.
3. Carefully stir the hummus.
4. Serve and enjoy.

Per serving: Calories: 219Kcal; Fat: 13.3g; Carbs: 19.4g; Protein: 7.7g; Sodium: 0.4g; Sugar: 0.6g.

632. SORGHUM BAKE

Preparation time: 10 minutes

Cooking time: 25 minutes

Servings: 4

Ingredients:

- 1 apple, chopped
- 1-ounce raisins
- 1 ½ cups water
- ½ cup sorghum

Directions:

1. Put sorghum in a sizable pan and flatten it.
2. Top the sorghum with raisins, apple, and water.
3. Cover the meal with baking paper and transfer in the preheated to 375⁰F oven.
4. Bake the meal for 25 minutes.
5. Serve and enjoy.

Per serving: Calories: 178Kcal; Fat: 1.1g; Carbs: 44.2g; Protein: 0.4g; Sodium: 0.01g; Sugar: 2.5g.

633. GARBANZO BEANS WITH MEAT STRIPS

Preparation time: 10 minutes

Cooking time: 10 minutes

Servings: 5

Ingredients:

- 2 tablespoons olive oil
- 10 ounces beef sirloin
- 1 cup garbanzo beans, cooked
- 1 teaspoon Cajun seasonings

Directions:

1. Rub the beef sirloin with Cajun seasonings and brush with a tablespoon of olive oil.
2. Grill the meat for 5 minutes on each side at 400⁰F.
3. Cut the meat into thin strips and mix with garbanzo beans and remaining olive oil.
4. Serve and enjoy.

Per serving: Calories: 299Kcal; Fat: 11.6g; Carbs: 24.3g; Protein: 24.9g; Sodium: 0.05g; Sugar: 4g.

634. LIGHT MORNING BEANS

Preparation time: 10 minutes

Cooking time: 5 minutes

Servings: 4

Ingredients:

- ¼ teaspoon garlic powder
- ½ white onion, diced
- ¼ cup cilantro, chopped
- 2 tablespoons apple cider vinegar
- 1 teaspoon ground coriander
- 2 cups fava beans, vanned
- 1 ½ tablespoon avocado oil
- 2 ounces tomato, chopped

Directions:

1. Heat the avocado oil in a saucepan.
2. Add onion and cook it until light brown.
3. Add tomato, garlic powder, cilantro, ground coriander, fava beans, and apple cider vinegar.
4. Cook the meal for 5 minutes on medium heat.
5. Serve and enjoy.

Per serving: Calories: 273Kcal; Fat: 1.9g; Carbs: 46.1g; Protein: 20g; Sodium: 0.01g; Sugar: 2g.

635. ROASTED SORGHUM

Preparation time: 10 minutes

Cooking time: 15 minutes

Servings: 4

Ingredients:

- ½ cup sorghum, cooked
- 1 tablespoon avocado oil
- 2 tablespoons cream cheese
- 1 carrot, diced
- 3 tablespoons dried parsley
- ½ teaspoon dried oregano

Directions:

6. Heat avocado oil and add the carrot in a sizable pan. Roast for 5 minutes.
7. Add cooked sorghum, parsley, oregano, and cream cheese.
8. Roast the meal for 10 minutes on low heat. Stir the mixture occasionally to avoid burning.
9. Serve and enjoy.

Per serving: Calories: 145Kcal; Fat: 1.7g; Carbs: 33.1g; Protein: 0.4g; Sodium: 0.01g; Sugar: 2.5g.

636. SORGHUM SALAD

Preparation time: 10 minutes

Cooking time: 10 minutes

Servings: 3

Ingredients:

- ¼ cup sorghum
- ¼ cup fresh cilantro, chopped
- 1 teaspoon ground cumin
- 2 tablespoons organic canola oil
- 2 ½ cups water
- 2 tablespoons apple cider vinegar
- 10 ounces butternut squash, chopped

Directions:

1. Put sorghum and butternut squash in the saucepan.
2. Add water and cook for 10 minutes.
3. Cool the ingredients and transfer in the salad bowl.
4. Add cilantro, ground cumin, organic canola oil, and apple cider vinegar.
5. Stir the meal well.
6. Serve and enjoy.

Per serving: Calories: 180Kcal; Fat: 9.5g; Carbs: 24.2g; Protein: 0.4g; Sodium: 0.01g; Sugar: 2.5g.

637. BEANS CHILI

Preparation time: 20 minutes

Cooking time: 60 minutes

Servings: 8

Ingredients:

- 1 red bell pepper, seeded and diced
- 1 sweet onion, chopped
- 2 teaspoons minced garlic
- 28 ounces low-sodium diced tomatoes

- 15 ounces sodium-free black beans, rinsed and drained
- 15 ounces sodium-free navy beans, rinsed and drained
- 1 green bell pepper, seeded and diced
- 2 tablespoons chili powder
- 1 teaspoon extra-virgin olive oil
- ¼ teaspoon red pepper flakes
- 2 teaspoons ground cumin
- 15 ounces sodium-free red kidney beans, rinsed and drained
- 1 teaspoon ground coriander

Directions:

1. In a large saucepan, heat the oil over medium-high heat.
2. Sauté the onion, red and green bell peppers, and garlic for about 5 minutes, or until the veggies have softened.
3. Toss in the tomatoes, black beans, red kidney beans, navy beans, chili powder, cumin, coriander, and red pepper flakes, as well as chili powder, cumin, coriander, and red pepper flakes.
4. Bring the chili to a boil, then turn it down to a low heat.
5. Cook, stirring occasionally, for 60 minutes
6. Serve immediately and enjoy.

Per serving: Calories: 480Kcal; Fat: 28.1g; Carbs: 45.1g; Protein: 15.1g; Sodium: 0.01g; Sugar: 4.0g

638. FRIED BEANS WITH YOGURT DRESSING

Preparation time: 10 minutes

Cooking time: 6 minutes

Servings: 4

Ingredients:

- ½ cup fresh cilantro, chopped
- 1 cucumber, chopped
- 1 teaspoon cayenne pepper
- 1 teaspoon smoked paprika
- 1/3 cup plain yogurt
- 1 tablespoon apple cider vinegar
- ½ cup black-eyed peas, canned, drained

Directions:

1. Add black-eyed peas in the hot skillet and roast for 6 minutes. Stir in the beans after 3 minutes of cooking.
2. Mix plain yogurt, smoked paprika, cayenne pepper, and apple cider vinegar.
3. Cool the fried black-eyed peas and mix them with cilantro and cucumber.
4. Add yogurt mixture and mix properly.

5. Let the meal rest before serving.
6. Enjoy.

Per serving: Calories: 53Kcal; Fat: 0.7g; Carbs: 8.8g; Protein: 3.3g; Sodium: 0.02g; Sugar: 0.9g.

639. GREEN BEANS WITH MEAT

Preparation time: 10 minutes

Cooking time: 45 minutes

Servings: 4

Ingredients:

- 1 teaspoon dried sage
- 12 ounces green beans, chopped
- 2 tablespoons low-sodium tomato paste
- 1 carrot, chopped
- 4 cups water
- 1 tablespoon organic canola oil
- 1-ounce pork shoulder, chopped

Directions:

1. In the saucepan, roast the pork shoulder with organic canola oil for 2 minutes per one side.
2. Add low-sodium tomato paste, carrot, green beans, and sage.
3. Add water and gently stir the mixture.
4. Cook the meal for 45 minutes on medium heat.
5. Serve and enjoy.

Per serving: Calories: 216Kcal; Fat: 14.3g; Carbs: 9.2g; Protein: 13.6g; Sodium: 0.06g; Sugar: 4.5g.

640. TUNISIAN STYLE GREEN BEANS

Preparation time: 15 minutes

Cooking time: 7 minutes

Servings: 3

Ingredients:

- 1 cup green beans
- 1 cup water
- ¼ teaspoon white pepper
- 1 teaspoon sesame seeds
- 2 tablespoons organic canola oil
- 1 tablespoon balsamic vinegar
- ¼ teaspoon dried tarragon

Directions:

1. Bring a cup of water to a slight boil before adding green beans.
2. Boil the beans for 7 minutes and cool them in ice water before chopping them roughly.
3. Add the cooked green beans in a bowl, add white pepper, organic canola oil, sesame seeds, balsamic vinegar, and dried tarragon.
4. Stir the meal well.

5. Serve and enjoy.

Per serving: Calories: 101Kcal; Fat: 9.9g; Carbs: 3g; Protein: 0.9g; Sodium; 0.05g: Sugar: 3.6g.

641. HERBED BROWN RICE WITH BEANS

Preparation time: 15 minutes

Cooking time: 15 minutes

Servings: 8

Ingredients:

- 1 large tomato, chopped
- ½ sweet onion, chopped
- ¼ teaspoon black pepper
- 1 teaspoon minced jalapeño pepper
- 1 teaspoon minced garlic
- 1 teaspoon chopped fresh thyme
- ¼ teaspoon sea salt
- 2 teaspoons extra-virgin olive oil
- 2 cups cooked brown rice
- 15 ounces sodium-free red kidney beans, rinsed and drained

Directions:

1. In a sizable skillet, heat the olive oil over medium-high heat.
2. Sauté the onion, jalapeno, and garlic for 3 minutes, or until softened.
3. Combine the beans, tomato, and thyme in a mixing bowl.
4. Cook, and stir frequently, for around 10 minutes, or until completely cooked.
5. Season with salt and pepper to taste.
6. Serve with a side of warm brown rice.
7. Enjoy.

Per serving: Calories: 200Kcal; Fat: 2.1g; Carbs: 37.1g; Protein: 9.1g; Sodium: 0.04g; Sugar: 2.0g

642. SPICY BROWN RICE WITH COLLARD

Preparation time: 14 minutes

Cooking time: 18 minutes

Servings: 4

Ingredients:

- 1 large egg
- 1 tablespoon extra-virgin olive oil
- 1 bunch collard greens, stemmed and chiffonade-style
- 1 red onion, thinly sliced
- ½ cup low-sodium vegetable broth
- 1 garlic clove, minced
- 1 carrot, cut into 2-inch matchsticks
- 1 cup cooked brown rice
- 1 teaspoon paprika
- ¼ tsp. salt
- 2 tablespoons coconut amino
- 1 teaspoon red pepper flakes

Directions:

1. In a Dutch oven or nonstick pan, heat the olive oil over medium heat until it shimmers.
2. Add the collard greens and cook until wilted, about 4 minutes.
3. In a Dutch oven, combine the carrots, onion, broth, coconut amino, and garlic; cover and cook for around 6 minutes, or until the carrots are soft.
4. Cook for 4 minutes after adding the brown rice. Throughout the cooking process, keep stirring.
5. Break an egg over the mixture, then heat and scramble it for 4 minutes, or until it is set.
6. Before serving, remove from the fire and season with red pepper flakes, paprika, and salt.
7. Serve and enjoy.

Per serving: Calories: 154Kcal; Fat: 6g; Carbs: 22g; Protein: 6g; Sodium: 0.03g; Sugar: 2g.

643. CARROTS, BROWN RICE, AND SCRAMBLED EGG

Preparation time: 15 minutes
Cooking time: 18 minutes
Servings: 4
Ingredients:

- 1 carrot, cut into 2-inch matchsticks
- 1 tablespoon extra-virgin olive oil
- 1 red onion, thinly sliced
- ½ cup low-sodium vegetable broth
- 1 garlic clove, minced
- 1 teaspoon paprika
- 1 bunch collard greens, stemmed and cut into chiffonade
- ¼ teaspoon salt
- 1 cup cooked brown rice
- 2 tablespoons coconut aminos
- 1 large egg
- 1 teaspoon red pepper flakes

Directions:

1. In a Dutch oven or nonstick pan, heat the olive oil over medium heat until it shimmers.
2. Add the collard greens and cook until wilted, about 4 minutes.
3. In a Dutch oven, combine the carrots, onion, broth, coconut aminos, and garlic; cover and cook for around 6 minutes, or until the carrots are soft.
4. Cook the brown rice in the oven for 4 minutes. Throughout the cooking process, keep stirring.
5. Break an egg over them, then heat and scramble it for 4 minutes, or until it is set.
6. Remove from the fire and season with red pepper flakes, paprika, and salt.

7. Enjoy.

Per serving: Calories: 154Kcal; Fat: 6g; Carbs: 22g; Protein: 6g; Sodium: 0.03g; Sugar: 2g.

644. CAROLINA GREEN BEANS

Preparation time: 8
Cooking time: 28 minutes
Servings: 8
Ingredients:

- 3 tablespoons extra-virgin olive oil, divided
- ¼ cup almond flour
- 8 ounces brown mushrooms, diced
- 3 garlic cloves, minced
- 1-pound green beans, trimmed, cut into bite-size pieces
- 1 cup low-sodium vegetable broth
- 1 cup unsweetened plain almond milk
- 1½ tablespoons whole-wheat flour
- 2 tablespoons dried minced onion

Directions:

1. Pre-heat the oven to 400⁰F.
2. Bring a sizable saucepan of water to a rolling boil.
3. Cook the green beans for 5 minutes, or until they are just barely soft but bright green. Drain the water and set it aside.
4. Once the 2 tablespoons oil are heated in a medium skillet over medium-high heat, toss in the mushrooms and combine. Cook for 3 -5 minutes, or until the mushrooms are golden brown and liquid has evaporated.
5. Stir in the garlic for approximately 30 seconds, or until it is barely aromatic.
6. Stir in the whole-wheat flour until everything is fully combined. Add broth before you bring to a simmer for a minute.
7. Reduce the heat to a low setting and stir in the almond milk.
8. Return to a low heat and cook for 7 minutes, or until the sauce has thickened. Turn off the heat.
9. Stir in the green beans and then turn on the heat.
10. Mix the almond flour, the remaining 1 tablespoon of olive oil, and the dried onion minces in a small bowl until well combined.
11. Sprinkle the mixture over the beans.
12. Cook for 20 minutes until it is bubbling and browned.
13. Serve and enjoy.

Per serving: Calories: 241Kcal; Fat: 20g; Carbs: 0.1g; Protein: 7g; Sodium: 0.05g; Sugar: 3.4g.

645. BLACK EYED BEANS AND RICE BOWL

Preparation time: 14 minutes
Cooking time: 47 minutes
Servings: 8
Ingredients:

- 2 celery stalks, thinly sliced
- 2 cups brown rice, rinsed 1 medium green bell pepper, chopped
- 1 tablespoon tomato paste
- 2 garlic cloves, minced
- 5 cups low-sodium vegetable broth, divided
- 2 bay leaves
- 1¼ cups frozen black-eyed peas
- 1 small yellow onion, chopped
- 1 teaspoon smoked paprika
- 1 teaspoon Creole Seasoning
- 1 tablespoon canola oil

Directions:

1. In a Dutch oven, warm the canola oil over medium heat.
2. Add onion, celery, tomato paste, garlic, and bell pepper in the oven. Cook, as you stir occasionally, for 5 minutes, or until the celery, onion, bell pepper, tomato paste, and garlic are softened.
3. Combine the rice, 4 cups broth, bay leaves, paprika, and Creole seasoning in a large mixing bowl.
4. Lower the heat, cover, and cook for 30 minutes, or until the rice is tender.
5. Add the remaining 1 cup of broth and the black-eyed peas and cook for 12 minutes, or until the peas soften, stirring occasionally.
6. Set the bay leaves aside and toss them out.
7. Enjoy.

Per serving: Calories: 185Kcal; Fat: 3.3g; Carbs: 35.6g; Protein: 4.6g; Sodium: 0.01g; Sugar: 5.8g.

646. EGGPLANT AND BULGUR PILAF WITH BASIL

Preparation time: 10 minutes
Cooking time: 60 minutes
Servings: 4
Ingredients:

- 1 cup chopped eggplant
- ½ sweet onion, chopped
- 2 teaspoons minced garlic
- 1 cup diced tomato
- 2 tablespoons chopped fresh basil
- ¼ teaspoon sea salt
- 1½ cups bulgur
- 4 cups low-sodium chicken broth

- ¼ teaspoon freshly ground black pepper

Directions:
1. Warm the oil in a big pan over medium heat.
2. Sauté the onion and garlic for 3 minutes or until softened and transparent.
3. Add the eggplant and cook for 4 minutes to soften it.
4. Combine the bulgur, broth, and tomatoes in a mixing bowl. Bring the water to a slight boil in a kettle.
5. Reduce the heat to low, cover, and cook for about 50 minutes, or until the water has been absorbed.
6. Add salt and pepper accordingly to the pilaf.
7. Garnish with basil leaves and serve.
8. Enjoy.

Per serving: Calories: 300Kcal; Fat: 4.0g; Carbs: 54.0g; Protein: 14.0g; Sodium: 0.36g; Sugar: 7.0g.

647. CURRIED BLACK-EYED PEAS

Preparation time: 15 minutes

Cooking time: 35 minutes

Servings: 12

Ingredients:

- 4 cups vegetable broth
- 1-pound dried black-eyed peas, rinsed and drained
- 1 cup chopped onion
- Lime wedges, for serving
- 1 cup coconut water
- 1 tablespoon minced garlic
- 1 teaspoon peeled and minced fresh ginger
- 1 tablespoon extra-virgin olive oil
- 4 large carrots, coarsely chopped
- 1½ tablespoons curry powder
- Kosher salt (optional)

Directions:
1. Combine the black-eyed peas, broth, coconut water, onion, carrots, curry powder, garlic, and ginger in an electric pressure cooker. Drizzle a topping of extra virgin olive oil.
2. Close and lock the pressure cooker lid. To close the valve, turn it to the closed position. Cook for 25 minutes on high pressure.
3. After cooking is complete, press 'Cancel' and let the pressure naturally release for 10 minutes before quick-releasing any leftover pressure.
4. Unlock and remove the cover once the pin has dropped.
5. Season with salt and squeeze fresh lime juice over each serving.
6. Enjoy.

Per serving: Calories: 113Kcal; Fat: 3.1g; Carbs: 30.9g; Protein: 10.1g; Sodium: 0.62g; sugar: 6.0g.

648. QUINOA WITH FRESH VEGETABLES

Preparation time: 15 minutes

Cooking time: 30 minutes

Servings: 12

Ingredients:

- 2 cups quinoa, well rinsed and drained
- 2 teaspoon extra-virgin olive oil
- 4 cups low-sodium vegetable broth
- 2 cups fresh or frozen corn kernels
- 4 teaspoons minced garlic
- 1 sweet onion, chopped
- 1 large green zucchini, halved lengthwise and cut into half disks
- ¼ teaspoon sea salt
- 2 red bell pepper, chopped into small strips after being sown
- ¼ teaspoon freshly ground black pepper
- 2 teaspoon chopped fresh basil

Directions:
1. Place the veggie broth in a medium saucepan over medium heat.
2. Bring the stock to a boil before stirring in the quinoa. Cover and reduce to a low heat setting.
3. Cook for 20 minutes, or until the quinoa has absorbed all of the broth. Set aside and leave aside to cool.
4. Heat the oil in a big skillet over medium-high heat while the quinoa is cooking.
5. Sauté the onion and garlic for 3 minutes, or until softened and transparent.
6. Sauté the zucchini, bell pepper, and corn for about 7 minutes, or until the vegetables are tender-crisp.
7. Turn off the heat in the skillet. Stir in the cooked quinoa and basil until everything is well-combined.
8. Season with a touch of salt and pepper before serving.
9. Enjoy.

Per serving: Calories: 159Kcal; Fat: 3.0g; Carbs: 26.1g; Protein: 7.1g; Sodium: 0.03g; Sugar: 3.0g.

649. KALE, SQUASH, AND BARLEY RISOTTO WITH PISTACHIO

Preparation time: 10 minutes

Cooking time: 14 minutes

Servings: 6

Ingredients:

- 2 cups cooked butternut squash, cut into ½-inch cubes

- ½ sweet onion, finely chopped
- 2 cups cooked barley
- 1 teaspoon minced garlic
- Sea salt, to taste
- 2 cups chopped kale
- 2 tablespoons chopped pistachios
- 1 teaspoon extra-virgin olive oil
- 1 tablespoon chopped fresh thyme

Directions:
1. Warm the oil in a big pan over medium heat.
2. Sauté the onion and garlic for 3 minutes, or until softened and transparent.
3. Stir in the barley and kale for about 7 minutes, or until the grains are heated through and the greens are wilted.
4. Combine the squash, pistachios, and thyme in a mixing bowl.
5. Season with salt and cook until the dish is heated, about 4 minutes.
6. Serve and enjoy.

Per serving: Calories: 160Kcal; Fat: 1.9g; Carbs: 32.1g; Protein: 5.1g; Sodium: 0.06g; Sugar: 2.0g.

650. NAVY BEANS WITH PICO DE GALLO

Preparation time: 20 minutes

Cooking time: 0 minutes

Servings: 4

Ingredients:

- ½ red bell pepper, seeded and chopped
- 2½ cups cooked navy beans
- ¼ jalapeño pepper, chopped
- 1 tomato, diced
- 1 scallion, white and green parts, chopped
- 1 teaspoon minced garlic
- ½ teaspoon ground coriander
- ½ cup low-sodium feta cheese
- 1 teaspoon ground cumin
- Pico de Gallo, for serving

Directions:
1. In a sizable mixing bowl, combine the beans, tomato, bell pepper, jalapeno, scallion, garlic, cumin, and coriander.
2. Heat the mixture slightly.
3. Serve with feta cheese on top.
4. Enjoy with Pico de Gallo.

Per serving: Calories: 225Kcal; Fat: 4.1g; Carbs: 34.1g; Protein: 14.1g; Sodium: 0.16g; sugar: 3.9g

651. AVOCADO AND FARRO

Preparation time: 5 minutes

Cooking time: 25 minutes

Servings: 4

Ingredients:

- 3 cups water
- 1 teaspoon ground cumin
- ½ teaspoon salt
- 1 cup uncooked farro
- 1 tablespoon extra-virgin olive oil
- 4 lemon wedges
- ½ teaspoon freshly ground black pepper
- ⅓ cup plain low-fat Greek yogurt
- 1 avocado, sliced
- 4 hardboiled eggs, sliced

Directions:

1. In a sizable saucepan over high heat, bring the water to a boil.
2. Pour the boiling water over the farro and whisk to fully submerge the grains.
3. Cook for 20 minutes after lowering the heat to medium-low. Drain and set the water aside.
4. Over medium-low heat, heat a medium skillet. Pour in the oil when the pan is heated, then add the farro, cumin, salt, and pepper. Cook, stirring periodically, for 5 minutes.
5. Top each portion of farro with one-quarter of the eggs, avocado, and yoghurt.
6. Serve with a squeeze of a lemon on top of each serving.
7. Enjoy.

Per serving: Calories: 333Kcal; Fat: 16.1g; Carbs: 31.9g; Protein: 15.1g; Sodium: 0.36g; Sugar: 2.0g

652. CHICKPEA SPAGHETTI BOLOGNESE

Preparation time: 5 minutes
Cooking time: 40 minutes
Servings: 4
Ingredients:

- 6 ounces extra-firm tofu
- 1 cup no-sugar-added spaghetti sauce
- ½ teaspoon ground cumin
- 1 low-sodium chickpeas, drained and rinsed
- 4 pounds deseeded spaghetti squash, halved lengthwise

Directions:

1. Preheat the oven to 400⁰F.
2. Season both sides of the squash with cumin and set cut-side down on a baking pan. Cook for 25 minutes at 350°F.
3. Meanwhile, simmer the spaghetti sauce and chickpeas in a medium skillet over low heat.
4. Squeeze off any excess water by pressing the tofu between two layers of paper towels.

5. Cook for 15 minutes after crumbling the tofu into the sauce.
6. Remove the squash from the oven and comb thin strands of flesh through each half with a fork.
7. Divide the spaghetti into four sections and drizzle one-quarter of the sauce over each.
8. Serve and enjoy.

Per serving: Calories: 276Kcal; Fat: 7.1g; Carbs: 24.8g; Protein: 7g; Sodium: 0.02g; Sugar: 7g.

653. BLACK BEAN AND CORN SOUP

Preparation time: 10 minutes
Cooking time: 25 minutes
Servings: 7
Ingredients:

- 1-pound chicken breast, boneless and skinless, cubed
- ½ onion, diced
- 5 cups low-sodium chicken broth
- ¼ teaspoon black pepper
- 1 washed and drained black beans with no salt added
- ½ teaspoon Adobo seasoning, divided
- 1 can fire-roasted tomatoes
- ½ teaspoon cumin
- 1 tablespoon chili powder
- ½ cup frozen corn
- 2 tablespoons olive oil

Directions:

1. Heat the olive oil in a sizable stockpot over medium-high heat until it shimmers.
2. Sauté the onion for 3 minutes, or until it is transparent.
3. Spread the Adobo seasoning and pepper over the chicken breasts. Cook for 6 minutes, or until gently browned, with the lid on. Halfway through the cooking period, give the pot a good shake.
4. Combine the other ingredients in a mixing bowl.
5. Reduce to a low heat and continue to cook for another 15 minutes, or until the black beans are tender.
6. Serve right away.
7. Enjoy.

Per serving: Calories: 170Kcal; Fat: 3.6g; Carbs: 7g; Protein: 20g; Sodium: 0.01g; Sugar: 3g.

654. LIME YOGURT CHILI SOUP WITH TOMATOES

Preparation time: 60 minutes
Cooking time: 1 hour 33 minutes
Servings: 8

Ingredients:

- ¼ cup low-fat Greek yogurt
- 1 medium onion, chopped
- 1 pound dried black beans, soaked in water for at least 8 hours, rinsed
- 1 tablespoon freshly squeezed lime juice
- 10 ounces diced tomatoes and green chilies
- 1 teaspoon ground cumin
- 6 cup vegetable broth, or water
- 3 garlic cloves, minced
- Kosher salt, to taste
- 2 tablespoons avocado oil

Directions:

1. In a sizable nonstick skillet, heat the avocado oil over medium heat until it shimmers.
2. Cook properly for around 3 minutes, or until the onion is clear.
3. In a large pot, combine the onion, tomatoes, green chilies, and their juices, black beans, cumin, garlic, broth, and salt. Stir everything together thoroughly.
4. Bring everything to a slight boil over medium-high heat, then set to a low setting. Cook for 1 hour and 30 minutes, or until the beans are soft.
5. Meanwhile, in a sizable bowl, combine the lime juice and Greek yoghurt. Stir everything together thoroughly.
6. Pour the soup into a sizable serving bowl and drizzle with lime yoghurt.
7. Serve and enjoy.

Per serving: Calories: 285Kcal; Fat: 6g; Carbs: 29g; Protein: 19g; Sodium: 0.05g; sugar: 3g;

655. KALE AND CARROTS SOUP

Preparation time: 8 minutes
Cooking time: 11 minutes
Servings: 4
Ingredients:

- ½ teaspoons freshly ground black pepper
- 2 carrot, chopped
- 2 cups canned lentils, drained and rinsed
- 2 cup chopped kale, stems removed
- 6 garlic cloves, minced
- 2 onion, finely chopped
- 2 cups unsalted vegetable broth
- 1 teaspoon sea salt
- 4 teaspoons dried rosemary
- 4 tablespoons extra-virgin olive oil

Directions:

1. Heat the olive oil in a sizable pot over medium-high heat until it shimmers.

2. Add the onion and carrot and cook for 3 minutes, stirring periodically, or until the vegetables soften.
3. Cook for an extra 3 minutes after adding the kale.
4. Cook, stirring regularly, for 30 seconds after adding the garlic.
5. Add the lentils, vegetable broth, rosemary, salt, and pepper and stir to combine.
6. Heat to a low boil, and reduce to low heat. Cook for an additional 5 minutes, stirring periodically.
7. Serve and enjoy.

Per serving: Calories: 160Kcal; Fat: 7g; Carbs: 19g; Protein: 4.96g; Sodium: 0.06g; Sugar: 15g.

656. KIDNEY BEANS BOWL

Preparation time: 10 minutes

Cooking time: 12 minutes

Servings: 8

Ingredients:

- 2 garlic cloves, minced
- 1 cup crushed tomatoes
- 1 medium yellow onion, chopped
- 1 teaspoon smoked paprika
- 2 cups low-sodium canned red kidney beans, rinsed
- 2 tablespoons olive oil
- Salt, to taste
- 1 cup roughly chopped green beans
- ¼ cup low-sodium vegetable broth

Directions:

1. In a nonstick skillet, warm the olive oil over medium heat until it shimmers.
2. In a large mixing bowl, combine the onion, tomatoes, and garlic. Sauté for 5 minutes, or until the onion is transparent and fragrant.
3. In a skillet, combine the kidney beans, green beans, and broth. Season with paprika and salt, then sauté until everything is nicely combined.
4. Cook for 7 minutes, or until the vegetables are soft, covered in the skillet.
5. Serve right away.
6. Enjoy.

Per serving: Calories: 187Kcal; Fat: 17.51g; Carbs: 34g; Protein: 13g; Sodium: 0.03g; Sugar: 4g.

657. LETTUCE WRAPS WITH CHESTNUTS

Preparation time: 10 minutes

Cooking time: 0 minutes

Servings: 2

Ingredients:

- 2 3/5 ounces package tuna packed in water, drained

- ½ cup drained and sliced canned water chestnuts
- 2 large butter lettuce leaves
- 1 teaspoon reduced-sodium soy sauce
- 1 tablespoon freshly squeezed lemon juice
- 1 teaspoon curry powder
- ½ teaspoon sriracha

Directions:

1. Combine the lemon juice, curry powder, soy sauce, and sriracha in a medium mixing bowl.
2. Combine the water chestnuts and tuna in a mixing bowl. To blend, stir everything together.
3. Wrap the lettuce leaves around the meat and serve.
4. Enjoy.

Per serving: Calories: 271Kcal; Fat: 14g; Carbs: 18g; Protein: 19g; Sodium: 0.01g; Sugar: 8.1g.

658. VEGGIE MACARONI PIE

Preparation time: 15 minutes

Cooking time: 25 minutes

Servings: 6

Ingredients:

- 2 celery stalks, thinly sliced
- 1-pound package whole-wheat macaroni
- 1 small yellow onion, chopped
- Salt, to taste
- ¼ teaspoon freshly ground black pepper
- 2 roasted red peppers, ¼-inch pieces, chopped
- 2 garlic cloves, minced
- 2 tablespoons chickpea flour
- 1 cup fat-free milk
- 2 cups grated reduced-fat sharp Cheddar cheese
- 2 large zucchinis, finely grated and squeezed dry

Directions:

1. Pre-heat the oven to 350⁰F.
2. Bring a water pot to a boil, then add the macaroni and cook until al dente, about 4 minutes.
3. Remove water from the macaroni and place it in a big mixing dish. Set aside 1 cup of the macaroni water.
4. In an oven-safe skillet, heat the macaroni water over medium heat.
5. In a large skillet, sauté the celery, onion, garlic, salt, and black pepper for 4 minutes, or until soft.
6. Fold in the cheese and milk after gently mixing in the chickpea flour. Whisk the liquid until it is thick and smooth.
7. Combine the cooked macaroni, zucchini, and red peppers in a large

mixing bowl. Stir everything together thoroughly.
8. Pre-heat the oven to 350°F and before covering the skillet with aluminum foil.
9. Bake for 15 minutes, or until the cheese has melted, then remove the foil and bake for 5 minutes more, or until the top is lightly browned.
10. Get the pie out of the oven and serve right away.

Per serving: Calories: 378Kcal; Fat: 4g; Carbs: 67g; Protein: 24g; Sodium: 0.02g; Sugar: 6g.

659. TOMATOES AND RED KIDNEY BEANS

Preparation time: 10 minutes

Cooking time: 12 minutes

Servings: 8

Ingredients:

- 1 medium yellow onion, chopped
- 1 cup roughly chopped green beans
- 2 garlic cloves, minced
- 2 tablespoons olive oil
- 1 cup crushed tomatoes
- Salt, to taste
- 2 cups low-sodium canned red kidney beans, rinsed
- ¼ cup low-sodium vegetable broth
- 1 teaspoon smoked paprika

Directions:

1. In a sizable nonstick skillet, heat the olive oil over medium heat until it shimmers.
2. In a large mixing bowl, combine the onion, tomatoes, and garlic. Sauté for 5 minutes, or until the onion is transparent and fragrant.
3. In a skillet, combine the kidney beans, green beans, and broth. Season with paprika and salt, then sauté until everything is nicely combined.
4. Cook for 7 minutes, or until the vegetables are soft, covered in the skillet.
5. Serve right away.
6. Enjoy.

Per serving: Calories: 187Kcal; Fat: 1g; Carbs: 20g; Protein: 13g; Sodium: 0.04g; Sugar: 4g.

660. GARLIC BEANS

Preparation time: 10 minutes

Cooking time: 10 minutes

Servings: 3

Ingredients:

- ½ teaspoon chili powder
- 1 ½ tablespoons olive oil
- 1 garlic clove, minced
- 1 cup red kidney beans, cooked

- 1 tomato, chopped

Directions:

1. Heat olive oil in the pan.
2. Add chopped tomato, and chili powder.
3. Cook the mixture for 3 minutes.
4. Add garlic and red kidney beans.
5. Stir the ingredients well and cook over the medium-low heat for 7 minutes.
6. Serve and enjoy.

Per serving: Calories: 273Kcal; Fat: 9.7g; Carbs: 39g; Protein: 14.1g; Sodium: 0.30g; Sugar: 2g.

CHAPTER 14: Vegetarian Recipes

661. VEGGIE NIÇOISE SALAD

Preparation time: 15 minutes
Cooking time: 20 minutes
Servings: 1
Ingredients:

- 1/8 teaspoon salt
- 16 ounces kidney beans, rinsed and drained
- 1 small red onion
- 6 large, hard-boiled eggs, quartered
- ¼ cup lemon juice
- 1-pound fresh asparagus, trimmed
- ½ pound fresh green beans, trimmed
- 1-pound small red potatoes (about 9), halved
- ¼ teaspoon coarsely ground pepper
- 12 cups torn romaine (about two small bunches)
- 2 teaspoons minced fresh oregano
- ½ cup Niçoise or kalamata olives
- 2 teaspoons minced fresh thyme
- 1 teaspoon Dijon mustard
- 1 garlic clove, minced
- 1/3 cup olive oil

Directions:

1. Whisk together the vinaigrette ingredients.
2. Toss kidney beans and onion with one tablespoon vinaigrette in a separate dish. Set aside the bean mixture and the rest of the vinaigrette.
3. Cover the potatoes with water in a saucepan. Bring the water to a boil.
4. Lower the heat and cook properly, covered, for 15 minutes, or until vegetables are soft. Drain.
5. Toss the potatoes with one tablespoon vinaigrette while still heated; leave aside.
6. Cook asparagus in a sizable saucepan of boiling water for 4 minutes, or until crisp-tender. Remove with tongs and before immersing in ice cold water. Pat dry after draining.
7. Cook green beans in the same saucepan of boiling water for 4 minutes, or until crisp-tender. Remove the beans and place them in a bowl of cold water. Pat dry after draining.
8. Toss asparagus with one tablespoon vinaigrette and green beans with two tablespoons vinaigrette before serving.
9. Toss the romaine with the rest of vinaigrette and serve on a plate.
10. Top with veggies, kidney bean mixture, eggs, artichoke hearts, and olives.
11. Enjoy.

Per serving: Calories: 366Kcal; Fat: 17.51g; Carbs: 9.79g; Protein: 12.8g; Sodium: 0.65g; Sugar: 5.1g

662. LENTIL SLOPPY JOES

Preparation time: 15 minutes
Cooking time: 33 minutes
Servings: 1
Ingredients:

- 1 medium green pepper, chopped
- ½ medium sweet red pepper, chopped
- 1 large, sweet onion, chopped
- 1 medium carrot, shredded
- 5 plum tomatoes, chopped
- 8 ounces tomato sauce
- 4 ½ teaspoons cider vinegar
- 2 teaspoons vegan Worcestershire sauce
- 2 teaspoons honey or maple syrup
- 2 tablespoons yellow mustard
- 14 whole-wheat hamburger buns, split and toasted
- 1 ½ teaspoons tomato paste
- 2 tablespoons olive oil
- ¼ teaspoon salt
- 1/8 teaspoon pepper
- 2 ½ cups reduced-sodium vegetable broth
- 1 cup dried red lentils, rinsed
- 6 garlic cloves, minced
- 2 tablespoons chili powder

Directions:

1. Heat the oil in a sizable skillet over medium-high heat.
2. Cook and stir until the onion, peppers, and carrot are crisp-tender, 8 minutes. Cook for a minute more after adding the garlic.
3. Bring the broth and lentils to a boil. Lower the heat and cook, uncovered, for around 15 minutes, or until lentils are cooked, stirring occasionally.
4. Combine chopped tomatoes, tomato sauce, chili powder, mustard, vinegar, Worcestershire sauce, honey, tomato paste, salt, and pepper in a mixing bowl.
5. Bring the water to a boil. Lower the heat and cook until the sauce thickens for about 10 minutes.
6. Serve with buns and enjoy.

Per serving: Calories: 254Kcal; Fat: 15.5g; Carbs: 10.7g; Protein: 4.96g; Sodium: 0.05g; Sugar: 3g

663. VEGETARIAN BLACK BEAN PASTA

Preparation time: 15 minutes
Cooking time: 7 minutes
Servings: 1
Ingredients:

- 1 tablespoon olive oil
- 2 cups fresh baby spinach
- 1 ¾ cups sliced baby portobello mushrooms
- 1 teaspoon dried rosemary, crushed
- 1 garlic clove, minced
- ½ teaspoon dried oregano
- 15 ounces black beans
- 14 ½ ounces diced tomatoes, undrained
- 9 ounces uncooked whole-wheat fettuccine

Directions:

1. Cook the fettuccine as per package instructions.
2. Heat the oil in a sizable pan over medium-high heat.
3. Cook and stir for 6 minutes, or until the mushrooms are soft. Cook for a minute more after adding the garlic.
4. Heat through the black beans, tomatoes, rosemary, and oregano. Stir in the spinach until it is properly wilted.
5. Drain the fettuccine and add it to the bean mixture, tossing to incorporate.
6. Serve and enjoy.

Per serving: Calories: 212Kcal; Fat: 4.5g; Carbs: 28g; Protein: 4.96g; Sodium: 0.02g; Sugar: 2.2g

664. FIERY STUFFED POBLANOS

Preparation time: 15 minutes

Cooking time: 20 minutes

Servings: 1

Ingredients:

- 1 medium zucchini, chopped
- 1 small red onion, chopped
- 8 poblano peppers
- 1 ½ teaspoons ground ancho Chile pepper
- 4 garlic cloves, minced
- 15 ¼ ounces whole kernel corn, drained
- ¼ teaspoon salt
- 1 tablespoon ground
- 2 teaspoons cumin
- ¼ teaspoon pepper
- 1 cup shredded reduced-fat Mexican cheese blend, divided
- ½ cup reduced-fat sour cream
- 14 ½ ounces fire-roasted diced tomatoes, undrained
- 3 green onions, chopped
- 1 cup cooked brown rice
- 1 can black beans

Directions:

1. Broil peppers 3 inches from the flame for 5 minutes or until the skins blister.
2. Rotate the peppers a quarter turn with tongs. Broil, often rotating, until both sides are blistered and browned.
3. Place the peppers in a sizable mixing bowl right away; cover and set aside for 20 minutes.
4. Meanwhile, roughly mash the beans in a small dish and leave them aside.
5. Cook and stir zucchini and onion in a large nonstick pan until Soft.Cook for a minute more after adding the garlic.
6. Combine the corn, tomatoes, rice, spices, and beans in a mixing bowl. Remove from the fire and mix in ½ cup of the cheese. Place aside.
7. Heat up your oven to 375° F. Remove the charred skins from the poblanos and set them aside. Remove the membranes and de-seed each pepper by cutting a longitudinal incision through the stem. Fill each pepper with 2/3 cup filling.
8. Place the peppers in a sizable baking dish sprayed with cooking spray.
9. Bake 22 minutes, or until cooked through, sprinkle with green onions and remaining cheese during the final 5 minutes of baking.
10. Toss with sour cream and serve.
11. Enjoy.

Per serving: Calories: 223Kcal; Fat: 32g; Carbs: 11g; Protein: 11g; Sodium: 0.58g; Sugar: 0.8g

665. ROASTED VEGETABLE STRATA

Preparation time: 15 minutes

Cooking time: 65 minutes

Servings: 1

Ingredients:

- 1 medium tomato, chopped
- ½ cup shredded sharp cheddar cheese
- 2 tablespoons olive oil
- 1-pound unsliced crusty Italian bread
- 1 each medium red, yellow, and orange peppers, cut into 1-inch pieces
- ½ cup shredded Asiago cheese
- 6 large eggs
- ½ teaspoon salt
- 2 cups fat-free milk
- 1 teaspoon dried oregano
- ½ teaspoon pepper
- 3 large zucchinis halved lengthwise and cut into 3/4-inch slices
- ½ teaspoon dried basil

Directions:

1. Preheat the oven to 400⁰F. Toss zucchini and peppers with oil and spices in a sizable baking dish.
2. Cook for 30 minutes, stirring once, until soft. Stir in the tomato and set aside to cool.
3. Bread should be sliced into 1-inch slices once the ends have been trimmed. Layer half of each of bread slice, roasted veggies, and cheeses in a greased baking dish: bread, roasted veggies, and cheeses. Repeat the layers.
4. Whisk properly the milk and eggs, then pour equally over the top. Refrigerate for 6 hours or overnight, covered.
5. Heat up your oven to 375°F. Remove the dish from the refrigerator while the oven warms up. Cook, uncovered, for 50 minutes, or until golden brown. Allow standing for 10 minutes before slicing.
6. If freezing, wrap the unbaked dish in plastic wrap and place it in the freezer. To use, defrost slightly in the refrigerator overnight. Thirty minutes before baking, remove from refrigerator.
7. Preheat the oven to 375° F.
8. Bake casserole as per package directions, adding time as needed to cook through and a thermometer inserted into the middle to read 165F°.
9. Serve and enjoy.

Per serving: Calories: 349Kcal; Fat: 14g; Carbs: 40g; Protein: 17g; Sodium: 0.64g; Sugars: 9g

666. PORTOBELLO POLENTA STACKS

Preparation time: 15 minutes

Cooking time: 27 minutes

Servings: 1

Ingredients:

- ¼ teaspoon pepper
- 4 slices tomato
- ½ cup grated Parmesan cheese
- 2 tablespoons balsamic vinegar
- 1 tablespoon olive oil
- 2 tablespoons minced fresh basil
- 18 ounces polenta, cut into 12 slices
- 4 large portobello mushrooms, stems removed
- ¼ teaspoon salt

Directions:

1. Pre-heat the oven to 400⁰F.
2. Warm the oil in a sizable saucepan over medium heat.
3. Cook, constantly stirring, until the garlic is soft, about 2 minutes. Set aside and stir in the vinegar.
4. Place the mushrooms, gill side up, in a sizable baking dish.
5. Brush with the vinegar mixture and season with salt and pepper.
6. Sprinkle with cheese and top with polenta and tomato slices.
7. Cook, uncovered, for 25 minutes, or until the mushrooms are soft.
8. Garnish with basil.
9. Enjoy.

Per serving: Calories: 243Kcal; Fat: 14.5g; Carbs: 9.7g; Protein: 4.8g; Sodium: 0.03g; Sugar: 4g

667. CHILI-LIME MUSHROOM TACOS

Preparation time: 15 minutes
Cooking time: 8 minutes
Servings: 1
Ingredients:

- 1 medium onion halved and thinly sliced
- 8 corn tortillas, warmed
- 1 tablespoon olive oil
- 1 medium sweet red pepper, sliced into strips
- 1 ½ teaspoons chili powder
- 1 cup shredded pepper jack cheese
- ¼ teaspoon crushed red pepper flakes
- 2 garlic cloves, minced
- ½ teaspoon salt
- ½ teaspoon ground cumin
- 2 tablespoons lime juice
- 1 teaspoon grated lime zest
- 4 large portobello mushrooms

Directions:

1. Remove the stems from the mushrooms and, if desired, remove the gills with a spoon. Slice the mushrooms into ½ inch pieces.
2. Heat the oil in a sizable pan over medium-high heat; sauté the mushrooms, red pepper, and onion until the mushrooms are soft, about 7 minutes. Cook and stir for a minute after adding the garlic spices, lime zest, and juice.
3. Serve in tortillas with cheese on top.

Per serving: Calories: 222Kcal; Fat: 23g; Carbs: 11g; Protein: 4.9g; Sodium: 0.17g; Sugar: 7g

668. CHEESE MANICOTTI

Preparation time: 15 minutes
Cooking time: 1 hour 5 minutes
Servings: 1
Ingredients:

- 1 cup shredded part-skim mozzarella cheese, divided
- 4 cups marinara sauce
- 8 ounces manicotti shells
- 1 cup grated Parmesan cheese, divided
- 15 ounces reduced-fat ricotta cheese
- ½ cup water
- 1 large egg, lightly beaten
- Additional parsley, optional
- ¼ teaspoon salt
- 1 small onion, finely chopped
- 2 tablespoons minced fresh parsley
- ½ teaspoon pepper

Directions:

1. Pre-heat the oven to 350°F.
2. Combine the fat ricotta cheese, egg, onion, salt, pepper, manicotti shells in a small mixing bowl; whisk in ½ cup mozzarella cheese and ½ cup Parmesan cheese.
3. Mix marinara sauce and water in a separate bowl; put ¾ cup sauce over the bottom of a sizable baking dish sprayed with cooking spray.
4. Fill uncooked manicotti shells with ricotta mixture and place on top of sauce. Finish with the remaining sauce.
5. Bake for 50 minutes, covered, or until pasta is tender.
6. Finish with the remaining ½ cup mozzarella and ½ cup Parmesan cheese.
7. Bake, uncovered, for around 15 minutes.
8. Top with extra parsley if desired.
9. Enjoy.

Per serving: Calories: 369Kcal; Fat: 17.6g; Carbs: 9.7g; Protein: 4.9g; Sodium: 0.8g; Sugar: 1.2g

669. GOLDEN BEET AND PEACH SOUP

Preparation time: 15 minutes
Cooking time: 45 minutes
Servings: 1
Ingredients:

- 2 medium fresh peaches, peeled and diced
- ¼ cup plain Greek yogurt
- Fresh tarragon sprigs
- 2 cups white grape-peach juice
- 1 tablespoon olive oil
- 2 tablespoons cider vinegar
- ¼ teaspoon finely chopped fresh tarragon

Directions:

1. Pre-heat the oven to 400°F. Bake the beets on a sizable baking sheet.
2. Drizzle oil over the vegetables and toss to coat. Cook for 45 minutes, or until the vegetables are soft. Allow cooling slightly.
3. Add the beets into a food processor. Blend in the juice and vinegar until smooth.
4. Refrigerate for at least one hour.
5. Refrigerate Greek yogurt and chopped tarragon.
6. Divide the beet mixture among individual dishes and top with a tablespoon of the yogurt mixture.
7. Serve with chopped peaches and tarragon sprigs on top.
8. Serve and enjoy.

Per serving: Calories: 159Kcal; Fat: 4g; Carbs: 31g; Protein: 3g; Sodium: 0.13g; Sugar: 4g

670. STIR-FRY RICE BOWL

Preparation time: 15minutes
Cooking time: 10 minutes
Servings: 1
Ingredients:

- 1 tablespoon canola oil
- 1 cup bean sprouts
- 1 tablespoon water
- 1 medium zucchini, julienned
- 1 tablespoon chili garlic sauce
- 1 cup fresh baby spinach
- 4 large eggs
- 2 medium carrots, julienned
- 1 tablespoon reduced-sodium soy sauce
- 3 cups hot cooked brown rice
- 1 teaspoon sesame oil
- ½ cup sliced baby portobello mushrooms

Directions:

1. Heat the canola oil in a large pan over medium-high heat.
2. Cook and stir carrots, zucchini, and mushrooms for 5 minutes, or until carrots are crisp-tender.
3. Cook and mix in the bean sprouts, spinach, water, soy sauce, and chili sauce until the spinach has wilted. Remove from the heat and keep warm.
4. In a big skillet with high sides, add 2 water. Bring to a slight boil, then reduce to a medium simmer.
5. Break cold eggs into a small bowl, one at a time.
6. Cook, uncovered, for 5 minutes, or until the whites are set, and the yolks are thickening but not hard. Remove the eggs from the water using a slotted spoon.
7. Serve rice in dishes with veggies on top. Drizzle sesame oil over the top.
8. Serve with a topping of poached egg on each plate.

Per serving: Calories: 380Kcal; Fat: 10g; Carbs: 57g; Protein: 17g; Sodium: 0.89g; Sugar: 3g

671. RICOTTA-STUFFED PORTOBELLO MUSHROOMS

Preparation time: 15 minutes

Cooking time: 10 minutes

Servings: 1

Ingredients:

- ¾ cup reduced-fat ricotta cheese
- 1/8 teaspoon pepper
- ¾ cup fresh basil leaves
- 6 large portobello mushrooms
- 6 slices large tomato
- ¾ cup grated Parmesan cheese, divided
- 3 tablespoons slivered almonds, toasted
- 2 tablespoons olive oil
- ½ cup shredded part-skim mozzarella cheese
- 1 small garlic clove
- 2 tablespoons minced fresh parsley
- 3 teaspoons water

Directions:

1. Combine ricotta cheese, ¼ cup Parmesan cheese, mozzarella cheese, parsley, and pepper in a small mixing basin.
2. Remove and discard mushroom stems; scrape and remove gills with a spoon. Fill the caps with the ricotta mixture. Serve with tomato slices on top.
3. Cover the grill over medium heat for 10 minutes or until mushrooms are tender. Using a metal spatula, remove it from the grill.
4. Meanwhile, pulse the basil, almonds, and garlic until finely chopped in a small food processor. Add the remaining Parmesan cheese and pulse just until combined.
5. While processing, gradually add oil and water until the required consistency is reached.
6. Before serving, drizzle over packed mushrooms.

Per serving: Calories: 201Kcal; Fat: 13g; Carbs: 9g; Protein: 12g; Sodium: 0.23g; Sugar: g

672. CUMIN QUINOA PATTIES

Preparation time: 15 minutes

Cooking time: 23 minutes

Servings: 1

Ingredients:

- ½ cup quinoa, rinsed
- 3 teaspoons ground cumin
- 1 cup water
- 1 medium carrot, cut into 1-inch pieces
- 2 tablespoons olive oil
- ¼ teaspoon salt
- Sour cream, salsa, and minced fresh cilantro, as needed
- 1/8 teaspoon pepper
- 3 green onions, chopped
- 1 large egg, lightly beaten
- 1 cup canned cannellini beans
- ¼ cup panko breadcrumbs

Directions:

1. Bring quinoa and water to a boil in a sizable saucepan.
2. Reduce heat to low and simmer, covered, for 15 minutes, or until liquid is absorbed. Set aside and fluff with a fork.
3. Pulse the carrot properly in a food processor until it is finely chopped. Process the beans until they are finely chopped.
4. Transfer the mixture to a large mixing bowl.
5. Combine cooked quinoa, breadcrumbs, green onions, egg, and spices in a mixing bowl. Form the mixture into eight patties.
6. Heat the oil in a sizable skillet over medium heat. Cook until a thermometer reaches 160°, 4 minutes per side, flipping gently.
7. Serve and enjoy.

Per serving: Calories: 235Kcal; Fat: 10g; Carbs: 2g; Protein: 8g; Sodium: 0.27g; Sugar: 2g

673. TUSCAN PORTOBELLO STEW

Preparation time: 15 minutes

Cooking time: 10 minutes

Servings: 1

Ingredients:

- 1 teaspoon dried thyme
- ½ teaspoon dried basil
- 3 garlic cloves, minced
- 2 tablespoons olive oil
- 1 medium onion, chopped
- 1 bay leaf
- ½ teaspoon dried rosemary, crushed
- ¼ teaspoon pepper
- 2 large portobello mushrooms, coarsely chopped
- 30 ounces cannellini beans, rinsed and drained
- ½ cup white wine
- 28 ounces diced tomatoes, undrained
- 2 cups chopped fresh kale
- ¼ teaspoon salt

Directions:

1. Sauté the mushrooms, onion, and garlic in oil in a large pan until soft. Pour in the wine or broth. Bring to a slight boil before simmering until the liquid has been reduced by half.
2. Combine the tomatoes, greens, and spices in a mixing bowl. Bring the water to a slight boil.
3. Lower the heat, before covering, and allowing to cook for 10 minutes.
4. Heat through the beans and remove the bay leaf.

Per serving: Calories: 309Kcal; Fat: 8g; Carbs: 9.79g; Protein: 4.96g; Sodium: 0.67g, Sugar: 0.4g

674. VEGETARIAN KETO BURGER ON A BUN

Preparation time: 10 minutes

Cooking time: 35 minutes

Servings: 2

Ingredients:

- 2 tablespoon freshly chopped basil
- Mushrooms, as desired
- Black pepper, as desired
- 2 medium-large flat mushrooms
- ½ teaspoon dried Freshly chopped oregano
- 1 crushed garlic clove
- 1 tablespoon of each
- Coconut oil or ghee, as desired
- ¼ teaspoon salt

For the Garnish:

- 2 keto buns
- 2 tablespoon mayonnaise
- 2 large organic eggs
- 2 slices cheddar or gouda cheese
- 2 tablespoon mayonnaise

Directions:

6. Prepare the mushrooms for marinating by seasoning with crushed garlic, pepper, salt, ghee (melted), and fresh herbs. Save a small amount for frying the eggs. Marinate for about one hour at room temperature.
7. Arrange the mushrooms in the pan with the top side facing upwards. Cook for about five minutes on med-high setting. Flip and keep cooking for another five minutes.

8. Remove the pan from the burner and flip the mushrooms over and add the cheese. When it is time to serve, put them under the broiler for a minute or so to melt the cheese.

9. With the remainder of the ghee, fry the eggs leaving the yolk runny. Remove from the heat.

10. Slice the buns and add them to the grill, cooking until crisp for about 2 to 3 minutes.

11. To assemble, add one tablespoon of mayonnaise to each bun and top them off with mushroom, egg, tomato, and lettuce.

12. Put the toppings on the buns and serve.

Per serving: Calories: 497Kcal; Fat: 33.4g; Carbs: 32.4g; Protein: 19.62g; Sodium: 0.87g; Sugar: 2g

675. PEPPER RICOTTA PRIMAVERA

Preparation time: 15 minutes

Cooking time: 6 minutes

Servings: 1

Ingredients:

- 6 ounces fettuccine, cooked and drained
- ½ cup fat-free milk
- 1 cup part-skim ricotta cheese
- 1 medium zucchini, sliced
- 1 medium sweet yellow pepper, julienned
- 1 cup frozen peas, thawed
- ¼ teaspoon dried oregano
- 1 garlic clove, minced
- 1 medium green pepper, julienned
- ¼ teaspoon dried basil
- 4 teaspoons olive oil
- ½ teaspoon crushed red pepper flakes
- 1 medium sweet red pepper, julienned

Directions:

1. Set aside the ricotta cheese and milk that have been whisked together.

2. Heat the oil in a large skillet over medium heat. Cook for a minute after adding the garlic and pepper flakes.

3. Add the remaining seven ingredients. Cook and stir properly over medium heat for 5 minutes, or until veggies are crisp-tender.

4. Top fettuccine with cheese mixture and veggies. To coat, toss everything together.

5. Serve right away.

Per serving: Calories: 229Kcal; Fat: 7g; Carbs: 31g; Protein: 4.96g; Sodium: 0.08g; Sugar: 6g

676. VEGETARIAN CROCK POT SPLIT PEA SOUP

Preparation time: 10 minutes

Cooking time: 10 minutes

Servings: 8

- 2 chopped potatoes
- 2 cubes low-sodium bouillon
- 2 chopped celery ribs
- 2 carrots
- 2 cup uncooked green split peas
- 8 cup water
- 3 bay leaves

Directions:

1. Place the bouillon cubes, split peas, and water in the Crock-Pot. Stir briefly to disperse the bouillon cubes.

2. Add the potatoes, celery, and carrots, along with the bay leaves.

3. Combine thoroughly by stirring.

4. Cover and simmer on the low setting of your Crock-Pot for at least 4 hours, or until the green split peas are tender.

5. Season properly with salt and pepper.

6. Set the bay leaves aside before serving and enjoy.

Per serving: Calories: 149Kcal; Fat: 1 g; Carbs: 30 g; Protein: 7 g; Sodium: 0.73g; Sugar: 3 g

677. SPINACH QUESADILLAS

Preparation time: 15 minutes

Cooking time: 5 minutes

Servings: 2

Ingredients:

- ¼ cup reduced-fat ricotta cheese
- 1 small tomato, chopped
- 6 flour tortillas
- 1 cup shredded reduced-fat Monterey Jack cheese
- 4 green onions, chopped
- 1 teaspoon ground cumin
- Reduced-fat sour cream, optional
- 3 ounces fresh baby spinach
- 2 tablespoons lemon juice
- ¼ teaspoon garlic powder

Directions:

1. Cook and stir the first six ingredients in a large nonstick pan until the spinach is wilted. Set aside and mix in the cheeses.

2. Place half of each tortilla on the spinach mixture; fold the other half over the contents.

3. Cook the mix over medium heat until golden brown for 2 minutes per side, on a grill covered with cooking spray.

4. Halve the quesadillas and serve with sour cream.

Per serving: Calories: 952Kcal; Fat: 48g; Carbs: 9.7g; Protein: 12g; Sodium: 0.12g; Sugar: 3.6g

678. MARKET BASKET SOUP

Preparation time: 15 minutes

Cooking time: 35 minutes

Servings: 3

Ingredients:

- 6 cups vegetable stock or water
- 2 bay leaves
- 1 tablespoon olive oil
- 1 large kohlrabi bulb, peeled and chopped
- 1 teaspoon coarsely ground pepper
- 4 celery ribs, chopped
- 2 medium carrots, chopped
- 3 garlic cloves, minced
- 2 medium tomatoes, chopped
- 2 tablespoons minced fresh tarragon
- 2 medium onions, chopped
- 2 cans great northern beans, rinsed and drained
- 2 tablespoons minced fresh parsley
- 2 tablespoons minced fresh thyme
- 1 teaspoon salt

Directions:

1. Heat the oil in a sizable stockpot over medium-high heat.

2. Cook for 5 minutes, or until the onions are softened, after adding the kohlrabi, celery, onions, and carrots.

3. Cook and stir for 5 minutes after adding the garlic, salt, and pepper.

4. Combine the stock, beans, and bay leaves in a mixing bowl.

5. Bring the water to a slight boil over medium-high heat.

6. Reduce heat to low and cook, covered, for 25 minutes, or until veggies are soft—Cook for 5 minutes more after adding the other ingredients.

7. Remove the bay leaves and serve.

Per serving: Calories: 130Kcal; Fat: 17.51g; Carbs: 9.79g; Protein: 5g; Sodium: 0.9g; Sugar: 4g

679. BOW TIE AND SPINACH SALAD

Preparation time: 9 minutes
Cooking time: 10 minutes
Servings: 2
Ingredients:

- 6 cups fresh baby spinach
- ¼ cup minced fresh basil
- 2 plum tomatoes, chopped
- ¼ cup chopped walnuts, toasted
- 2 cups uncooked multigrain bow tie pasta
- 15 ounces garbanzo beans, rinsed and drained
- ½ cup cubed part-skim mozzarella cheese
- 1 medium sweet red pepper, chopped
- ¼ teaspoon salt
- ½ cup pitted Greek olives, halved
- 2 cups fresh broccoli florets
- 1/3 cup reduced-fat sun-dried tomato salad dressing

Directions:

1. Cook the pasta according to package instructions. Drain and place in a sizable mixing bowl.
2. Pasta should be topped with beans, veggies, cheese, olives, and basil.
3. Drizzle with dressing and season with salt, then toss to coat.
4. Garnish with walnuts before serving.

Per serving: Calories: 318Kcal; Fat: 13g; Carbs: 6g; Protein: 13g; Sodium: 0.67g; Sugar: 8g

680. VEGETARIAN ANTIPASTO SALAD

Preparation time: 10 minutes
Cooking time: 0 minutes
Servings: 8
Ingredients:

- 1 cup cubed light mozzarella cheese
- ½ cup sliced black olives
- 1 cup halved marinated mushrooms
- 1 cup chopped canned artichokes
- 1 cup chopped roasted red peppers
- 4 cups chopped romaine lettuce
- ½ cup chopped fresh basil
- Dressing of your choice, as desired

Directions:

1. Toss all the ingredients in a large bowl and serve.
2. Enjoy!

Per serving: Calories: 167Kcal; Fat: 3.5g; Carbs: 9g; Protein: 5g; Sodium: 0.48g; Sugar: 2g

681. QUINOA-STUFFED SQUASH BOATS

Preparation time: 10 minutes
Cooking time: 27 minutes
Servings: 1
Ingredients:

- 1/8 teaspoon pepper
- 3 teaspoons olive oil, divided
- 1 teaspoon salt, divided
- ½ teaspoon grated lemon zest
- 1 ½ cups vegetable broth
- 1 cup quinoa, rinsed
- ¼ cup dried cranberries
- 1 teaspoon lemon juice
- ½ cup crumbled goat cheese
- 15 ounces garbanzo beans, rinsed and drained
- 1 green onion, thinly sliced
- ¼ cup salted pumpkin seeds or pepitas, toasted
- 1 teaspoon minced fresh sage
- 4 delicata squash

Directions:

1. Pre-heat the oven to 450 degrees. Halve each squash lengthwise; remove and discard seeds. Brush the cut sides lightly with one teaspoon oil and season with pepper and ½ teaspoon salt. Align the cut side facing down on a baking pan. Bake for 12 minutes, or until the potatoes are cooked.
2. Bring the quinoa and broth to a boil in a large saucepan. Reduce heat to low and simmer, covered, for 15 minutes, or until liquid is absorbed.
3. Then, stir in the garbanzo beans, cranberries, green onion, sage, lemon zest, lemon juice, and the remaining oil and salt, spoon into the squash. Cheese and pumpkin seeds should be sprinkled on top.

Per serving: Calories: 237Kcal; Fat: 8.1 g; Carbs: 32.7 g; Protein: 4.96g; Sodium: 0.05g; Sugar: 4.2 g

682. VEGETARIAN LENTILS AND EGGS ON A TOAST

Preparation time: 5 minutes
Cooking time: 10 minutes
Servings: 1

Ingredients

- ½ yellow sliced bell pepper
- ½ orange sliced bell pepper
- ⅛ tablespoon powder chipotle
- ½ tablespoon powder garlic
- 2-ounce vegetable broth with low-sodium
- 2 eggs
- Grounded black pepper of your preference
- 1 drained 15-ounce canned lentils with low-sodium
- 1 medium diced onion
- ¼ sliced avocado
- ½ tbsp. paprika, which is smoked
- 2 tablespoon fresh parsley, torn
- Spray of olive-oil
- 2 slices of whole grained bread
- 2 minced cloves of garlic
- ½ red sliced bell pepper
- ½ sliced lemon

Directions:

1. In vegetable broth, cook garlic and onions in a large pan over medium to high heat until they become translucent and stir it time to time.
2. Cook it for 4 minutes after adding bell peppers. Also, stir it from time to time. Mix in chipotle powder, lentils, black pepper, garlic powder, and paprika.
3. Reduce the heat flame to medium, and cook it for 3-4 min and stir it frequently. In that time, cut out a hole in every piece of the bread. For this, use plain edge type of small cutter which is round and the bread should be toasted.
4. The frying pan is coated with a spray oil, cook eggs.
5. Separate the lentil mixture into two plates, and topping is done of each through an egg, then slice the toast with the hole over the yolk of the egg.
6. Parsley is sprinkled on top and garnishes the plate with lemon and avocado. Squeeze the juice of the lemon on the lentil mixture.

Per serving: Calories: 226Kcal; Fat: 2g; Carbs: 6g; Protein: 5g; Sodium: 0.5g; Sugar: 3g

683. ASPARAGUS TOFU STIR-FRY

Preparation time: 10 minutes
Cooking time: 16 minutes
Servings: 2

Ingredients:

- 2 teaspoons minced fresh ginger root, divided
- 1 ¼ cups vegetable broth
- 4 teaspoons reduced-sodium soy sauce
- 2 cups hot cooked brown rice
- 2 tablespoons sliced almonds, toasted
- ½ teaspoon sugar
- 1 tablespoon cornstarch
- 14 ounces extra-firm tofu, drained, and sliced into cubes
- 1 yellow summer squash, halved and sliced
- 3 teaspoons canola oil, divided
- 1-pound fresh asparagus
- ¼ teaspoon pepper
- 2 green onions, thinly sliced
- ¼ teaspoon salt

Directions:

1. Combine the cornstarch, sugar, broth, and soy sauce in a small bowl until combined; put aside.
2. Stir-fry 1 teaspoon ginger in 1 teaspoon oil in a large nonstick pan or wok for 1 minute. Stir-fry the asparagus for 2 minutes. Stir in the squash for 2 minutes more.
3. Stir in the onions for 1 minute more, or until the veggies are crisp-tender. Take out and keep warm.
4. Stir-fry the tofu, salt, pepper, and remaining ginger in the remaining oil for 9 minutes, or until lightly browned. Take out and keep warm.
5. Stir the cornstarch mixture into the pan. Bring to a boil and simmer, constantly stirring, for 2 minutes, or until thickened. Heat through the asparagus mixture and tofu.
6. Serve with rice and a sprinkling of almonds.

Per serving: Calories: 157Kcal; Fat: 7.0 g; Carbs: 15.6 g; Protein: 8.7g; Sodium: 0.05g; Sugar: 3.4 g

684. VEGETARIAN CLUB SALAD

Preparation time: 10 minutes
Cooking time: 22 minutes
Servings: 3
Ingredients:

- 1 cup diced cucumber
- 1 teaspoon dried parsley
- 3 large hard-boiled eggs
- 1 tablespoon milk
- 2 tablespoons of each: Mayonnaise & Sour cream
- ½ teaspoon of each: Onion powder & Garlic powder
- 4 oz. cheddar cheese
- 1 tablespoon Dijon mustard
- ½ cup cherry tomatoes
- 3 cups torn romaine lettuce

Directions:

1. Slice the hard-boiled eggs and cube the cheese. Cut the tomatoes into halves and dice the cucumber.
2. Prepare the dressing (dried herbs, mayo, and sour cream) mixing well.
3. Add one tablespoon of milk to the mixture - and another if it is too thick.
4. Layer the salad with vegetables, cheese, and egg slices. Scoop a spoonful of mustard in the center along with a drizzle of dressing.
5. Toss and enjoy!

Per serving: Calories: 336Kcal; Fat: 26.32g; Carbs: 9.79g; Protein: 16.82g; Sodium: 0.4g; Sugar: 2g

685. VEGETARIAN KEBABS

Preparation time: 10 minutes
Cooking time: 6 minutes
Servings: 4
Ingredients:

- 2 zucchinis, trimmed
- 2 tablespoons balsamic vinegar
- 1 teaspoon dried parsley
- 1 tablespoon olive oil
- 2 sweet peppers
- 2 tablespoons water
- 2 red onions, peeled

Directions:

1. Cut the sweet peppers and onions into sizable size squares.
2. Then slice the zucchini.
3. String all vegetables into the skewers.
4. In the shallow bowl, mix up olive oil, dried parsley, water, and balsamic vinegar.
5. Sprinkle the vegetable skewers with olive oil mixture and transfer in the preheated to 390°F grill.
6. Cook the kebabs for 3 minutes on each side or until the vegetables are light brown.
7. Serve and enjoy.

Per serving: Calories: 205Kcal; Fat: 3.9g; Carbs: 13g; Protein: 2.4g; Sodium: 0.01g; Sugar: 2g

686. VEGETARIAN LASAGNA

Preparation time: 10 minutes
Cooking time: 30 minutes
Servings: 6
Ingredients:

- ½ cup bell pepper, diced
- 1 cup low-sodium vegetable broth
- 1 cup spinach, chopped
- 1 teaspoon chili powder
- 1 cup tomatoes, chopped
- 4 ounces cottage cheese
- 1 tablespoon olive oil
- 1 cup carrot, diced
- 1 eggplant, sliced

Directions:

1. Put carrot, bell pepper, and spinach in the saucepan.
2. Add olive oil and chili powder and stir the vegetables well. Cook them for 5 minutes.
3. After this, make the layer of sliced eggplants in the casserole mold and top it with vegetable mixture.
4. Add tomatoes, vegetable stock and cottage cheese.
5. Bake the lasagna for 30 minutes at 375F.

Per serving: Calories: 171Kcal; Fat: 3g; Carbs: 9.7g; Protein: 4.1g; Sodium: 0.12g; Sugar: 1g

687. ONE POT HOT CORN

Preparation time: 10 minutes
Cooking time: 20 minutes
Servings: 12
Ingredients:

- 6 ears corn

Directions:

1. Remove the corn husks and silk.
2. Each ear should be cut or broken in half.
3. Fill the bottom of the electric pressure cooker with 1 cup of water.
4. Place a wire rack or trivet on the table.
5. Cut-side down, stand the corn upright on the rack.
6. Close and lock the pressure cooker's lid. To close the valve, turn it to the closed position.
7. Cook for 5 minutes on high pressure.
8. After completion, press 'Cancel' and release the pressure quickly.
9. Unlock and remove the cover once the pin has dropped.
10. To remove the corn from the pot, use tongs.

11. Season properly with salt and pepper.
12. Serve immediately away.

Per serving: Calories: 164Kcal; Fat: 17.1g; Carbs: 13.9g; Protein: 2.1g; Sodium: 0.14g; Sugar: 5g

688. GARLIC ONION AND TOMATO

Preparation time: 10 minutes
Cooking time: 20 minutes
Servings: 2
Ingredients:

- 1 chopped onion
- 2 tablespoons extra-virgin olive oil
- 2 minced garlic cloves
- A pinch red pepper flakes
- 14-ounce crushed tomatoes
- 1 tablespoon Italian seasoning
- 2 cups green beans, fresh or frozen
- ½ cup dried whole-wheat elbow macaroni
- 3 cups low-sodium vegetable broth
- 1 red bell pepper, seeded and chopped
- ½ teaspoon sea salt

Directions:

1. Warm the olive oil in a sizable saucepan over medium heat till it shimmers.
2. Add onion and bell pepper in the saucepan. Cook, as you stir regularly, for about 3 minutes, or until the onion and bell pepper begin to soften.
3. Add garlic. Cook, as you stir occasionally, for 30 seconds, or until the garlic is aromatic.
4. Bring the mixture to a slight boil, stirring in the tomatoes, green beans, vegetable broth, and Italian seasoning.
5. Combine the elbow macaroni, red pepper flakes, and salt in a large mixing bowl. Cook for extra 8 minutes, or until the macaroni is cooked through, stirring periodically.
6. Remove the pan from the heat and place it in a large mixing bowl to cool for 6 minutes before serving.

Per serving: Calories: 202Kcal; Fat: 17.51g; Carbs: 29.2g; Protein: 5.2 g; Sodium: 0.13g; Sugar: 2.9g

689. BUTTER YAMS

Preparation time: 7 minutes
Cooking time: 45 minutes
Servings: 8
Ingredients:

- 2 tablespoons unsalted butter
- ⅛ teaspoon ground cloves
- 1½ teaspoons ground cinnamon
- Juice of 1 large orange
- ¼ teaspoon ground ginger
- ¾ teaspoon ground nutmeg
- 2 medium jewel yams cut into 2-inch dices

Directions:

1. Pre-heat the oven to 350⁰F.
2. Arrange the yam dices in a single layer on a rimmed baking sheet. Remove from the equation.
3. In a medium saucepan over medium-low heat, combine the butter, orange juice, cinnamon, ginger, nutmeg, and garlic cloves. Cook, stirring constantly for 3 to 5 minutes, or until the sauce thickens and bubbles.
4. Toss the yams in the sauce to thoroughly coat them.
5. Pre-heat the oven to 400°F before baking for 40 minutes, or until the potatoes are soft.
6. Allow 8 minutes for the yams to cool on the baking sheet before serving.

Per serving: Calories: 129 Kcal; Fat: 2.8g; Carbs: 24.7g; Protein: 2.1g; Sodium: 0.07g; Sugar: 2.9g;

690. LEMONY BROCCOLI

Preparation time: 8 minutes
Cooking time: 24 minutes
Servings: 8
Ingredients:

- 2 tablespoons freshly squeezed lemon juice
- ¼ teaspoon ground black pepper
- ¼ teaspoon salt
- 2 tablespoons extra-virgin olive oil
- 3 garlic cloves, minced
- 2 large broccoli heads, cut into florets

Directions:

1. Pre-heat to 425⁰F and grease a large baking sheet.
2. Combine the broccoli, olive oil, garlic, salt, and pepper in a large mixing basin. Toss until the broccoli is well covered. Place the broccoli on the baking sheet that has been prepped.
3. Roast for about 25 minutes, or until the broccoli is browned and fork-tender, in a pre-heated oven, flipping halfway through.
4. Set aside and place it on a dish to cool for 5 minutes.
5. Serve with a squeeze of lemon juice on top.

Per serving: Calories: 133Kcal; Fat: 2.1g; Carbs: 3.1g; Protein: 21.2g; Sodium: 0.04g; Sugar: 1.1g

CHAPTER 15: Meat Recipes

691. HORSERADISH-ENCRUSTED BEEF TENDERLOIN

Preparation time: 25 minutes
Cooking time: 1 hour 30 minutes
Servings: 1
Ingredients:

- ¼ teaspoon dried thyme
- ¼ teaspoon pepper
- 1 whole garlic bulb, outer skin removed
- 1/3 cup soft breadcrumbs
- 3-pound beef tenderloin roast
- ¼ teaspoon salt
- 1/3 cup prepared horseradish
- 1 teaspoon olive oil
- ¼ teaspoon dried basil

Directions:

1. Brush the garlic bulb with oil. Wrap tightly in heavy-duty foil.
2. Bake for 35 minutes at 425°F or until tender. Allow cooling for 15 minutes. Reduce the oven temperature to 400°F.
3. Combine the softened garlic, horseradish, salt, basil, thyme, and pepper in a small bowl. Toss in the breadcrumbs to coat.
4. Spread on top of the tenderloin and place in a big shallow roasting pan on a rack.
5. Wait for 55 minutes, or until meat reaches desired doneness.
6. Allow for a 10-minute rest before slicing.
7. Serve and enjoy.

Per serving: Calories: 241 Kcal; Fat: 10.6g; Carbs: 1.4g; Protein: 33.1g; Sodium: 0.80g; Sugar: 0.3g

692. TERIYAKI BEEF STEW

Preparation time: 15 minutes
Cooking time: 8 hours 30 minutes
Servings: 1
Ingredients:

- 2 tablespoons sesame seeds
- 2 garlic cloves, minced
- 2 tablespoons cornstarch
- 12 ounces ginger beer or ginger ale
- Hot cooked rice, optional, as needed
- 2 cups frozen peas, thawed
- ¼ cup teriyaki sauce
- 2 pounds beef stew meat
- 2 tablespoons cold water

Directions:

1. Brown the meat in batches in a sizable nonstick pan and then place in a 3-quart slow cooker.
2. Transfer the meat into a small dish and combine the ginger beer, teriyaki sauce, garlic, and sesame seeds.
3. Cook on low for around 8 hours, or until the meat is soft.
4. Stir together cornstarch and cold water until smooth; gradually add to the stew. Mix in the peas.
5. Cook, covered, for 30 minutes on high, or until thickened.
6. If preferred, serve with rice and enjoy.

Per serving: Calories: 370Kcal; Fat: 25g; Carbs: 7g; Protein: 28g; Sodium: 0.58g; Sugar: 0.6g

693. TENDER MAPLE-GLAZED PORK CHOPS

Preparation time: 15 minutes
Cooking time: 20 minutes
Servings: 1
Ingredients:

- 1 tablespoon olive oil
- 1 tablespoon Dijon mustard
- 2 teaspoons Worcestershire sauce
- 4 boneless pork loin chops
- 1 teaspoon minced fresh thyme
- ½ teaspoon pepper
- ½ cup brewed coffee
- ½ teaspoon salt
- ¼ cup maple syrup

Directions:

1. Sprinkle thyme, salt, and pepper over the pork chops.
2. Brown the chops in oil in a large skillet. Take out and keep warm.
3. To the skillet, add the remaining ingredients. Bring the ingredient mixture to a boil and simmer until the liquid has been reduced by half.
4. Return the pork chops to the skillet. Lower the heat before covering, and cook for 12 minutes, turning once until meat is tender.
5. Serve with your favorite sauce.
6. Enjoy.

Per serving: Calories: 316Kcal; Fat: 13g; Carbs: 15g; Protein: 4.96g; Sodium: 0.46g; Sugar: 0.12g

694. SHREDDED PORK WITH BEANS

Preparation time: 30 minutes
Cooking time: 8 hours
Servings: 1
Ingredients:

- Hot cooked rice, as needed
- 3 pounds pork tenderloin, sliced
- 24 ounces Picante sauce
- 30 ounces black beans, rinsed and drained

Directions:

1. Place the meat, beans, and Picante sauce in a 5-quart slow cooker.
2. Cook on the mixture on low for 8 hours, or until the meat is tender.
3. Return the shredded pork to the slow cooker.
4. If preferred, serve with rice.
5. Enjoy.

Per serving: Calories: 380Kcal; Fat: 22g; Carbs: 14g; Protein: 29g; Sodium: 0.11g; Sugar: 5.3g

695. FAVORITE BEEF ROAST DINNER

Preparation time: 25 minutes
Cooking time: 8 hours
Servings: 1
Ingredients:

- 1 teaspoon dried thyme
- 4 ½ teaspoons dried minced onion
- 1 teaspoon garlic salt
- 1 tablespoon Worcestershire sauce
- 1 teaspoon dried oregano
- 4 medium potatoes, peeled and quartered
- ½ pound fresh baby carrots
- 1 teaspoon pepper
- 4-pound boneless beef chuck roast
- 1 teaspoon celery seed
- 3 garlic cloves, minced

Directions:

1. In a slow cooker, mix carrots, potatoes, and beef chuck roast. Finish with the remaining ingredients.
2. Cook for around 8 hours on low, or until the meat and veggies are cooked.
3. Skim the fat from the cooking fluids and serve with the roast and veggies.
4. Enjoy!

Per serving: Calories: 368Kcal; Fat: 16g; Carbs: 19g; Protein: 35g, Sodium: 0.34g; Sugar: 3g

696. LAMB CHOPS WITH ORANGE SAUCE

Preparation time: 20 minutes
Cooking time: 12 minutes
Servings: 1
Ingredients:

- 8 small lean lamb chops
- ½ cup freshly squeezed orange juice
- 2 tablespoons orange zest
- 1/8 teaspoon freshly ground black pepper
- Nonstick cooking spray
- 1 cup sliced fresh mushrooms
- 1 teaspoon fresh thyme
- ½ cup dry white wine

Directions:

1. Combine the orange juice, orange zest, thyme, and pepper in a small baking dish and stir properly.
2. Place the lamb chops in a baking tray and trim away any extra fat. Spoon the orange juice mixture over the chops; cover and chill for 4 hours, flipping chops regularly.
3. Coat a big skillet with nonstick cooking spray and heat medium-high until hot. Reserve the marinade, remove the chops and place them in the skillet.
4. Brown the chops on all sides in a pan, then transfer to a dish lined with paper towels.
5. Reduce the heat to medium and sauté the mushrooms until just tender. Bring to a boil with the reserved marinade and wine.
6. Return the lamb chops into the skillet; cover, decrease the heat to low and cook for 12 minutes.
7. Serve the lamb chops on a dish with the orange sauce spooned on top.
8. Enjoy.

Per serving: Calories: 383Kcal; Fat: 11.1g; Carbs: 21.9g; Protein: 46.7g; Sodium: 0.49g; Sugar: 9g

697. ROPA VIEJA

Preparation time: 25 minutes
Cooking time: 10 hours 3 minutes
Servings: 1
Ingredients:

- ½ teaspoon salt
- 6 ounces tomato paste
- 1 large carrot, sliced
- 1 large onion, thinly sliced
- ½ teaspoon pepper
- 2 cups beef broth
- 1 small sweet red pepper
- ½ cup dry vermouth
- 1 Cubanelle or mild banana pepper
- 2 pounds beef flank steak

- 3 sprigs of fresh oregano
- Hot cooked rice, as needed
- ½ cup dry red wine

Directions:

1. Cut the meat into six pieces and season with pepper and salt.
2. Brown the meat in batches in a sizable pan over medium-high heat.
3. Place the beef in a 5- or 6-quart slow cooker.
4. Add the broth, vermouth, wine, and tomato paste to the pan.
5. Cook for 3 minutes, occasionally stirring, to dislodge browned parts from the pan.
6. Pour over the meat onion, carrot, red pepper, Cubanelle pepper, and oregano on top. Cook, covered, over low heat for 10 hours, or until meat is cooked.
7. Remove and discard the oregano sprigs.
8. Set the meat aside and shred it with two forks.
9. Return to the slow cooker and heat until well heated.
10. Serve with rice with optional oregano.

Per serving: Calories: 285 Kcal; Fat: 21.2g; Carbs: 0.9g; Protein: 21.9g; Sodium: 0.06g; Sugar: 1.5g

698. LAMB PROVENÇAL

Preparation time: 10 minutes
Cooking time: 10 minutes
Servings: 1
Ingredients:

- 6 cloves garlic, crushed
- 2 onions, chopped
- 1 sprig rosemary
- 400g chopped tomatoes
- 1 sprig thyme
- 2 tsps. rapeseed oil
- 1 yellow and one green pepper, chopped into large chunks
- 1 tsp. dried oregano
- 20g chopped fresh parsley
- 400g lean lamb steaks
- 3 courgettes
- Provençal sauce, as desired

Directions:

1. In a sizable pan, heat the oil and stir in the onions for 2 minutes over medium heat.
2. Stir in the red, yellow, and green peppers for another 2 minutes.
3. Stir in the garlic and courgettes for 3 minutes.
4. Stir in the tomatoes after adding the rosemary, thyme, oregano, and parsley to the veggies. Cook, covered, for 10 minutes, stirring periodically.

5. Meanwhile, grill the lamb steaks until done to your liking.
6. Remove the meat from the heat, cover, and set aside for 3 minutes to rest.
7. Serve with a green salad and the Provençal sauce.

Per serving: Calories: 200Kcal; Fat: 15.0g; Carbs: 1.0g; Protein: 15.0g; Sodium: 0.23g; Sugar: 0.1g

699. PORK CHOPS WITH HERB-CRUSTED CRUST

Preparation time: 5 minutes
Cooking time: 10 minutes
Servings: 3
Ingredients

- 1 ½ pounds boneless chops, pork loin
- ¼ teaspoon black pepper
- ½ teaspoon chili powder
- 1 teaspoon oregano, dry
- ½ teaspoon thyme, dry
- 1 tablespoon olive oil
- 1 teaspoon dried rosemary
- ½ teaspoon garlic powder

Directions:

1. Combine thyme, rosemary, oregano, garlic powder, chili powder, black pepper, garlic powder, and black pepper in a bowl. Mix thoroughly.
2. In a pan, heat the olive oil above a medium flame.
3. Season both sides of the pork chops with the herb mix.
4. Cook the pork chops for approximately 5 minutes on each side.
5. Serve and enjoy.

Per serving: Calories: 277Kcal; Fat: 18.0g; Carbs: 5.0g; Protein: 23.0g; Sodium: 0.22g; Sugar: 0.05g

700. MEAT LOAVES, STOVETOP

Preparation time: 10 minutes
Cooking time: 40 minutes
Servings: 2
Ingredients

- ½ pound lean ground beef
- ½ cup Italian tomato sauce
- 3 tablespoons milk
- 1/8 teaspoon salt
- ½ teaspoon cornstarch
- 2 tablespoons quick-cooking oats
- 1 tablespoon chopped onion
- ¼ cup cold water
- 2 meatloaves

Directions:

1. In a sizable nonstick skillet, brown loaves on all sides and drain.
2. Combine the cornstarch, tomato sauce and water until smooth. Pour over meatloaves and bring to a boil. Lower the heat to medium-low; cover and cook until meat is no longer pink for 20 minutes.
3. Combine the oats, onion, milk, and salt in a mixing bowl.
4. Over the mixture, crumble the meat and stir gently but thoroughly.
5. Divide the dough into two loaves. Brown your loaves on both sides in a pan and drain.
6. Whisk together the cornstarch, tomato sauce, and water before smoothening to prepare the sauce.
7. Pour the sauce over the meatloaves.
8. Bring the water to a boil.
9. Reduce flame to low, close the lid, and simmer for 20 minutes.
10. Serve and enjoy.

Per serving: Calories: 300Kcal; Fat: 11.0g; Carbs: 24.0g; Protein: 26.0g; Sodium: 0.17; Sugar: 0.11g

701. BEEF GOULASH

Preparation time: 15 minutes

Cooking time: 56 minutes

Servings: 6

Ingredients:

- 2 bay leaves
- 1 cup low-sodium beef broth
- 1 tablespoon olive oil
- 2 tablespoons tomato paste
- 2 teaspoons hot smoked paprika
- Sea salt, as needed
- Black pepper, as needed
- 1 green pepper, chopped
- 1 red pepper, chopped
- 3 onions, quartered
- 3 garlic cloves, diced fine
- 1 orange pepper, chopped
- 1 can tomatoes, chopped
- 3 cups water
- 2 pounds chuck steak, trim the fat, and cut into bite-sized pieces
- 1 tablespoon paprika

Directions:

1. Heat oil in a sizable soup pot over medium-high heat. Add the steak and cook until browned, stirring often.
2. Add onions and keep cooking for another 5 minutes or until soft. Add garlic before cooking for an extra minute, stirring often.
3. Add remaining ingredients, then bring to a boil. Lower the heat to a low simmer for 50 minutes, stirring

occasionally. The Goulash is done when the steak is tender.
4. Stir well, then add to serving bowls and enjoy!

Per serving: Calories: 321Kcal; Fat: 15.7g; Carbs: 12.39g; Protein: 34.8g; Sodium: 0.13g; Sugar: 1.5g

702. CURRIED LAMB ARRANGED ON RICE

Preparation time: 5 minutes

Cooking time: 45 minutes

Servings: 2

Ingredients

- ¼ teaspoon ground ginger
- 1 cup beef broth
- 2 teaspoon curry powder
- ½ cup chopped onion
- ½ cup carrot, grated
- 1 ½ tablespoons flour, all-purpose
- 1 minced clove garlic
- 2 cups cooked rice
- 1 tablespoon margarine
- ¾ teaspoon salt
- 1-pound lean lamb
- 1 medium-sized chopped, seeded and peeled tomato

Directions:

1. Heat a big nonstick skillet.
2. Add in the margarine, onion, garlic, and meat to cook for 5 minutes.
3. Combine the salt, broth, curry powder, tomato, ginger, and flour in a large mixing bowl. Stir everything well together.
4. Cook for approximately 40 minutes, or until lamb is cooked.
5. Stir periodically, and if the liquid dries, add a little water.
6. In a small nonstick saucepan, combine the grated carrot and rice. Bring to a boil.
7. Distribute the rice among four serving dishes and top with the meat.

Per serving: Calories: 282Kcal; Fat: 10g; Carbs: 31g; Protein: 28g; Sodium: 0.14g; Sugar: 2.3g

703. ROAST BEEF IN THE AIR FRYER

Preparation time: 5 minutes

Cooking time: 45 minutes

Servings:

Ingredients:

- ½ teaspoon coarsely ground black pepper
- 3 tablespoons olive oil
- ½ tablespoon garlic powder
- 1 tablespoons rosemary

- 2 pounds beef roast

Directions:

1. Pre-heat the air fryer to 360°F.
2. On a plate, combine herbs and oil. On the plate, roll the roast in the blend to coat the entire surface of the beef.
3. Set the beef in a single layer in the air fryer basket. Set the timer for 45 minutes for tool-rare beef and 51 minutes for the tool. Check the beef using a meat thermometer to ensure it is cooked to your preference.
4. Cook for an additional 6-minutes if desired.
5. Transfer the roast from the air fryer to a plate and tent with lightweight aluminum foil.
6. Allow to cool before serving.

Per serving: Calories: 666 Kcal; Fat: 54g; Carbs: 0.3g; Protein: 43g; Sodium: 0.35g; Sugar: 1.8g

704. ROAST BEEF

Preparation time: 5 minutes

Cooking time: 45 minutes

Servings: 4

Ingredients:

- ¼ teaspoon pepper
- 1000g beef joint
- 1 tablespoon extra-virgin olive oil
- ¼ teaspoon salt

Directions:

1. Rub the oil all over the beef.
2. Season with salt and pepper to taste.
3. Position the seasoned beef on the air fryer oven rotisserie.
4. Set the timer for 45 minutes and the temperature to 380⁰F. Ascertain that the beef is rotated.
5. After 45 minutes, check if the roast beef is ready and slice it into pieces.
6. Serve and enjoy.

Per serving: Calories: 666 Kcal; Fat: 54g; Carbs: 2.9g; Protein: 43g; Sodium: 0.66g; Sugar: 1.9g

705. ROASTED BEEF WITH SHERRY AND PEPPER SAUCE

Preparation time: 10 minutes

Cooking time: 1 hour 40 minutes

Servings: 4

Ingredients:

- 1 cup beef broth, no salt
- 2 tablespoon sherry
- ¼ teaspoon Himalayan pink salt, fine
- ¼ teaspoon black pepper, ground
- 1½ pounds rump beef roast
- 3 small onions, minced
- 2 teaspoons garlic, minced

- 1 tablespoon green peppercorns
- 3 teaspoons olive oil, divided
- 2 tablespoons almond flour

Directions:

1. Pre-heat the oven to 300⁰F.
2. Season the beef roast liberally with fine Himalayan pink salt and freshly ground black pepper.
3. Cook 2 teaspoons of olive oil in a sizable cast-iron pan over medium-high heat until hot.
4. Brown the beef on both for about 10 minutes, then transfer to a baking dish.
5. Roast the meat until it's done to your liking, about 1½ hours for medium. Add the pepper sauce after the roast has been in the oven for 1 hour.
6. Fry the minced onion in the remaining 1 teaspoon olive oil in the same skillet over medium-high heat for 4 minutes, or to tenderness.
7. Cook for 1 minute after adding the minced garlic and green peppercorns. To deglaze the pan, whisk in the sherry.
8. Cook for 1 minute, stirring frequently, after whisking in the almond flour to produce a thick paste.
9. Whisk in the no-salt beef broth for 4 minutes, or until the sauce thickens and becomes glossy. Season the sauce with fine Himalayan pink salt and ground black pepper.
10. Carve the steak and serve it with a large dollop of sauce.
11. Enjoy.

Per serving: Calories: 330Kcal; Fat: 18g; Carbs: 4g; Protein: 36g; Sodium: 0.06g; Sugar: 4.52g

706. LAMB CHOPS WITH LIME

Preparation time: 10 minutes
Cooking time: 10 minutes
Servings: 4
Ingredients:

- 2 tablespoons mint, chopped
- ¼ teaspoon black pepper, ground
- 12 lamb chops
- ¼ cup lime juice
- 2 tablespoons lime zest
- 2 tablespoons parsley, chopped
- ¼ cup olive oil
- ¼ teaspoon Himalayan pink salt, ground

Directions:

1. Combine the olive oil, lime juice, lime zest, chopped parsley, chopped mint, ground Himalayan pink salt, and ground black pepper in a small mixing dish.

2. Pour the mixture into a lidded marinating dish.
3. Cover the marinating dish with the lid and add the lamb chops. To blend, stir everything together.
4. Refrigerate the dish with the marinated lamb for 4 hours, flipping it many times.
5. Pre-heat the broiler in the oven.
6. Remove the chops from the dish and place them on a baking sheet lined with aluminum foil. Remove the rest of the marinade and discard it.
7. Cook the lamb chops for 4 minutes on each side under the broiler.
8. Before serving, let the lamb chops rest for 5 minutes.
9. Enjoy.

Per serving: Calories: 413Kcal; Fat: 29g; Carbs: 0.7g; Protein: 31g; Sodium: 0.16g; Sugar: 3.42g

707. OVEN BARBECUED PORK CHOPS

Preparation time: 15 minutes
Cooking time: 20 minutes
Servings: 4
Ingredients:

- ¼ teaspoon freshly ground pepper
- 1 ¾ pounds ¾-inch-thick pork rib chops, bone-in, trimmed off fat
- 1 clove garlic, minced
- 1 medium onion, diced
- ½ cup barbecue sauce
- ¼ teaspoon salt
- 3 teaspoons canola oil, divided
- ⅓ cup orange juice

Directions:

1. Pre-heat oven to 425⁰F.
2. Sprinkle pork chops with pepper and salt.
3. Heat 2 teaspoons oil in a sizable oven proof skillet over high heat.
4. Add pork chops and cook until they begin to brown, 1 to 2 minutes per side. Transfer to a plate.
5. Add 1 teaspoon oil to the skillet. Add onion and cook properly, stirring, until softened, for 4 minutes.
6. Add the garlic and cook properly, stirring, until fragrant, 30 seconds.
7. Add orange juice and cook until most of the liquid has evaporated, 30 seconds to 1 minute.
8. Add the barbecue sauce. Return the pork chops to the sizable skillet, turning several times to coat with the sauce.
9. Transfer the sizable skillet to the oven and bake until the pork chops are pink in the center, about 10 minutes.

10. Serve the sauce over the pork chops right away.
11. Enjoy!

Per serving: Calories: 196Kcal; Fat: 9.9g; Carbs: 10g; Protein: 20g; Sodium: 0.26g; Sugar: 1.45g

708. LAMB KOFTA WITH CUCUMBER SALAD

Preparation time: 10 minutes
Cooking time: 15 minutes
Servings: 4
Ingredients:

- 1-pound ground lamb
- 2 teaspoons ground coriander
- 3 garlic cloves, minced
- ¼ teaspoon red pepper flakes
- 1 teaspoon sea salt, divided
- 2 cucumbers, peeled and chopped
- ¼ cup red wine vinegar
- 1 tablespoon fresh mint, chopped
- ½ red onion, finely chopped
- 1 teaspoon ground cumin

Directions:

1. Pre-heat the oven to 375⁰F.
2. Using a parchment paper, line a rimmed baking sheet.
3. In a sizable bowl, whisk together the vinegar, red pepper flakes, and ½ teaspoon salt. Add the cucumbers and onion and toss to combine. Set aside.
4. In a sizable bowl, mix the lamb, coriander, cumin, garlic, mint, and remaining ½ teaspoon salt.
5. Form the mixture into 1-inch meatballs and place them on the prepared baking sheet.
6. Bake until the lamb reaches 140⁰F internally for about 15 minutes.
7. Serve with the salad on the side.
8. Enjoy.

Per serving: Calories: 346Kcal; Fat: 27g; Carbs: 6g; Protein: 20g; Sodium: 0.26g; Sugar: 1.5g

709. AUTUMN PORK CHOPS

Preparation time: 15 minutes
Cooking time: 31 minutes
Servings: 4
Ingredients:

- 1 teaspoon chopped fresh thyme
- 1 apple, peeled, cored, and sliced
- 2 tablespoons granulated sweetener
- 4 pork chops, about 1 inch thick
- 1 tablespoon extra-virgin olive oil
- Sea salt, as needed
- Freshly ground black pepper, as needed
- ¼ cup apple cider vinegar
- ½ red cabbage, finely shredded

- 1 sweet onion, thinly sliced

Directions:

1. In a sizable bowl, whisk together the vinegar and sweetener. Set it aside.
2. Season the pork with salt and pepper.
3. Place a sizable skillet over medium-high heat and add the olive oil.
4. Cook the pork chops until no longer pink, turning once, about 8 minutes per side.
5. Transfer the chops to a medium plate and set aside.
6. Add the cabbage and onion to the skillet and sauté until the vegetables have softened, about 5 minutes.
7. Add the vinegar mixture and the apple slices to the skillet and bring the mixture to a boil.
8. Lower the heat before simmering covered, for 5 additional minutes.
9. Place the pork chops back to the sizable skillet, along with any accumulated juices and thyme, cover, and cook for 5 more minutes.
10. Serve and enjoy.

Per serving: Calories: 224Kcal; Fat: 8g; Carbs: 12g; Protein: 26g; Sodium: 0.36g; Sugar: 2.5g

710. HERBED MEATBALLS

Preparation time: 10 minutes
Cooking time: 15 minutes
Servings: 4
Ingredients:

- ¼ teaspoon freshly ground black pepper
- ½ pound lean ground pork
- 2 teaspoons minced garlic
- 1 sweet onion, finely chopped
- ¼ cup bread crumbs
- ½ pound lean ground beef
- 2 tablespoons chopped fresh basil
- 1 egg
- ¼ teaspoon sea salt

Directions:

1. Pre-heat the oven to 350⁰F.
2. Using a parchment paper, line a sizable baking tray and set it aside.
3. In a sizable bowl, mix together the pork, beef, onion, bread crumbs, basil, garlic, egg, salt, and pepper until very well mixed.
4. Roll the meat mixture into 2-inch meatballs.
5. Transfer the meatballs to the baking tray and bake until they are browned and cooked through, about 15 minutes.
6. Serve the meatballs right away with your favorite marinara sauce and some steamed green beans.
7. Enjoy.

Per serving: Calories: 33Kcal; Fat: 19g; Carbs: 12g; Protein: 24.7g; Sodium: 0.32g; Sugar: 2.9g

711. TORTILLAS WITH STEAK AND GUACAMOLE

Preparation time: 10 minutes
Cooking time: 9 minutes
Servings: 4
Ingredients:

For the Guacamole

- 1 tablespoon fresh lime juice
- 4 ripe avocados, peeled and pitted
- 1 teaspoon garlic, minced
- 1 shallot or onion, minced
- ¼ teaspoon salt
- 1 tomato chopped, remove the pulp
- ¼ tsp. chili flakes (optional)

For the Filling

- 8 lettuce leaves or low-carb tortillas
- 1 cup guacamole
- 3 tablespoons olive oil, divided
- 1 finely sliced red and green bell pepper
- 2 teaspoons ground coriander
- 2 teaspoons ground cumin
- 1 tablespoon chili powder
- 1 teaspoon salt
- 1-pound frying steak, thinly sliced
- 1 onion, thinly sliced

Directions:

1. To prepare the guacamole, mash the ripe avocados with a fork in a medium-sized bowl until slightly lumpy.
2. Mix in the minced garlic, onion, diced tomato, chili flakes (if using), and lime juice until everything is well combined. Season with salt and pepper to taste. Refrigerate until ready to use.
3. In a medium bowl, whisk together 2 tablespoons olive oil, chili powder, coriander, cumin, and 1 teaspoon salt. Add the thinly sliced frying steak and toss to coat.
4. Heat a heavy-bottomed skillet over medium-high heat until it is smoking hot, then add the seasoned steak pieces and cook for 4 minutes. Take the object out of the room and put it away.
5. Add the chopped onions and bell peppers to the pan with the remaining 1 tablespoon olive oil and sauté for 5 minutes, until lightly browned. To taste, mix with salt and pepper.
6. Place the thinly cut steaks and vegetables in the center of the lettuce leaves or low-carb tortillas and top with homemade guacamole.
7. Serve and enjoy.

Per serving: Calories: 547Kcal; Fat: 42.0g; Carbs: 10g; Protein: 18.1g; Sodium: 0.56g; Sugar: 4.0g

712. BAKED BASIL MEATBALLS

Preparation time: 9 minutes
Cooking time: 15 minutes
Servings: 4
Ingredients:

- ½ pounds ground pork, lean
- 2 teaspoons garlic, minced
- ¼ teaspoon Himalayan pink salt, ground
- Marinara sauce, as desired
- Non-stick cooking spray
- 1 onion, finely chopped
- Vegetable of your choice, as needed
- ¼ cup breadcrumbs
- 2 tablespoons basil, chopped
- ½ pound ground beef, lean
- 1 egg
- ¼ teaspoon black pepper, ground

Directions:

1. Pre-heat the oven to 350⁰F.
2. Set aside a baking tray that has been sprayed with nonstick cooking spray.
3. Toss the ground pork, ground beef, chopped onion, breadcrumbs, chopped basil, minced garlic, egg, ground Himalayan pink salt, and ground black pepper together in a large mixing basin.
4. Make medium-sized meatballs out of the ground beef.
5. Place the meatballs on a sizable baking pan and bake for 15 minutes, or until browned and well cooked.
6. Serve the meatballs with marinara sauce and cooked green beans or any other vegetable.

Per serving: Calories: 332Kcal; Fat: 21.2g; Carbs: 19g; Protein: 24g; Sodium: 0.76g; Sugar: 4.56g

713. SPICED LAMB VEGETABLE CASSEROLE

Preparation time: 10 minutes
Cooking time: 2 hours 11 minutes
Servings: 4
Ingredients:

- 2 tablespoons canola oil
- 2 teaspoons parsley, chopped for garnish
- ¼ teaspoon cloves, ground
- 1½ pounds organic lamb shoulder, cut into chunks
- ½ sweet onion, finely chopped
- 1 tablespoon ginger, grated
- 1 teaspoon cinnamon, ground

- 2 teaspoons mint, finely chopped
- 1 teaspoon cumin, ground
- 2 white sweet potatoes, peeled and diced
- 2 teaspoons garlic, minced
- 2 cups beef broth, low sodium
- ¼ teaspoon Himalayan pink salt, fine
- ¼ teaspoon black pepper, ground

Directions:

1. Pre-heat the oven to 300⁰F.
2. Heat the canola oil in a big heavy-bottomed pan over medium-high heat.
3. Cook for 6 minutes, tossing periodically, until the lamb chunks are browned.
4. Fry for 5 minutes with the chopped onion, grated ginger, minced garlic, ground cinnamon, ground cumin, and ground cloves.
5. Bring the stew to a boil with the diced sweet potatoes and low sodium beef stock.
6. Place the lamb mixture in an oven-safe casserole dish and cover with a lid or aluminum foil before baking. Cook for 2 hours, stirring occasionally, or until the meat is cooked.
7. Remove the stew from the oven and season with ground black pepper and fine Himalayan pink salt.
8. Garnish with chopped parsley and serve hot.
9. Enjoy.

Per serving: Calories: 545Kcal; Fat: 35g; Carbs: 16g; Protein: 32g; Sodium: 0.66g; Sugar: 5.23g

714. ROASTED PORK TENDERLOIN AND APPLE SLAW

Preparation time: 10 minutes

Cooking time: 20 minutes

Servings: 4

Ingredients:

- Himalayan pink salt, ground
- ½ red cabbage, thinly sliced and core removed
- 1 tablespoon apple cider vinegar
- ½ cup parsley, roughly chopped
- 1 Granny Smith apple, cored, seeded cut into wedges
- 2 tablespoons avocado oil, divided
- 1 tablespoon mint, chopped
- ¼ teaspoon black pepper, ground
- 1 tablespoon rosemary, chopped
- 1¼ pounds pork tenderloin, boneless and patted dry
- ½ red onion, thinly sliced

Directions:

1. Pre-heat the oven to 425⁰F.
2. In a sizable cast-iron pan, heat 1 tablespoon avocado oil over medium heat until hot.
3. Rub the ground Himalayan pink salt, ground black pepper, and finely chopped rosemary all over the dried pork.
4. Place the pork in a sizable pan and sear for about 10 minutes, or until both sides are browned.
5. Combine the apple wedges, sliced cabbage, and sliced onion in a large mixing bowl with the remaining 1 tablespoon avocado oil.
6. In the cast iron pan, scatter the mixture around the meat.
7. Arrange the pan to the oven and roast the pork for 10 minutes.
8. Set aside the cooked pork on a chopping board to cool.
9. Mix the apple wedges and cabbage with the apple cider vinegar, chopped mint, and chopped parsley in the pan.
10. Serve the pork slices with the slaw and enjoy.

Per serving: Calories: 263Kcal; Fat: 11g; Carbs: 10g; Protein: 28g; Sodium: 0.76g; Sugar: 4.51g

715. LAMB AND MUSHROOM CHEESE BURGERS

Preparation time: 15 minutes

Cooking time: 14 minutes

Servings: 4

Ingredients:

- ¼ teaspoon freshly ground black pepper
- 1 tablespoon minced fresh basil
- 8 ounces grass-fed ground lamb
- ¼ teaspoon salt
- ¼ cup crumbled goat cheese
- 8 ounces brown mushrooms, finely chopped

Directions:

1. In a large mixing bowl, combine the lamb, mushrooms, salt, and pepper, and mix well.
2. In a small bowl, mix the goat cheese and basil.
3. Form the lamb mixture into 4 patties, reserving about ½ cup the mixture in the bowl. In each patty, make an indentation in the center and fill with 1 tablespoon the goat cheese mixture.
4. Use the reserved meat mixture to close the burgers. Press the meat firmly to hold together.
5. Heat the barbecue or a large skillet over medium-high heat. Add the

burgers and cook for 7 minutes on each side, until cooked through.

6. Serve.

Per serving: Calories: 172 Kcal; Fat: 21.2g; Carbs: 2.9g; Protein: 11.7g; Sodium: 0.56g; Sugar: 1g

716. PORK TENDERLOIN

Preparation time: 10 minutes

Cooking time: 30 minutes

Servings: 6

Ingredients:

- 1 ½ pounds pork tenderloin

Directions:

1. Pre-heat the Air Fryer to 370⁰F.
2. Arrange the pork tenderloin in the Air Fryer basket.
3. Cook at 400⁰F for approximately 30 minutes, flipping halfway through for an even cook.
4. Serve.

Per serving: Calories: 419Kcal; Fat: 5g; Carbs: 0.56g; Protein: 26g; Sodium: 0.36g; Sugar: 1.52g

717. THYME PORK STEAK

Preparation time: 20 minutes

Cooking time: 12 minutes

Servings: 2

Ingredients:

- 1 tablespoon balsamic vinegar
- 1 tablespoon dried thyme
- 2 pork steaks
- 1 tablespoon olive oil

Directions:

1. Rub the meat with dried thyme and brush with balsamic vinegar and olive oil.
2. Leave the meat for 15 minutes to marinate.
3. Preheat the skillet until hot.
4. Put the steaks in the hot skillet and roast for 6 minutes per side.
5. Serve and enjoy.

Per serving: Calories: 285 Kcal; Fat: 21.2g; Carbs: 0.9g; Protein: 21.9g; Sodium: 0.06g; Sugar: 1.5g

718. PULLED PORK SANDWICHES WITH APRICOT JELLY

Preparation time: 5 minutes

Cooking time: 7 minutes

Servings: 4

Ingredients:

- 2½ tablespoons apricot jelly
- Avocado oil cooking spray
- ½ cup chopped green bell pepper
- 2 slices reduced fat provolone cheese

- 8 ounces store-bought pulled pork
- 4 whole-wheat sandwich thins

Directions:

1. Heat the pulled pork according to the package instructions.
2. Heat a medium skillet over medium-low heat. When hot, coat the cooking surface with cooking spray.
3. Put the bell pepper in the skillet and cook for 5 minutes. Transfer to a sizable bowl and set aside.
4. Meanwhile, tear each slice of cheese into 2 strips, and halve the sandwich thins so you have a top and bottom.
5. Lower the heat and place the sandwich thins in the skillet cut-side down to toast, about 2 minutes.
6. Remove the sandwich thins from the skillet.
7. Spread one-quarter of the jelly on the bottom ½ of each sandwich thin, then place one-quarter of the cheese, pulled pork, and pepper on top. Cover with the top ½ of the sandwich thin.
8. Serve and enjoy.

Per serving: Calories: 250Kcal; Fat: 21.2g; Carbs: 34.1g; Protein: 16.1g; Sodium: 0.42g; Sugar: 8g

719. PORK CARNITAS

Preparation time: 20 minutes

Cooking time: 5 hours

Servings: 6

Ingredients:

- 1 tablespoon whole black peppercorns
- 1 teaspoon dried oregano, crushed
- ⅓ cup purchased salsa (Optional)
- 2 tablespoons lime juice
- 2 scallions, thinly sliced
- 14 ounces of reduced-sodium chicken broth
- ⅓ cup light dairy sour cream (optional)
- 3 bay leaves
- 2 pounds boneless pork shoulder roast, sliced into small pieces
- ¼ teaspoon salt
- 2 teaspoons finely shredded lime peel
- ¼ teaspoon ground pepper
- 2 teaspoons cumin seeds
- 4 cloves garlic, minced
- 12 crisp corn tortillas

Directions:

1. Sprinkle the pork appropriately with salt and pepper and place in a 4-quart slow cooker.
2. Cut a 6-inch square from a double thickness of cheesecloth.
3. Place the garlic, peppercorns, cumin seeds, oregano, and bay leaves in the center of the cheesecloth square.
4. Pull up the cheesecloth corners and tie it with kitchen twine. Add to the pot over low heat. Add the broth.
5. Cover and cook on low for around 12 hours or on high for 5 hours.
6. Remove meat from the pot.
7. Discard the bouquet and cooking liquid.
8. Using 2 forks, coarsely shred the meat. Discard fat.
9. Sprinkle meat with lime juice and lime zest. Toss to mix.
10. Serve over tortillas. Top with scallions and, if not cooked, sour cream and salsa.
11. Enjoy!

Per serving: Calories: 318Kcal; Fat: 10g; Carbs: 24g; Protein: 32g; Sodium: 0.42g; Sugar: 1g

720. EASY JUICY PORK CHOPS

Preparation time: 5 minutes

Cooking time: 15 minutes

Servings: 2

Ingredients:

- 2 tablespoons unsalted butter, divided
- ½ teaspoon garlic powder
- ½ teaspoon cumin
- 1 teaspon chili powder
- ¼ teaspon dried oregano
- 4 ounces boneless pork chops
- ¼ teaspoon powdered black pepper

Directions:

1. Combine chili powder, garlic powder, cumin, pepper, and oregano in a small bowl. On pork chops, rub dry rub. Pork chops should be placed in the air fryer basket.
2. Pre-heat the oven to 400^0F and set a timer for 15 minutes.
3. When thoroughly cooked, the internal temperature should be at least 145^0F.
4. Serve warm, with 1 tablespoon butter on top of each serving.
5. Enjoy.

Per serving: Calories: 313Kcal; Fat: 5g; Carbs: 26g; Protein: 24g; Sodium: 0.12g; Sugar: 0.1g

CHAPTER 16: Fish and Seafood

721. LIMES AND SHRIMPS SKEWERS

Preparation time: 15 minutes
Cooking time: 6 minutes
Servings: 4
Ingredients:

- ½ teaspoon white pepper
- 1-pound shrimps, peeled
- 1 teaspoon lemon juice
- 1 lime, cut into wedges

Directions:

6. Sprinkle the shrimps with white pepper and lemon juice.
7. String the lime wedges and lime in the wooden skewers one-by-one.
8. Preheat the grill to 400⁰F.
9. Put the shrimp in a grill and cook for around 3 minutes from each side or until the shrimps become light pink.
10. Serve and enjoy.

Per serving: Calories: 141Kcal; Fat: 2g; Carbs: 3.7g; Protein: 26g; Sodium: 0.28g; Sugar: 3g

722. TUNA TACOS

Preparation time: 15 minutes
Cooking time: 0 minutes
Servings: 4
Ingredients:

- 3 tablespoons plain yogurt
- ½ teaspoon cayenne pepper
- 4 pitas
- 7 ounces tuna, shredded and canned
- ¼ cup broccoli rice, cooked

Directions:

1. Mix the canned tuna with cayenne pepper, broccoli rice, and plain yogurt.
2. Fill the pittas with tuna mixture and roll into tacos.
3. Serve and enjoy.

Per serving: Calories: 274Kcal; Fat: 5g; Carbs: 6.2g; Protein: 19.6g; Sodium: 0. 35g; Sugar: 2g

723. CRUSTED SALMON WITH HORSERADISH

Preparation time: 10 minutes
Cooking time: 13 minutes
Servings: 2
Ingredients:

- 1 teaspoon coconut flakes
- 1 tablespoon olive oil
- 8 ounces salmon fillet, sliced
- ¼ teaspoon ground coriander
- 1-ounce horseradish, grated

Directions:

1. Mix ground coriander, horseradish, and coconut flakes.
2. Heat up olive oil in a skillet.
3. Put the salmon fillets in a sizable skillet and top with the horseradish mixture.
4. Cook the fish for around 5 minutes on medium heat.
5. Flip the fish on the side and cook for 8 minutes more.
6. Serve and enjoy.

Per serving: Calories: 220 Kcal; Fat: 14.4g; Carbs: 1.7g; Protein: 22.2g; Sodium: 0.09g; Sugar: 3g

724. CURRY SNAPPER

Preparation time: 10 minutes
Cooking time: 15 minutes
Servings: 4
Ingredients:

- 1 tablespoon olive oil
- ¼ cup water
- 1-pound snapper fillet, chopped
- 1 cup celery stalk, chopped
- ½ cup yogurt
- 1 teaspoon curry powder

Directions:

1. Roast the snapper fillet in the olive oil for 2 minutes per side.
2. Add celery stalk, curry powder, yogurt, and water.
3. Stir in the fish until you get a homogenous texture.
4. Close the lid and simmer the fish for 10 minutes on medium heat.
5. Serve and enjoy.

Per serving: Calories: 195Kcal; Fat: 5.9g; Carbs: 3.2g; Protein: 29.5g; Sodium: 0.10g; Sugar: 3.2g

725. SHRIMP PUTANESCA

Preparation time: 5 minutes
Cooking time: 20 minutes
Servings: 3
Ingredients:

- ¼ cup olives, sliced
- 1 tablespoon olive oil
- ¼ cup water
- 1 teaspoon chili flakes
- ½ onion, diced
- 5 ounces shrimps, peeled
- 1 teaspoon garlic, diced
- 1 cup tomatoes, chopped

Directions:

1. Heat olive oil in the saucepan.
2. Add shrimps and chili flakes. Cook the shrimps for 4 minutes.
3. Stir them well and add diced onion, garlic, tomatoes, olives, and water.
4. Close the lid and sauté the meal for 15 minutes.
5. Serve and enjoy.

Per serving: Calories: 128 Kcal; Fat: 6.7g; Carbs: 5.8g; Protein: 11.7g; Sodium: 0.21g; Sugar: 2.3g

726. FISH PUTTANESCA

Preparation time: 10 minutes
Cooking time: 20 minutes
Servings: 2
Ingredients:

- 1 teaspoon low-sodium tomato paste
- 8 ounces tilapia fillet
- 1 tablespoon olive oil
- ¼ cup water
- 2 ounces onion, diced
- ¼ teaspoon garlic powder
- ½ teaspoon mustard
- 3 kalamata olives, sliced
- 1 teaspoon fresh cilantro, chopped

Directions:

1. Heat the oil in a sizable skillet and add fish fillets. Roast them for 3 minutes per side.
2. Remove the fillets from the skillet.
3. Add all the remaining ingredients in the skillet and roast them for 10 minutes.
4. Stir well and add fish.
5. Close the lid before cooking the meal for another 7 minutes.
6. Serve and enjoy.

Per serving: Calories: 180Kcal; Fat: 9g; Carbs: 4.1g; Protein: 21.9g; Sodium: 0.10g; Sugar: 1.3g

727. BAKED TUNA WITH FETA

Preparation time: 10 minutes
Cooking time: 40 minutes
Servings: 6
Ingredients:

- 5 ounces Feta, crumbled oil.
- 1 teaspoon allspices
- 1 tablespoon olive oil
- 12 ounces tuna fillet, roughly chopped
- ½ teaspoon dried rosemary

Directions:

1. Sprinkle the tuna fillet cubes with allspices, dried rosemary, and olive
2. Line a sizable baking tray with parchment paper and put the fish inside.
3. Flatten it in one layer.
4. Top the tuna with crumbled Feta and cook at 365⁰F for 40 minutes.

Per serving: Calories: 289Kcal; Fat: 25g; Carbs: 1.3g; Protein: 15.3g; Sodium: 0.26g; Sugar: 1.5g

728. SHEET-PAN SEABASS

Preparation time: 10 minutes
Cooking time: 40 minutes
Servings: 3
Ingredients:

- 1 bell pepper, roughly chopped
- 8 ounces seabass, trimmed, chopped
- 2 tablespoons olive oil
- 1 tomato, chopped
- 1 teaspoon allspices

Directions:

1. Line the baking tray with baking paper.
2. Put fish, bell pepper, and tomato in the tray.
3. Sprinkle the ingredients with allspices and olive oil. Gently stir them.
4. Bake the meal at 375⁰F for 40 minutes.
5. Serve and enjoy.

Per serving: Calories: 282 Kcal; Fat: 14.3g; Carbs: 9.1g; Protein: 0.6g; Sodium: 0.36g; Sugar: 1.7g

729. STUFFED BRANZINO

Preparation time: 15 minutes
Cooking time: 30 minutes
Servings: 3
Ingredients:

- ½ teaspoon ground turmeric
- 10 ounces branzino, trimmed
- 1 tablespoon olive oil
- ¼ teaspoon sesame seeds
- 3 ounces red kidney beans, canned
- ½ teaspoon white pepper

Directions:

1. Mix ground turmeric, white pepper, and sesame seeds.
2. Rub the fish with spices and brush with olive oil.
3. Fill the fish with red kidney beans and secure with toothpicks.
4. Wrap the branzino in the foil and bake at 400⁰F for 30 minutes.

5. Serve and enjoy.

Per serving: Calories: 231Kcal; Fat: 17.51g; Carbs: 9.79g; Protein: 24g; Sodium: 0.06g; Sugar: 0.4g

730. COD WITH POMEGRANATE SAUCE

Preparation time: 10 minutes
Cooking time: 15 minutes
Servings: 4
Ingredients:

- 1 teaspoon olive oil
- ½ teaspoon chili powder
- 1-pound cod fillet
- ½ teaspoon dried mint
- 1 teaspoon whole-grain flour
- ½ cup pomegranate juice

Directions:

1. Chop the cod fillet roughly and roast with olive oil for 2 minutes per side.
2. Mix pomegranate juice with dried mint, flour, and chili powder.
3. Pour the liquid over the fish and close the lid.
4. Simmer the fish for 10 minutes on low heat.
5. Serve and enjoy.

Per serving: Calories: 123Kcal; Fat: 2.3g; Carbs: 5.3g; Protein: 20.4g; Sodium: 0.08g; Sugar: 2.1g

731. COD RELISH

Preparation time: 10 minutes
Cooking time: 5 minutes
Servings: 4
Ingredients:

- ½ teaspoon white pepper
- 1-pound cod fillet, chopped
- 1 teaspoon dried oregano
- 1 onion, diced
- 3 tablespoons olive oil
- 1 cup green peas, cooked

Directions:

1. Heat a sizable pan with 1 tablespoon oil over medium-high heat and add the cod fillets. Cook for 2 minutes on each side.
2. Put the fish in the serving plates.
3. In the mixing bowl, mix all remaining ingredients and shale well.
4. Top the fish with onion mixture.
5. Serve and enjoy.

Per serving: Calories: 223Kcal; Fat: 11.7g; Carbs: 8.2g; Protein: 22.6g; Sodium: 0.07g; Sugar: 2.2g

732. SEARED MACKEREL

Preparation time: 10 minutes
Cooking time: 5 minutes
Servings: 2
Ingredients:

- 1 tablespoon avocado oil
- 8 ounces mackerel fillets
- ¼ teaspoon ground turmeric

Directions:

1. Cut the mackerel into 2 fillets and sprinkle with ground turmeric from both sides.
2. Pre-heat avocado oil until shimmering.
3. Put mackerel in the hot oil and roast for 2 minutes.
4. Flip the fish on another side and cook for 2 minutes more.
5. Serve and enjoy.

Per serving: Calories: 321Kcal; Fat: 21.3g; Carbs: 3.4g; Protein: 27.4g; Sodium: 0.48g; Sugar: 3g

733. SALMON TAPAS

Preparation time: 10 minutes
Cooking time: 2 minutes
Servings: 2
Ingredients:

- 4 ounces salmon, canned, shredded
- 2 ounces low-sodium Cheddar cheese, shredded

Directions:

1. Make 2 rounds in the skillet from low-sodium Cheddar cheese and cook them until cheese is melted. Cool the cheese rounds.
2. Put the shredded salmon on the cheese rounds and roll them.
3. Serve and enjoy.

Per serving: Calories: 189Kcal; Fat: 12.9g; Carbs: 0.4g; Protein: 18.1g; Sodium: 0.2g; Sugar: 0.9g

734. DILL STEAMED SALMON

Preparation time: 10 minutes
Cooking time: 0 minutes
Servings: 4
Ingredients:

- 1 teaspoon chili flakes
- 1 red onion, diced
- 2 tablespoons dill, chopped
- 1-pound steamed salmon, chopped
- 1 tablespoon cream cheese

Directions:

1. Mix all ingredients in the bowl and carefully stir until homogenous.
2. Serve and enjoy.

Per serving: Calories: 174Kcal; Fat: 8g; Carbs: 3.5g; Protein: 22.8g; Sodium: 0.06g; Sugar: 2.2g

735. PAPRIKA SCALLOPS

Preparation time: 10 minutes

Cooking time: 5 minutes

Servings: 4

Ingredients:

- 1-pound scallops
- 1 teaspoon smoked paprika Cooking spray

Directions:

1. Sprinkle scallops with smoked paprika.
2. Spray the skillet with cooking spray, add scallops, and cook for 2 minutes per side.
3. Serve and enjoy.

Per serving: Calories: 127Kcal; Fat: 3.8g; Carbs: 3g; Protein: 19.1g; Sodium: 0.35g; Sugar: 3.4g

736. COD IN TOMATOES

Preparation time: 4

Cooking time: 10 minutes

Servings: 16 minutes

Ingredients:

- 1 teaspoon scallions, chopped
- ½ teaspoon minced garlic
- 4 cod fillets, boneless
- 1 tablespoon avocado oil
- ½ cup water
- 1 cup plum tomatoes, chopped

Directions:

1. Heat a sizable pan with the oil over medium-high heat, add the garlic and the fish and cook for around 3 minutes per side.
2. Top the fish with the remaining ingredients and cook for 10 minutes more.
3. Serve and enjoy.

Per serving: Calories: 110Kcal; Fat: 2g; Carbs: .9g; Protein: 20.7g; Sodium: 0.09g; Sugar: 0.9g

737. SWEET HALIBUT

Preparation time: 10 minutes

Cooking time: 12 minutes

Servings: 6

Ingredients:

- ½ teaspoon ground coriander
- ¼ cup water
- 1 teaspoon lime zest
- 1 tablespoon liquid honey
- 1-pound halibut
- 1 teaspoon olive oil

Directions:

1. Chop the halibut roughly and sprinkle with ground coriander.
2. Roast the chopped fish with olive oil for 1 minute per side.
3. Mix water with liquid honey.
4. Pour water over fish, add lime zest, and close the lid.
5. Cook it for 10 minutes on low heat.
6. Serve and enjoy.

Per serving: Calories: 198Kcal; Fat: 1.2g; Carbs: 2.9g; Protein: 13.9g; Sodium: 0.07g; Sugar: 2.3g

738. SPINACH HALIBUT

Preparation time: 10 minutes

Cooking time: 6 minutes

Servings: 4

Ingredients:

- 1 teaspoon olive oil
- 4 halibut fillets
- 2 tablespoons spinach, blended

Directions:

1. Melt the olive oil in the skillet and add fish fillets.
2. Cook them for 3 minutes per side.
3. Top the cooked halibut with spinach.
4. Serve and enjoy.

Per serving: Calories: 327Kcal; Fat: 7.7g; Carbs: 1.79g; Protein: 60.5g; Sodium: 1.3g; Sugar: 0.8g

739. NUTMEG COD

Preparation time: 10 minutes

Cooking time: 7 minutes

Servings: 5

Ingredients:

- 2 tablespoons avocado oil
- 1 tablespoon lemon juice
- 5 cod fillets
- 2 tablespoons ground nutmeg

Directions:

1. Pre-heat the grill to 390⁰F.
2. In the shallow bowl, mix ground nutmeg, lemon juice, and avocado oil.
3. Carefully brush every cod fillet with a nutmeg mixture from each side and put it in the grill.
4. Grill the fish for around 3 ½ minutes per side.
5. Serve and enjoy.

Per serving: Calories: 113Kcal; Fat: 2.8g; Carbs: 1.8g; Protein: 20.3g; Sodium: 0.07g; Sugar: 2.3g

740. PAPRIKA TUNA STEAKS

Preparation time: 10 minutes

Cooking time: 4 minutes

Servings: 4

Ingredients:

- 1 teaspoon ground paprika
- 1 teaspoon avocado oil
- 4 tuna steaks, boneless

Directions:

1. Rub the fish with paprika and sprinkle with avocado oil.
2. Transfer the tuna steaks in the pre-heated to 400⁰F grill and cook for 2 minutes per side.
3. Serve and enjoy.

Per serving: Calories: 159Kcal; Fat: 5.6g; Carbs: 0.4g; Protein: 25.5g; Sodium: 0.04g; Sugar: 2g

741. POACHED SALMON

Preparation time: 7 minutes

Cooking time: 9 minutes

Servings: 6

Ingredients:

- ¼ teaspoon cumin seeds
- 1 cup organic almond milk
- ¼ cup fresh cilantro, chopped
- 1-pound salmon fillet, chopped

Directions:

1. Bring the milk to a boil and add cumin seeds, and cilantro.
2. When the mixture starts to boil, add chopped salmon fillet and poach it for 9 minutes over medium heat.
3. Serve and enjoy.

Per serving: Calories: 210 Kcal; Fat: 9.8g; Carbs: 1.4g; Protein: 29.5g; Sodium: 0.19g; Sugar: 2g

742. SALMON AVOCADO SALAD

Preparation time: 10 minutes

Cooking time: 0 minutes

Servings: 1

Ingredients:

- 3 ounces cooked salmon, flaked
- ¼ tablespoon lemon juice
- 3 tablespoons avocado, peeled, pitted and chopped
- ¼ tablespoon olive oil
- Salt, to taste
- Black pepper, to taste
- 3 tablespoons cucumber, chopped
- ½ cup lettuce, chopped

Directions:

1. In a salad bowl, add all the recipe ingredients and stir to combine.
2. Serve immediately.

Per serving: Calories: 206Kcal; Fat: 14.2g; Carbs: 4g; Protein: 17.3g; Sodium: 0.05g; Sugar: 0.8g

743. SALMON ZUCCHINI SALAD

Preparation time: 10 minutes

Cooking time: 10 minutes

Servings: 1

Ingredients:

For dressing

- ⅛ tablespoon Dijon mustard
- ¼ teaspoon red pepper flakes, crushed
- ½ tablespoon olive oil
- ½ tablespoon balsamic vinegar

For salad

- 1 teaspoon basil, chopped
- 3 ounces smoked salmon
- ½ zucchinis, spiralized with blade

Directions:

For the dressing:

1. In a small blender, add all the recipe ingredients and pulse until smooth.

For the salad:

2. In a suitable bowl, add all the recipe ingredients and mix. Place the dressing over salad and toss to coat well.
3. Serve immediately.

Per serving: Calories: 179Kcal; Fat: 11g; Carbs: 3.6g; Protein: 15.9g; Sodium: 0.4g; Sugar: 1.8g

744. FISH WRAPS

Preparation time: 10 minutes

Cooking time: 30 minutes

Servings: 2

Ingredients:

- 2 tablespoons olive oil
- 6 oz tilapia fillet, chopped
- ½ teaspoon dried cilantro
- 1 carrot, peeled and sliced into strips
- 1 yellow onion, sliced

Directions:

1. Mix carrot strips with onion, olive oil, and dried cilantro.
2. Make pockets from the baking paper and add the carrot mixture inside.
3. Top the vegetables with tilapia and transfer in the baking tray.
4. Bake the fish for 30 minutes at 375⁰F.
5. Serve and enjoy.

Per serving: Calories: 225Kcal; Fat: 14.8g; Carbs8.1g; Protein: 16.7g; Sodium: 0.64g; Sugar: 4g

745. SALMON MOZZARELLA SALAD

Preparation time: 10 minutes

Cooking time: 0 minutes

Servings: 1

Ingredients:

- 3 tablespoons tomato, chopped
- ½ tablespoon dill, chopped
- Salt, as required
- 2 tablespoons part-skim mozzarella cheese, cubed
- 3 ounces cooked salmon, chopped
- 1 cup baby spinach
- ½ teaspoon lemon juice

Directions:

1. In a salad bowl, add all the recipe ingredients and stir to combine.
2. Serve immediately.

Per serving: Calories: 268Kcal; Fat: 11.4g; Carbs: 5.3g; Protein: 36.8g; Sodium: 0.3g; Sugar: 1.1g

746. EASY CRAB CAKES

Preparation time: 10 minutes

Cooking time: 8 minutes

Servings: 1

Ingredients:

- ¼ pound lump crabmeat, drained
- ¼ tablespoon old bay seasoning
- ¼ teaspoon Worcestershire sauce, low-sodium
- 2 tablespoons onion, chopped
- ¾ tablespoon blanched almond flour
- ¼ teaspoon black pepper
- ¼ teaspoon yellow mustard
- ¾ tablespoon olive oil
- 1 tablespoon egg white
- ½ tablespoon low-fat mayonnaise
- ¼ tablespoon dried parsley, crushed

Directions:

1. Heat the olive oil in a prepared wok over medium-high heat and sauté onion for almost 10 minutes.
2. Remove the frying pan from heat and set it aside to cool slightly.
3. Place cooked onion and remaining ingredients except for crabmeat in a suitable mixing bowl and mix until well combined. In the bowl of onion mixture, add the crabmeat and gently stir to combine. Make 2 equal-sized patties from the mixture.
4. Arrange the patties onto a foil-lined tray and refrigerate for almost 30 minutes.
5. In a large frying pan, heat the remaining oil over medium-low heat and cook the crab patties for almost 4 minutes per side or until desired doneness.
6. Serve hot.

Per serving: Calories: 253Kcal; Fat: 19g; Carbs: 5.1g; Protein: 15.6g; Sodium: 0.89g; Sugar: 1.9g

747. AVOCADO SHRIMP SALAD

Preparation time: 10 minutes
Cooking time: 0 minutes
Servings: 1
Ingredients:

- ¼ pound cooked shrimp
- ½ of a small avocado, peeled, pitted and cubed
- ½ tablespoon olive oil
- ¼ teaspoon ground cumin
- Salt, as required
- ½ tablespoon lime juice
- ½ scallion, chopped

Directions:

1. In a salad bowl, add oil, lime juice, cumin and salt and beat until well combined.
2. In the salad bowl, add shrimp, avocado and scallion and gently toss to coat well.
3. Serve immediately.

Per serving: Calories: 285Kcal; Fat: 15.5g; Carbs: 7.5g; Protein: 27.1g; Sodium: 1.2g; Sugar: 0.5g

748. GREENS SHRIMP SALAD

Preparation time: 10 minutes
Cooking time: 6 minutes
Servings: 1
Ingredients:

- ¼ tablespoon lime juice
- 1 tablespoon olive oil
- ½ garlic clove, crushed
- ¼ teaspoon salt
- ¼ teaspoon black pepper
- ¾ cup baby arugula
- ¼ pound shrimp, peeled and deveined
- ¾ cup baby spinach

Directions:

1. In a suitable wok, heat the oil over medium heat and sauté garlic for almost 1 minute.
2. Add the shrimp with salt and black pepper and cook for almost 5 minutes. Remove it from the heat and set it aside to cool.
3. In a salad bowl, add the shrimp, arugula, spinach, remaining oil, lime juice, salt and black pepper and gently toss to coat.
4. Serve immediately.

Per serving: Calories: 266Kcal; Fat: 14.5g; Carbs: 3.6g; Protein: 27g; Sodium: 0.05g; Sugar: 0.4g

749. CORN SHRIMP SALAD

Preparation time: 10 minutes
Cooking time: 0 minutes
Servings: 1
Ingredients:

- ¼ tablespoon olive oil
- 1 cup lettuce, torn
- 2 tablespoons onion, sliced
- ¼ pound cooked shrimp
- ¼ teaspoon salt
- ¼ teaspoon black pepper, to taste

Directions:

1. In a salad bowl, add shrimp, corn, onion, oil, salt and black pepper and toss to coat well.
2. Serve immediately.

Per serving: Calories: 180 Kcal; Fat: 5.5g; Carbs: 5.1g; Protein: 26.3g; Sodium: 0.45g; Sugar: 1.4g

750. TUNA EGG SALAD

Preparation time: 10 minutes
Cooking time: 0 minutes
Servings: 1
Ingredients:
For dressing

- ¼ teaspoon salt
- ¼ teaspoon black pepper
- ½ tablespoon dill, minced
- ¼ tablespoon lime juice
- ½ tablespoon olive oil

For salad

- ¼ cup tomato, chopped
- 1 cup spinach, torn
- 1 hard-boiled egg, peeled and sliced
- 3 ounces canned water-packed tuna, drained and flaked

Directions:

1. Place dill, oil, lime juice, salt, and black pepper in a suitable bowl and beat until well combined.
2. Place the torn spinach onto a serving plate and top with tuna, egg and tomato.
3. Drizzle with dressing and serve.
4. Enjoy.

Per serving: Calories: 241Kcal; Fat: 12.4g; Carbs: 4.1g; Protein: 28.8g; Sodium: 0.06g; Sugar: 1.7g

CHAPTER 17: Appetizers, Soups and Snacks

751. PESTO CAULIFLOWER

Preparation time: 10 minutes
Cooking time: 30 minutes
Servings: 4
Ingredients:

- ¼ cup pesto sauce
- ¼ teaspoon salt
- 4 cups cauliflower
- ¼ teaspoon pepper
- ¼ cup parmesan cheese

Directions:

1. Mix the pesto sauce and cauliflower in a mixing dish.
2. Mix until the cauliflower is covered in pesto sauce.
3. Spread the cauliflower uniformly on the baking sheet.
4. Apply salt and pepper to taste and parmesan cheese to be used as a topping.
5. Bake at 350⁰F for 30 minutes.
6. Serve and enjoy.

Per serving: Calories: 98.5Kcal; Fat: 8.4g; Carbs: 4.4g; Protein: 2.7g; Sodium: 0.8g; Sugar: 3g

752. ROASTED ITALIAN GREEN BEANS AND TOMATOES

Preparation time: 5 minutes
Cooking time: 10 minutes
Servings: 4
Ingredients:

- 1 tablespoon Italian seasoning
- ½ pound fresh green beans, trimmed and halved
- 1 tablespoon olive oil
- ½ pound tomatoes, trimmed

Directions:

1. Heat oven to 425⁰F.
2. Put green beans in a sizable baking pan.
3. The baking pan should be coated with cooking spray.
4. Mix oil, Italian seasoning, and salt. Sprinkle it over beans and bake for 10 minutes.
5. Insert tomatoes into the pan.
6. Roast the beans until they become crisp-tender. Tomatoes are softened by leaving them for an additional 6 minutes.
7. Serve and enjoy.

Per serving: Calories: 52.6Kcal; Fat: 0.1g; Carbs: 12.4g; Protein: 2.6g; Sodium: 0.01g; Sugar: 8.86g

753. RICE CAKES WITH FIRE JELLY

Preparation time: 5 minutes
Cooking time:
Servings: 4
Ingredients:

- 2 tablespoons minced fresh jalapeño chili pepper
- 1 tablespoon fresh rosemary, chopped
- 12 eaches miniature salt-and-pepper rice cakes
- 1/3 cup fat-free cream cheese
- 1/3 cup sugar-free apricot preserves

Directions:

1. Mix sugar-free preserves and chili pepper in a small bowl.
2. Place rice cakes with cream cheese; use the preserve mixture for topping.
3. Sprinkle with rosemary at the end.
4. Serve and enjoy.

Per serving: Calories: 54.8Kcal; Fat: 0.8 g; Carbs: 10.8g; Protein: 3.9g; Sodium: 0.02g; Sugar: 1.2g

754. GRILLED PEACHES

Preparation time: 5 minutes
Cooking time: 10 minutes
Servings: 6
Ingredients:

- 6 tablespoons fat-free whipped topping
- 6 fresh peaches, ripe
- 1 tablespoon olive oil

Directions:

1. Lightly grease a grill pan and preheat it over medium heat.
2. Halve the peaches and remove the pits.
3. Brush the cut sides with olive oil or spritz with cooking spray.
4. Place the peaches cut-side down on the grill for 5 minutes.
5. Flip the peaches before cooking for another 5 minutes until tender.
6. Spoon the peaches into bowls and serve with fat-free whipped topping.

Per serving: Calories: 99.7Kcal; Fat: 2.1g; Carbs: 17.7g; Protein: 1.9g; Sodium: 0.56g; Sugar: 15.4g

755. BAKED OMELET MIX

Preparation time: 10 minutes
Cooking time: 40 minutes
Servings: 12
Ingredients:

- 12 eggs, whisked
- 5 ounces feta cheese, crumbled
- 1 tablespoon dill, chopped
- ¼ teaspoon salt
- 1 teaspoon lemon pepper
- 4 teaspoons olive oil
- 8 ounces spinach, chopped
- 2 cups almond milk
- 12 ounces canned artichokes, chopped
- 2 garlic cloves, minced
- 1 teaspoon oregano, dried

Directions:

1. Heat a sizable pan with the oil over medium-high heat, add the garlic and the spinach and sauté for 3 minutes.
2. In a baking dish, combine the eggs with the artichokes and the rest of the ingredients.
3. Add the spinach mix as well, toss a bit, bake the mix at 375⁰F for 40 minutes, divide between serving plates.
4. Enjoy.

Per serving: Calories: 185.8Kcal; Fat: 12.4g; Carbs: 4.8g; Protein: 9.8g; Sodium: 0.5g; Sugar: 4.0g

756. ZUCCHINI MINI PIZZAS

Preparation time: 20 minutes
Cooking time: 5 minutes
Servings: 24
Ingredients:

- 1 zucchini, cut into ¼ inch slices diagonally
- 1/3 cup pizza sauce
- 1/8 teaspoon salt
- 1 teaspoon basil, minced
- ½ cup onion, chopped
- ½ cup pepperoni, small slices
- 1 cup tomatoes
- 1/8 teaspoon pepper
- ¾ cup mozzarella cheese, shredded

Directions:

1. Pre-heat your broiler.
2. Keep the zucchini in 1 layer on your greased baking sheet.
3. Add the onion and tomatoes. Broil each side for 2 minutes till they

become tender and crisp. Sprinkle pepper and salt.
4. Top with cheese, pepperoni, and sauce. Broil for a minute until the cheese melts.
5. Sprinkle basil on top.
6. Serve and enjoy.

Per serving: Calories: 28.7Kcal; Fat: 1.9g; Carbs: 1g; Protein: 2.2g; Sodium: 0.4g; Sugar: 1g

757. MARINATED MUSHROOM WRAPS

Preparation time: 15 minutes
Cooking time: 0 minutes
Servings: 2
Ingredients:

- 1 ripe Hass avocado, pitted and peeled
- 2 cups fresh baby spinach leaves
- 1 medium red bell pepper, cut into ¼ inch strips
- 1 ripe tomato, chopped
- 3 tablespoons soy sauce
- ¼ teaspoon salt
- ¼ teaspoon freshly ground black pepper
- 3 tablespoons fresh lemon juice
- 1½ tablespoons toasted sesame oil
- 2 portobello mushroom caps, cut into ¼ inch strips
- 2 whole-grain flour tortillas

Directions:

1. In a sizable bowl, combine the soy sauce, 2 tablespoons of the lemon juice, and the oil.
2. Add the portobello strips, toss to combine, and marinate for 1 hour or overnight.
3. Drain the mushrooms and set aside.
4. To assemble wraps, place 1 tortilla on a work surface and spread with some of the mashed avocado.
5. In the lower third of each tortilla, arrange strips of the soaked mushrooms and some of the bell pepper strips.
6. Sprinkle with the tomato and salt and black pepper to taste. Roll up tightly and cut in half diagonally.
7. Repeat with the remaining ingredients and serve.
8. Enjoy.

Per serving: Calories: 314Kcal; Fat: 21.7g; Carbs: 7.3 g; Protein: 22.9g; Sodium: 0.06g; Sugar: 4.3g

758. LEMON FAT BOMBS

Preparation time: 15 minutes
Cooking time: 0 minutes
Servings: 10

Ingredients:

- 1/8 teaspoon
- 1 teaspoon vanilla extract, unsweetened
- 1 tablespoon Erythritol sweetener
- ¼ cup avocado oil
- 3 tablespoons lemon juice
- 1 zest lemon
- 1 tablespoon coconut cream, full-fat
- ¾ cup coconut butter, full-fat

Directions:

1. Place all the ingredients for fat bombs in a blender and pulse until well combined.
2. Take a baking dish, line it with parchment sheet, then transfer the fat bomb mixture on the sheet and place the sheet into the freezer for 45 minutes until firm enough to shape into balls.
3. Set the baking sheet aside from the freezer, roll the fat bomb mixture into ten balls, and arrange the fat bombs on the baking sheet in a single layer.
4. Return the baking sheet into the freezer, let chill until hard and set, and then store in the freezer as desired.
5. Serve when required.

Per serving: Calories: 163.7Kcal; Fat: 16.1g; Carbs: 0.4g; Protein: 1.8g; Sodium: 0.01g; Sugar: 0.8g

759. DARK CHOCOLATE ALMOND YOGURT CUPS

Preparation time: 10 minutes
Cooking time: 0 minutes
Servings: 6
Ingredients:

- 3 cups plain nonfat Greek yogurt
- ½ teaspoon almond extract
- ¼ teaspoon liquid stevia extract
- 2 ounces dark chocolate, chopped
- ½ cup slivered almonds

Directions:

1. Whisk together the yogurt, almond extract, and liquid stevia in a medium bowl.
2. Spoon the yogurt into four dessert cups.
3. Sprinkle with chopped chocolate and slivered almonds.
4. Serve and enjoy.

Per serving: Calories: 169.5Kcal; Fat: 7.2g; Carbs: 10.6g; Protein: 15.1g; Sodium: 0.05g; Sugar: 7.7g

760. CREAMY AND AROMATIC CHICKEN

Preparation time: 15 minutes
Cooking time: 20 minutes
Servings: 4
Ingredients:

- ¼ cup heavy whipping cream
- 1 scallion, white and green parts, chopped
- 4 boneless, skinless chicken breasts
- 1 tbsp. extra-virgin olive oil
- ½ sweet onion, chopped
- 2 teaspoons fresh thyme, chopped
- ¼ teaspoon salt
- ¼ teaspoon freshly ground black pepper
- 1 cup low-sodium chicken broth

Directions:

1. Pre-heat the oven to 375⁰F.
2. Rub the chicken with salt and pepper.
3. Heat the olive oil in a sizable ovenproof pan over medium-high heat until shimmering.
4. Put the chicken in the skillet and cook for 10 minutes or until well browned. Flip halfway through. Transfer onto a platter and set it aside.
5. Add the onion to the skillet and sauté for 3 minutes or until translucent. Add the thyme, the broth, and simmer for 6 minutes or until the liquid reduces in half. Mix in the cream, then put the chicken back into the skillet.
6. Arrange the skillet in the oven and bake for 10 minutes.
7. Remove the skillet from the oven and serve them with scallion.

Per serving: Calories: 286.5Kcal; Fat: 13.9g; Carbs: 3.7g; Protein: 34.5g; Sodium: 0.9g; Sugar: 0.8g

761. MU SHU CHICKEN

Preparation time: 20 minutes
Cooking time: 6 hours
Servings: 6
Ingredients:

- 12 ounces chicken thighs, skinless, boneless
- 6 whole wheat flour tortillas
- 3 garlic cloves, minced
- ½ cup hoisin sauce
- 2 tablespoons water
- ¼ cup green onions
- 1 tablespoon cornstarch
- 1 tablespoon reduced-sodium soy sauce
- 16 ounces cabbage with carrots, shredded

- 4 teaspoons toasted sesame oil
- 1 cup carrots, coarsely shredded

Directions:

1. Combine the hoisin sauce, water, sesame oil, cornstarch, and soy sauce in a bowl.
2. In a slow cooker, combine shredded carrots and coleslaw mix.
3. Cut the chicken into 1/8-inch slices, then cut each slice in half lengthwise. Place the chicken on top of the cabbage mix. Drizzle with ¼ cup of the hoisin mixture.
4. Heat tortillas according to package directions. Fill tortillas with chicken mixture.
5. Top with green onions and serve.
6. Enjoy.

Per serving: Calories: 268.7Kcal; Fat: 7.6g; Carbs: 33.2g; Protein: 16.3g; Sodium: 0.3g; Sugar: 6.3g

762. CHOCO PEPPERMINT CAKE

Preparation time: 15 minutes

Cooking time: 3 hours

Servings: 4

Ingredients:

- 1 cup water
- 1/3 cup oil
- 3 eggs, beaten
- ¼ teaspoon peppermint extract
- Cooking spray
- 15 ounces chocolate cake mix

Directions:

1. Spray slow cooker with oil.
2. Mix all the ingredients in a bowl.
3. Use an electric mixer on medium speed setting to mix ingredients for 2 minutes.
4. Pour mixture into the slow cooker. Cover the sizable pot and cook on low for 3 hours.
5. Let cool before slicing and serving.

Per serving: Calories: 184.7Kcal; Fat: 7.1g; Carbs: 26.5g; Protein: 4.1g; Sodium: 0.2g; Sugar: 8g

763. COUNTRY-STYLE WEDGE SALAD WITH TURKEY

Preparation time: 10 minutes

Cooking time: 5 minutes

Servings: 4

Ingredients

- 2 hard-cooked eggs, chopped
- 1 cup halved grape or cherry tomatoes
- 1 head butterhead lettuce, quartered
- ¼ cup red onion, finely chopped
- ¼ teaspoon cracked black pepper
- 1 recipe buttermilk-avocado dressing

- 2 cups cooked turkey breast, shredded
- 4 slices less-fat bacon, low-sodium, crisp-cooked, and crumbled

Directions:

1. Arrange a quarter of lettuce on each plate. Drizzle half of the dressing over wedges.
2. Top with the turkey, eggs, and tomatoes. Drizzle with the remaining dressing.
3. Sprinkle with onion, bacon, and pepper.

To make the buttermilk-avocado dressing:

4. In a blender, combine ¾ cup buttermilk, ½ avocado, 1 tablespoon of parsley, ¼ tsp. each salt, onion powder, dry mustard, and black pepper, and 1 garlic clove, minced.
5. Cover and blend until smooth.
6. Serve and enjoy.

Per serving: Calories: 227.8Kcal; Fat: 8.6g; Carbs: 7.6g; Protein: 29.3g; Sodium: 0.1g; Sugar: 1.3g

764. BALSAMIC CHICKEN

Preparation time: 10 minutes

Cooking time: 23 minutes

Servings: 6

Ingredients:

- ½ teaspoon dried thyme
- 6 chicken breast halves, skinless and boneless
- 1 teaspoon dried rosemary
- 1 teaspoon garlic salt
- 2 tablespoons olive oil
- 1 onion, thinly sliced
- 14 ½ ounces tomatoes, diced
- ¼ teaspoon ground black pepper
- ½ cup balsamic vinegar
- 1 teaspoon dried oregano
- 1 teaspoon dried basil

Directions:

1. Season both sides of your chicken breasts thoroughly with pepper, salt and garlic.
2. Take a skillet and place it over medium heat.
3. Add some oil and cook the seasoned chicken for 4 minutes per side until the breasts are browned.
4. Pour the diced-up tomatoes and balsamic vinegar over the chicken, and season with rosemary, basil, thyme, and rosemary. Simmer the chicken for about 15 minutes until they are no longer pink.
5. Serve and enjoy.

Per serving: Calories: 195.8Kcal; Fat: 6.7g; Carbs: 6.8g; Protein: 23.7g; Sodium: 0.1g; Sugar: 9.6g

765. BUFFALO CHICKEN AND CHEESE MEATBALLS

Preparation time: 5 minutes

Cooking time: 15 minutes

Servings: 6

Ingredients:

- 1 tablespoon olive oil
- ½ cup buffalo sauce
- 1 ½ pounds ground chicken
- 2 medium egg whites
- ½ cup green onions, chopped
- ½ cup Blue cheese

Directions:

1. Pre-heat the oven to 400⁰F.
2. Using a parchment paper, line a baking tray.
3. In a sizable mixing bowl, add the egg whites, ground chicken, ¾ of buffalo sauce, and scallions. Mix well.
4. Take the blue cheese and crumble it well. Now add the crumbled cheese to the chicken mixture and fold it gently.
5. Use a medium spoon to scoop out the mixture. Roll it into balls measuring about an inch. Place the prepared meatballs onto the lined baking sheet. Redo the process with the rest of the meat and cheese mixture.
6. Place the baking tray into the preheated oven and bake for around 15 minutes.
7. Meanwhile, take a small bowl and add in the olive oil and buffalo sauce. Whisk well to combine.
8. Once the meatballs are done, transfer them onto a fresh sheet of parchment paper. Drizzle the meatballs with prepared buffalo sauce and olive oil mixture.
9. Place the meatballs back to the oven and bake for another couple of minutes.
10. Serve and enjoy.

Per serving: Calories: 291Kcal; Fat: 14.5g; Carbs: 0.8g; Protein: 23.4g; Sodium: 0.6g; Sugar: 0.9g

766. TURKEY SCALOPPINI

Preparation time: 14 minutes

Cooking time: 10 minutes

Servings: 4

Ingredients:

- 1 garlic clove, minced
- 2 tablespoons chopped fresh rosemary
- 1 cup low-sodium chicken broth
- ½ cup whole-wheat flour
- ¼ teaspoon freshly ground black pepper

- 3 tablespoons extra-virgin olive oil
- ½ teaspoon sea salt
- 2 tablespoons salted butter, very cold, cut into small pieces
- 12 ounces turkey breast, cut into ½ inch-thick cutlets and pounded flat
- ½ cup dry white wine

Directions:

1. Preheat the oven to 200⁰F. Line a baking sheet with parchment paper.
2. In a medium bowl, whip together the flour, salt, and pepper.
3. In a large skillet over medium-high heat, warm the olive oil until it shimmers.
4. Working in batches with one or two pieces of turkey at a time, dredge the turkey cutlets in the flour and pat off any excess. Cook in the hot oil until the turkey is cooked through, about 3 minutes per side. Add more oil if needed.
5. Place the cooked cutlets on the lined baking sheet and keep them warm in the oven while you cook the remaining turkey and make the pan sauce.
6. Once all the turkey is cooked and warming in the oven, add garlic to the pan. Cook for 30 seconds while you stir constantly.
7. Add the wine and use the side of a spoon to scrape any browned bits off the bottom of the pan. Simmer, stirring, for 1 minute. Add the rosemary and chicken broth. Simmer, stirring, until it thickens, 2 minutes more.
8. Whisk in the cold butter until incorporated. Place the turkey cutlets back into the sauce and turn once to coat.
9. Serve with any remaining sauce spooned over the top.

Per serving: Calories: 343.8Kcal; Fat: 19.8g; Carbs: 14.6g; Protein: 23.7g; Sodium: 0.3g; Sugar: 1.1g

767. VEGETABLE BEEF SOUP

Preparation time: 10 minutes

Cooking time: 15 minutes

Servings: 4

Ingredients:

- 1/8 teaspoon freshly ground black pepper
- ½ teaspoon sea salt
- 1 onion, chopped
- 2 cups peas
- 1 carrot, chopped
- 2 celery stalks, chopped
- 1 teaspoon dried rosemary
- 6 cups low-sodium beef or chicken broth

- 1-pound ground beef

Directions:

1. Cook the ground beef, crumbling with the side of a spoon, until browned, about 5 minutes.
2. Add the onion, celery, carrot, and rosemary. Cook, stirring properly, until the vegetables start to soften for about 5 minutes.
3. Add the broth, salt, pepper, and peas. Bring to a simmer.
4. Reduce the heat and simmer, stirring, until warmed through, about 5 minutes more.
5. Serve and enjoy.

Per serving: Calories: 354.7Kcal; Fat: 16.5g; Carbs: 17.5g; Protein: 34.5g; Sodium: 3.0g; Sugar: 3.4g

768. CARROT GINGER SOUP

Preparation time: 5 minutes

Cooking time: 20 minutes

Servings: 4

Ingredients:

- ¼ cup fat-free sour cream
- 1 tablespoon fresh grated ginger
- 1-pound carrots, peeled and chopped
- 1 tablespoon olive oil
- ¼ teaspoon salt
- ¼ teaspoon pepper
- 1 medium yellow onion, chopped
- 3 cups fat-free chicken broth

Directions:

1. Heat the olive oil in a sizable saucepan over medium heat.
2. Add the onions and sauté for 5 minutes until softened.
3. Stir in the broth, carrots, and ginger then cover and bring to a boil.
4. Reduce heat and simmer for 20 minutes. Stir in the sour cream before setting aside.
5. Blend using an immersion blender until smooth and creamy.
6. Season properly with salt and pepper then serve hot.
7. Serve and enjoy.

Per serving: Calories: 269.6; Fat: 22.1g; Carbs: 10.9g; Protein: 4.96g; Sodium: 0.3g; Sugar: 7.3g

769. MUSHROOM SOUP

Preparation time: 10 minutes

Cooking time: 10 minutes

Servings: 2

Ingredients:

- 1 teaspoon dried thyme
- 1 cup Cremini mushrooms, chopped
- ½ teaspoon dried oregano
- 1 bell pepper, chopped

- 1 tablespoon olive oil
- 1 cup Cheddar cheese, shredded
- 2 cups water
- ½ teaspoon salt
- 1 tablespoon fresh parsley, chopped

Directions:

1. Pour olive oil in the pan. Add mushrooms and bell pepper.
2. Roast the vegetables for 5 minutes over medium heat. Then sprinkle them with thyme, salt, and dried oregano. Add parsley and water. Stir the soup well.
3. Cook the soup for 10 minutes.
4. After this, blend the soup until it is smooth and simmer it for 5 minutes more.
5. Add cheese and stir properly.
6. Serve and enjoy.

Per serving: Calories: 319.7Kcal; Fat: 25.7g; Carbs: 7g; Protein: 16.2g; Sodium: 2g; Sugar: 15g

770. 7-MINUTES EGG DROP SOUP

Preparation time: 5 minutes

Cooking time: 7 minutes

Servings: 4

Ingredients:

- 8 thinly sliced medium mushrooms
- 4 large eggs
- 1 teaspoon fresh ginger, grated
- 4 cups chicken broth
- 1 teaspoon black pepper
- ¼ teaspoon sea salt
- 4 teaspoons coconut aminos
- 4 medium green onions, thinly sliced

Directions:

1. Add the chicken broth, coconut aminos, ginger, mushrooms, black pepper, and onions into a medium-sized saucepan.
2. Place the pan on a high flame and let it come to a boil. Reduce the flame and cook for a couple of minutes more.
3. Crack the eggs in a cup and whisk them well.
4. Slowly pour the whisked eggs in a stream into the simmering soup. Keep stirring to get some smooth egg ribbons.
5. Stir in the salt as soon as you finish cooking the soup.
6. Serve and enjoy.

Per serving: Calories: 107Kcal; Fat: 5.8g; Carbs: 4.8g; Protein: 10.7g; Sodium: 0.3g; Sugar: 0.9g

771. CLASSIC TOMATO SOUP

Preparation time: 10 minutes

Cooking time: 15 minutes

Servings: 4

Ingredients:

- ½ teaspoon salt
- ¼ teaspoon dried oregano
- 2 teaspoons vegetable oil
- ¼ teaspoon ground pepper
- 1 ½ cups water
- 2 teaspoons brown sugar
- ¼ cup chopped celery
- 15 ounces diced tomatoes
- ½ teaspoon dried basil
- ¼ cup chopped onion

Directions:

1. On a large skillet and heat some oil.
2. Add onion and celery into the skillet and cook for 4 minutes. Add the remaining ingredients.
3. Boil and simmer for 10 minutes.
4. Garnish with basil and serve.
5. Enjoy.

Per serving: Calories: 75.4Kcal; Fat: 1.8g; Carbs: 12.7g; Protein: 2.3g; Sodium: 0.1g; Sugar: 5.8g

772. CREAMY TOMATO SOUP

Preparation time: 10 minutes

Cooking time: 40 minutes

Servings: 4

Ingredients:

- ½ cup heavy cream
- 1-pound fresh tomatoes, core removed
- 4 cups chicken broth
- ¼ teaspoon salt
- 4 cloves garlic, peeled
- ¼ teaspoon pepper
- ¼ cup olive oil

Directions:

1. Pre-heat the oven to 400⁰F.
2. Using aluminum foil sheet, line the baking tray.
3. Add the tomatoes on a sizable baking tray and the garlic cloves alongside the tomatoes.
4. Season both tomatoes and garlic with pepper and salt, and drizzle with olive oil.
5. Place the baking tray into a ready oven and roast for around 30 minutes.
6. Transfer the roasted tomatoes and garlic along with the juices and 2 cups of broth into the blender.
7. Blend the tomatoes and garlic into a smooth puree-like consistency.
8. Take a large saucepan and place it over a medium flame. Pour the prepared tomato puree into the saucepan.
9. Stir in the heavy cream and remaining broth; cook over a medium flame for around 10 minutes.

10. Season with black pepper and salt as per your taste. Mix well.
11. Transfer into a bowl and garnish with a dash of cream and freshly cracked pepper.

Per serving: Calories: 123Kcal; Fat: 19.1g; Carbs: 6.1g; Protein: 6.9g; Sodium: 0.02g; Sugar: 3.2g

773. ALMOND COCONUT BISCOTTI

Preparation time: 5 minutes

Cooking time: 50 minutes

Servings: 2

Ingredients:

- 1⅓ cups unsweetened coconut, grated
- 2 teaspoons baking powder
- ⅔ cup Splenda
- 1 egg, room temperature
- ½ teaspoon salt
- 2 ½ cups flour
- ½ cup margarine, melted
- ¾ cup almonds, sliced
- 1 egg white, room temperature
- 1 teaspoon vanilla

Directions:

1. Heat oven to 350°F.
2. Using a parchment paper, line a baking sheet.
3. In a sizable bowl, combine all the dry ingredients.
4. In a separate mixing bowl, beat the other ingredients together.
5. Add ingredients together and mix until thoroughly combined.
6. Divide dough in half. Shape each half into a loaf measuring 8x2¾ inches. Place loaves on pan 3 inches apart.
7. Bake the loaves for 30 minutes until golden brown. Cool them on a wire rack for 10 minutes.
8. With a serrated knife, cut loaf diagonally into ½-inch slices.
9. Place the cookies, cut side down, back on the pan, and bake another 20 minutes, or until firm and nicely browned.
10. Store in an airtight container before serving.

Per serving: Calories: 274Kcal; Fat: 18g; Carbs: 27.18g; Protein: 5g; Sodium: 0.2g; Sugar: 1.2g

774. FRESH BROCCOLI SOUP

Preparation time: 20 minutes

Cooking time: 43 minutes

Servings: 8

Ingredients:

- 2 chopped celery ribs
- 1 ½ pounds broccoli, cut into small pieces
- 2 tablespoons lime juice
- ½ pounds sliced mushrooms.
- 2 chopped carrots
- 1 tbsp. vegetable oil
- ¼ cup chopped onion
- 32 ounces vegetable broth
- 1 minced garlic clove
- 2 cups water
- 1 tablespoons soy sauce

Directions:

1. Add vegetable oil to a sizable frying pan and heat.
2. Fry the mushrooms for 5 minutes.
3. Stir with soy sauce and take off from the heat.
4. Put broccoli, carrots, onion, water, celery, garlic and broth to the same pan.
5. Let it boil and simmer for 30 minutes. Blend the hard-remaining vegetables in the soup.
6. Put it back to the pot and add cauliflower and mushrooms.
7. Cook for 8 extra minutes and turn off the heat.
8. Serve immediately and enjoy.

Per serving: Calories: 68.7Kcal; Fat: 1.7g; Carbs: 10.8g; Protein: 4.1g; Sodium: 0.2g; Sugar: 3.8g

775. LOW CARB CREAM BOUILLON

Preparation time: 5 minutes

Cooking time: 21 minutes

Servings: 4

Ingredients:

- 3 cups chicken broth
- 1 tablespoon taco seasoning
- 8 ounces cream cheese
- ½ cup heavy cream
- 1 tablespoon avocado oil
- ¼ teaspoon salt
- 1-pound chicken breast
- 10 ounces diced chilies

Directions:

1. Heat oil in a sizable pot.
2. Add taco seasoning and diced chilies into the pot and cook for a minute.
3. Add the broth and chicken and simmer for 20 minutes.
4. Reserve the chicken pot.
5. Add cream cheese and heavy cream to the bouillon.
6. Add the salt to taste and serve.
7. Enjoy.

Per serving: Calories: 478.5Kcal; Fat: 36.8g; Carbs: 6.8g; Protein: 30.2g; Sodium: 0.02g; Sugar: 3.8g

776. ALMOND CHEESECAKE BITES

Preparation time: 5 minutes
Cooking time: 0 minutes
Servings: 6
Ingredients:

- ¼ cup almond butter
- 2 drops liquid Stevia
- ½ cup reduced-fat cream cheese, soft
- ½ cup almonds, ground fine

Directions:

1. In a sizable bowl, beat cream cheese, almond butter, and Stevia on high speed until the mixture is smooth and creamy. Cover and chill for 30 minutes.
2. Mold the mixture into 12 balls using your hands.
3. Place the ground almonds on a shallow plate.
4. Roll the molded balls in the nuts and ensure to completely cover all sides.
5. Store in a container covered with a lid.
6. Refrigerate and serve when desired.

Per serving: Calories: 186Kcal; Fat: 16g; Carbs: 6.3g; Protein: 6.7g; Sodium: 0.09g; Sugar: 1g

777. CRACKERS

Preparation time: 7 minutes
Cooking time: 12 minutes
Servings: 15
Ingredients:

- 1 beaten large egg
- 2 cups blanched almond flour
- ½ teaspoon sea salt

Directions:

1. Pre-heat your oven to 350°F.
2. With parchment paper, line a baking sheet, then combine the almond flour and the salt in a large bowl. Crack in the egg and mix very well until you form a large ball of dough.
3. Place your dough between 2 large pieces of prepared parchment paper. Using a rolling pin, roll the dough into a rectangular shape.
4. Slice the dough into rectangles, prick with a fork, and place on a baking sheet that has been prepared and lined.
5. Bake the crackers for 12 minutes.
6. Allow the crackers to cool for 10 minutes.
7. Serve the crackers immediately or store them in a jar.
8. Enjoy.

Per serving: Calories: 79Kcal; Fat: 6.7g; Carbs: 2.79g; Protein: 3.18g; Sodium: 0.07g; Sugar: 1.5g

778. CHEESY TACO BITES

Preparation time: 5 minutes
Cooking time: 6 minutes
Servings: 12
Ingredients:

- 2 cups shredded cheddar cheese
- 2 tablespoon chili powder
- 1 teaspoon salt
- 2 tablespoons cumin
- Pico de Gallo, for garnishing
- 8 teaspoons coconut cream, for garnishing

Directions:

1. Pre-heat your oven to 350°F.
2. Place 1 tablespoon piles of cheese on a baking sheet lined with parchment paper, leaving 2 inches between each.
3. Bake for 5 minutes with the baking sheet in the oven.
4. Remove from the oven and allow the cheese to cool for 1 minute before gently lifting and pressing each into the cups of a tiny muffin tray.
5. Be careful to push the cheese's edges to make the shape of little muffins.
6. Allow the cheese to cool completely before removing it while you're baking the cheese and making your cups.
7. Fill the cheese cups halfway with coconut cream and top with Pico de Gallo.
8. Serve and enjoy.

Per serving: Calories: 96.19Kcal; Fat: 15g; Carbs: 3.58g; Protein: 4.7g; Sodium: 0.4g; Sugar: 1.4g

779. ALMOND FLOUR CRACKERS

Preparation time: 5 minutes
Cooking time: 15 minutes
Servings: 8

Ingredients:

- 1½ cups almond flour
- ¼ cup Stevia
- ½ cup coconut oil, melted

Directions:

1. Heat oven to 3500F. Line a cookie sheet with parchment paper.
2. In a sizable mixing bowl, combine all ingredients and mix well.
3. Spread dough onto prepared cookie sheet, ¼-inch thick. Use a paring knife to score into 24 crackers.
4. Bake for 15 minutes or until golden brown.
5. Separate and store in an air-tight container.
6. Serve and enjoy.

Per serving: Calories: 224Kcal; Fat: 23g; Carbs: 9g; Protein: 3.89g; Sodium: 0.01g; Sugar: 4.0g

780. ASIAN CHICKEN WINGS

Preparation time: 5 minutes
Cooking time: 30 minutes
Servings: 12
Ingredients:

- 24 chicken wings
- 6 tablespoons soy sauce
- 6 tablespoon Chinese Five Spice
- ¼ teaspoon salt
- ¼ teaspoon pepper
- Non-stick cooking spray

Directions:

1. Heat oven to 350⁰F. Spray a baking sheet with cooking spray.
2. Combine the soy sauce, Five Spice, salt, and pepper in a large bowl. Add the wings and toss to coat.
3. Pour the wings onto the prepared pan. Bake for 15 minutes.
4. Turn the chicken over and cook for another 15 minutes until the chicken is cooked through.
5. Serve with your favorite low-carb dipping sauce.

Per serving: Calories: 232 Kcal; Fat: 15g; Carbs: 2.76g; Protein: 20.44g; Sodium: 0.5g; Sugar: 1.8g

CHAPTER 18: Desserts

781. CRISPY APPLE SLICES

Preparation time: 20 minutes

Cooking time: 35 minutes

Servings: 8

Ingredients:

- 3 tablespoons plant-based butter
- 5 cups Granny Smith apples
- 1 teaspoon lemon juice
- ¾ teaspoon apple pie spice, divided
- ½ cup rolled oats
- ¼ cup and 2 tablespoons Splenda
- 3 tablespoons flour

Directions:

1. Pre-heat the oven to 375°F.
2. Combine apples, 2 tablespoons Splenda, lemon juice, and ½ teaspoon apple pie spice in a bowl until apples are well coated. Place apples in a greased square baking pan.
3. Combine oats, flour, ¼ Splenda, and remaining apple pie spice in a bowl.
4. Add butter and mix properly until mixture resembles coarse crumbs.
5. Sprinkle the crumbs evenly over apples.
6. Bake the apple crisp for 35 minutes, or until apples are tender and topping is golden brown.
7. Serve warm.

Per serving: Calories: 153Kcal; Fat: 5g; Carbs: 27g; Protein: 1g; Sodium: 0.05g; Sugar: 18g

782. BLACKBERRY CROSTATA

Preparation time: 10 minutes

Cooking time: 22 minutes

Servings: 6

Ingredients:

- 3 tablespoons Splenda, divided
- 1 9-inch pie crust, unbaked
- Juice and zest, 1 lemon
- 2 tablespoons butter, soft
- 2 cup fresh blackberries

Directions:

1. Heat oven to 425°F.
2. Using a parchment paper, line a sizable baking sheet and unroll pie crust in pan.
3. In a medium bowl, combine blackberries, 2 tablespoons of Splenda, lemon juice, zest, and cornstarch.
4. Spoon onto the crust but leave a 2-inch edge. Fold and crimp the edges.
5. Top the berries with 1 tablespoon of butter.
6. Brush remaining butter around edges of crust and sprinkle crust and fruit with the remaining Splenda.
7. Bake the mixture for approximately 22 minutes or until golden brown.
8. Chop and cool before eating.

Per serving: Calories: 206Kcal; Fat: 11g; Carbs: 24g; Protein: 2g; Sodium: 0.43g; Sugar: 9g

783. APRICOT SOUFFLÉ

Preparation time: 5 minutes

Cooking time: 33 minutes

Servings: 6

Ingredients:

- ¼ teaspoon cream tartar
- ¼ cup warm water
- ⅛ teaspoon salt
- 4 egg whites
- 3 egg yolks, beaten
- ¾ cup sugar-free apricot fruit spread
- ⅓ cup dried apricots, diced fine
- 2 tablespoons flour
- 3 tablespoons plant-based butter

Directions:

1. Pre-heat the oven to 325°F for 10 minutes.
2. In a sauce pan, melt plant-based butter over medium heat. Stir in flour and cook until bubbly.
3. In a sizable bowl, stir together the fruit spread and water and add it to the saucepan with the apricots. Cook, stirring, 3 minutes or until mixture thickens. Whisk in egg yolks.
4. Let cool to room temperature, stirring occasionally.
5. Beat the egg whites, salt, and cream of tartar in a medium bowl on high speed until stiff peaks form. Gently fold into cooled apricot mixture.
6. Spoon the apricot batter into a 1-½ quart soufflé dish.
7. Bake the soufflé for 30 minutes, or until puffed and golden brown.
8. Serve immediately.

Per serving: Calories: 116Kcal; Fat: 8g; Carbs: 7g; Protein: 4g; Sodium: 0.4g; Sugar: 1g

784. BAKED MAPLE CUSTARD

Preparation time: 5 minutes

Cooking time: 1 hour 15 minutes

Servings: 6

Ingredients

- Nonstick cooking spray
- 2 ½ cup half-and-half
- 2 teaspoon vanilla
- 3 cup boiling water
- ¼ cup Splenda
- 2 tablespoons sugar free maple syrup
- ½ cup egg substitute
- A dash nutmegs

Directions:

1. Heat oven to 325°F.
2. Lightly spray 6 custard cups or ramekins with cooking spray.
3. In a large bowl, combine half-and-half, egg yolks, Splenda, vanilla, and nutmeg.
4. Pour evenly into prepared custard cups.
5. Place the cups in a 13x9-inch baking dish.
6. Pour boiling water around the cup, being careful not to splash it. Bake the cups for 1 hour and 15 minutes.
7. Remove the cups from the pan and let them cool completely.
8. Cover and let cool overnight.
9. Drizzle with maple syrup before serving.

Per serving: Calories: 190Kcal; Fat: 12g; Carbs: 15g; Protein: 5g; Sodium: 0.56g; Sugar: 8g

785. AUTUMN SKILLET CAKE

Preparation time: 10 minutes

Cooking time: 30 minutes

Servings: 10

Ingredients:

- 1 teaspoon pumpkin spice
- ¼ teaspoon salt
- 2 tablespoons planted-based butter, melted
- 2 cup almond flour, sifted
- 2 teaspoons cinnamon
- 1 cup fresh cranberries
- 3 eggs, room temperature
- 1 teaspoon ginger
- ¼ teaspoon nutmeg
- 4 ounces reduced-fat cream cheese, soft
- 3 tablespoons fat free sour cream
- ¾ cup Splenda
- ¾ cup pumpkin puree
- 1 ½ tablespoons baking powder
- Nonstick cooking spray

Directions:

1. Pre-heat the oven to 350°F.
2. Grease a sizable cast iron skillet or cake pan with cooking spray.

3. In a bowl, beat Splenda, butter and cream cheese until thoroughly combined.

4. Add eggs, each at a time, beating after adding each egg.

5. Add pumpkin and spices in the butter mix and combine. Add the dry ingredients and mix well. Stir in the sour cream. Pour into prepared pan.

6. Sprinkle cranberries over the batter and with the back of a spoon, push them half-way into the batter.

7. Bake for 30 minutes or until the cake passes the toothpick test. Cool completely before serving.

Per serving: Calories: 280Kcal; Fat: 17g; Carbs: 23g; Protein: 7g; Sodium: 0.06g; Sugar: 16g

786. APPLE PEAR AND PECAN CUPS

Preparation time: 10 minutes
Cooking time: 23 minutes
Servings: 24
Ingredients:

- ½ cup pecan pieces
- ½ teaspoon vanilla
- 1 tablespoon Splenda
- 1 ¼ cups water, divided
- Nonstick cooking spray
- 1 teaspoon cinnamon
- 1 red delicious apple, sliced, leave peel on
- ¼ teaspoon nutmeg
- 1 tablespoon plant-based butter
- 1 ripe pear, sliced, leave peel on
- 3 eggs
- ½ cup plain fat-free yogurt
- 1 tablespoon lemon juice
- 1 Granny Smith apple, sliced, leave peel on
- 1 package spice cake mix

Directions:

1. Pre-heat the oven to 350°F for 10 minutes.

2. Grease jelly-roll pan with the nonstick cooking spray.

3. In a sizable bowl, beat cake mix with 1 cup water, eggs and yogurt until smooth.

4. Pour the cake batter into prepared sizable pan and bake for 20 minutes until fully cooked. Cool completely.

5. Toss pecans over med-high heat in a skillet until lightly browned.

6. In a skillet, add the remaining ¼ cup water, sliced fruit, juice and spices and boil to medium heat for 3 minutes until fruits are tender crisp.

7. Remove the fruits from heat and stir in Splenda, plant-based butter, vanilla, and toasted pecans. Spoon evenly over cake.

8. Slice and serve.

Per serving: Calories: 130Kcal; Fat: 5g; Carbs: 20g; Protein: 2g; Sodium: 0.17g; Sugar: 10g

787. CHOCOLATE ORANGE BREAD PUDDING

Preparation time: 10 minutes
Cooking time: 35 minutes
Servings: 8
Ingredients:

- ¾ teaspoon cinnamon
- 1 teaspoon low-sugar vanilla
- 1 ½ cups skim milk
- 2 teaspoons orange zest, grated
- ¼ cup Splenda
- 4 cups French baguette cubes
- 3 eggs, lightly beaten
- ¼ cup sugar-free chocolate ice cream topping
- 4 cups French baguette cubes
- 3 tablespoons unsweetened cocoa powder

Directions:

1. Heat oven to 350°F.

2. In a medium bowl, combine the Splenda and cocoa. Whisk milk, egg, zest, vanilla, and cinnamon until well combined.

3. Place square bread on an 8-inch square baking sheet. Pour the milk mixture over the top.

4. Bake for 35 minutes or until a medium knife is clean. Let cool for 10 minutes.

5. Place the cake on a sizable serving plate and sprinkle lightly with an ice cream topping.

6. Serve and enjoy.

Per serving: Calories: 139Kcal; Fat: 2g; Carbs: 23g; Protein: 6g; Sodium: 0.01g; Sugar: 9g

788. BROILED STONE FRUIT

Preparation time: 5 minutes
Cooking time: 6 minutes
Servings: 2
Ingredients:

- Nonstick cooking spray
- 1 peach
- 2 tablespoons sugar-free whipped topping
- 1 nectarine
- 1 tablespoon Splenda

Directions:

1. Heat the oven for baking. Place foil on a thin baking sheet and spray with the cooking spray.

2. Cut the peach and nectarine in half and remove the seeds.

3. Place one side off the prepared plate. Broil for 3 minutes.

4. Turn fruit over and sprinkle with Splenda.

5. Cook for another 3 minutes.

6. Transfer 1 fruit each to a bowl and top with 1 tablespoon of the whipped topping.

7. Serve and enjoy.

Per serving: Calories: 101Kcal; Fat: 1g; Carbs: 22g; Protein: 1g; Sodium: 0.89g; Sugar: 19g

789. CAFÉ MOCHA TORTE

Preparation time: 15 minutes
Cooking time: 25 minutes
Servings: 14
Ingredients:

- ¼ cup brewed coffee, room temperature
- 8 eggs
- Nonstick cooking spray
- 1 cup plant-based butter, cut into cubes
- 1-pound bittersweet chocolate, chopped

Directions:

1. Pre-heat the oven to 325°F.

2. Spray cooking spray on the 8-inch springform pan. Line bottom side with parchment paper and spray again.

3. Wrap the outer part with a double layer of foil and place them in a sizable baking sheet.

4. Add water in a sizable pot and bring to a boil. Beat eggs in a large bowl on medium speed until doubled in size, about 5 minutes.

5. Place chocolate, plant-based butter, and coffee in a microwave-safe bowl stirring every 30 seconds, until chocolate melts and the mixture is soft.

6. Fold ⅓ of the eggs in the chocolate until almost combined. Add the remaining egg, ⅓ at a time and fold until combined.

7. Pour into the prepared pan. Pour boiling water around a sizable pan until it reaches halfway up the side.

8. Bake for around 25 minutes or until the cake is slightly puffed and the edges are just starting to harden.

9. Set aside from the double boiler and allow to cool completely.

10. Cover with plastic wrap and let cool for 6 hours or overnight.

11. About 30 minutes before cooking, brush the edges and remove both sides of the pan.

12. Cut and serve.

Per serving: Calories: 260Kcal; Fat: 21g; Carbs: 12g; Protein: 5g; Sodium: 0.05g; Sugar: 0.5g

790. PEANUT BUTTER PIE

Preparation time: 10 minutes
Cooking time: 0 minutes
Servings: 8
Ingredients:

- ½ teaspoon sugar-free vanilla
- 9-inch reduced-fat graham cracker pie crust
- 1 ½ cups skim milk
- 1 package sugar-free instant vanilla pudding mix
- 1 ½ ounces sugar-free peanut butter cups, chopped
- ⅓ cup reduced-fat peanut butter
- 1 ½ cups frozen fat-free whipped topping, thawed and divided

Directions:

1. In a large bowl, combine milk and pudding until thickened.
2. Add the peanuts, vanilla, and 1 cup of whipped cream and whisk. Stir in peanut butter cups.
3. Pour over in pie crust and spread whipped cream more on top. Cover and chill at least 4 hours before eating.

Per serving: Calories: 191Kcal; Fat: 6g; Carbs: 27g; Protein: 4g; Sodium: 0.76g; Sugar: 6g

791. CHOCOLATE CHERRY CAKE ROLL

Preparation time: 10 minutes
Cooking time: 15 minutes
Servings: 10
Ingredients:

- 1 cup sugar-free cool whip, thawed
- ½ cup Splenda for baking
- Nonstick cooking spray
- ¼ teaspoon baking soda
- 10 maraschino cherries, drained and patted dry
- ⅔ cup maraschino cherries, chop, drain and pat dry
- Unsweetened cocoa powder, as needed
- ½ cup reduced-fat cream cheese, soft
- 4 eggs, room temperature
- ⅓ cup flour
- ¼ cup unsweetened cocoa powder
- 1 tablespoon sugar-free hot-fudge ice cream topping
- ¼ teaspoon salt

Directions:

1. Pre-heat the oven to 375⁰F. Spray a large sheet baking pan and spray with the cooking spray.
2. In a sizable bowl, combine the flour, ¼ cup cocoa powder, baking soda, and salt.

3. Beat the eggs in a large bowl at high speed for 5 minutes,
4. Slowly add the sweetener and continue beating until the mixture is thick and lemon-colored. Stir in the dry ingredients.
5. Spread evenly over the prepared pan. Bake for 15 minutes.
6. Place a clean paper towel on the cutting board and sprinkle with cocoa powder.
7. Place the cake on a towel and carefully remove the parchment.
8. Start at the short end and wrap a towel around it. Cool on a wire rack for 1 hour.

Preparing the filling:

9. In a sizable bowl, beat the cream cheese until tender. Add ½ cup of the whipped topping and mix gently and slowly until combined. Stir in another ½ cup of whipped topping. Fold the chopped cherries.
10. Unwrap the cake and remove the towel. Spread the filling to within 1-inch of the edges.
11. Roll the cake again and cut off the ends.
12. Cover and refrigerate overnight.
13. Reheat fudge toppings, drizzle over cake, garnish with whole cherries and serve in slices.

Per serving: Calories: 163Kcal; Fat: 3g; Carbs: 25g; Protein: 5g; Sodium: 0.04g; Sugar: 12g

792. UNBAKED BLUEBERRY CHEESECAKE

Preparation time: 5 minutes
Cooking time: 0 minutes
Servings: 8
Ingredients:

- 1 tablespoon plant-based butter, melted
- 1 envelope unflavored gelatin
- 1 teaspoon sugar-free vanilla
- 1 cup sugar-free frozen whipped topping, thawed
- ¾ cup blueberries
- 1 cup boiling water
- 16 ounces fat free cream cheese, softened
- 8 zwieback toasts
- ⅓ cup Splenda

Directions:

1. Place the toast and plant-based butter in the food processor. Pulse until mixture resembles coarse crumbs.
2. Press the mixture to the bottom of the 9 inches spring foam.
3. Place gelatin in a medium bowl and add boiling water. Stir until gelatin is completely dissolved.

4. In a sizable bowl, whisk the cream cheese, Splenda, and vanilla on medium speed until combined. Beat the whipping toppings.
5. Add the gelatin in a stream while stirring at a low speed.
6. Increase speed to medium and hold for 4 minutes or until smooth and creamy.
7. Gently fold in the berries and spread over the crust.
8. Cover and refrigerate for 3 hours or until frozen.
9. Serve and enjoy.

Per serving: Calories: 316Kcal; Fat: 23g; Carbs: 20g; Protein: 6g; Sodium: 0.1g; Sugar: 10g

793. CINNAMON BREAD PUDDING

Preparation time: 10 minutes
Cooking time: 45 minutes
Servings: 6
Ingredients:

- 2 cups skim milk
- 4 tablespoons plant-based butter, sliced
- ¼ teaspoon salt
- 1 ½ teaspoons cinnamon
- 4 cups day-old French bread, cut into ¾-inch cubes
- 2 egg whites
- 1 egg
- 5 teaspoon Splenda

Directions:

1. Pre-heat the oven to 350⁰F.
2. In a suitable saucepan, bring the milk and plant-based butter to a boil. Remove from the heat and stir until the plant-based butter is completely dissolved. Let cool for 10 minutes.
3. Beat eggs and whites in a sizable bowl until foamy. Add Splenda, spices, and salt. Whisk until smooth, then add the cold milk and bread.
4. Transfer the mixture to a 1½-quart baking sheet. Place on a rack in the roasting pan and add 1-inch of hot water to the roasting pan.
5. Bake for 45 minutes until the pudding hardens and the knife in the middle is clean.
6. Serve and enjoy.

Per serving: Calories: 362Kcal; Fat: 10g; Carbs: 25g; Protein: 14g; Sodium: 0.02g; Sugar: 10g

794. GERMAN CHOCOLATE CAKE BARS

Preparation time: 10 minutes
Cooking time: 15 minutes
Servings: 20
Ingredients:

- ½ cup and 2 tablespoons powdered sugar substitute
- 1 ½ cups almond flour cracker crumbs
- 2 cups unsweetened coconut flakes
- Nonstick cooking spray
- ¾ cup chopped pecans
- ¾ cup dark baking chocolate, chopped
- 1 cup coconut milk, divided
- ½ cup coconut oil

Directions:

1. Spray an 8 x 8-inch baking sheet with cooking spray.
2. In a large bowl, combine the coconut, ½ cup sugar substitute, cracker crumbs, and pecans and mix.
3. Add ½ cup of milk and oil to a suitable saucepan and cook over medium heat until oil and mixture are heated through. Pour in the coconut mixture and stir to combine.
4. Spread evenly on a baking dish and let cool for 2 hours.
5. In a clean saucepan, put the chocolate and milk over medium-low heat. Continue cooking, stirring, until the chocolate melts and the mixture is tender. Add 2 tablespoons of the sugar substitute and stir to combine.
6. Pour chocolate over the coconut layer and let cool for 1 hour or until firm.
7. Cut into squares to serve.

Per serving: Calories: 245Kcal; Fat: 19g; Carbs: 9g; Protein: 3g; Sodium: 0.02g; Sugar: ?g

795. UNSWEETENED CHOCOLATE COFFEE CUPCAKES

Preparation time: 10 minutes
Cooking time: 25 minutes
Servings: 24
Ingredients:

- ½ cup plant-based butter, melted
- 1 cup almond flour, sifted
- 4 ounces unsweetened chocolate
- 3 teaspoon baking powder
- 2 eggs
- ½ cup fat free sour cream
- ½ cup coconut flour
- ½ teaspoon-salt
- 2 cup Splenda
- 1 cup strong coffee, room temperature

Directions:

1. Pre-heat the oven to 350⁰F.
2. Line 12 muffin cups with cupcake liners.
3. Melt the chocolate.
4. Add the Splenda, almond and coconut powder, baking powder, and sea salt.
5. In a small bowl, combine the coffee, sour cream, and butter. Add the butter mixture to the dry ingredients and keep beating on low speed until well combined.
6. Add and beat the eggs properly, one at a time. Stir in chocolate until well combined.
7. Pour batter into ready cups and bake for 25 minutes.
8. Let cool completely before serving.

Per serving: Calories: 173Kcal; Fat: 9g; Carbs: 20g; Protein: 2g; Sodium: 0.06g; Sugar: 16g

796. MINI BREAD PUDDINGS

Preparation time: 5 minutes
Cooking time: 35 minutes
Servings: 12
Ingredients:

- 1 teaspoon vanilla
- ⅛ teaspoon nutmeg
- 6 slices cinnamon bread, cut into cubes
- 1 ¼ cups skim milk
- ½ cup egg substitute
- ⅓ cup Splenda
- ⅛ teaspoon salt
- 1 tablespoon plant-based butter, melted

Directions:

1. Pre-heat the oven to 350⁰F. Line in 12 medium muffin cups.
2. In a large bowl, combine milk, egg yolks, Splenda, vanilla, salt, and nutmeg until blended.
3. Add the cubed bread and stir until moist. Take 15 minutes of rest. Pour evenly into the prepared baking dish. Sprinkle plant-based butter evenly on top.
4. Bake the bread for 35 minutes or until puffed and golden.
5. Remove from the oven and let cool completely.

Per serving: Calories: 105Kcal; Fat: 2g; Carbs: 15g; Protein: 4g; Sodium: 0.03g; Sugar: 9g

797. MOIST BUTTER CAKE

Preparation time: 15 minutes
Cooking time: 35 minutes
Servings: 14
Ingredients:

- 1 cup Splenda, divided
- 3 eggs
- 2 tablespoons water
- Butter flavored cooking spray
- ¾ cup plant-based butter, divided
- ½ cup fat free sour cream
- 1 teaspoon baking powder
- 2 cup almond flour, packed
- 1 tablespoon and 1 teaspoon low-sugar vanilla, divided

Directions:

1. Pre-heat the oven to 350⁰F.
2. Sprinkle cooking oil to bake on a Bundt cake pan.
3. In a sizable bowl, combine the flour, sour cream, ½ cup of plant-based butter, 3 eggs, ⅔ cup of Splenda, baking powder, and 1 teaspoon of vanilla and whisk until well combined.
4. Pour into prepared pan and bake for 35 minutes.
5. Melt ¼ cup of plant-based butter in a small saucepan over medium heat.
6. Add ⅓ cup of Splenda, a tablespoon of vanilla, and water and stir. Keep stirring until Splenda is completely dissolved.
7. Using a skewer, poke holes across the cake. Pour the syrup mixture evenly over the cake so that all the holes are filled. Turn the pan for a few minutes until the syrup is absorbed into the cake. Leave to cool for 1 hour.
8. Turn onto the plate, cut, and serve.

Per serving: Calories: 259Kcal; Fat: 17g; Carbs: 18gg; Protein: 4g; Sodium: 0.2g; Sugar: 10g

798. CINNAMON PEARS

Preparation time: 10 minutes
Cooking time: 20 minutes
Servings: 2
Ingredients:

- 2 pears, sliced into wedges
- 1 teaspoon ground cinnamon
- 1 teaspoon maple syrup

Directions:

1. Place the pears in the casserole mold in one layer.
2. Sprinkle the fruits with ground cinnamon and maple syrup.
3. Bake the pears at 365⁰F for 20 minutes.
4. Serve and enjoy.

Per serving: Calories: 183Kcal; Fat: 6.1g; Carbs: 35g; Protein: 0.9g; Sodium: 0.04g; Sugar: 3.2g

799. STRAWBERRY COMPOTE

Preparation time: 14 minutes

Cooking time: 15 minutes

Servings: 6

Ingredients:

- 1 tablespoon fresh mint
- ½ cup cherries, raw
- 3 cups strawberries
- 3 cups of water

Directions:

1. Mix strawberries, cherries, fresh mint, and water in a saucepan.
2. Bring the mixture to boil and remove from heat.
3. Cool the compote and serve it with ice cubes.
4. Enjoy.

Per serving: Calories: 31 Kcal; Fat: 0.3g; Carbs: 7.4g; Protein: 0.7g; Sodium: 0.05g; Sugar: 1.42g

800. OATMEAL COOKIES

Preparation time: 10 minutes

Cooking time: 15 minutes

Servings: 4

Ingredients:

- 3 bananas, mashed
- 1 cup oatmeal, grinded
- 1 teaspoon honey
- 1 teaspoon vanilla extract

Directions:

1. Mix mashed bananas and oatmeal.
2. Add vanilla extract and honey. Stir the mixture well.
3. Using a parchment paper, line the baking tray.
4. Prepare small cookies from the banana mixture with the help of a spoon and put them in a prepared baking tray.
5. Bake the cookies for 15 minutes at 360⁰F or until the cookies are light brown.
6. Serve and enjoy.

Per serving: Calories: 165Kcal; Fat: 1.6g; Carbs: 35.6g; Protein: 3.7g; Sodium: 0.01g; Sugar: 2.05g

801. SWEET PEANUTS

Preparation time: 10 minutes

Cooking time: 2 minutes

Servings: 3

Ingredients:

- 1 teaspoon ground cinnamon
- 1 tablespoon honey
- 2 ounces peanuts, chopped

Directions:

1. Mix ingredients in the ramekin and microwave for 2 minutes.
2. Carefully whisk the mixture and cool.
3. Serve and enjoy.

Per serving: Calories: 126Kcal; Fat: 9.3g; Carbs: 8.1g; Protein: 4.9g; Sodium: 0.15g; Sugar: 3.3g

802. SAVORY FRUIT SALAD

Preparation time: 10 minutes

Cooking time: 0 minutes

Servings: 2

Ingredients:

- 1 teaspoon lime zest, grated
- ½ cup strawberries halves
- 4 ounces mango, chopped
- ¼ cup yogurt
- ½ cup grapes, halved
- 1 tablespoon liquid honey

Directions:

1. In a sizable salad bowl mix up strawberries, grapes, mango, and lime zest.
2. Add yogurt before sprinkling the salad with liquid honey.
3. Shake it gently.
4. Serve and enjoy.

Per serving: Calories: 110 Kcal; Fat: 0.5g; Carbs: 26.4g; Protein: 2.7g; Sodium: 0.03g; Sugar: 3.1g

803. AVOCADO MOUSSE

Preparation time: 10 minutes

Cooking time: 0 minutes

Servings: 2

Ingredients:

- 2 teaspoons liquid honey
- 1 avocado, peeled, pitted
- ½ cup skim milk
- 1 tablespoon cocoa powder
- 1 teaspoon vanilla extract

Directions:

1. Chop avocado and put it in the food processor.
2. Add milk, vanilla extract, and cocoa powder.
3. Blend the mixture until smooth.
4. Pour the cooked mousse in glasses before topping with honey.

Per serving: Calories: 264Kcal; Fat: 20.5g; Carbs: 19.2g; Protein: 4.5g; Sodium: 0.03g; Sugar: 1.32g

804. BANANA ICE CREAM

Preparation time: 8 minutes

Cooking time: 0 minutes

Servings: 4

Ingredients:

- 2 cups Greek yogurt
- ½ teaspoon vanilla extract
- 2 bananas, peeled, chopped, frozen

Directions:

1. Put bananas in the food processor.
2. Add Greek yogurt and vanilla extract and blend the mixture until smooth.
3. Pour the cooked ice cream in the ramekins and freeze for 15 minutes in the freezer.

Per serving: Calories: 130Kcal; Fat: 2.2g; Carbs: 17.6g; Protein: 10.7g; Sodium: 0.03g; Sugar: 3.2g

805. PEACH CRUMBLE

Preparation time: 15 minutes

Cooking time: 25 minutes

Servings: 2

Ingredients:

- 1 teaspoon olive oil
- 2 tablespoons olive oil
- 1 cup peach, chopped
- ½ teaspoon ground cinnamon
- 4 tablespoons oatmeal, grinded
- 1 teaspoon ground nutmeg

Directions:

1. Mix olive oil and oatmeal. After getting a smooth dough, crumble the mixture with your fingertips.
2. Rub the sizable baking pan with olive oil and put the peaches inside.
3. Sprinkle the peaches with a topping of ground nutmeg and cinnamon.
4. Top the fruits with crumbled dough.
5. Bake the meal for 25 minutes at 360⁰F or until you get the light brown crust.
6. Serve and enjoy.

Per serving: Calories: 197Kcal; Fat: 15g; Carbs: 15.1g; Protein: 2.3g; Sodium: 0.13g; Sugar: 4.02g

806. BEANS BROWNIES

Preparation time: 15 minutes

Cooking time: 15 minutes

Servings: 6

Ingredients:

- 1 tablespoon lemon juice
- 1 teaspoon olive oil

- 1 cup black beans, cooked and mashed
- 3 tablespoons liquid honey
- 1 teaspoon baking powder
- 5 ounces whole-grain oats
- 1 tablespoon cocoa powder
- 1 teaspoon vanilla extract

Directions:
1. Mix the mashed black beans with cocoa powder, whole-grain oats, honey, baking powder, lemon juice, and vanilla extract.
2. Add olive oil and stir the mass properly with the help of a spoon.
3. Line the baking tray with baking paper.
4. Transfer the brownie mixture in the baking tray and flatten it well. Cut the brownie into bars.
5. Bake the dessert in the preheated oven to 360⁰F for 15 minutes.
6. Cool the cooked brownies well.
7. Serve and enjoy.

Per serving: Calories: 244 Kcal; Fat: 2.9g; Carbs: 45.8g; Protein: 10.3g; Sodium: 0.05g; Sugar: 2.03g

807. CHOCOLATE RASPBERRY SOUFFLÉS

Preparation time: 10 minutes
Cooking time: 10 minutes
Servings: 6
Ingredients:

- cup fresh raspberries
- egg whites
- ½ ounces dark chocolate, chopped
- teaspoon Splenda
- teaspoon plant-based butter, soft

Directions:
1. Pre-heat the oven to 400⁰F for 10 minutes.
2. Grease the 6 small ramekins with plant-based butter.

3. Add rasberry in a blender and puree well.Stain the puree and add 1 tablespoon splenda in it and set aside.
4. In a mixing bowl, beat egg whites until thickened and start adding the remaining Splenda, gradually, until the mixture forms stiff glossy peaks.
5. Gently fold ⅓ of the egg whites into the raspberry puree.
6. Fold the raspberry puree mixture into the remaining egg whites.Fold gently until evenly mixed.
7. Spoon the raspberry egg mixture into the ramekins filling them ½ full.
8. Divide the chopped chocolate between the ramekins and then fill to the top with soufflé mixture.
9. Place ramekins on a baking sheet and bake for 9 minutes until golden brown and puffed up.
10. Serve immediately.

Per serving: Calories: 60Kcal; Fat: 1g; Carbs: 8g; Protein: 3g; Sodium: 0.24g; Sugar: 2.42g

808. LEMON MUFFINS

Preparation time: 10 minutes
Cooking time: 14 minutes
Servings: 12
Ingredients:

- 1 teaspoon baking powder
- 1 tablespoon lemon juice
- 3 eggs, beaten
- 2 cups whole-grain flour
- 1 tablespoon lime zest, grated
- ¼ cup organic almond milk
- 1 teaspoon vanilla extract
- 2 tablespoons liquid honey

Directions:
1. Mix all ingredients in the mixing bowl and blend with the help of the immersion blender until smooth.
2. Pour the batter in the muffin molds.
3. Bake the muffins for 14 minutes at 355⁰F.
4. Serve and enjoy.

Per serving: Calories: 97Kcal; Fat: 1.5g; Carbs: 18g; Protein: 4.2g; Sodium: 0.02g; Sugar: 3.02g

809. FRAGRANT APPLE HALVES

Preparation time: 10 minutes
Cooking time: 10 minutes
Servings: 4
Ingredients:

- 1 teaspoon vanilla extract
- 1 teaspoon ground cinnamon
- 2 apples, halved
- 2 tablespoons chia seeds

Directions:
1. Rub the apples with vanilla extract and ground cinnamon and transfer in the preheated to 375⁰F oven.
2. Bake the apple halves for 10 minutes.
3. Sprinkle the apples with chia seeds.
4. Serve and enjoy.

Per serving: Calories: 155Kcal; Fat: 2.6g; Carbs: 34.4g; Protein: 1.8g; Sodium: 0.03g; Sugar: 2.13g

810. CARDAMOM BLACK RICE PUDDING

Preparation time: 10 minutes
Cooking time: 20 minutes
Servings: 4
Ingredients:

- 2 cups brown rice
- 2 cups water
- ½ cup agave syrup
- 1 teaspoon ground cardamom

Directions:
1. Mix rice, water, and ground cinnamon.
2. Cook the rice for 20 minutes.
3. Add agave syrup and stir the pudding well.
4. Serve and enjoy.

Per serving: Calories: 413Kcal; Fat: 0.9g; Carbs: 93.4g; Protein: 1.8g; Sodium: 0.04g; Sugar: 1.45g

30-Day Meal Plan

Days	Breakfast	Lunch	Dinner	Dessert
1	Beautiful Buckwheat Waffles	Pepper-Infused Tuna Steaks	Lamb with Prunes**Error! Bookmark not defined.**	Strawberry Pie
2	Appetizing Crepes with Berries	Persian Chicken	Lemon Garlic Shrimp	Healthy Broccoli Muffins
3	Poached Eggs	Vegetable Biryani	Spicy Lamb Curry	Oatmeal Cakes With Mango
4	Savory Breakfast Pancakes	Chicken Meatballs Curry	Greek Baked Cod	Vanilla Pastry Cream
5	Spiced Morning Chia Pudding	Baked Tilapia	Pesto Pork Chops	Papaya Cream
6	Pumpkin Pie Yogurt Bowl	Turkey Sausages	Lime Asparagus Spaghetti	Mango Bowls
7	Egg White Breakfast Mix	Pork Loin and Orzo	Beef with Carrot & Broccoli	Pineapple Pudding
8	Scrambled Eggs with Smoked Salmon	Lime Asparagus Spaghetti	Tandoori Lamb Tail	Pear Jam
9	Baking Powder Biscuits	Zero-Fussing Pork Meal	Chopped Tuna Salad	Creamy Butternut Porridge
10	Veggie Scramble	Cod and Cauliflower Chowder	Smoked Lamb	Chocolate Pudding
11	Breakfast Fruits Bowls	Tuna Bowl With Kale	Sweet Life Bowl	Rice Pudding
12	Mushrooms and Cheese Omelet	Lemon Chicken Mix	Turkey Verde With Brown Rice	Avocado and Sauerkraut
13	Steel Cut Oat Blueberry Pancakes	Tomato and Avocado Salad	Greek Chicken Bites	Ricotta Ramekins
14	Strawberry Sandwich	Deliciously Simple Beef	Salmon Broccoli Bowl	Tapioca Pudding
15	Scrambled Eggs with Mackerel	Chicken Marsala	Stuffed Eggplant Shells	Mango Mug Cake
16	Spinach Frittata	Swordfish with Lemony Parsley	Herbed Chicken	The Best Jam Ever
17	Breakfast Burgers with Avocado Buns	Spicy Roasted Leg of Lamb	Grilled Lamb Gyro Burger	Ruby Pears Delight
18	Golden Milk	Tofu and Tomato	Ropa Vieja	Pumpkin Cheesecake
19	Spiced Popcorn	Zesty Chicken	Kale Cod Secret	Picositos Brownies
20	Buckwheat Granola	Tilapia with Limey Cilantro Salsa	Pork and Chestnuts Mix	Orange Cake
21	Gingerbread Oatmeal	Smokey Turkey Chili	Millet Tabbouleh, Lime and Cilantro	Fruit Crepes
22	Oats with Berries	Fish Curry Dinner	Ground Lamb with Peas	Chocolate Coffee Pots de Crème
23	High-Protein Breakfast Bowl	Oregano Pork	Fresh Tuna Steak and Fennel Salad	Raspberry Curd
24	Yogurt, Berry, and Walnut Parfait	Beans and Cucumber Salad	Cauliflower Tomato Beef	Butterscotch Lava Cakes
25	Vegan "Frittata"	Cauliflower Tomato Beef	Grilled Steak	Vanilla Cake

26	Cherry-Coconut Pancakes	Rosemary Chicken	Fresh Tuna Steak and Fennel Salad	Berry Compote
27	French Toast with Applesauce	Salmon Ceviche	Roasted Brussels Sprouts	Ripe Banana Pudding
28	Pumpkin Cookies	Chicken Tacos	Baked Lamb with Spinach	Apple Couscous Pudding
29	Greek Yogurt Oat Pancakes	Cauliflower Mashed Potatoes	Rosemary Pork Chops	Cocoa and Pears Cream
30	Sweet Potato Toast Three Ways	Chicken Shawarma	Coconut Milk-Baked Sole	Refreshing Curd

Measurement Conversion Chart

Volume Equivalents (Liquid)

US Standard	US Standard (ounces)	Metric (approximate)
2 tablespoons	1 fl. oz.	30 mL
¼ cup	2 fl. oz.	60 mL
½ cup	4 fl. oz.	120 mL
1 cup	8 fl. oz.	240 mL
1½ cups	12 fl. oz.	355 mL
2 cups or 1 pint	16 fl. oz.	475 mL
4 cups or 1 quart	32 fl. oz.	1 L
gallon	128 fl. oz.	4 L

Volume Equivalents (Dry)

US Standard	Metric (approximate)
⅛ teaspoon	0.5 mL
¼ teaspoon	1 mL
½ teaspoon	2 mL
¾ teaspoon	4 mL
1 teaspoon	5 mL
1 tablespoon	15 mL
¼ cup	59 mL
⅓ cup	79 mL
½ cup	118 mL
⅔ cup	156 mL
¾ cup	177 mL
1 cup	235 mL
2 cups or 1 pint	475 mL
3 cups	700 mL
4 cups or 1 quart	1 L

Oven Temperatures

Fahrenheit (F)	Celsius (C) (approximate)
250°F	120°C
300°F	150°C
325°F	165°C
350°F	180°C
375°F	190°C
400°F	200°C
425°F	220°C
450°F	230°C

Weight Equivalents

US Standard	Metric (approximate)
½ ounce	1g
1 ounce	3g
2 ounces	6g
4 ounces	11g
8 ounces	22g
12 ounces	34g
16 ounces or 1 pound	45g

Conclusion

After reading this book, it is hoped that you will find a better understanding of what inflammation is, how it affects you and your body, and even better, that you have hopefully learned how you can move forward into a better lifestyle that includes a reduction of inflammation.

Because there is still so much for the medical communities to understand, not only about what chronic, low-level inflammation does to the human body, how it happens, and the seemingly endless search on how to reduce—or even eventually cure—inflammation, it falls on those who suffer to do what they are able to in order to keep themselves healthy and feeling the best they can. This means you!

Where you go from here and how you choose to proceed in living your life is entirely in your hands. Always be up front with your medical provider, as he or she can help you to steer clear of potentially harmful choices.

Always, always listen to your body and what it is trying to say. Try to look past the actual pain and discomfort of the signals your body is sending, and see what it is trying to tell you of the underlying causes and triggers. Don't just try to suck it up and live with it. This will only add stress to a situation that has been continuing to reach unbearable heights. We have already learned that stress and depression and/or anxiety that its causes can exacerbate an already untenable situation of inflammation in the body.

Body and situational awareness are not a joke. They are key to finding the best way of communicating back and forth with your body to find any and all ways that you can to make it more comfortable. Reducing stress and pain will only help you in the reduction of inflammation. Maybe it has been so long since you have felt healthy, or even halfway to normal, that it is hard to remember what that means in terms of feeling "better".

With dedication, a slow and steady pace, and working hard to become more aware of your body and your lifestyle choices, you can start making a difference in how you feel. The end result could leave you both amazed by and head over heels in love with the reminder of what feels "better" really means for the long-term.

If you're suffering from chronic pain or inflammation from an injury, this cookbook is an easy, effective way to reduce your pain and inflammation without drugs. Once you've followed the program outlined in this book, you can be pain-free in just a few weeks.

Printed in Great Britain
by Amazon

84277893R00104